Radical Passion

New Directions in German-American Studies

Werner Sollors
General Editor

Vol. 1

A Longfellow Institute Book

PETER LANG
New York • Washington, D.C./Baltimore • Boston • Bern
Frankfurt am Main • Berlin • Brussels • Vienna • Canterbury

Radical Passion

Ottilie Assing's Reports from America and Letters to Frederick Douglass

Edited, Translated, and Introduced by
Christoph Lohmann

PETER LANG
New York • Washington, D.C./Baltimore • Boston • Bern
Frankfurt am Main • Berlin • Brussels • Vienna • Canterbury

Library of Congress Cataloging-in-Publication Data

Assing, Ottilia.
Radical passion: Ottilie Assing's reports from America and letters to Frederick
Douglass / edited, translated, and introduced by Christoph Lohmann.
 p. cm. — (New directions in German-American studies; vol. 1)
Includes bibliographical references and index.
1. Assing, Ottilia. 2. Douglass, Frederick, 1817?–1895—Friends and associates
Biography. 3. Abolitionists—United States Biography. 4. Women abolitionists—
United States Biography. 5. Women social reformers—United States Biography.
6. German American women Biography. 7. Assing, Ottilia Correspondence.
8. Douglass, Frederick, 1817?–1895 Correspondence. 9. Antislavery movements—
United States—History—19th century Sources. 10. Afro-Americans—Relations
with Germans—History—19th century Sources. I. Lohmann, Christoph K.
II. Douglass, Frederick, 1817?–1895. III. Title. IV. Series: New directions
in German-American studies (New York, New York); vol. 1.
E449.A8   973.8'092—dc21   [B]   99-20055
ISBN 0-8204-4526-6
ISSN 1524-7813

Die Deutsche Bibliothek-CIP-Einheitsaufnahme

Assing, Ottilie:
Radical passion: Ottilie Assing's reports from America
and letters to Frederick Douglass / ed., transl.,
and introduced by Christoph Lohmann.
–New York; Washington, D.C./Baltimore; Boston; Bern;
Frankfurt am Main; Berlin; Brussels; Vienna; Canterbury: Lang.
(New directions in German-American studies; Vol. 1)
ISBN 0-8204-4526-6

Cover design by Lisa Dillon

© 1999 Peter Lang Publishing, Inc., New York

All rights reserved.
Reprint or reproduction, even partially, in all forms such as microfilm,
xerography, microfiche, microcard, and offset strictly prohibited.

Acknowledgments

I am very grateful to my friend and colleague Maria Diedrich of the University of Münster, author of *Love Across Color Lines: Ottilie Assing & Frederick Douglass* (Hill & Wang, 1999), the first full-length biography of Assing, which was my principal source for the explanatory notes related to Assing's life. With Professor Diedrich's permission, I used her forthcoming book in manuscript form, realizing that its final published form may well differ in some details. It is, of course, Terry H. Pickett's fortuitous discovery of Assing's correspondence with her sister that precipitated the recent interest in Assing and Douglass, and I am grateful to him for his scholarship and advice. I also wish to thank Maria Diedrich, David Blight (Amherst College), Jonathan Elmer (Indiana University), Henry Louis Gates Jr. (Harvard University), Wolfgang Hochbruck (University of Stuttgart), Werner Sollors (Harvard University), and John Stauffer (Harvard University), for reading and commenting on the contents of this volume in various stages of completion. Research grants from the U.S. Educational (Fulbright) Commission in Germany, the Office of International Programs at Indiana University, the Longfellow Institute at Harvard University, and the Department of English at Indiana University have made it possible for me to collect the materials for this volume in archives located in Germany, Poland, and the United States. Members of the staff at the Deutsches Literaturarchiv in Marbach, the Jagiellonian University Library in Krakow, the Library of Congress, and the National Park Service in Washington (especially Gay C. Bindocci) have been invariably helpful and courteous; but Ann Bristow and her staff in the Reference Department of the Indiana University Library in Bloomington deserve my very special thanks for going far beyond the call of duty in helping me with their meticulous research. It was both instructive and a pleasure to try out some versions of my translation on audiences at a conference on "The German-American Tradition: German-American History and Literature in the Context of American Multilingualism" at Harvard University and at a presentation to the Friends of the Nantucket Atheneum, where Frederick Douglass gave his first antislavery speech in 1841 and where, more than a century and a half later, he remains a person of special historical significance.

My wife and partner in translation projects, Pamela Fezandié Lohmann, is my most patient and loving critic, even when she does not formally appear on the title page as cotranslator. I can best express my gratitude for all her support and suggestions by dedicating this volume to her.

Ottilie Assing
National Park Service, Frederick Douglas National Historic Site

Contents

Series Editor's Foreword   xi

Introduction   xiii

Reports and Essays, 1852–1865   1

1. From Hamburg to New York   3
2. Schenectady–Barnum–Curiosities–Life in a Republic–Mrs. Trollope   8
3. The Tombs–The Washington Exhibition–Minstrels   13
4. From New York to Schenectady–The Shakers   19
5. A Small Western Town   25
6. Winter Portrait of a Small Western Town   29
7. From West to East   33
8. An Antislavery Meeting   35
9. An Excursion to Sing Sing   40
10. Rambles Through New York   47
11. Colored People in New York   54
12. American Types: Women–Irish–Blacks–Chinese–Indians–Gypsies   60
13. Preface to the German Translation of *My Bondage and My Freedom*   68
14. The Presidential Election and Slavery   71
15. The Election–Art and Industry Exposition–Women's Rights   78
16. Kansas and the Extension of Slavery   84
17. Wendell Phillips–A "Gift Enterprise"   88
18. Hoboken   90
19. Meeting of the Antislavery Societies: Frederick Douglass   94
20. The Money Crisis–Antislavery Movements   96
21. A Negro Colony in Canada   99
22. The Mayoral Election–A Fugitive Slave   103
23. The Kansas Controversy–Lola Montez–Public Lectures   106
24. Revivals–Women's Rights–Female Dress Reform–Women and Work   110
25. Feeding the Poor–Penny Boardinghouses–Emigration Ships   116
26. Opera–Musard's Orchestra–A Rogues' Gallery–Barnum   119
27. Kansas–Anniversaries   123
28. An Excommunication–Slavery and the Germans   127
29. Malcontents–Indians–James Monroe–A Marylander Without Slaves   132
30. A Captured Slave Ship–Retreat of Reverend Brownlow   135
31. Revivals and Spiritualism   137
32. State and Congressional Elections–Slavery   139
33. New Efforts to Colonize the Negroes   141

34.	Democrats Congratulated	143
35.	Cuba–Public Lectures–Mount Vernon–Buying a Slave's Freedom	146
36.	A Fashionable Preacher	150
37.	Anniversaries	152
38.	Slave Trade–Hatred of America	154
39.	A Visit with Gerrit Smith	158
40.	Frederick Douglass	163
41.	The Insurrection at Harpers Ferry	165
42.	The Aftermath of John Brown's Trial	170
43.	John Brown's Execution and Its Consequences	175
44.	Literary War of the North Against the South–The Octoroon	181
45.	Lecturers–Painting–The Cooper Institute	184
46.	Mormonism–Preparations for the Presidential Election	187
47.	Presidential Candidates–Anniversaries–Humboldt's Letters	190
48.	Election Prospects–Southern Fear–A Convention of Infidels	194
49.	The Presidential Election–Republicans and Democrats	198
50.	Developments in the Southern Part of the Union	202
51.	The Public Crisis	205
52.	Outbreak of Hostilities–Martial Spirit	207
53.	The War	211
54.	War–Douglas's Death– Missouri Germans–A Black Hero–Barnum	215
55.	Civil War–Frémont and the Government–A Rogues' Gallery	220
56.	War–Slavery–The Charleston Fire–An Important Document	224
57.	Slavery and Government–Women and Slavery–Soldiers–Supplies	228
58.	Drastic Change–Southern Knighthood–Executing a Slave Trader	232
59.	The War–The Slavery Question–Color Prejudice	236
60.	General Hunter and the Government–Blacks–The Homestead Bill	239
61.	The Emancipation of Slaves	243
62.	Consequences of War–Congressional Elections–McClellan	248
63.	New Defeats–Corruption–Religious Conditions	252
64.	Emancipation Proclamation–Conditions in Mississippi	256
65.	Humbug–Psychology–Dwarves–Behavior of Negroes in the South	260
66.	American Conditions–Mob Rule	265
67.	Colored Troops–Cost Increases–Luxury–Worker Unrest–Bloomerism	269
68.	Anniversary of the Anti-Slavery Society	274
69.	Effects of War on Social Conditions and on Slavery	276
70.	A Negro Regiment–Radical Germans	280
71.	The Presidential Election	283
72.	The Presidential Election	288
73.	Christmas and New Year's–Slavery–Everett–A New German Book	294
74.	The Constitutional Abolition of Slavery	298
75.	A Public Celebration–Corruption	303
76.	Thrills of Victory and Depths of Mourning	306

77. The Trial–A Funeral Procession–Reconstruction 310
78. Lincoln's Assassins–Jefferson Davis–Emancipation 314
79. Presidential Policies–Persecution of Negroes–Embittered Southerners 319
80. Victorious South–Half- and Whole-hearted–Black Literary Institute 323

Appendix: Letters to Frederick Douglass, 1870–1879 327

Index 369

Series Editor's Foreword

The German-American Tradition Reconsidered

Most countries are bilingual. The fact seems simple—less than 200 nation-states exist today, and approximately 6,000 languages are spoken—but multilingualism has not been recognized by branches of nationalist history-writing. Even today, notions of "one nation, one language" enjoy unmerited, and at times dangerous, popularity.

The United States is a case in point. The fact that Americans have expressed themselves in more than a hundred languages is obscured by the battle about "Official English." These are not just unrecorded spoken languages by immigrants and Native Americans; there are over 100,000 American texts written in languages ranging from Amerindian tongues and from Spanish, French, Dutch, German, and Russian colonial writings to immigrant literature in all European, many Asian, and some African languages. The list of multilingual American newspapers under the surveillance of the U.S. Postmaster in 1917 is 60 single-spaced pages and contains over 2,000 titles of periodicals in languages including Ruthenian, Syrian, Bohemian, "Spanish-Jewish" (Ladino), Tagalog-Visayan, Rumanian, and bilingual and trilingual formats, such as Polish-Latin, Danish-Norwegian-Swedish, and German-Hungarian. These oft-ignored texts raise important issues about language policies, national identity, and education, and they are especially suited to the kind of international scholarly collaboration that the Longfellow Institute at Harvard University has begun to stimulate.

Though it has been a stepchild of German Studies and American Studies, the German-American tradition is particularly rich, extending from the seventeenth century to the present. It has been impressive quantitatively. The German Society of Pennsylvania holds 70,000 titles (among which are many German-Americana), and new electronic bibliographies show that in the Harvard library system alone exist over 25,000 German-language works published in the United States, making German by far the largest single non-English language group among American imprints. In addition, more than 5,000 German-language Newspapers and periodicals have been identified. How many more might the Library of Congress, the New York Public Library, and the University of Chicago Archives hold?

We have known for a very long time that German-American literature is historically long-lasting and quantitatively significant—but, you may ask, how about the quality of that literature? Are there any "good" texts among them or at least "interesting" or otherwise "important" ones? What do they tell us that we don't already know from "better sources"? And, given the antiquarian and dusty feeling that surrounds the term "German-American," do these works connect with, and relate to, the work of such flourishing fields as Cultural Studies?

The purpose of this series is to reconnect German-American Studies with current trends in German Studies and American Studies and to present it as a field that deserves reconsideration now, after the century in which two World Wars and their legacies consigned German-America to near-oblivion. The series also examines America's largest linguistic, ethnic, and literate minority in international, polyethnic, and multilingual contexts.

One of the first German-American writers was Francis (or Franz—he used both versions of his name) Daniel Pastorius, who co-authored the first protest against African slavery in the English colonies in 1688 (for which he later was memorialized by John Greenleaf Whittier). He also wrote the first practical legal treatise in British North America, which included provisions for mediation instead of litigation. His most important and intriguing manuscript, the multilingual collection of excerpts, advice to his children, and autobiographical observations, is titled "Bee Hive" (1696). At least scholars are familiar with Pastorius's works. But this is not the case for the many German-American autobiographies, essays, poems, plays, and novels that still await twentieth-century readers. Such works include Franklinian autobiographies before Franklin; incisive political and economic analyses of the United States; memorable observations on subjects ranging from slavery to the emergence of prefabricated housing; early candid literary representations of lesbian love; interracial novels of manners; pioneering journalistic accounts of America's ethnic diversity, of rural life, and of the rise of urban life; haunting poetic articulations of labor issues, women's rights, and environmental concerns; expressions of exile and hope, nostalgia and despair; and comedies of manners and serious drama in High and Low German, Yiddish, English, and the mixed language sometimes called "Germerican."

These works raise many questions: Was there ever a unified German-American tradition, or do the heterogeneous linguistic, religious, and regional groups and unrepresentative writers and thinkers dominate the scene? How did German-language writers in the United States position themselves in relation to the various German-speaking areas and countries in Europe, and how did they interact with different ethnic and linguistic groups in the United States? Which new general insights from Germany, Austria, and Switzerland, into emigration, American cultural and ethnic relations, and transatlantic history can be gained by new scholarship and freshly presented historical sources?

It is the purpose of this series to subject the large topic of German-America to new cultural scrutiny. It does so as an international collaborative effort among scholars from disciplines ranging from modern languages to political history and from American Studies to anthropology, who present independently conceived publications. Reimagined as part of multilingual America, the examinations of the German-American tradition in this series offer new approaches to German-American studies and force new thinking about what constitutes "German literature" and what greatly unrecognized, multilingual features define "American literature."

Introduction

> . . . like Harriet Martineau, like Frances Trollope and Fredrika Bremer, likeTocqueville and [Alexander von] Humboldt, she would write about the land, the people, their institutions, their cultures, the art they produced, the literature they wrote, and the songs they sang. Those back home would be fascinated by . . . the radical readings she had to offer.
>
> [Ottilie Assing and Frederick Douglass] both believed in . . . human perfectibility and progress, and both saw themselves as members of an enlightened vanguard whose duty it was to mold public opinion toward a perceptual and practical change that would contribute to achieving an ideal society. Both strove to radicalize public sentiment. . . . Where such accord prevailed, working together became an act of love, a sensuous encounter.
>
> Maria Diedrich[1]

> For much of Douglass's mature career, Assing was his principal intellectual consort; the two read widely together—Goethe, Feuerbach, Dickens, Shakespeare and Marx. Theirs was a salon for two.
>
> Henry Louis Gates, Jr.[2]

When Ottilie Assing arrived in New York on September 27, 1852, she was greatly relieved that the ordeal of a five-week transatlantic voyage from Hamburg was finally over. She had traveled first-class on the *Indian Queen* and did not suffer the horrors of seasickness, yet the crossing was "nothing but a series of miseries and inconveniences" that even a determined program of reading failed to alleviate. "Ah!" she exclaimed as she disembarked, "[I'll take] one deep breath, the first on firm soil, and then onward into the city!"

But the young woman's "deep breath" was more than an expression of relief from the tedium and inconvenience of transatlantic travel. As she breathed the air of the American continent and gazed at the beckoning panorama of New York, she felt free, independent, and on the verge of new possibilities. She had left behind the clutter of a complicated family situation; she had emerged from suicidal depression and personal tragedy; and, most of all, she had distanced herself from the disappointment over a failed revolution that had raised and dashed so much hope for Germany as a nation and for herself as an idealistic radical.

Before her lay a land in which only she would be responsible for herself, a country that was professing—though surely not always acting on—the ideals she most admired. Liberty, equality, social justice; a rational, secular, enlightened system of government; and the absence of an oppressive church and overbearing aristocracy were the principles by which this young American republic was expected to conduct itself—even as the dark cloud of slavery was casting an ever more ominous shadow across the political landscape.

As Ottilie Assing took a first look at her New World, she saw America as the stage on which the drama of radical social and political change was to be enacted, with herself as a keen observer and incisive commentator—or, better yet, a deeply engaged participant. But she could not yet see the twisting plot that lay ahead or her own remarkable role in it over the next three decades.

*

Assing was born in 1819, the older of the two daughters of David and Rosa Maria Assing. Her father was a prominent, though troubled and brooding, physician and poet in Hamburg; her mother, a lively, energetic, cheerful woman, a teacher with a gift for Romantic poetry, song, and stories. David had grown up as David Assur in the orthodox Jewish community of Königsberg, but his move to Hamburg, after receiving his medical degree in 1807, was only a continuation of his intellectual development toward contemporary Enlightenment thought. His decision to be baptized in 1815 was not so much an act of religious transformation as a response to a social necessity in anticipation of his marriage to Rosa Maria Varnhagen in 1816. In fact, David and Rosa Maria made it a point to bring up their children as freethinking atheists, as true daughters of the Enlightenment, who saw themselves as members of a universal human race of thought and reason rather than as followers of any religious tradition or denomination.

However, German anti-Semitism, though not nearly as lethal as it was to become in the twentieth century, was a force to be reckoned with no matter how well Jews adapted themselves to the social and cultural majority. Even the famous Rahel Levin, a central figure in the literary and artistic world of Berlin, was obliged to convert to Christianity and rename herself before her marriage in 1814 to Rosa Maria's brother, Karl August Varnhagen von Ense (who was to play an important role in the lives of the two Assing daughters). But that formality failed to assuage the prejudices of those who determined social codes, and Varnhagen von Ense's political career never flourished again because of his marriage to a Jew. The Assings also were not spared the stings of anti-Semitic sentiments in Hamburg: not only was there a clear dividing line between the Jewish artistic and professional middle class and the prosperous mercantile circles of this Hanseatic city, but Ottilie always remembered the ugly anti-Jewish riots that flared up during her youth, leaving a deep fear and hatred of discrimination and mob violence throughout her life.

The great fire that ravaged Hamburg in early May 1842—just a few days after David Assing's death and two years after Rosa Maria's—though sparing the family's house, was important in determining the question whether the two sisters,

Ottilie and Ludmilla, would accept "Uncle Varnhagen's" invitation to live with him in Berlin. They had received only a small inheritance and their income could be stretched by living in Varnhagen's house and assuming the role of social companions. Also, for two intelligent, well-educated, intellectually ambitious young women it must have been a welcome challenge to try to fill the shoes of a Rahel Levin in the cultural world of Berlin. All in all it seemed to be a perfect arrangement, and Ottilie thanked her uncle for offering "such an opening" for herself and Ludmilla.

As it turned out, it was a perfect arrangement for Ludmilla; for Ottilie it was a disaster. The relationship between the two sisters had always been full of tensions, rivalries, and even animosities, but the new life with their 57-year-old uncle brought these problems to a boil. While Ludmilla finally felt appreciated as she catered to the considerable needs of her ailing (or hypochondriac) uncle, Ottilie bridled at the demands made on her and the restrictions to her independence. Politically, she was close to the Young Germany movement of young, idealistic, committed, and uncompromising nationalists and antimonarchists, and from her perspective Varnhagen's reputation as a liberal nationalist was utterly undeserved. Most likely she agreed with Friedrich Engels' comment that Varnhagen was a "cowardly rascal" for whom social status was more important than political principle.

After less than six months, this eminently proper *ménage à trois* erupted in an ugly scene that had dramatic consequences. Losing control of himself in an argument with Ottilie, Varnhagen slapped her; she stormed out of the house, was gone throughout the night, and did not reappear until the following day when she presented herself pale and bleeding at the house of one of her friends. She had fled to a public park and stabbed herself several times in the chest with a dagger, inflicting wounds severe enough to lose consciousness for most of the night. She finally managed to drag herself to her friend's house, profoundly distraught, but also probably somewhat savoring the role of Romantic heroine that she had admired in her mother's poems and stories since early childhood. It was an eerie dress rehearsal for Ottilie's death in 1884.

She returned to Hamburg in the fall of 1843—after less than a year in Berlin—setting the stage for another complicated living arrangement. This time, however, the *ménage à trois* flew in the face of her own family's moral standards and of bourgeois propriety in general. For a while, Ottilie supplemented her modest inherited income by writing on literature, art, and the theater for local newspapers, and in that capacity she got involved in a heated controversy over the control and direction of Hamburg's theaters. Espousing the cause of what she considered pure art, which was embattled against more philistine interests, she soon became closely associated and passionately involved with Jean Baptiste Baison, an actor widely admired throughout the German states.

Always intent upon living an emotional life that enacted her political and social convictions, Ottilie Assing accepted Jean Baptiste and Caroline Baison's invitation to move in with them as their children's governess. That in itself may have been a questionable departure from traditional bourgeois mores, but what truly shocked all but Ottilie's most loyal and radical friends was that Caroline absented herself more and more from her family, leaving children and husband to Ottilie's passionate affections. While the good burghers of Hamburg stared in disbelief and disapproval, the three principals considered this a quite delightful arrangement, one that in no way diminished the close friendship between the two women.

But by January 1849 Ottilie's life had taken another tragic turn. During the preceding year, the much hoped-for revolution had spread from France to Germany only to collapse within a few months as a result of lacking internal cohesion and bloody external assaults on the disorganized forces of liberal nationalism. This defeat of her most cherished political dreams was devastating enough; but Baison's increasingly precarious financial situation, the wounds inflicted on him during the brutal cultural wars in Hamburg, and finally his physical collapse in the fall, left Ottilie in emotional despair, which was perhaps even more difficult to bear than the dashed political hopes. Baison died in January, leaving Assing bereft and with little else to her name than a scandalous reputation and the plan to write Baison's biography. She did and had it published as *Jean Baptiste Baison: Ein Lebensbild* in 1851, but not without making an effort—a quite transparent one, as it turned out—to conceal her authorship; the title page revealed only that "An Actor" had authored the following text.

It was time to make a new beginning. Like so many millions of emigrants who left behind the calamities of the Old World, Ottilie Assing turned from her own and her country's calamitous experiences looking to America. She stepped aboard the *Indian Queen* on August 16, 1852, more than ever reaching out for that personal independence and political freedom she had tried so hard—and failed—to find at home.

*

Freedom and independence, however, meant first of all securing a sufficient income to maintain herself. In the early, most difficult months in New York this meant trying to sell some artwork, coloring daguerreotypes, and—like so many nineteenth-century immigrant women—working as a seamstress; but within six months Assing began to rely on her work as a journalist.[3] More than a year before she left Hamburg she had procured an arrangement with Johann Friedrich Cotta to write occasional reports for his *Morgenblatt für gebildete Leser* (Morning Journal for Educated Readers).[4] This and Cotta's other paper, the *Allgemeine Zeitung* (General Newspaper), represented a decidedly liberal—sometimes even radical—point of view that was quite in keeping with Assing's own politics, and they appealed to an influential intellectual elite in and beyond Germany. Heinrich Heine was so impressed with the *Allgemeine* (which also published some of his own work) that he praised it for its wide-ranging influence: "it so truly deserves its worldwide renown as authoritative source that one could well call it the common newspaper of Europe."[5] It was the kind of forum Assing was eager to use for expressing her unequivocal opinions and for shaping European perceptions of the United States during a dozen years of increasingly bitter and violent sectional conflicts over slavery.

During the first 18 months or so as a commentator on the American scene she was casting about for an appropriate subject matter, a special angle of vision, a "handle," that would differentiate her reporting from that of so many other expatriate German "forty-eighters" who also tried to make a living by their pens. She began with two rather standard pieces that she wrote for the journal *Jahreszeiten* (Seasons), detailing her arrival in and early impressions of New York. These were followed by *Morgenblatt* pieces about a visit to the New York City jail; a Shaker colony near Albany; her long winter sojourn with German settlers in the "small western town" of Sheboygan, Wisconsin (she loathed the frontier and the American provinces and could not wait to return to New York in the spring of 1854); kaleidoscopic observations and "rambles through New York"; as well as a look at New York schools and the American education system in general. There are a few hints scattered throughout these pieces that Assing was curious about matters of race—a glimpse of Washington's black "companion" in Leutze's famous painting of "Washington Crossing the Delaware"; seating herself next to an African-American woman on the train to Schenectady; and observing a black inmate in the New York City jail—but these do not amount to anything like a major theme.

But beginning with Assing's attendance at the annual meeting of the American Anti-Slavery Society in May 1854, there is a noticeable and important shift in her writings toward a preoccupation with African Americans, with racial relations, with slavery, and with the antislavery struggle. As an observer with a keen eye for social injustices and political flashpoints, Assing quickly became aware that the whole complex of black-white relations was increasingly becoming *the* dominant issue, *the* potential powder keg, of the brave new world she had adopted as her home. It was not an issue that came as a surprise for her because she had read deeply and widely about the United States before she left Germany. Without apparently realizing how problematic the founders' own implications in slavery were, she had come to idealize the Enlightenment statesmen—especially Thomas Jefferson—who had stood at the beginning of the American Republic and constructed something of a model for the unified German nation that the Young Germany movement hoped to create. Even before disembarking from the *Indian Queen*, Assing had known about and begun to despise the abomination of slavery that contrasted so sharply with the noble principles of the Declaration of Independence, that besmirched the Constitution, and that was spreading ever more ominously westward across the American landscape. If nothing else, Assing had read Alexander von Humboldt and deeply agreed with his views on race and slavery. "Without doubt," he had written in 1826, "slavery is the greatest of all evils that have afflicted mankind"; and in his famous *Kosmos*, published half a dozen years before Assing left Hamburg for New York, he had commented even more explicitly: "no race is nobler than any other. All are equally entitled to freedom, which in the state of nature belongs to the individual and which in civilization belongs as a right to the entire population through political institutions."[6] Some years later, in 1860, commenting on the publication of *The Letters of Alexander von Humboldt to Varnhagen von Ense*, Assing expressed her admiration for Humboldt's views: "The enlightened and freethinking public is of course rejoicing that Humboldt is one of their own. . . . [His] boldly liberal thought and his opinions about slavery and American democracy rile Democrats and the religiously orthodox."

Of all the societies holding their May "anniversary meetings" in New York, Assing thought the Anti-Slavery Society the most important in regard to substance and the most satisfactory in regard to rhetorical performance. In 1854 she listened attentively to William Loyd Garrison, sympathetically to Robert Purvis (a "rather dark mulatto"), and with rapture to Wendell Phillips, as they spoke against slavery and the Kansas-Nebraska Bill in Chapin's church on Broadway. Garrison, much to Assing's satisfaction, proclaimed that "everybody in this country, in heaven and in hell knows that we are right when we stand up for the rights of every human being on this earth." As for Purvis, she commented rather smugly and condescendingly that although "not particularly outstanding" as a speaker, he was the type of man who "will be favorably received and met with interest by any European." But Phillips impressed her immensely with his "verbal dexterity and . . . incisive, ironic, and dialectical mind." She quoted his speech at length and was thrilled to hear him make the point that the injustice of slavery was greater than the sanctity of the Union: "A Union that was brought into being by an Adams, a Hancock, and a Jay," he proclaimed, "has never required the glue of the slaves' blood!" From this moment on, the antislavery cause became central to Assing's thinking and writing, and Wendell Phillips was forever enshrined in her Pantheon of great orators for justice.

But she was still searching for an authentic representative of the slavery experience, a black American whose voice and personal guidance might give her a better, deeper, more direct understanding of slavery and racial prejudice, which she could then in turn employ to enlighten her German audience. It had to be a person of color, a former slave, someone with compelling narrative and rhetorical skills, a revolutionist of radical fervor, with a broad, idealistic vision of the future. Assing did not find him among the Methodist faithful who attended the black revival camp meeting she visited in Sing Sing on the Hudson in the summer of 1855. In fact, though surprisingly sympathetic in her treatment of such religious enthusiasm, this anticlerical extremist and self-professed rationalist found most of the proceedings either repugnant or amusing. The pulpit-thumping was too loud and the preaching too shrill, and conversions were a deplorable spectacle of religious irrationality and the ministers, on the whole, nothing but exhorters of the worst fire-and-brimstone kind. She described one of them who approached her later in the well-worn words of European anticlericalism: "the fire in his eyes had a disgustingly sensual quality that I had already noticed earlier from a distance"; with a curt reply she "made short shrift of his insinuating ways."

It is surprising, therefore, that the first heroic black figure that appears in Assing's reports turns out to be a minister: Rev. James W. C. Pennington of Shiloh Presbyterian Church in New York City. In preparation for an article on "Colored People in New York," Assing had "plucked up [her] courage" and introduced herself as the "correspondent of Mr. Cotta's *Morgenblatt*" to the author of a slave autobiography, *The Fugitive Blacksmith,* and the man who had recently caused considerable commotion trying to make it possible for blacks to ride on New York omnibuses. Pennington had received an honorary doctorate from the University of Heidelberg, and that must have counted for something with Assing as she accepted the friendship that Rev. Pennington and his wife extended to her, and she began to write her first extensive piece on race and slavery.

Her long essay, "Colored People in New York," sounded a whole new note in the treatment of that subject—new, at least, to most Europeans and probably also to many white Americans. Pennington, she pointed out, was not the kind of subservient Christian martyr made so acceptable to American and European whites by Harriet Beecher Stowe's Uncle Tom just a few years earlier. "[He] is not one of those saccharine personalities," Assing wrote, "in whom a soft concept of Christianity has smothered the ability to hate.... He speaks out with bitterness and hatred against slavery and its supporters." He was, in her rendition, the prototypical revolutionary whom she had learned to idealize in her years of association with the Young Germany movement—only now the scene had shifted to America, and the cause was no longer a free and unified Germany but a Union freed of the curse of slavery. Carried away by her enthusiasm for her new project and her newfound hero, Assing wrote more than 25 pages, far longer than anything Cotta could print in either of his two papers. Her denunciation of slavery and northern race prejudice, coupled with her encomium on Pennington's narrative style, courage, and agreeable yet determined and steadfast character, included long translated passages from *The Fugitive Blacksmith,* resulting in an unwieldy, uneven piece. Cotta tucked the manuscript away in his archives, leaving his readers unaware of the new journalistic wind that was beginning to blow across the Atlantic.

The friendship with the Penningtons did not last very long, possibly because of the fundamental conflict between Assing's determined rejection of all forms of religion and Pennington's evident commitment to his faith. But it became clear to Assing that if she wanted to write with authority about race and the potential revolution against slavery in America she would have to get to the heart of it—she would have to become personally acquainted with Frederick Douglass, the editor of the *North Star* and author of *My Bondage and My Freedom,* a book that had set her afire with ideas and projects as soon as she had read it after its publication in 1855. Most immediately her project was to translate this extraordinary autobiography and make it available to her German readers as *Sclaverei und Freiheit* (1860), and for that purpose she needed to meet with Douglass, obtain his agreement, and ask his help. Reading Douglass's account of the first 38 years of his life revealed to Assing an even more striking potential revolutionary than Pennington: here was a man of great power of expression, strength of character, firmness of principle, and personal determination. She needed to meet Douglass not just for immediate practical reasons; she wanted to commune with him on their common vision of the great new American revolution—the overthrow of the slavery system.

*

When Assing finally met Douglass in the summer of 1856 he was all she had hoped he would be, only more so:

> At first I went to meet Frederick Douglass in his newspaper office, which is marked by a sign in large letters above the entrance: THE NORTH STAR OFFICE.... As I did not find him there, I went to his home about a half hour outside the city [of Rochester]. The handsome villa, surrounded by a large garden, is situated on a hill overlooking a charming landscape.—Douglass is a rather light mulatto of unusually tall, slender, and powerful stature. His features are striking: the prominently domed forehead with a peculiarly deep cleft at the base of the nose, an aquiline nose, and the narrow, beautifully carved lips betray more of his white than his black origin. The thick hair, here and there with touches of gray, is frizzy and unruly but not woolly. His whole appearance, stamped by past storms and struggles, bespeaks great energy and will power that shuns no obstacle and has been the sole source of his success in reaching his present prominence in the face of all odds.... Despite all the vicissitudes, his whole being expresses a richly endowed, original, happily mature nature. Everything about him is fresh, genuine, true, and good. Endowed with an exceptional talent for conversation, he knows how to inspire and elevate others, and in conversation proves to be cheerful, animated, witty, and knowledgeable. Glowing with passion for the cause to which he has dedicated his life, he is far too wide-ranging in his interests as not to engage other worthy causes with energy. We touched upon a wide variety of things—large and small, general and personal—in the course of our conversation, and everywhere I encountered understanding and sympathy.

It was the beginning of an intense intellectual and emotional relationship that would result in yet another *ménage à trois,* not a permanent arrangement but one in which Ottilie Assing would join the Douglass household for several months during the summer for the next 22 years.[7] During the rest of the year, Douglass and Assing would see each other frequently in New York or in Hoboken (where Assing had moved not long after her arrival in the United States). They would go to meetings, plays, and social occasions and sometimes travel together; they would exchange weekly letters (only a very small number of which have survived; they are printed in the Appendix of the present volume) and read and converse on literature, philosophy, and, of course, on politics and the need for radical social change. At times Assing would assist Douglass in his writing,[8] just as he would give her an understanding of the slavery issue that she needed for her reports.

It was a relationship deeply fulfilling for Assing despite the limitations that Douglass's responsibilities as a husband and father necessarily placed on it; but part of her fulfillment was the very satisfaction of violating every traditional value and standard of bourgeois society. Their passion for each other—and the evidence suggests that at least for some years it was both mutual and sexual—transcended not only conventional notions of the institution of marriage but also the even more powerful social taboos of race. For Assing that meant enacting the autonomy she had always longed for but found impossible to achieve within the constraints of family and friends and social conditions in Germany. It also meant actually living the principles she believed in: opposing the kind of white racial prejudice she despised wherever she saw it—even as elements of typical nineteenth-century racial thinking revealed themselves in her own writings. She was so convinced that the relationship between her and Douglass was fundamentally right that by 1864 she felt free to inveigh publicly against the social prohibitions surrounding the "amalgamation" issue. Evidently mistaking a racist political hoax for a serious and supportive discussion of miscegenation, she praised a pamphlet that had appeared in December 1863, "Miscegenation: The Theory of the Blending of the Races Applied to the American White Man and the Negro," and took it as proof that things had changed for the better:

> As little as two years ago, any word in favor of mingling the races would have caused a unanimous outcry of shock and horror. It was the very issue on which even declared abolitionists . . . could not overcome their prejudice. Many who treated the colored man as an equal . . . would have revolted against the thought of darkening their pure Anglo-Saxon blood by mixing it with the African. And those who had perhaps no personal objections were loath to incur the rejection and contempt of the masses.

As wrong as she appears to have been about both the seriousness of the pamphlet and the evidence of social progress, she was clearly flaunting her own radical unconventionality, her contempt for the contempt of the masses.

Assing's close relationship with Douglass profoundly shaped her thinking and writing about the dramatic events of the 1856–1865 period. Much as she admired William Lloyd Garrison and Wendell Phillips and the work that had been done by the American Anti-Slavery Society, she completely sided with Douglass and the National Abolitionists in the conflict over whether or not the Constitution sanctioned slavery. The Garrison faction's attack on the Constitution, she believed, "will never gain the support of the broad mass of the people, who are loyal to the Constitution and the Union." Douglass, on the other hand, "defend[s] the Constitution in word and spirit against the charge that it is proslavery" and is convinced that "any tendency towards dissolving the Union is cowardly because it can only result in an exacerbation of the slaves' condition in the South." Assing was present at the debate on this issue between Douglass and Charles Lenox Remond in 1857, and she was delighted to report that Douglass displayed "such power of mind, wit, and humor as to devastate his opponent."

In another controversy that occurred later that year within the antislavery movement, Assing again sided with Douglass even though it meant opposing Gerrit Smith, a man she came to admire greatly. At the National Compensation Convention in Ohio in the summer of 1857, Smith and others had proposed that the

North should raise funds to purchase the freedom of the slaves. This was anathema to Assing because she felt that paying slave owners was to accede to their premise that slaves were property, a concession that amounted to a tacit legalization of slavery. "[T]his point of view," she wrote, "has been met with the most determined opposition on the part of genuine and active abolitionists." Among this group of true abolitionists she counted, of course, "Frederick Douglass, the celebrated fighter for the freedom of his race, [who] has argued . . . with the full force of his mind, the brilliance of his rhetoric, and the fire of his convictions" against the compensation idea. Assing's phrasing here clearly suggests that she had read or listened to Douglass's arguments, accepted them as her own, and repeated them in her report.

Assing also identified herself closely with Douglass in her severe criticism of any kind of colonization scheme. In December 1858, she lashed out against both earlier efforts to promote Liberia and more recent attempts on the part of the African Colonization Society to remove African Americans to Yoruba. Such plans, she argued, rather than facilitating the abolition of slavery, will only weaken the abolitionist movement "by losing people who would otherwise dedicate their abilities and energies more effectively to the emancipation and progress of the colored race in the United States." Any colonization scheme was, in Assing's view, inspired and supported by the slavery interests because "they hate and fear the educated, skilled, and capable among the colored people with a special passion" and therefore "do everything possible to get them to emigrate and . . . to eliminate them as a threat to the 'peculiar institution'." None of these ideas is "well received among the Negroes themselves," she wrote; and certainly Frederick Douglass "is one of the most outspoken opponents": "this excellent man, on the basis of his work and his personality, has achieved more for the abolition movement and in the fight against color prejudice than all those who have emigrated to Liberia."

On some of the larger political issues of the day, Assing associated herself strongly with the view that the abolition of slavery could not be a half-hearted affair open to compromise: an unbending moral commitment to it rather than a politically pragmatic pursuit of any number of other agendas—such as the preservation of the Union—was central to her thinking and writing. It is a theme that runs consistently through her reports from the election of 1856 to the end of the Civil War, and the more she wrote about it, the more unbending she became. Her comments about the speech that Senator Henry Wilson of Massachusetts gave before the New York Trade Council during the campaign of 1856 show her early ambivalence between a purist and a pragmatist attitude:

> Although the passionate abolitionist and friend of the Negro must have been cool to his argument opposing any intervention against slavery where it has traditionally existed and setting limits only to its extension, such a pronouncement must be seen in a different light, not only because an audience consisting mostly of merchants is least likely to be swayed by philanthropic considerations, but because outspoken, passionate abolitionists are generally regarded as muddle-headed idealists.

In that election, quite predictably, she supported Frémont, a man she typically saw in romantic, heroic dimensions, even though he had to present himself publicly as less of an abolitionist than she supposed him to be at heart—because "[t]hose who believe that the general public can be swayed by anything other than material advantages are flattering themselves with illusions"; "one has to be satisfied with whatever good is being done, and, without questioning people's motives too closely, hope for a better future."

In 1860 she was again a Frémont supporter, but now because she saw him as a radical purist opposed to Lincoln's far more moderate position and willingness to compromise with the South. After Lincoln was nominated, she referred to him as "a relatively obscure person, who has not been daring in his commitment to the fight for human rights, progress, and dignity." The only hope she saw was that the Democrats greeted Lincoln's nomination with "horror and anger," a sign that perhaps boded well for his "free[ing] the country from the hated yoke of slavery and its willing servants." After Frémont dropped out of the race, leaving her no alternative, Assing supported Lincoln, and of course she was pleased with his victory over the Democrats; but in her estimate Lincoln always remained a man whose commitment to the antislavery cause was deeply suspect, as were his accommodations to the interests of the hated "slavocracy." Thus, she wrote at the very beginning of the Civil War:

> In Pensacola, several slaves took refuge at Fort Pickens in the belief that they would find protection under the Union flag. But the commander returned them in chains to their owners. . . . [He] is mean and cowardly enough to assure the rebels that there is not a single abolitionist under his command and that he would not tolerate any tampering with the system of slavery. The president and his cabinet act in the same spirit. John Brown, Jr., the son of the venerable martyr killed by the Virginians . . . offered to organize several black regiments and to conduct raids with them into the rebel states, but his offer was categorically rejected by the government.

The contrast she is defining here between the firm radicalism of John Brown's son (the reincarnation of his father's noble spirit) and Lincoln's questionable tactics shows Assing's deep suspicion of Lincoln's motives, especially when seen in the larger context of her extensive treatment of John Brown's martyrdom.[9]

By early 1862, Assing was convinced that "the government in Washington seems to regard slavery as an institution more hallowed and sacrosanct than any other property right or social contract." She went so far as to claim that "the actual seat of the treasonous conspiracy is located there [in Washington], and many employees in many branches of government hardly bother to conceal their sympathies for the slaveholders." Even Lincoln's preliminary Emancipation Proclamation of September 1862 failed to assuage Assing's misgivings about the president. Her analysis of this surprising step—"The Emancipation of the Slaves"—was not an expression of satisfaction or victory but a further questioning of Lincoln's purity of motive and effectiveness as a leader of the free North. The true abolitionists, she felt, looked at the president's declaration and doubted whether it "was intended to bring about the unconditional abolition of slavery"; they feared that, although the measure may look good on paper, it would never be fully implemented. In her view, the problem was as always Lincoln's lack of absolute moral commitment:

> [I]ts effectiveness will be largely destroyed because it is now a necessary measure of war rather than an act of justice and humanitarianism. It comes too late, the president having resisted for too long everything that resembles an act of emancipation in the hope that nobler motives might prevail. His hand was finally forced by desperate circumstances resulting from a series of bloody defeats. . . . A measure that would have been regarded by the civilized world as an act of virtue, can now only be seen as a concession to the force of circumstances.

Those who were deeply committed to abolitionism as a moral and revolutionary cause, like Douglass and herself, increasingly felt that Lincoln did not stand with them but with the Unionists, whom they deemed capable of striking any deal with the South as long as it would lead to the reestablishment of the Union.

Perhaps the key issue that bound Assing and Douglass together in their opposition to the compromising ways of the Lincoln administration was the battle over the recruitment of black regiments for the Union forces and, once that battle had been won, for equal treatment of black soldiers within the army. These steps seemed essential to them if the war was to be primarily a fight against slavery rather than for national unity; they were essential steps also if it was to be not just a war fought *on behalf of* black Americans but *by* them—a war which would contain at least some element of black self-determination rather than a war that was part of a long series of historical events in which the white majority determined the fate of the black minority. When Lincoln finally relented—even though only out of necessity rather than on the basis of moral principle—Assing was jubilant at the results: "Wherever blacks have stood face to face with the enemy, they have displayed a courage and discipline that would have done honor to the best-trained white troops," she told her readers, citing the bravery of the famous Massachusetts 54th Regiment at Fort Wagner. But at the same time she bemoaned the fact that black soldiers received less pay and were given no opportunity to become officers. The whole problem seemed to her exemplified in the contempt with which Douglass himself was treated by the secretary of war, who at first wanted to appoint Douglass to recruit black soldiers in the South but then backed away from his offer. "In a situation in which Douglass . . . cannot become a captain or a major," Assing wrote, "there is no shadow of hope for all the rest."

Assing's view of Lincoln remained virtually unchanged until his assassination, and even then she drew a line between Lincoln's popularity with the masses and her own lingering misgivings about him. "Even if the stalwart and radical abolitionists

... were often displeased with his temporizing and indecisiveness ..., their discontent contained much of the sorrow one feels for errors committed by a friend and ally." The president, she felt, had been "lenient and conciliatory to a fault" because such a policy was popular with the majority of the people of the North, not because it was the right thing to do. He had played to the broad electorate, who suffered "from a certain lack of conscience and firm conviction as well as the ability to rise to the higher level of moral indignation"—a charge she often leveled at the people in general, revealing how much her own democratic convictions were undercut by middle-class European suspicions of the uneducated and unkempt masses. But if moral indignation could hardly be expected from the populace at large, it was a grave fault in anyone who would be a leader, especially one claiming to be opposed to slavery. In the end, however, Assing joined the rising chorus of praise for Lincoln, the martyr, when she wrote that "his death even reconciled his opponents and erased his errors; and his name will henceforth shine in the annals of history as that of a martyr to liberty, greatness, and unity of his people." But this sentence, which concludes her report "Thrills of Victory and Depths of Mourning," sounds more like a somewhat hollow rhetorical flourish in tune with popular sentiment at a time of deep national mourning than her usual radical criticism. *De mortuis nil nisi bonum!*

Assing continued to stand with Douglass in the aftermath of the Civil War as his pursuit of abolition was transformed into an energetic campaign to obtain civil rights for African Americans. She had been thrilled when Congress finally passed the Thirteenth Amendment abolishing slavery in January 1865,[10] but just a few months later she began to agitate for the enfranchisement of black men on both moral and political grounds:

> The educated European does not need to be told that humanitarianism and justice demand that the Negroes should immediately be given the same rights that the white population enjoys; anything less makes a mockery of the so-called republican idea of equality. But even without considering this general principle, the enfranchisement of the Negro is such an absolute political necessity that nothing but ill will or incurable stupidity can oppose it.

She attended the annual meeting of the American Anti-Slavery Society that year, where this issue came up for debate, and William Lloyd Garrison argued that the society, having accomplished its purpose, should be dissolved. Wendell Phillips and Frederick Douglass, however, insisted on redefining the goals of the abolitionist movement and to carry on the struggle, and Assing considered this position "the only one that is correct." She expressly told her readers that "Frederick Douglass, the most gifted and prominent representative of the colored race and one of the nation's foremost orators, is now dedicating the full power of his irresistible eloquence to this task; indeed, it seems beyond comprehension that any person who is at all receptive to the truth should not see the justice of a demand when it is presented by a man who in his own person, talent, and conduct so brilliantly contradicts all those hateful, hackneyed sophistries and old saws about the 'Negro's incompetence' and an 'inferior race'."

Just as Assing had vacillated between hopefulness and despair in the days before the abolition of slavery—at times believing that the great new revolution must and would succeed, at times fearing that halfway measures, compromises, corruption, and military incompetence would undo everything—she felt uncertain about the future that African Americans could look forward to. Observing Andrew Johnson and his administration's retreat from strong and affirmative policies in support of the freed slaves and the black population as well as the deeply entrenched racial prejudices among the white population, she felt nothing but the deepest pessimism:

> I have repeatedly expressed the opinion that the abolition of slavery was not a measure arising from the nation's sense of humanity and justice but simply an act necessitated by circumstances; one has to worry, therefore, that the task of emancipation will for the near future remain little more than a mere patchwork. The lack of concern about the future of the freed slaves and the rest of the colored population in the South as well as the general refusal of the masses to grant them civil rights are dark and ominous clouds on the horizon. The abolition of slavery is, of course, a first step, but the great work of liberation remains incomplete unless further, equally necessary steps follow.

But her old enthusiasm for and belief in America that had brought her to these shores at a time of despair over the insufficiencies of the Old World had not been entirely extinguished by America's own shortcomings. Somewhere deep inside her she felt that there was at least a faint possibility that the "dark and ominous clouds on the horizon" might in due time be dispelled:

> Whatever storms and turmoil may lie ahead and harm the nation's development, there can be no doubt that we are moving towards the great goal of full emancipation, of civil equality of all blacks. Slavery has received its death blow and will never again grow into a dominating power, and civil equality is the logical and inevitable consequence of this initial great step. Despite all opposition, it will sooner or later be the law of the land, for the spirit of the century, of civilization, and progress sternly demands it, and because it is the precondition for the republic's greatness, stability, and survival.

She was, after all, a student of the Enlightenment and a woman of her own time, sharing a belief in progress and the "advance of civilization": it sustained her and Douglass and so many others engaged in the battle for social justice even when the immediate future looked grim.

*

In her reports and essays, Ottilie Assing took up many other topics besides those relating to matters of race and slavery. She was fascinated with the wide spectrum that America presented to her observation and commentary. Given her background, one would expect her to be interested in the theater, and she certainly commented on it with her usual gusto—mostly thrashing the poor quality of plays presented on the American stage and lambasting the even poorer actors, who, as far as she was concerned, seemed to be capable of little more than shouting and sawing the air with their arms. She was curious about popular entertainments in general, saw and wrote about a minstrel show, and again and again returned to that most curious of American curiosities, Barnum's American Museum in New York—the home of humbug. Art exhibits always drew her attention, and she made it her specialty to inform her European readership of the development of American painting, which at first she considered quite inferior to the accomplishments of European artists, but gradually came to respect and like, having an eye for spotting talents that today are part of the canonical list of nineteenth-century American painters.[11]

Her interest in social reform movements and organizations, of course, also drew her to observe the "anniversary meetings" of the burgeoning women's movement, and in her own personal and professional conduct she exemplified many of the goals that various women's organizations advocated. It did not escape her notice that there were important connections between the antislavery movement and the various women's reform societies, that women were an active force against slavery, and that Frederick Douglass nurtured these connections by lending his support to many of the women's causes. But Assing was sometimes as ready to ridicule what she considered to be excesses—for example, Bloomerism and dress reform in general—as she was frank in her admiration of women she greatly admired for their courage and accomplishments. Reporting on the Women's Rights Convention in December 1856, she included the following comment:

> Lucy Stone Blackwell, presiding over the meeting, effectively erased the poor impression she had made upon me at an antislavery meeting some time ago. Her appearance does not elevate her above the average, but she soon reveals an ability for clear thinking, logical argument, and quick repartee that makes insignificant and mediocre men—who most jealously guard their privileges—feel intensely uncomfortable.

Assing felt that the goals of the convention were eminently sound and reasonable and that none of them—with the exception of the demand for women's right to vote—"would offend a fair-minded man." And even the issue of the vote was presented most sensibly by Lucy Stone, who pointed out that in other places where women had the vote "children continued to be born . . . and dinners prepared, no less than elsewhere."

In March 1858, Assing commented at greater length about the women's movement. She was particularly impressed by the differences between the "literary and theoretical" nature of the movement in Germany, which the general public decried as radical and revolutionary, and the practical, "more concrete forms" that the movement took in America. For instance, women in Massachusetts had submitted a petition to the legislature for the right to vote, basing their appeal on the same principles that had been used in America's fight for independence from England—taxation without representation; they had taken Wendell Phillips as their attorney, and a commission was currently considering their plea. Though Assing was doubtful that anything would come of it, she still felt that the American circumstances were far more promising than those in Germany:

> Imagine what would happen if the women of any German state were to turn with their appeal to the legislative chamber or to some governmental ministry! Here, on the other hand, where the population consists of the most diverse elements, where all sorts of religious sects coexist side by side, tolerance is the first condition of peaceful coexistence and, for the most part, is actually practiced. Hence, people are more disposed to making allowance for any sort of endeavor as long as it does not directly violate the social order; they do not consider it their obligation to suppress everything only because they do not approve of it.

It struck Assing as remarkable that women of very different backgrounds—Quakers, freethinkers, and those of Puritan faiths—would come together to fight for common goals, and if these goals included the right to vote, so much the better. There was no question in her mind that it was "humiliating for women of excellent education, who are equal to well-informed men in their knowledge of the country and its condition, to be excluded for incompetence." Why should virtually illiterate Irishmen and Germans who do not speak English be permitted to vote after five years of residence in the United States, but not educated women?

In this longer discussion of the women's movement, Assing's assessment of Lucy Stone was far less complimentary than it had been two years earlier: "[She] does not say anything that has not been said before and offers nothing but commonplaces, which her monotonous delivery makes the more tiresome. There is no trace of originality or genius, and her appearance is that of a solid middle-class woman." On the other hand, Lucretia Mott "makes an excellent impression; regardless of her advanced age she actively participates in every important movement with unusual intellectual vigor." But the most impressive of all was Ernestine Potowski Rose, a Polish Jew and reformer, who had been influenced by Robert Dale Owen in England before coming to the United States. Assing admired her for her lack of eccentricity, her "broadly educated, independent, and lucid mind ... [and] knowledge of two continents [that] has broadened her horizon; experience and understanding have matured her opinions." Here was someone with whom she could identify so much that by praising Rose, Assing seems to offer a representation of herself as an exemplary advocate of women's rights, whose lack of excess and "baroque appearance" would do more to further the movement "than any refusal to pay taxes or any penchant for sermonizing can ever achieve."

This and many other of her comments show that she felt both connected with and distant from the women's movement, that she agreed with its goals but was critical of many of its methods. This ambivalence came to a head during the years of conflict between the National Woman Suffrage Association and Frederick Douglass over the content and adoption of the Fifteenth Amendment. Gaining the vote for black American men was for Douglass a matter of survival in a country dominated by racial strife and legalized subjugation of African Americans; he was not about to jeopardize his goals by joining them to the even more controversial demands made by Elizabeth Cady Stanton and Susan B. Anthony. The women suffragists, on the other hand, felt increasingly angry at the prospect of having white, educated, middle-class women be excluded from a widening franchise that included lower-class, uneducated, and often illiterate former slaves. Much as Assing supported the demand for women's right to vote, her commitment to civil rights for black Americans and her personal commitment to Douglass could finally leave no doubt that she would again stand at his side, even if it meant abandoning the women who had fought so passionately and so earnestly for his cause over so many years.

What complicated Assing's relations to both the antislavery and the women's movement, however, was her aggressive stance as an atheist and freethinker. For her, all forms of religion were so much opium for the masses—irrational, socially regressive, antidemocratic, and as much of a humbug as Barnum and spiritualist table-rappers rolled into one. She saved her most scathing contempt for preachers and pulpit thumpers, whom she invariably saw as hypocrites and allies of the most retrograde elements in society, primarily of course the "slavocracy" of the South. As was pointed out earlier, when she encountered black preachers at the Sing Sing camp meeting, she cast them in the stereotypical role of the lecherous priest or the shouting fanatic and enthusiast, without the least perception of the black church's role in the struggle for freedom and equality. She saw religious revivals sweeping the country like an enormous plague or like a replay of the Salem witchcraft hysteria:

> In the eyes of the objective, unprejudiced observer, the whole phenomenon . . . resembles those medieval epidemics in which the populations of entire regions and provinces, who believed that they were possessed by the devil, screamed, ranted, and raved until they lay in convulsions. It is a well-known fact that the eastern states experienced a good deal of such devilish mischief, and the modern "religious revivals" are but a new form, a new epidemic.

Part and parcel of that epidemic were the activities of the American Tract Society, an organization that "has never accomplished anything good through the dissemination of its tracts, and no sensible person would ever expect anything reasonable and useful from that quarter." But the real problem as Assing saw it was that this nationwide Christian organization was so afraid to offend its constituency in the South that it passed a resolution at its annual meeting in 1858 (and reaffirmed it in 1859) "not to mention slavery in any of its tracts and not to permit any condemnation of either the principle or the practice of slavery." This was proof that a "cowardly, hypocritical, servile, greedy priesthood" was spreading its poison everywhere, accumulating power, and ruthlessly "excommunicating" those in its ranks who dared to speak up for justice.

Even someone as strongly identified with the antislavery movement as Henry Ward Beecher was given only the most grudging recognition for taking that stand; mostly Assing considered him a man of decidedly mediocre mind and a great craving for public approbation—in other words, a thorough conformist. His antislavery inclination, she thought, was little more than playing to the preferences of his parishioners: "in a free state and a decidedly abolitionist parish it does not take much heroism or self-denial to be an abolitionist." And if his abolitionism did not amount to much, neither did the rest of his claim to fame. "Beecher is not a man who dominates and reforms his times and environment, as his admirers claim; quite to the contrary, he is their product because he accommodates himself to them, makes concessions, and carefully avoids confronting them too harshly. He knows that his influence and success depend upon the masses and therefore pulls every conceivable lever to gain the applause of the many-headed monster." Yet, all in all, Beecher fared better than most other clerics in Assing's accounts.

So pervasive was her sense of the evils of religion that Assing found it difficult to explain why some of her heroized figures seemed to draw strength and courage and a sense of justice and equality from the very religion she so heartily despised. In John Brown she considered it a strange aberration, an almost inexplicable inconsistency. She thought of Gerrit Smith as one of the most dedicated and unselfish abolitionists, but she was disturbed at the observance of religious forms when she visited him and his family at their home. Clearly, the Reverend Pennington exemplified that religious faith could be the basis of progressive social action, yet his and Assing's friendship may have ended over that very issue. It could also not have escaped Assing that the New England abolitionist movement, which she greatly admired despite some differences, had very strong ties to the ministries of various churches and denominations.

As for Frederick Douglass himself, Assing was convinced that whatever religious inclination he had were merely superficial and conventional vestiges, nothing but pieces of the eggshell that a fledgling revolutionary of the modern and enlightened variety would sooner or later have to cast off if he wanted to spread his formidable wings of intellect and revolutionary fervor—of course, with some assistance from his radical European companion and confidante! In an extraordinary passage written sometime in 1868–1869, part of a lecture prepared for the Hoboken Association of Freethinkers, a German-American emigré group, Assing spoke directly to that point (in her own English):

> A prominent feature in FD is his receptibility for new impressions and truths, his readiness to adopt and appropriate them, if they offer

themselves in a shape at all acceptable. Few men of mature age are capable of renouncing lifelong errors, where by such renunciation not only all opinions, but even outward relations undergo a complete revolution. It requires as much courage as honesty; particularly if the old error is still cherished by the crowd, while the new truth excites their anger. FD has shown that courage and honesty. I have mentioned that he had freed himself of Church orthodoxy at an early time. The pious slaveholders, the position taken by the Church generally towards slavery, had enlightened him about the villainies inside of it, and the notorious immorality of the Methodist ministers, to whose Church he once belonged, could neither fill him with much reverence. His sound sense could not long be imposed upon by such gross nonsense as hell and devil, and the numberless obscenities and contradictions of the Bible necessarily awakened his doubt of its divine origin. Enabled by his whole nature to take the freest views, I should like to say: a born free-thinker, his opinions were notwithstanding that partial enlightenment, yet very unconnected, vague and conflicting, as they necessarily must be, because they lacked all scientific foundation. He was in this respect in about the same position with those who denounce the Pope and Priesthood and hold them responsible for all the abuses in the Church, yet cling to the "only true faith," and do not see that Pope and Priesthood are merely the necessary results of that faith; that indeed they cannot be different from what they are, as long as that faith and church are existing.—Moreover, philosophical, systematical unbelief had hardly ever approached FD. Most of those with whom he associated, were no further advanced than he was, while many remained yet in dark orthodoxy, and consequently no liberating influence from outside had reached him. It is not much longer than ten years, when he became acquainted with the great free ideas of our century. They struck him like a ray of light, and accomplished a complete revolution in his opinions. He was then over forty years old, but he was too true, too much open to every truth, to resist it, no matter how many cherished illusions were destroyed. I add with gratification that it was German radicalism, that worked that revolution, and that to our great, venerated Feuerbach above all others, our thanks are due for having pointed out the path to intellectual liberty to the distinguished man, after he had freed himself of the fetters of slavery.[12]

Assing, in other words, claimed that while Douglass freed himself from physical slavery through an admirable act of great courage, she was the necessary agent whose ministrations freed him from the intellectual and spiritual bondage of Christian faith: if *his* act made him a "man" in body, *hers* helped him to the full realization of freedom of thought. It is a claim that Assing often repeated in her letters to her sister and comments on in a letter of May 15, 1871, to Ludwig Feuerbach, the author of *The Essence of Christianity*, which she and Douglass had read together in the late 1850s. Also, in one of the surviving letters to Douglass,

Assing suggested that "deliverance from religious bondage" should be among the topics he might take up in extending his autobiography.

Taken literally and as a whole, her comments seem as overstated and presumptuous as they are self-serving and, therefore, deserve to be treated with considerable skepticism. However, Douglass did express views at about this time that show how far he had departed from Christian orthodoxy. He emphasized man's responsibility for his own salvation through social action and argued that it was the enlightenment of the age and the progress of rationalism, rather than God's infinite mercy, that have brought about advances in justice and equality. To what extent his development toward religious liberalism was self-generated and tentative rather than the radical result of Assing's insistent atheism (or at least a consequence of the books to which she introduced him) is still an open question. All that can be said with certainty now is that Assing's claim to have liberated Douglass's mind from the shackles of orthodoxy reflects her own profound need to invest the most important political companion in her life and the object of her greatest passion with her own antireligious ideology because for her social radicalism and rationalism were inseparable.[13]

*

In 1865 Cotta's *Morgenblatt* ceased publication, and the steady stream of Assing's reports and essays came to a halt. She continued to write (mostly on art) for other German publications and earned some money tutoring, translating, and working for a German bank in New York, but her passionate interest in American political and social issues continued to play itself out in working with Frederick Douglass. The focus of their life shifted to Washington after Douglass became editor of the *New National Era* in 1870 and particularly after the Douglasses' house in Rochester was lost to a fire of suspicious origin in 1872.[14] But during the decade of the 1870s their relationship developed severe strains, both personal and political in nature. Assing became increasingly dissatisfied with her role as "the other woman," and it seems that the more demands she made on Douglass to abandon his marriage to Anna and to regularize his relationship with Ottilie the more severe the strains became. Some of this dynamic can be seen in Assing's plans for an extended visit to Europe that she had been thinking about for several years. Nothing could have brought her and Douglass closer—both physically and emotionally—than a triumphant series of visits to her family and old friends; nothing could have extended Assing's program of exposing Douglass to the riches of European culture more dramatically than a tour of the great cities of Europe. It had been a dream of hers for a long time, and in 1876–1877 it was time to make it a reality. But in the end she had to travel by herself with little more than Douglass's word that he might follow her in the spring, and even that plan eventually had to be sacrificed to Douglass's much desired appointment as Marshal of the District of Columbia.

After her return from Europe, Assing resumed her habit of spending several months every year with the Douglasses, but these Washington visits suffered from internal and external pressures and problems. Assing presumed to give Douglass blunt advice about how to deal with the financial and marital problems of his children, who were in the habit of dumping these at their parents' doorstep, crowding the house, and draining their resources. She was not overly subtle in criticizing Douglass's increasing tendency to play the role of the loyal Republican who, for the sake of securing his own political spoils, refrained from criticizing the administration's retreat from protecting the freedmen in the South against economic exploitation, political disenfranchisement, and downright physical terror. She expressed her alarm at his new tendency to preach a bootstrap philosophy to black Americans that was more in keeping with the Social Darwinism of the Gilded Age than loyal to the revolutionary principles she and Douglass had so passionately espoused in earlier years. And if all this meddling and prodding and appealing were not enough, she also began to feel that Douglass's emotional and sexual interests were beginning to turn away from her, causing vituperative outbursts against anyone she suspected of attracting his attentions. There is a tone of ominous foreboding in one of her letters to Douglass that reveals how fragile their relationship had become:

> I shall start [for Washington] whenever it will be convenient for you. I don't fully understand your apprehensions, if they refer to me I have only to remind you of all which I wrote you months ago and which then you thought quite satisfactory. My *feelings* for you can never change, but if all this, after all, is nothing to *you,* or if *you* anticipate for yourself more pain than pleasure, you know that you may shake me off whenever you please.

With these words Assing wanted to persuade herself that she still was—or could again become—the autonomous, radical, independent woman scorning bourgeois institutions, values, and behavior who had arrived in New York a quarter of a century earlier. But things had changed, and more than anything else she longed for a haven of emotional peace and stability with Douglass. The irony was that her continuing adherence to radical principles of social justice, her growing suspicion of the Republican party, her presumptuous role as an adviser in financial and family matters, and her ever greater emotional demands on Douglass exerted pressures on their relationship that it finally could not sustain.

Even Anna Douglass's death in 1882 did not lead to the fulfillment of Ottilie Assing's deepest wish—to marry Douglass after all these years of longing, hoping, and defying the most sensitive social taboos. Instead, a year-and-a-half later, he chose as his wife Helen Pitts, a younger woman who had first entered their lives in 1878. After that first meeting, as if divining what the future would bring, Assing wrote about her in words of such extreme hostility that they must be seen as a reflection of her inner panic and despair. Having gone to Europe upon notice of her sister Ludmilla's death, Assing received the news of Douglass's marriage, and it appears that this devastating information made her change her plans for returning to her American "home." Visiting Paris, ill with breast cancer, and abandoned by the person who had been the center of her being for 28 years, she took her life in the Bois de Boulogne on August 21, 1884—completing an attempt she had made more than 40 years earlier in Berlin's Tiergarten. She made Frederick Douglass the heir of her worldly possessions, gave strict instructions to burn all her correspondence, including the letters Douglass had sent her over the years, but she left to the world a remarkable collection of her own essays, reports, and letters that remain a testimony to her radical passion.

Notes

1. Much of this Introduction draws on Maria Diedrich's biography of Ottilie Assing, *Love Across Color Lines: Ottilie Assing & Frederick Douglass* (Hill & Wang, 1999). The author has kindly made available to me her book in preliminary manuscript form and has given me permission to include her findings in my account. References to that text are not individually identified by footnotes or endnotes.

2. "A Dangerous Literacy: The Legacy of Frederick Douglass," *New York Times Book Review* (28 May 1995), 16.

3. Assing had lost most of her parental inheritance helping out Baison before her departure from Hamburg. Her financial situation was precarious until she received a bequest from her uncle Varnhagen after his death in 1858.

4. Cotta's *Morgenblatt* contains 125 pieces by Assing, a number that counts as separate entries the several reports that began in one issue of the paper and were continued in the next. These reports appeared in the period August 1851 through December 1865 and are available on microfiche from Deutsches Literaturarchiv, Marbach. The first 13 reports were written before Assing left Hamburg for New York, and the last one has a November 1865 dateline from London; the rest were written in the United States and carry a New York dateline, although Assing lived and worked primarily in Hoboken, New Jersey. In addition to the pieces that appeared in the *Morgenblatt*, two reports were published in *Jahreszeiten* and one in *Die Gartenlaube*, and it may well be that over time additional articles in these and other journals and newspapers will be identified as being from Assing's pen (see n. 11, below). Finally, seven manuscripts (one of which is fragmentary) are located in the Assing Papers, Deutsches Literaturarchiv, and two manuscript fragments in the Douglass Papers, Library of Congress. The present volume offers a selection in English translation of approximately half of Assing's currently identified journalistic output, with a rather strong bias in favor of her treatment of social and political issues, especially topics related to race, slavery, and abolition. Many of the texts are given in their entirety; editorial omissions within a text are marked by three asterisks (***).

5. Quoted in Hartmut Keil, "German Immigrants and African Americans in Mid-Nineteenth-Century America" (typescript supplied by the author).

6. The connections between Alexander von Humboldt and Ottilie Assing are discussed in Keil's essay.

7. In the fall of 1859, Assing gave her readers a glimpse of the highly idealized charms of her summer retreat at the Douglasses'. She described the house near Rochester as an Edenic retreat, "an island, a small separate world," a "magic castle," "where those who have the courage to defy disgraceful prejudice find a rich intellectual life and are received with great kindness, generosity, and a rather un-American heart-felt warmth." Many years later, in a letter to her sister Ludmilla of January 29, 1874, she gave a more troubling description of the complexities of her long sojourns in the Douglass home and her feelings about Anna Murray Douglass: "For seventeen years [Douglass and I] have not been married but joined in the most profound and mutual affection, more lasting than that of many who are married, but without the least prospect that it will ever be different—and, to make matters worse, kept from each other by a veritable ogre who herself knows nothing of either giving or respecting love. What a fate!" (Varnhagen Papers, Jagiellonian University, Krakow).

8. Because Assing's writings have so far not been widely available and the present volume is the first extensive English translation of her work, no full-scale systematic study has yet been undertaken to determine Assing's influence on Douglass's thought and writing. Maria Diedrich, Assing's biographer, presents some remarkable instances of the close working relationship between them and generally concludes that Assing and Douglass lived for some years in a "professional symbiosis," with Assing serving as Douglass's "secretary, ghostwriter, and inspiration" (see n. 14, below).

9. In the fall of 1859, Assing wrote three long hagiographic pieces on John Brown's raid on Harpers Ferry, his trial, and his execution; she sent them to Cotta, but they were never published in the *Morgenblatt* or elsewhere. The publication of these essays in English translation in the present volume is based on the manuscripts in the Deutsches Literaturarchiv, Marbach. About 10 years later, in March or April 1869, Assing prepared a lecture on Brown to be given to the Hoboken Association of Freethinkers or Association of Non-Believers ("Vereinigung Ungläubiger"), to which she referred in a letter to Ludmilla of March 28, 1869: "I know more about him [Brown] than most people do, as I was, so to speak, one of the conspirators. The outlines of his deed are generally known but very little about its origin and development as well as about his early history and true character" (Varnhagen Papers). The fragmentary manuscript of that lecture (the final 19 of 26 pages), in Assing's original English, is located in the Frederick Douglass Papers, Library of Congress.

10. She commented on the process in her report "The Constitutional Abolition of Slavery" (March 1865), but her deep personal satisfaction and her jubilation that the much longed-for social revolution had finally succeeded are expressed even more clearly in a letter to her sister of February 3, 1865: "For the last several days I have been intoxicated with happiness about the passage of the Constitutional amendment in Congress eliminating slavery forever from this country. Reality sometimes trumps everything that the richest imagination can invent. Five years ago none of us thought we would live to see the day of liberation, and now there is the prospect that we will experience many other good things. Of course, the radical reversal in the attitudes and views of the nation must be solely attributed to the revolution. The regular development of nations proceeds so slowly that a century of it is hardly as much as five years in the life of an individual; but when you unleash a revolution, a short time will produce such progress among the people as fifty or even a hundred years of peace would not have accomplished. By taking this step, the nation has decided its fate and is now looking toward a great future" (Varnhagen Papers).

11. Most of Assing's art criticism has been omitted here largely because of my personal preference for her writings on social and political issues. But much work remains to be done in this respect, particularly because in addition to the identified pieces in the *Morgenblatt* there are a number of art reviews in the *Zeitschrift für bildende Kunst* and other German publications in the 1870s that may or may not be by Assing. Some of these are identified by the initials "O.A." or "A." and deal with the American art scene, but their authorship has not yet been definitively established.

12. MS fragment (11 of probably 19 pages), Douglass Papers, Library of Congress. This text was the basis of a lecture by Assing on Douglass, given at a meeting of the Hoboken Association of Freethinkers on December 11, 1870.

13. In her biography of Assing, Maria Diedrich states the issue succinctly: "The bone of contention between them was religion." While for the atheist Assing the whole matter was relatively clear and simple, Douglass struggled with conflicting feelings. Although he became an ordained minister shortly after his escape from slavery in 1838, Douglass was not deeply religious, and he condemned the role many white churches played in abetting slavery. On the other hand, the liberatory and sustaining faith of Father Lawson and the community-building power of the black church exerted a strong influence on him.

14. Three passages from Assing's letters to her sister Ludmilla from this period suggest that Assing was deeply involved in Douglass's journalistic work and may in fact have acted as his ghostwriter. She wrote on December 3, 1870: "The long articles I am writing for the New Era are also keeping me very busy." On August 24, 1871, writing from Rochester, she informed her sister: "During the week we

[Douglass and I] write our editorials for the New Era; in this way, the perfect togetherness is a great pleasure and gives me no little satisfaction, especially when—as was the case recently—one of my articles, on the assumption that it had been written by Douglass himself, was reprinted in another newspaper." And again on October 29, 1871: "On his way to Washington, Douglass also spent a day and two nights with me [in Hoboken]. I have the satisfaction to hear that my articles are given some attention in Washington and are reprinted now and then in other papers. When Douglass is on his winter [lecture] tour, I will again have to do most of the work" (Varnhagen Papers).

Reports and Essays, 1852–1865

1

From Hamburg to New York[1]

Land, ahoy! How infinitely long a sea voyage seems while it is in progress, but only as fleeting as a moment as soon as you are done with it! I believe it has been but a few days since that evening when I took leave of my friends on board the ship and saw them disappear in the darkness. The moment when you set foot again on firm ground is like the awakening from a dream, a leaden nightmare. Even so happy a voyage as I had, without any bouts of seasickness, is nothing but a series of miseries and inconveniences. In spite of all its grandeur and beauty the sea remains forever a hostile element. The raw power of nature may to a certain extent be tamed, but suddenly its inherent wrath is aroused and, mocking all efforts at resistance, it swallows its conqueror just as the tiger or the hyena after many years of training will tear apart their trainer in an unguarded moment. What beauty and profound truth are expressed in the myth of the giant Anteus, who, as the son of the earth, remained invincible as long as his feet were planted on the ground but became as weak as a child when Hercules lifted him up. We are all like small versions of Anteus, and I, the most pronounced, the weakest of all who have ever wandered this planet. There were days when a longing for earth, trees, flowers, and fresh water all but drove me to despair; and not a night went by when I did not dream of the land and all the glories it had to offer.

Conditions on board ship are truly insufferable! To be forced to live in the company of strangers in such a small space is in itself intolerable for any well educated person, and it becomes altogether a torture if one has the misfortune to fall in with boring, mostly uneducated people. There were eight persons in first class: primarily Captain Drummond, a small, humorous, jolly American, friendly, benevolent, and generous; furthermore, a handful of questionable characters; and finally, more to the captain's than to my own delight, several women who, although they had paid only for second-class accommodations, were admitted into first class, I don't know at whose behest. A five-year-old child as well as a black cat, being considered no more than half persons, traveled at half-price; the cat served as a general toy for everyone suffering from boredom and enjoyed everyone's attention so much that she was called "the cat of social status."

"Oh, for a tiny little stall of straw, but a stall all to myself!" I often sighed when sitting in the cabin at night surrounded by people carrying on their shallow talk "with little wit but much contentment" or playing "Black Peter" because it was impossible to get together a party for Whist even in the first-class cabin. I had only one comfort, one protection against the ever-mounting pyramid of boredom: reading *Die Ritter vom Geist*,[2] which I had the pleasure to enjoy for the second time in full measure, made me forget the company, the sea, and its discomforts.

Better by far was the company in second class, representing as it did the good elements of the German people from all social levels. There were young scholars, sober farmers with wives and children who intended to buy a homestead in Wisconsin, craftsmen, an actor, and—political refugees, without whom hardly a ship sails for America these days. On evenings when the weather was fair they would all gather on deck as a choir, and it might well be the last time in your life for hearing the sad and joyful sounds of German folk and student songs wafting over the waves. Even some ridiculous specimens of humanity were present, most notably among them a former sergeant of the Wellington Regiment stationed in Altona, who stood out as one of the silliest bipeds I have ever encountered. Instead of dealing with the inevitable discomforts with humor and cheer, he took everything seriously and even with a kind of sentimental bathos that made him confide with sighs and heartbreaking emotion to everyone who would listen the tragic story of the precious food supplies he had taken along but which had all been spoiled. All on board knew about every last egg, herring, bouillon cube, and chocolate bar that Herr Keil had bought, and they also knew that for the same money that he had spent on this hoard of goods he could have traveled first class.

I was even more amused by a veterinarian who both mentally and physically might have been Shakespeare's model for Bardolph, Sir John Falstaff's friend. The deep, nasal voice, the pock-marked face, the crude jokes, the unpolished manners, and even the old-fashioned student clothes—all were appropriate for a gathering at the Boar's Head Tavern. And I silently concluded that this latter-day Bardolph, had he lived at the time of Queen Elizabeth, would not have hesitated to join the corpulent knight in the honorable trade of the highwayman.

The passengers in steerage were kept completely separate from the rest, but I found it entertaining to stand on the afterdeck and to look down on their picturesque activities as they received their midday meal. It amazes me that no artist has had the idea to make the sundeck above the steerage of an emigrant ship the subject of a large genre painting instead of repeating again and again the well-worn Tyrolean, the Italian women at the fountain, the farmers gathered at the pub, etc. What variety of groups and of physiognomies! Some are eating, others are washing dishes or playing cards, while someone is taking a nap, and a group of boys are launching little carved boats on a puddle. One day we even had an instance of popular justice being administered when a young country bumpkin who wanted to steal some butter was caught as he tried to slip the loot into his pocket; he had his hands tied and was put on public display after having his face smeared with the stolen butter.

A few events now and then disrupted the normal round of monotony. The first one was a violent storm that caught up with us eight days after we had set out to sea; and, as we were close to the English coast, it posed a not inconsiderable danger. This is clearly the appropriate occasion for presenting a highly poetic description, but I have to admit that I was not ready to step out into the pouring rain in my flimsy overcoat, and inside the ship there was nothing but a chaos of flying plates and glasses, of up-ended chairs and banging doors. One seasick passenger after another was dragged by the stewart to his bed, and I can only speak of my own good luck that I remained untouched by it all. The storm howled, the masts cracked, the rudder creaked, the sailors shouted as they ran hither and yon; and although everyone and everything joined in the cacophony of noise, I finally fell asleep and did not wake up until the next morning when all was quiet again. However, because the wind was still unfavorable, instead of sailing through the English Channel, the captain decided to go around England. This took us as far as the sixtieth degree of northern latitude, and one morning we found ourselves close to the coast of Scotland. It presented a magnificent view: the cliffs of sheer rock, bleak and forlorn, rising above a sea that in these latitudes has an even more sinister character. It seemed plausible to me that the people who inhabit these desolate regions so isolated from the rest of the world and so exposed to the horrors of nature should have the faculty of second sight.

After three long weeks the wind finally changed: a favorable east wind filled the sails and propelled us forward at the speed of a steamship. Life on board revived, and the expectation of the impending arrival at their destination made everyone forget present discomforts; even those who were seasick recovered, and all were glad to watch the preparations for a triumphant arrival in port: the ship was painted, freshly tarred and cleaned, and the masts were scrubbed down. The passenger list was updated to make a second edition, which, in its long extension of one sheet glued to another, soon began to resemble Don Juan's register. Every passenger was obliged to step up to give his name, occupation, and age, and I served as an interpreter. Here, on the far reaches of the ocean, these citizens of Saxony, Hessia, Hannover, and Mecklenburg, these inhabitants of Reuss, Greiz, and Schleiz, were given a common fatherland for the first time; even the proudly superior Prussians and Austrians all became Germans. The large number of children presented a special problem for the captain, who again and again had to ask whether Friedrich, Johanna, or Otto were *masculine* or *feminine*. And the captain paid hardly more attention to the distinctions among occupations, elevating farmhands, day laborers, and plain workers all to the rank of *farmer* because, so he said, "It looks better!"

But despite its comical aspects this inquiry had a sad side as well, for if even the educated, intelligent person must struggle to survive in these strange surroundings, what is to become of the mass of uneducated humanity—their very faces a picture of incomprehension—who flood into the New World without knowing either the conditions or the language and possessing no means of support? The country people have some advantage because the soil can be tilled in any language, but those who perish on the streets of New York disappear in the silence of history. Learn English! Learn English! I want to shout at all Germans, because who can be sure that he won't some day want or have to seek his fortune beyond the ocean? And no matter what occupation he may choose, "Do you speak English?" is always the first question the American asks of the foreigner.

Finally, on September 25, we saw land—both glad and apprehensive, because who knows what fate awaits us on this part of the earth which now still appears like a cloud before us? The shore became more and more distinct, and in the evening a boat dropped off the pilot who was to steer the ship into New York harbor the next morning. As a first greeting from the new continent we received the latest newspapers, but I looked in vain for any news from Europe. The American pilot, incidentally, does not bear the least resemblance to his German counterparts who look no different from regular sailors; instead he presents himself as an elegant gentleman in black tails and waistcoat according to the latest fashion magazine, adorned by a gold watch chain, well-trimmed beard, and scented hair. You should have seen the two Yankees, the pilot and the captain! Two Germans, one returning home after many months abroad, would have talked and chatted for hours! But not these two. Having greeted each other, they stood silently shoulder to shoulder: one Yankee clasped his collar and stared straight ahead without a word, while the other kept mum smoking his cigar. And sitting in the cabin after dinner over ample supplies of wine and brandy did not improve things. The captain sat in one corner and the pilot across from him on the sofa, busily stroking the cat of social status that had curled up next to him. Every ten minutes they exchanged a word or two about the trip or the weather until I could not stand the anxious silence any longer and started a conversation with the pilot, who continued to pet the cat. Before long, he began to thaw out, started laughing and making jokes and speaking of Kinkel, Alboni, and Kossuth,[3] generally revealing himself to be a man of some education.

In bright moonlight the ship anchored off Staten Island, whose lighthouses greeted us with welcoming beams. Scenic descriptions are not my thing, but this view is charming and unforgettable, and as I watched a shooting star I made the wish to own one of the handsome villas along the shore. If my wish comes true, all my friends are invited to stay with me!

The next morning, having undergone a somewhat perfunctory quarantine inspection, we continued briefly until we entered the enormous harbor of New York. While the ship stopped in the river, who could contain his impatience? Boats come alongside to take us ashore. Ah! one deep breath, the first on firm soil, and then onward into the city!

Notes

1. On Board the "Indian Queen," September 27, 1852; *Jahreszeiten* (November, 1852): 1505-1512.

2. Karl Gutzkow (1811-1878), *Die Ritter vom Geist* (1850-1851), a novel in nine volumes. Gutzkow, a journalist, writer, and member of the liberal nationalist movement known as "Young Germany," was part of Assing's circle of political and literary friends.

3. Gottfried Kinkel (1815-1882), a German poet, journalist, politician, and art historian, was an active supporter of the German revolution of 1848 who was closely associated with Carl Schurz, the most prominent German emigrant to

America after the collapse of the revolution. Marietta Alboni (1826–1894), an Italian contralto, toured American opera houses in 1852 after having achieved great success in many European countries. Louis Kossuth (1802–1894), a hero of the unsuccessful Hungarian effort to gain independence from Austria in 1848–1849, was celebrated as a proponent of freedom and democracy on his tour of the United States in 1850.

2

Schenectady—Barnum—Curiosities—Life in a Republic—Mrs. Trollope[1]

Since I last wrote, I undertook a trip of no less than sixty German miles from New York to Schenectady, about as far as from Hamburg to Frankfurt, but what a difference! I left on Friday and returned Tuesday, having taken nothing but a small travel bag and paid no more than two dollars round-trip! That's how people travel in America! My intention to sail up the Hudson to Albany early in the morning was unfortunately foiled by the fact that the morning steamer had had one of the frequent accidents that occur over here; "she was broken," was the brief announcement, and I had to wait patiently till evening, being thereby deprived of seeing the much-praised scenery along the banks. But what an American steamboat! You may know the exterior from the panorama of the Mississippi, but the interior of these floating palaces comes as a great surprise. Enormous salons, one above the other, as we would not find them in our most elegant houses: heavy silk curtains, magnificent carpets, and every comfort—of which I would gladly have dispensed with only the Bibles that were lying on every table because they seemed to me inappropriate here. However, the biggest surprise came when we went for supper down to a third salon (it corresponded to the "basement," the ground floor of all houses, where meals are commonly served); two long dining tables were set next to each other, which all but disappeared in this enormous room, and we were served a most elegant supper that at home we would expect only at a ball. Best of all, however, were the waiters, ten or twelve blacks and colored people, all dressed in snowy white tails, nimbly and silently vaulting hither and yon. It was the first moment in which I felt non-European, or rather that I was no longer in Europe. There were beds available for anyone who chose, but I preferred lying down on a simple bench and slept till we arrived in Albany the next morning.

There is a significant difference in climate: the day before I had felt nearly too warm under a light stole of lace, but in Albany I saw fires in the stoves. After flying by train from Albany to Schenectady in half an hour, I was met at the station by my friend, with whom I spent three very pleasant days. It rained so hard during the first two days that we could not think of going out but sat and talked; on the third day the weather cleared, and my friend, who knows several professors' families (Schenectady being a university town),[2] introduced me to her acquaintances. Among them I got to know women as charming as any in Europe, particularly a lady president who reminded me of Anna von Harder in *Die Ritter vom Geist*—Anna von Harder in an American version.[3] I also made the acquaintance of a German, Doctor ——, a lively young man whose eyes radiate intelligence. He came here as a political refugee and at first supported himself by playing the guitar in inns and lodging houses, but he was so successful with the public that he was soon given an appointment at the university. We also went for a walk that took me into a most beautiful region, which would have been famous back home but receives almost no notice here. Close to the town runs the Mohawk (well known through *The Last of the Mohicans*), and there are mountains and the most gorgeous vegetation in the world. It was the first time that I had seen sycamores, and I took several leaves with me, which measure almost a foot in width and three-quarters of a foot in length. I also got to know a new kind of cat—supposedly the true American variety; they are silvery-gray, without any stripes or other colors, like the fur of the gray Russian squirrel. Someone claimed the other day that all animals over here are tamer and more intelligent, but I hope to find out for myself. I also noticed the brilliant colors of the countryside, reminding me somewhat of Italy; the trees in their fall colors glowed in red and yellow as I have never seen before. It was also amusing to see a small fire alarm: as soon as the call went out, citizen volunteers rather than paid firemen pulled the engines and ladders through the streets, and it was funny to see elegant gentlemen pulling the fire engine while covering themselves with umbrellas.

Shortly after returning to New York, I visited Barnum's American Museum, a most remarkable place.[4] Not that I was interested in the stuffed animals, the old weapons, or the Chinese toys, all of which I have seen better elsewhere; however, the incredibly amusing mixture, the unique pell-mell of objects, shows the American naiveté in these matters. I was often reminded of primitive tribes that wear padlocks and brass buttons like decorative necklaces. On entering the ground level, the visitor is welcomed with a kind of circus music, and you ask yourself what such music has to do with a museum. An enormous dragon made of paper, leather, and God knows what other materials hangs suspended above the stairs just as one can see in old paintings, and the only thing missing is St. George slaying it. And there is a cheerful chaos as you enter: here, under a collection of animal skeletons, a proud flag that was used in the War of Independence; there, next to an Egyptian mummy, a piece of lace allegedly once worn by Marie Antoinette; next to that some sort of deep-sea creature. Beneath a collection of bugs you can see a painting of Christ and next to it an Indian idol with an ancient candle snuffer placed between the feet. The Venus of Medici and Pope Leo X meet in the midst of a collection of stuffed birds, and Jenny Lind stands next to a copy of the Kohi-Noor diamond. Among what is billed as paintings of Herculaneum are a number of small steel engravings of Paris like those found in any guidebook, and mixed in among them all are long rows of portraits of presidents, generals, and other patriots. There is also a small theater where plays are performed in broad daylight, and the top floor holds a menagerie of live animals, consisting of several ostriches, a young bear, a few snakes, and finally a cage in which birds, cats, weasels, rats, etc. live in peaceful harmony—they call it "the happy family."

There is never a day here when one doesn't make some curious discovery. It was only today that I read in the *Herald*, the most widely read newspaper, that a Dr. Lawson, for the charge of one dollar, promises to tell "lovers" the secret formula that will forever assure the bonds of love between them. All sorts of miracle cures are sold from carts in the streets, but no one seems to ask how many people are killed by these quackeries. Also, the fact that any former barber or tailor has the right to call himself Doctor and go merrily about treating people without having passed an examination seems too liberal an application of the freedom of occupational choice. And one would wish for better police protection, since the frequent cases of assault and murder in the public streets are not exactly conducive to one's comfort; and the fact, as people explain, that these crimes are always perpetrated by foreigners is surely of little consequence to the victims.

I have already become quite accustomed to life over here. It is a pleasure to deal with the charms of a new place! Every day you see new faces, have new experiences, and see new sights. Of course, if you are mostly bent on admiring poets and art, you will be disappointed; but what you will find instead is the poetry of reality, and so far it has amply compensated me for this dearth. Especially if you bring a good deal of European civilization and culture with you and have made it part of your inner self, your mind surely cannot starve over here.

I have already met the most diverse and peculiar types of humanity, among them a particularly amusing lady who belongs to the sect of the Millerites. With unctuous piety she told me how she had learned from the Bible that the world would come to an end this year, but that she and a few other select persons would go directly to heaven. Expecting the apocalypse, she completely refuses to take care of her affairs and has run away from two husbands who would not be converted to her beliefs, and for the past nine years she has lived at her relatives' expense, staying with one or the other of them uninvited and never leaves until bidden.

But it is a daily delight to know that I am living in a republic and to witness the happiness of the people and their conscious enjoyment of that happiness. The behavior of the lowest classes has nothing of the servile demeanor that they are made to adopt among us in early youth; they are free, friendly, and outgoing and meet you as equals without being pushy or cringing. With us, liberty is an ideal that we strive for but have not reached; here, where everyone has and enjoys liberty, you learn to take a double delight in it. Even animals enjoy these privileges: I have had my initial impression confirmed that they are generally treated better here than with us. Horses are directed only by verbal commands; they all look well cared for and, I am told, are rarely made to feel the whip—and in all my wanderings through the streets I have never heard a single crack of a whip. Dogs are also said to be seldom put on a chain.

In the company of my landlady, I undertook a most delightful tour to Yorkville, a village lying at a distance of about one German mile. The contrast between the crowds of New York and this little growing village (to which the stage will take you for 6 cents, about three and a half schillings) can hardly be greater; but I was even more pleased with the aspect of the little country house belonging to the family of my landlady's cook. Stepping in, we could hardly have wished for a cleaner and more comfortable home despite the cramped quarters. The people are Irish, and one is doubly glad for them as one remembers the deprivation and poverty which is the fate of the Irish at home. A cheerful fire in the fireplace and carpets throughout the house conveyed a pleasant impression. The parlor contained a small statue of the Virgin, surrounded by Catholic books of devotion in costly bindings. Ellen's brother, Jack, plays the role of the housewife and, besides all his other duties, keeps the entire house clean; he welcomed us as politely as I would wish any millionaire would do and told us that he had been offered a well-paying position but did not want to give up his independence.

A comical aspect of the Americans is their naive love of uniforms and playing at soldiers. Giving expression to the principle of complete freedom in this matter as well, each battalion of the citizens' militia sports a different uniform, thus creating a veritable sample collection of European uniforms—the Austrians' white coats and bear caps, the red pantaloons of the French, the red coats of Denmark, etc., while another battalion parades with guns wearing white leather straps, black tails, and round hats.

I am reading Mrs. Trollope's book about America.[5] Although it may contain some truths, too much is seen as through dark glasses, reminding me of Nicolai[6]: just as he sees only vermin in Italy, she finds nothing but chewing tobacco and feet on the table in America. This lady is entirely incapable of recognizing and respecting the beauty of republican equality.

Notes

1. New York, November 21, [1852], *Die Jahreszeiten* (January, 1853): 105–112.

2. The reference is to Union College, founded in 1795; its long-time president (1804–1866) was Eliphalet Nott. Assing's comments and descriptions here anticipate some of the details she would give about eighteen months later, in a piece for the *Morgenblatt* (see Essay 4), about another visit with her friend Amalie Schoppe, who lived in Schenectady.

3. Assing had read Gutzkow's *Die Ritter vom Geist* for the second time on her transatlantic voyage (see Essay 1, n. 2). The "lady president" was Urania Sheldon Nott, who, according to Assing's biographer, Maria Diedrich, had charge of the girls' school where Schoppe taught German and French.

4. Phineas Taylor Barnum (1810–1891) had become famous through his American Museum in New York, with his European and American tours of Tom Thumb, and by managing the triumphant tour of Jenny Lind ("the Swedish Nightingale") that began in New York City in September 1850.

5. Frances Trollope (1780–1863), *The Domestic Manners of the Americans* (1832).

6. Gustav Nicolai (b. 1795) was the author of *Italien wie es wirklich ist* (The Real Italy), a critical book about Italy, first published in 1834; the book's subtitle explains its purpose: "a report on a strange trip to the Hesperian fields, as a voice of warning to all those who long to be there."

3

The Tombs—The Washington Exhibition—Minstrels[1]

The landlord of the lady in whose boardinghouse I am living here, an almost eighty-year-old doctor, had his watch stolen by a poor drunkard of a tailor who was kept for a variety of small domestic services, and although there was no proof, he had him arrested on mere suspicion. This is a peculiarity of the law here which seems remarkable to our European concepts of justice. Anybody can have anyone arrested on any suspicion. If the suspect is able to post bond, he remains at liberty for the time being, assuming that it is not a matter of a serious crime; if not, he is marched off to jail, and it is left to later investigation to determine the validity of the charges. It is self-evident that this system, which is reminiscent of the *lettres de cachet*, invites private revenge. I personally have experienced that a particular acquaintance was charged by a jealous and disdained rival for the affections of a lady with threatening his life; he was arrested and escaped prison only by immediately posting bond.

A few days after the arrest of the thief, who had meanwhile confessed to stealing the watch, the inquiry was to begin. Mrs. S., the lady of the house, had also been requested to appear to tell what she knew about the matter, and because she was reluctant to go by herself and the old doctor could hardly be relied upon, I accompanied her to the jail. The city prison, which the people have given the sinister name "The Tombs," is a new building whose sides, with air holes resembling embrasures, give the appearance of an old castle, while in front a flight of steps leads up to an entrance hall supported by mighty columns. Musty, stifling air assaults the visitor even here; it is as if all the horrors of our social conditions, which in normal life we ignore with foolish egotism, were coming to weigh on our breast like an oppressive burden. This sensation increased as we stepped from the entrance hall into the large, circular court room. At its center are various partitions for judges and clerks, closest to the entrance several rows of benches for witnesses, and in the back, behind a barrier, the poor devils who were stupid enough to steal watches and silver spoons instead of millions. One look at these pitiful figures reveals the entire misery of our social conditions: that horrible war of annihilation that people fight among themselves, which neither individual nor communal philanthropic endeavors will ever bring to an end. For this reason I never could understand the optimistic courage with which so many are ready to pronounce verdicts of condemnation upon others. Whoever is courageous enough to be honest with himself and the world has to admit that once we subtract everything we have become through education, knowledge, and beneficial influences almost nothing remains; and no one can guarantee whether under exactly opposite circumstances he would be one iota better than the worst among those whom he is so ready to condemn. Once you are what good fortune has made you, it is easy to predict the future and not to clash with the police; but it is presumptuous to consider it anything but good fortune.

I was suddenly torn from these thoughts: the proceedings relating to the theft of the watch were next, beginning a strange scene. While the old, deaf doctor gave a long speech of accusation and explanation, Mrs. S., without being heard by him, told the judge in hushed tones that the poor accused had a wife and three children at home who would be exposed to extreme misery if he were locked up. This made so much sense to the judge that he suggested to release the prisoner, and since the doctor had no objections, having had his watch restored to him, the quaking sinner was set free after a short admonition henceforth to abstain from theft and drink. In my own mind I compared this to our native German states, where the poor man, having confessed his crime, would not have gotten away with anything less than two to three years imprisonment to satisfy the *fiat justitia*.

Following this happy conclusion of the bargain, Mrs. S. proposed that we visit the interior of the jail; and, having obtained the necessary permission, we commenced our excursion. Galleries run on three levels like balconies in a theater around a large elongated rectangle that is lighted from above, giving access to the iron-grate doors of the prisoners' cells, of which there are fifty on each floor. Since prisoners are kept here only for minor crimes and while awaiting trial, the horrors of Pennsylvania's solitary confinement—a method of torture unbecoming a free country (my old acquaintance, Dr. Julius, an eager proponent of the prisons of Pennsylvania,[2] would scream if he were to read these lines)—are not employed, and some of the prisoners started to engage us in easy conversation, while others withdrew to a corner out of a sense of shame. Some of the cells were occupied by two, three, or more prisoners, which given the small size of the rooms struck me as a great cruelty. The cells are very clean, heated by pipes, and on first glance not at all abhorrent; yet they are all—even the empty ones with wide open doors—filled with a peculiarly musty, stifling air, the cause of which was not explained to me until later. The whole building rests on swampy ground, is damp from top to bottom, and—a shameful situation for a republic—so unhealthy that completely well persons have become sick after three or four days of incarceration evidently in consequence of the harmful influences of the location. Even worse things occur in this place: only a few days ago the papers carried an official report from the grand jury to the aldermen of the City of New York regarding the death of four persons who, together with two who were saved, had been placed in one cell and were asphyxiated by coal gas. The situation was handled with such carelessness that after the first one had been found dead the guards removed him without any further inspection of the cells.

After having visited the galleries on all levels, we were guided to the women's prison across the courtyard where the executions take place, a chilly and frightening place lying to the north. We encountered the prisoners all sitting in a courtyard, some of them sewing, others chatting or smoking short Irish pipes. If the spectacle of the men is unpleasant, that of the women is horrifying and pitiful at once. A man can go through a lot and take a deep fall, yet get to his feet again; whereas a woman, if she has fallen to a certain level, must be considered lost. The final offense which has brought them here and usually was only the last drop that caused the cup of misery to overflow is nothing compared to all that went before; and most of their faces have been unmistakably branded by meanness, depravity, and vice. Here I saw creatures that can haunt one's dreams, yet even in all this misery and corruption there are distinctions by rank. An old Negro woman (incidentally, an old good-for-nothing who had been picked up for the third or fourth time) sat by herself at one end of the courtyard while the other women all sat close to each other at the other end. But even The Tombs have their humorous side: among these thirty or forty mostly very chatty women there was hardly a single one who was not, according to her own story, the very essence of angelic and persecuted innocence. Some claimed that the police persecuted them maliciously; and a garrulous old woman, who had tried to steal from a cobbler, told a story of wanting to buy a pair of shoes and being arrested for nothing with such comic naivete that the others all burst out laughing. Yet another one was also picked up just as she set out to visit her relatives in the country, and she was greatly worried about what they thought about her long delay. Mrs. S. advised her to tell them that she had been on a pleasure trip, a suggestion that she immediately took to heart. After more than two hours in The Tombs we stepped into the outside world, and I gulped the air as if I had just been released after a long term in prison. Freedom! Freedom!

Longing for more cheerful, comforting impressions, I sought refuge in the Washington Exhibition on the way back. One can breathe more freely there! Art is a beautiful truth and reality, of which neither disappointments nor failures can deprive us. Happy is he who is receptive to art and can momentarily forget himself and the world in its presence. This exhibition consists of 160 paintings by American and foreign artists brought together here from private and public collections. Unlike European exhibitions, which are open only in the mornings and afternoons, this one maintains splendidly lighted salons until ten o'clock in the evening. What people can see at that time in the pictures and how they judge them, heaven only knows; but I understand that the largest crowd of visitors comes in the evenings. It can't be a surprise to see that the most remarkable works in this collection are by foreigners. Art cannot burst forth over night like springtime, and rather than denying both a present and a future to American art—as so many of the thousands of resident "Americaphobes" do—we would prefer to wait with hopeful expectations what flowers will eventually develop from these buds. Meanwhile America has had the good fortune to find in Leutze,[3] a German, a painter for its young history. Although naturalized in America, he received his artistic training during a ten-year sojourn in Europe.

His "Washington Crossing the Half-frozen Delaware," the centerpiece of this exhibition, is one of the most remarkable works of modern art. Conception and technique are on an equally high plane, and a simple nobility heightens its grand impression. Nothing is forced or *outré* nor is the artist trying for effects; all is truth, simple truth, which—ennobled by beauty—is the highest and the only end of art. The victory of the power of man battling the elements, enhanced by idealistic enthusiasm, is here presented with overwhelming truth and faithfulness to nature. Anyone who has never seen one of the mighty, fierce American rivers at the beginning or end of the winter, before the ice has formed or entirely melted, has no conception of the force and thunderous noise with which the massive ice floes crash into each other, shatter into fragments, and pile up into towering glaciers. To dare a crossing at such a season seems like madness, and even the most courageous sailors today will undertake it at best with a boat containing no more than three or four persons. The oars are all but useless in such an undertaking, and the sailor in the bow trying to propel the boat forward by means of a long pole-oar finds himself more outside the vessel on the ice than inside. The figure of Washington, standing in the center of the boat, his coat lifted by the wind, presenting his profile to the viewer, is marked by the power and confidence heightened by enthusiasm for and commitment to the cause. No less successfully rendered are the other figures: Monroe, Greene (the Scotsman), Washington's loyal black companion,[4] the officers, and the soldiers.

* * *

Among New York institutions of entertainment, the minstrels, also called the Ethiopian Opera Company, occupy an important place; they are, in fact, far too typical as to remain unmentioned. Indeed, Christy,[5] their founder, is in a sense one of America's men of fame—something he never fails to mention in each of his flyers. It is on his minstrel stage that he first introduced "Old Folks at Home," which was as successful as "Yankee Doodle" in finding its way to the hearts and throats of the masses, and even today it echoes in every street, cranked out by a thousand hurdy-gurdies. A theater-like building on Broadway above Grand Street carries the inscription: "Christy's Opera House," where performances are offered every night. Upon entering we find ourselves in a large concert hall, at the end of which a raised orchestra platform also serves as a stage. Large palm-leaf fans are placed on the benches for cooling the ladies, for whom the front rows have been reserved out of that consideration they can generally expect to enjoy here—as the flyer points out. One glance at the audience and its generally loud and vulgar apparel reveals to us that it is primarily the middle class that has come here for its entertainment, even though a large number of the men appear to be of the upper class.

The hall is filling up rapidly, and by eight o'clock it is crowded. A short delay is greeted by an outburst of noisy impatience. Finally the company appears on stage: nine pitch-black fellows dressed in black tails, among them Christy as their leader, play a Negro melody. Their long hair, bright red lips, and entire physiognomy reveals them at first glance to be not real but merely made-up Negroes—among them an honest "Herr" Meyer, according to the program. Two violins play the leading melodies; the other instruments are a guitar, two banjos—a genuine Negro instrument, something between a drum and a guitar—a concertina, a triangle, a tambourine, and castanets, the last two being played by the comedians of the company, who accompany the music by making faces and filling the breaks with joking and grimacing. Their jokes are so cheap that any clown in a European circus would be loath to serve them up; they are good enough, however, for this grateful audience, which greets every silliness with happy laughter. The first segment consisted of a few so-called Ethiopian songs, rendered by generally poor voices, accompanied by the said instruments, and spiced with the facial contortions of the comedians, one of whom parodied a Tyrolean yodeler with earsplitting sounds. An assortment of burlesque dances, some of them in female costume, is performed during the second segment; and in the third, the plantation Negroes appear with their songs and dances. The witty conclusion, giving the whole performance an appropriate ending, has the two comedians, again cast in the main roles, covering each other with flour, and even this brand-new joke is greeted by the audience with ecstatic delight.

That reasonable people would wish to amuse themselves with this nonsense more than once seems quite impossible, as one looks in vain for even a spark of true humor and wit. The minstrels lack even the enticement of novelty, since Christy's company, the first and the oldest according to the program, was founded as long ago as 1842 and now has found a rival in Wood. In earlier years it used to tour other cities but recently has not left New York, yet the hall is always crowded. Christy has become a rich man, and his minstrels are likely to flourish for another decade. There is an odd conflict between the intelligent, quiet, and reasonable nature of the Americans in all practical matters and their childish naivete and lack of judgment in regard to art. This, of course, does not apply to the educated elite, which is finally very much alike throughout the world with only shades of difference here and there. But one can experience the most fantastic things, even with altogether reasonable people, and nothing is too silly and senseless not to attract admirers as long as it is properly designed to pique their curiosity. One example is the so-called "happy families" that were first introduced by Barnum, the father of humbug, and presented in his museum. Having spread here and there in a small way, they can now be found on Broadway, in the Bowery, and elsewhere, where one can see the advertisement: "Happy Family. Admission 12 ½ Cents." If you let yourself be tempted and enter, you will probably find two dogs, a cat, a few rabbits, rats, mice, and birds together in a cage being stared at in happy contemplation by numerous visitors who don't seem to realize that it really isn't much of a trick to get animals to live peacefully with each other by training them early and feeding them amply. One look at the plump figures of the animals suffices to explain the miracle. But, no matter, the "happy family" is still something to marvel at.

Notes

1. New York, May [1853], *Morgenblatt*, 47:27:643–646.

2. Nicolaus Heinrich Julius (1783–1862), *Die amerikanischen Besserungssysteme* [The American System of Corrections] (Leipzig, 1837).

3. The German-American painter Emmanuel Gottlieb Leutze (1816–1868) completed his most famous painting, "Washington Crossing the Delaware," in 1851.

4. Most likely Assing knew that the figure represents Washington's slave, but she may have been reluctant to reveal to her German audience that the hero of the American Revolution was a slaveholder.

5. Founded in 1842 in Buffalo by Edwin P. Christy (1815–1862), the Christy Minstrels made their New York City debut in 1846 and provided popular entertainment for many years, especially featuring such songs by Stephen Foster as "Swanee River" (also called "Old Folks at Home").

4

From New York to Schenectady—The Shakers[1]

The journey to the West has begun. It was on June 18, and the world was glowing in those radiant, warm colors that only the southern sun can paint when I left New York at around the noon hour. The depot of the Hudson Railroad lies at the center of the city, and instead of the little carriages common in northern Germany they here use enormous cars accommodating forty or fifty persons, who sit, two and two, on little benches on either side of each window, leaving the middle open as an aisle. Most of the cars were well occupied, and since I had to give up the idea of having a bench to myself, I simply sat down next to an old Negro woman. If I had the good or bad fortune to be an important person, this would have been interpreted as an abolitionist demonstration, but under the circumstances it was at most seen as the inexperience of a "greenhorn." No matter! The colored people meet all approaches by whites with friendly courtesy. Considering the prevailing prejudice, it is remarkable that the black and colored people are not stuffed into separate cars or so carefully segregated on the railroads as they are in the theaters and similar places. In this regard alone republican equality rules: he who pays, whether white or black, travels in the same car. But there is a separate class of cars for immigrants only, in which people are said to have suffocated—the "emigrants-train" that transports them at little cost to the interior of the country.

Meanwhile everyone has settled down in the cars; a clock strikes the time of departure: "All right!" The train leaves. It is of course forbidden to go under steam in the city, so four horses effortlessly pull each enormous car along the tracks in the streets along the Hudson up to the lonely streets at the northern end of the city where there is another depot. Here the horses are unhitched; a single push and the whole row of cars is coupled together; another, and the locomotive is attached. In less than a minute everything is accomplished, and the train is flying along like the wind, as it would only in America. Farewell, New York, loveliest of cities, darling of the gods, risen from the sea! How I love you with your ever beaming skies, with your colorful, turbulent street-life!—The route from New York to Albany follows the Hudson all the way. It is a magnificent route: the mighty river to the left, with hills rising on the far side fringed by forests and dotted by charming mansions; on the right the chain of the Catskill Mountains, which at every turn offer ever new and beautiful vistas. In order to avoid the detours necessitated by the bends in the river, the train at times runs straight through them, so that while at one moment you are completely surrounded by water, the next you are engulfed by the darkness of a tunnel. How wrong those are who say that the poetry of travel has been destroyed by modern steam transportation! True, the acquaintances one makes along the way, the adventures of the wayside inns have come to an end; but what is such mail-coach romance compared to the greater poetry that lies in the lightning leaps from one country, from one people to another? The seven-league boots that our parents admired when they were children have been far surpassed, and yet it is said that poetry is in decline. Whoever grasps the poetry of the present reality will always be richly rewarded and will rarely have to complain about disappointments and lost illusions.

In the afternoon the train stopped at the edge of the river. We cross it on a steam ferry and find ourselves in Albany, the capital of the State of New York where the governor resides. I much enjoyed its location on a hill, from which one has a view of the river and the opposite bank. The city itself, full of life and activity, with wide streets, and like most American cities dotted with green, park-like squares, makes a pleasing impression. However, there was not much time to satisfy my curiosity because after a short while the locomotive snorted and we were on our way again. The train dashes through the lower part of the city, and only its bell, rung by the conductor, announces the approach of the black monster. There is no sign of barriers here or at places where country roads cross the tracks; a simple marker—Crossing of the Railroad. Look out for the Cars!—is the only warning. The carelessness with which Americans deal with life is unbelievable. Everything is assessed by its basic monetary value: Time is money! is the generally accepted saying. Indeed, time is assessed with anxious care as if it were cash and currency, even at dinner, where Americans never remain over long conversations as we do, often forgetting with pleasure the actual purpose of the meal. Only life itself seems to have no value here, is treated almost like an outlaw, and is daily put at risk with cheerful carelessness. Hence the innumerable railroad accidents, hence the daily murders in the streets of the large cities, especially New York, that the police has hitherto been unable to stop. Hence also the uncontrolled public advertisement and sale of all sorts of miracle potions, even of poison, which can be obtained in every apothecary's shop. Hence the licensing of every quack, every escaped barber's apprentice, every apothecary's assistant who wants to play doctor.

The train takes half an hour from Albany to Schenectady, which was my immediate goal because I intended to spend several days with my dear friend of many years, Amalie Schoppe,[2] the author of fiction and books for young people, well-known and popular throughout Germany. She met me at the railroad station, and soon we sat together in lively, intimate talk as we often had done on the other side of the ocean. This excellent woman, who far surpasses all her writings in her qualities of mind and heart, in the genuineness and truth of her whole being, and in her personal charm and originality, had enough courage and enterprise at age sixty to follow her son across the sea after he had accepted a very good position as an engineer for the new Albany–Schenectady railroad line. For almost two years she has been living in this city in the most agreeable circumstances among the best educated families, tutoring some of their daughters, beloved and esteemed by all who meet her, having a sprightly and stimulating mind, maintaining a youthful interest in all current developments.

In the evening we took a splendid walk through the town of Schenectady, one of the oldest cities of the State of New York, which has a university[3] and was founded by Dutch settlers. The location of the town is charming: surrounded by wooded hills affording the most pleasant views, it lies in a beautiful valley formed by the Mohawk, well-known through Cooper's "Last Mohican." In earlier years Indians often raided and set fire to the town, and to this day there is a monument marking the spot which their anger reached during the last assault. Situated on top of a hill with a perfect view of the town and the mountains beyond are the university building—"The College"—and the quarters of most of the professors, to whom Amalie Schoppe introduced me and where I was given a hearty welcome and spent some pleasant hours. The pleasure I take in being with educated Americans rises with each new acquaintance. Except for a certain inflexible orthodoxy, they are quite free of prejudice, open-minded, and receptive to every new, fresh impulse no matter where it may come from. The prejudice they are accused of having against Germans is in reality only a certain reluctance to accept the broad masses and is completely justifiable in light of the majority of adventurers and riff-raff that flood the United States year after year by the thousands. The individual educated German, on the other hand, may always count on a friendly reception, if he is deserving of it in terms of his personal character, and will never be mortified by any hint of prejudice.

Ten miles from here lies a colony of Shakers, those sectarians who dance during their worship services. To see such a sight is too interesting for any traveler to pass up, so we are planning an excursion for tomorrow. Early the next day we got on the way in a light buggy. The day was warm but cloudy, just right for driving on the unshaded country road. At first we traveled along the old Albany road for about five miles, then turned off to follow small lanes through magnificent country, almost losing our way, until we finally, after two hours, arrived at the Shaker colony. It consists of three friendly villages fifteen minutes distance from each other, each with its own entrance, closed by an iron gate. The church lies in the last village. On weekdays every stranger arriving here is hospitably greeted and served; on Sundays, however, such a show of hospitality would be considered a sacrilege, and even our horse, who was beginning to have sinful longings for a measure of oats, had to content itself with the pasture, along with other horses of nearby visitors that we found grazing at the entrance.

A path made of neatly laid flagstones leads from the entrance to the church, a simple elongated rectangle with two narrow doors, of which the right is designated for women, the left for men. We enter and find ourselves in a large hall with benches running along the walls. On the end where we entered are seven to eight inclined rows of benches for visitors (the Shakers are clearly counting on an audience), who soon appeared in large numbers. These seats are separated in front from the hall by means of a balustrade; on the other end of the hall are two doors for the congregation. The only adornment is exceptional cleanliness—benches and floor shine; otherwise the place is dominated by a sense of soberness that I have generally found in the churches of American sects. It always reminds me of Councilor Blaustrumpf in Gutzkow's *Blasedow*,[4] whose wish to eliminate everything related to Catholicism made him build a church in the shape of a plain cube, which he then wished to name, not after some saint, but simply "house of spiritual exercise."

The sect of the Shakers was founded during the last century by an Englishwoman, Anna Luze.[5] Having once been the mistress of an English officer, she moved from one man to another for a long time and came to America after a colorful and adventure-filled life. In her later years—like so many good-for-nothings making the best of things—she got religion and asked her followers to renounce all the things that no longer tempted her. Celibacy is the cardinal principle of the Shakers: men and women live separately and only meet for worship services. Although married couples are accepted into the community, they are divorced from the moment of their admission—a situation that has reportedly now and then been used to get rid of a wife or husband cheaply, without costly divorce proceedings. As the sect, therefore, can replenish itself only from the outside, its numbers will always remain rather limited; at present it is estimated at no more than 20,000 in the United States. However, since all unnatural conditions exert their vengeance, this prohibition among the Shakers sometimes leads to illicit relations, which, if discovered, are punished by expulsion from the community. Private property is also prohibited, and all individual possessions become the property of the community, which is very wealthy and owns large tracts of land. The Shakers grow garden, orchard, and field products of outstanding quality; and they manufacture and trade in medicines and materials made of wool, cotton, and linen. Like the Quakers, they have no ministers; whoever feels that the spirit is moving him can get up and preach. Worldly amusements are, of course, not permitted; however, the Shakers are said to compensate for all these sacrifices—like so many pious people—through a life of ease and comfort and particularly excellent cooking. As I was told, many a shiftless fellow has taken advantage of this during the hard winter months and let himself be admitted to and fed by the community only to disappear without a trace in the spring.

After about half an hour, both doors to the hall opened and the congregation appeared, the sisters from the right, the brethren from the left: about 120 persons of all ages, ranging from white-haired old men to children of eight to ten years. The men's clothes resemble those worn by farmers in some parts of Germany: dark trousers, dark blue jackets with long tails, long gray overcoats; the hair, cropped short on the side and growing longer in the back, is also much like that of many of our compatriots. The women's dress is more unusual, and there can hardly be anything less becoming than the diagonally cut, reddish-brown, half-woolen dresses with straight waists running just below the breast covered by square white silk kerchiefs that are carefully pinned at the neck. But the most tasteless part are the white caps half covering forehead and cheeks and thoroughly disfiguring even the prettiest of faces.

All sat down on the benches in silence, the women spreading on their laps the excessively large kerchiefs like napkins. They remained seated for about a quarter of an hour, and I took the occasion to look at them more closely. But I looked in vain for a figure of beauty, a pretty or intelligent face. Nothing but ugly and stupid faces; nothing but heavy, cloddish figures with large feet and hands: no beauty, no intelligence! Of course, anyone who still has a hopeful future in this world, who knows how to give and enjoy, whose spirit reaches beyond the sober realities of the workaday world, whose imagination longs for the stimulation of art and beauty—such a person would never join the Shakers, with whom intellect, imagination, and a sense of beauty are by definition elements of evil.

Suddenly the congregation rose: men and women placed themselves in long facing rows bowing deeply to each other. They began to intone a song which was even more horrible than what I had heard among the Methodists: the tune like a popular street song, the sound a lovely combination of shouting, screaming, grunting, and roaring. Then a few speakers stepped up, but their words were so few and so faint at the other end of the hall that nothing could be heard except for the request addressed to the visitors not to disturb the congregation by leaving the service but to remain till the end, to keep quiet any children who might be present (one was just shouting loudly), and to wipe their shoes upon entering—a reminder that came a bit late now that all benches were occupied. After a few more songs had been screeched, another speaker stepped forward who gave a long sermon mostly directed at the visitors, accusing them of sinful worldliness and bidding them to turn within themselves and contemplate their actions. He did not really speak better or worse, more or less intelligently, than any of a hundred other sectarian preachers, but we found it tedious all the same. But even this trial finally came to an end; the congregation sat down after another song to rest for a few minutes, but then jumped to its feet again.

The men tear off their jackets, and men and women on both sides arrange themselves in rows. Four men and four women in the middle—probably the elders—begin to sing a cheerful tune, moving their hands to the beat, and the dance can begin. A few who may be impeded by ill health or old age remain standing along the walls and content themselves with moving their hands, but I also saw aged men and women with snowy white hair hop merrily along. At first the dance consists mostly of a kind of *chassé en avant* and *en arrière* and a few movements to the left and to the right, not unlike a contradance, but that pattern soon comes to an end. Brethren and sisters join in several large circles, of which the smaller one in the center is made up of younger people and children, the older folks moving in the outer circle. The segregation between men and women is maintained to the point that two men always walk next to two women without holding hands. Everyone jumps merrily by himself moving their hands to the beat and occasionally clapping. The tempo picks up, and they dance a few figures with a sure sense of rhythm but heavy-footed and graceless. Stepping lightly on the tips of one's toes and turning one's feet sideways are unheard of here: with feet stiffly pointing forward, they jump up and down with all their weight.

The dance lasted about forty-five minutes including a few short moments of rest, then they suddenly stood still, the earlier speaker said a few words again, calling the dance "a recreation to the honor of God," and then added: "The assembly is dismissed!" They all withdrew as quietly and seriously as they had come. We stepped outside, too, and started on our return. What we had seen would have been comical if the stupidity and narrow-mindedness which so many people freely accept did not make such a depressing and revolting impression.

Notes

1. From the Northern United States, October [1853], *Morgenblatt*, 47:51:1221–1224.

2. Amalie Schoppe (1791–1858), a friend of Rosa Maria Assing, had founded a school for girls in Hamburg but moved to Schenectady, N.Y., in 1851 to live with one of her sons. She wrote more than 200 popular novels, some under the male pseudonym "Adalbert von Schonau."

3. Union College, founded in 1795.

4. Gutzkow's comic novel, *Blasedow und seine Söhne* (Blasedow and His Sons) was published in 1838 (see Essay 1, n. 2).

5. Evidently an error—on either the printer's or Assing's part—for Ann Lee, the English-born founder of the Shakers, who came to America in 1774, where she lived and worked until 1784. Her original community was located in what is now Colonie, N.Y., where one can still visit Ann Lee's grave in the Shaker cemetery and view the remains of the settlement that survived until 1921.

5

A Small Western Town[1]

For three and a half days I had been floating around on the lakes before we finally landed at the small Wisconsin town where I intended to stay for a while.[2] A few people were standing on the dock; there was no trace of the crowds that I had seen in other places where we had stopped. When I asked for Mr. ——, I was addressed in German by an elderly man: "Are you coming directly from Berlin?" Once a royal Prussian prison guard in Spandau,[3] an American citizen for twenty years, and now the proprietor of a local inn, he still retained much of the Berlin manner, despite the long distance in time and space. He offered to show me the way, but I looked in vain for something resembling a town, because even though this place has the honor to be known as a city, it has the looks of a village, like all recently established western towns. Paved streets and street lamps are an unknown luxury and "the cattle plods along in darkness"; cows and pigs casually roam the streets, and if you can spend a half hour or so you may eventually spy a human biped. The houses are all made of wood and stand in rows only along Main Street; on the elevation above, the country lanes winding through the meadows are looked upon as streets in anticipation of future houses, which at this point appear only here and there with much space in between, because this one-horse town has been conceived on a grand scale.

In Europe, cities are the result of progressive development, here they are based on speculation. Over there, circumstances and the general condition of things first prompted a few people to settle in a particular place, and by and by a few shacks became a village and then a city. Here, people determine that a city is to be established in a particular place; they set out long and wide streets, name them, and seek to attract settlers through advertisements and agents. If the speculation was successful, such a city will blossom at an incredible rate; if, however, the conditions are unfavorable, there will be a disproportion between the size of the town and the population. Such a town with its handful of inhabitants and long undeveloped streets gives the impression of a small child in a man's coat. Furthermore, if the area is flat and not very attractive, as is the case here, one is inclined to call the town merely a place for things that are still missing: there is still room for a neighborhood, room for a city, room for people, and room in which to be happy.

On the other hand, even a place like this has its charms. In front of our house is a spot of greenery where beautiful pines stand in magnificent clusters, a piece of the virgin forest as it used to grow everywhere until a few years ago, with the blue gleam of Lake Michigan shimmering behind. Fires made by neighborhood children from wood shavings and branches often shine in the evening, and at a distance one can see flames burning the cut trees—clean-up work in the fashion characteristic of this country of bountiful forests. Beautiful green snakes now and then find their way into the garden, and enormous bullfrogs also come to greet us. There are such quantities of insects as I have never seen before: billions of flies, grasshoppers, crickets, spiders, butterflies, dragon flies, bugs, and other insects swarm, fly, chirp, whistle, hum, and buzz day and night to gladden one's heart. The forest begins only a few steps from our house, and although in the immediate vicinity of the town it is robbed of its most beautiful specimens by the cutting of almost all the tall trees, hence offering little protection against the heat of the sun, it still has many picturesque parts. Especially at night, when the trees give off an unusual scent, it is a pleasure that always gives me new delight when I go for a ride or walk through "the bush," as it is locally called.

Pictures of a swamp would be an appropriate title for any description of local conditions because, truthfully, this town, like so many around here, is nothing but a large stagnant swamp, a small hamlet, compared to which many a German country village looks like an Eldorado. No trade, no industry, no factories: hence, neither life nor progressive conditions. At least three-quarters of the population is German, and most of them are of the kind best described as riff-raff and ne'er-do-wells. This is neither a unified nor a divided, neither a young nor an old Germany: it is just a rabble of the worst kind. This riff-raff—who of course do not have the deep republican roots of the American people, among whom a person of the lowest standing knows how to encounter the highest-ranking citizen as an equal without causing the least offense—avenge themselves here for everything of which they were deprived at home just because they are in the majority. They are mean-spirited and insulting towards the so-called aristocrats, among whom they include even the most honorable democrat if he has money and education; and he has to suffer their insults quietly for fear of physical assault. Just a few years ago, a mob forced its way into a ball given by the so-called local dignitaries, appropriated the gentlemen's hats and coats, and managed to chase away the assembled guests because any serious attempt at resistance would have led to a bloody fray.

Besides these people, there is the class of so-called dignitaries: the solid, stolid, smug middle-class from the German provinces—the most boring society I have ever come across. One has to put up with the pleasure of their company or suffer public notoriety. The worst of it are the ladies' visits for coffee between two and six, and it has happened that, seeing them coming from afar, we locked the doors all around and threw ourselves flat on the floor to escape detection through the many low windows. If the visitors don't find anyone home, instead of leaving a calling card they will write their name in the sand. A major topic of conversation, besides the town gossip, are the vegetable gardens; and when people visit each other, they will follow the usual inquiries about everyone's health with questions how the cabbage and beets are doing, whether the corn is coming along, and how big the cucumbers are. Then everyone steps out into the garden, inspects each cabbage leaf, checks each bean, and remains for hours exposed to the burning sun. These people are so sociable that they invent a different name for each meeting, but they always invite the same people for the same purpose: there is a garden society, a choral group, a coffee circle, a firemen's meeting, and an antitemperance society—always the same people meeting under a different name on different days.

If this region has little to offer for a civilized person, it is most suitable for the farmer, who can find cheap land, fertile soil, and a healthy climate that is free of the fevers that afflict the neighboring states of Michigan, Ohio, and Illinois. Many peasants from Württemberg, Prussia, and Switzerland, most of whom arrive here virtually penniless, have risen to be wealthy farmers within a few years, especially those who have brought along their sons as laborers, avoiding dependence on hired labor. On the other hand, educated people coming from larger cities, inveterate urbanites lacking agricultural experience and physical stamina, make a fatal mistake when they imagine they can succeed as farmers from one day to another in America—in Wisconsin or in any other state; yet it is a mistake that thousands of educated and intelligent people have made. In fact, with the exception of those who have stayed to live in the cities, there is only a small number who have not learned this painful lesson: a farm in a beautiful setting, perhaps surrounded by virgin forest—how poetic, how romantic! But then they drop into the prosaic pothole of the most miserable reality.

The first mistake is often made before leaving Europe by hiring managers, carpenters, as well as male and female farmhands and paying for their transatlantic voyage, and it is not unusual to see families setting out with two or three such appendages. But upon arriving in America they usually experience the pleasure of having these people, whose service is essential, politely express their gratitude for the free voyage and then go off on their own. It would be folly to try to stop such traitors by force, since they are bound by no law, and finally one has to resign oneself, seeking comfort in the realization that it is better to be rid of such deadbeats. The next step is buying a farm—that is, a piece of woodland of so many acres with a log cabin. Even if some of the land has already been cleared, much still needs to be done: trees must be cut, the land plowed, and cattle purchased; the log cabin will have to do until a house can be built; meanwhile the expectation of future improvements provides comfort for the lack of amenities. Wages for labor are high, and there is no end to bother and drudgery, not even counting the pleasure of boarding a horde of rough laborers for months at a time. Naturally, the greenhorn is cheated right and left, and every item runs twice its estimate; but there is no turning back now.

When the hardest work is finally done, the worst misery is about to begin. If the farmer, considering the high cost of labor, wishes to avoid substantial losses, he has to put his own hand to the wheel; but if his hands have been exposed to the air only in kid gloves, if he has used no other tools than the writing pen, he cannot cut trees, saw wood, or plow the earth. He who has spent his days in the regulated temperature of a study or an office is not cut out to labor in the heat and frost of the outdoors, to walk through miles of forest mornings and nights to gather the cows for milking. His wife, sisters, and daughters—ladies who used to think that life without servants was impossible—not only have to do the heavy housework but milk the cows, feed the pigs, and tend to the vegetable garden. Many a mishap is the consequence: the chickens lay their eggs in the woods; the precious young pigs are either stolen or exchanged by villainous neighbors; the frost kills the vegetables that haven't been protected in time. In the end, to stave off the worst shortages, one is forced to buy things in town that one ought to have produced in abundance. Among my acquaintances is a former doctor who also caught the farming fever, and I have often seen him riding six miles to the nearest town to buy meat, eggs, butter, and "greeneries," as he used to call them.

Such miseries quickly destroy one's illusions, and fortunate is he who manages to get rid of his farm without too great a loss. I am convinced that educated people, such genuine products of civilization as scholars and artists, will always feel most comfortable in the cities of the East, where education, art, and knowledge are advancing with every passing day, and where new movements and refreshing change offer rich opportunities for all activities.

Notes

1. From the Northern United States, December [1853], *Morgenblatt*, 48:2:48 and 48:3:71–72 (1854).

2. According to Maria Diedrich, Assing had traveled to Sheboygan, Wisconsin, at the invitation of Adolph Rosenthal and his family, friends from Berlin who had emigrated in the early 1850s.

3. The Prussian military prison in Berlin, which finally served the Allies after World War II for the incarceration of Nazi war criminals, was not razed until 1987.

6

Winter Portrait of a Small Western Town[1]

Just as in the United States in general, autumn is the most pleasant time of year in Wisconsin. The rather sober, northern light of summer gives way to a peculiarly colorful atmosphere: the greens of the trees change to reds and yellows, and the sky and earth glow in a wide range of shades. In October the sun still has the strength of summer, and everyone basks in these final smiles of nature. But these joys do not last long, and, with the sudden changes of temperature so typical of North America, one has to be prepared for waking up one morning behind frost-covered windows and seeing yesterday's bright show of flowers burnt to the ground by the frost.

Although it is only a cold snap that will not last, the colors of the landscape have faded into the gray sky of late autumn. The forty-fourth parallel notwithstanding, the pouring rain often reminds me of the dark November days back in the northern parts of Germany. Yet, usually in December, winter sets in as we hardly know it: the temperature falls well below twenty degrees Reaumur; several feet of snow cover the ground; and when a blizzard strikes, as it often does from the northwest, drifts pile up that make you sink in above your knees. The steamships stop running on Lake Michigan, and a mail coach—similar to our means of conveyance before the railroad—is the only connection to the East and the civilized world.

At night one can often see the northern lights, not red as they are with us, but white like pale omens of the cold of winter. Suddenly the weather breaks and gets warmer, but it only lasts a day or two, then changes back to freezing cold. All other vehicles being banned, sleigh bells jingle everywhere, and on bright days one can see farmers from near and far, drawing sleighs with oxen along the good roads, streaming towards town, while the townspeople indulge in their passion for pleasure excursions. No weather is bad enough to keep them at home, and a temperature of twenty-four degrees with sharply blowing winds will not prevent the women with all their children big and small from going on distant outings.

A passion for pleasures is, incidentally, one of the most noticeable characteristics of German middle-class women here; rarely does one see that sense of quiet domesticity that is still so common among the small-town bourgeoisie in Germany. Of course there is no trace of the higher, more refined delights because they are not available, and even if they were, they would not be appreciated. Hence, public dances are all the more important, and old and young, dignitaries and servants are equally eager participants. Grandmothers compete with their daughters on the dance floor, and children and dogs—all of them dragged along—wriggle underfoot until the former finally fall asleep stretched out on coats and cloaks in the dressing room.

In spite of the severe cold, the climate is exceptionally healthy, and in spite of the sudden changes in the weather there is not much talk of the common cold that is so pervasive with us, let alone of any of the more serious illnesses. In fact, despite the thin wooden walls of which houses are constructed here, thanks to the use of excellent stoves people suffer less from the cold than they do in the more elegant residences of European cities. Even the poorest person has a good cooking stove in the single room that serves him as a kitchen, living room, and bedroom, and the surrounding forest offers an abundance of firewood if he is willing to gather it. As I have had occasion to mention before, the adventurer and the speculator who wants to make a quick fortune will find his expectations dashed, but not the true proletarian who has crossed the ocean to escape unemployment, high taxes, and low wages. Even without assistance he will always find a better place here for himself and his family than in the dark dungeons of poverty in our cities or the miserable mud huts in so many of our country villages. Both the countryside and the cities of this country offer an abundance of real estate, which the owner in many cases has left unused and unimproved for many years, but on which a poor man is permitted to build his shanty and grow his supply of potatoes, vegetables, and feed for his pig, which is essential to such an operation. Neither is there any lack of work, so that many people achieve a certain level of wealth that would have been impossible under the pressure of poverty in Europe.

In order to enjoy a variety of entertainment during the long winter it would be necessary to engage in lively sociability, but that is still an unfamiliar luxury in these small German-American towns of the West; and although this town has a population of nearly three thousand (of which more than two-thirds are Germans) and offers two German, two English, and one Dutch newspaper, the life of the intellect and of what might be called society are nonexistent. Whoever is averse to visiting the breweries and saloons is condemned to a life of complete loneliness; and even if one were satisfied with the society of solid and provincial citizens from all the different Germans states, anxious considerations and petty animosities among them would make pleasant sociability unthinkable.

Germans and Americans have no social contact whatsoever; they live side by side in strict separation, and since they meet only to conduct business, most of the men learn only very inadequate English, the women with few exceptions none, even after many years. All they know is that awful "yes," "no," and "well"—the sure sign of all the half- and uneducated Germans who have breathed American air for four weeks. The less English such a "greenhorn" understands—and often he is limited to these three words—the more unfailingly he will use them. Walking through the town, one can see horrors of orthography: "fresch butter," "coffe," and "te," and even a lawyer is not ashamed to present himself as a "notary publick." Furthermore, the mixture of picked-up corrupted English words and German dialects makes an incomparable gibberish: Anglicized Saxon, Swabian, and Berlin speech that is incomprehensible to any German in Germany or to any Englishman; only a German-American can understand it. Who could guess the meaning of such a sentence as this: "I like not, dass du die spoons in die bashket or zehr about gelayed hast"? Which is supposed to mean: "I don't like that you have placed the spoons in the basket or next to it." Or that "die bell has gerunged" means nothing other than "the bell has rung"; or that "ein harts kaes" doesn't mean "a hard cheese" but "a hard case"?

The American habit of forming religious sects is also something the Germans quickly learn to imitate. Besides American Presbyterians, Episcopalians, Baptists, and Methodists, there are Catholics, Reformed and Traditional Lutherans, a Christian and a Free Assembly, German Methodists, German Catholics, and Albrecht Brethren (of which, incidentally, there are only four families).[2] This adds up to twelve sectarian churches for three thousand inhabitants, to which one needs to add the large number of freethinkers, who use their republican freedom to belong to no church at all.

The only general stir that ever touches this forsaken corner of limited interests is caused by the annual elections for the State Assembly, which were this year met with unusual interest because the legislature considered adoption of the "Maine liquor law," which would prohibit the sale and production of spirits throughout the state. The Americans residing here, almost all of whom belong to the Temperance Party, are making every effort to get one of their own elected. They are motivated far more by the intention to close all saloons and thereby shut down the gathering places and sole means of communication among the Germans, to paralyze their objectionable influence, and to exclude them from public offices, than by any philanthropic considerations. From a strictly philanthropic perspective, the implementation of the "Maine liquor law" has little to recommend itself, since it prohibits only the production and sale but not the import of spirits, thus leaving ample possibility for the poisoning to proceed secretly and quietly.

Emissaries of temperance societies have crisscrossed the country to convert people to cold water; even Barnum himself, the father of humbug and the enemy of all that is serious, was willing to speak in favor of the law; and one evening two ladies appeared, Mrs. Fowler and Mrs. Nicholls, in the company of a Mr. Booth, to offer their lectures in one of the churches. These ladies wore elegant dresses and neither looked nor acted like the kind of emancipated creature one would normally expect in a woman who presents herself in public under such circumstances. Their confident and modest demeanor, to which Mrs. Fowler added a pleasantly youthful personality, did not make the repulsive impression that I had expected. Their lectures, however, suffered greatly from being both monotonous and boring, although they flowed well enough—which is not remarkable, considering the fact that the ladies had given them night after night for a whole month in different locations—and the content also never rose above the commonplaces one has heard a hundred times from every street-corner moralist. The dull gray of their talks lacked spark despite some feeble but futile efforts; and everything was cast in a mold of prudish religiosity that was completely inappropriate, as the subject was one of general human interest, not a matter of faith. It took American heroism for enduring this sort of tedium and to listen without fatigue to the lectures of these two persons, each of whom—a watch before her on the table—spoke for a full hour.

In these proceedings, Mr. Booth played by far the most insignificant and negligible part; his speech distinguished itself by its vacuity and dearth of ideas.

Toward the end he explained to the audience without the least embarrassment the expenses he and the ladies had incurred in traveling, which was probably a lie, since the temperance societies usually reimburse their emissaries for travel expenses. Then he called on his "Christian friends" to show their support by contributing a few dollars, which they willingly did. We would consider such begging a matter of shame, but people here are so casual about matters of money that nobody seemed to object.

Despite their efforts, the temperance people came up short in the election. A freethinking German, a thoroughly modern and well-educated man, was given a handsome majority, and, according to reports, the majority of the legislature seems to be opposed to the "Maine liquor law," so it is unlikely that it will be passed in Wisconsin.

Toward the end of February, the cold weather finally begins to relent. There are still some cold and stormy days, but the hard freeze of the winter is over. Now and then, on a few days in March, one can feel the coming of spring: the ice floes on the lake begin to melt, the first steamboats tie up at the dock, communications with the East come back to life, and immigrants start pouring in from all directions.

Notes

1. *Morgenblatt*, 48:19:445–447 (1854).

2. Jacob Albrecht (1759–1808), a German-American Methodist lay preacher in Pennsylvania, founded an independent German-speaking Methodist society that, after 1816, became known as the *Evangelische Gemeinschaft* (Evangelical Community).

7

From West to East[1]

Farewell, friends of the West, who gave me a better home than I had in the old world! Finally we must part! Mighty Lake Michigan is roaring; the steamer is rocking on the waves; red sparks flying from the smokestack compete with lightning that now and then flashes on the horizon. The departure signal is given and the steamer takes off into the night. A long final look at the shore as it disappears from view; only the lighthouse provides a sense of direction until everything is swallowed up in the darkness of night.

The journey from north to south along the western shore of Lake Michigan offers nothing remarkable. The country is flat and boring, and on that gloomy, foggy morning it had a doubly gloomy and dull appearance, which was heightened by the fact that winter still seemed to hold on in this rough climate, despite the advanced date—it was April 20—and our location at 44 degrees latitude. Trees and shrubs stuck out their branches like besoms, and the grass was hardly yet turning green. The visitor who expects nature to be impressive in these parts will be generally disappointed, but the farmer finds sufficient reward in the prosaic health of the excellent soil. There is also nothing exotic by way of compensation: the Indians, of whom we dream at home and who in fact inundated the country only a few years ago, have long since retreated to their settlements near Green Bay, so that I met only a single one during my ten-month stay in Wisconsin. Manitowoc, Kenosha, Waukesha, Sheboygan, Waukegan—how unusual, how strange, how promising the sounds of these names and what expectations they raise! But what you find instead are—German Podunks! Let me say it again: we who are educated and have certain expectations of nature, art, literature, and society have come too early to the American West by a hundred years. Only a profound and sweeping change of conditions in Europe is likely to bring more of the cultural elite to these parts, who by acting in concert might gain a decisive influence and succeed in a greater emphasis on intellectual principles.

The only exception among all the towns and cities in the state is Milwaukee, where one can have somewhat higher expectations largely because of the incredible speed with which its population has grown in just a few years. German manners and culture have been to a degree successful: reading circles, musical societies, and other such benefits can be enjoyed, and I understand that Effelen's monthly journal, "Atlantis," with its mostly learned content, is largely a success. I should also mention one recent incident, which must be seen as a sign of the effect the better European element has here. For a number of years, a Negro has lived in Milwaukee, freely plying his trade even though it was known that he had escaped from the South. Suddenly a southern slaveholder appeared, recognized the Negro as his property, and demanded that he be immediately turned over to him. According to the laws of the Untied States, any colored person suspected of being an escaped slave is to be arrested by court order. Since he enjoys neither the right to a public hearing nor the right to a trial by jury, the authorities had no choice. The poor devil was captured and would surely have been turned over had the people not rebelled and practiced lynch law in reverse. In a most orderly fashion, without any excessive behavior, they stormed the jail, set the prisoner free, and left the owner empty-handed; of course he sued for compensation, but the outcome can be easily predicted.

Before I leave Wisconsin, I must mention what happened to the "Maine liquor law"—the law for the suppression of alcoholic beverages—that has been threatening the state. In spite of all efforts by the opponents of such restrictive legislation, it was passed by a significant majority in the state senate, with the proviso, however, that it be submitted to the people for a final vote. Dissatisfied with such a victory, the cold-water advocates of the second house demanded by a two-thirds majority the immediate implementation of the law without further appeal to the people. However, with the senate insisting on its resolution, the assembly, sure of victory, just as insistent, and the constitution not permitting the passage of any law without agreement between the two houses, the very fanaticism of the water party spared the state a law circumscribing liberty despite the majority it had received in both houses. Such a law would not only have the disadvantage of being widely violated by the secret sale of fraudulently produced spirits that occurs wherever the "Maine law" is in force; it would also be detrimental to immigration: immigrants, who are the chief guarantee for the future development of the West, would surely turn elsewhere if such a prohibition, hated by every German, were passed.

Chicago, the capital of the State of Illinois, lies at the southern end of Lake Michigan. This city, which has developed in a remarkably short time and with a speed possible only in America, already is said to have a population of 80,000 and is a picture of the most heartening progress. Imposing buildings are under construction on all sides, most of the streets have been improved with excellent boardwalks, and everywhere life is pulsing busily. Present accomplishments suggest a bright future. As soon as the nearby swamps have been drained the city will be a healthier place than it is now, for every year it is plagued by fevers, which, though not deadly, are protracted, exhausting, and recurring. The air is already warmer here than up in Wisconsin, the April lawns are green, trees and shrubs are heavy with buds, and the colors of the land are brighter and warmer. In Chicago we disembark from the steamer and proceed by railroad through the fertile, flat, and fever-wracked State of Michigan. After approximately twelve hours we reach Detroit, its capital, whence one of the magnificent steamboats that I have previously described takes us across Lake Erie to Buffalo.

Notes

1. New York, June [1854], *Morgenblatt*, 48:29:692–693.

8

An Antislavery Meeting[1]

May is the month in which public clubs and societies hold their annual meetings in New York. Members of the Antislavery Society, Bible Society, Temperance Society, Missionary Society, Prison Reform Society, and every other kind of society arrive in droves, and no day goes by without the announcement of at least six or seven such "anniversary meetings" morning, noon, and night, mostly in churches. Schools schedule vacations for this time, and the papers outdo each other in offering lengthy reports. Among all of them, however, it is the Antislavery Society that can claim for itself the most widespread interest, an interest that has recently been spurred again by the infamous bill offered by Senator Douglas. It asked Congress to approve the admission of the Territory of Nebraska into the Union as a slavery state, even though it is situated north of the 36th parallel, the legally established northern boundary for slavery. A howl of indignation swept the country, and while on one side Congress is receiving petitions opposing the Nebraska bill, the supporters of slavery are running up all their sails to push it through.

Recently, the excitement and anger of the friends of freedom increased as a result of a letter from the Irishman Mitchel,[2] who, while asking Americans to sympathize with his own oppressed compatriots, openly declares himself in favor of slavery. Thus, among all domestic issues dealt with by the parties, slavery is given the greatest attention. In earlier days, antislavery meetings were often stormy events because opponents came to pick fights, in which people attacked each other with sticks and hurled chairs, so that the more timid were afraid to attend. However, since emancipation has gained much ground in recent years and even become somewhat fashionable in the North, such outbursts are no longer a cause of much anxiety. On this, the twentieth-anniversary meeting of the society, it was the first time that a church—Chapin's Church on Broadway—had been made available. Hitherto, members of the clergy, much to their shame, had stood out as supporters of slavery and stubbornly kept the doors of their churches closed to the emancipation movement.

Chapin's Church on Broadway, halfway between the fashionable north end and the commercial south end of the city, is so elegantly and comfortably furnished as one would wish in a place where church attendance is a matter of fashion and churches are the meeting places of the wealthy. Floors, stairs, and galleries are covered with expensive carpeting; red velvet pews invite comfortable relaxation, perchance even sweet naps; and the eye lingers with pleasure over the delicate Gothic pillars and arches that support the ceiling and over the tastefully shaped quatrefoils adorning balustrades and galleries. Like in all English churches that I have seen so far, the pulpit is located opposite the entrance below the altar, and in front of it, slightly lower, there is a spacious platform for seating the president, the speakers, etc.

The church was filled from top to bottom with an elegant audience, offering a pleasing view from the gallery. The introduction took the form of those ceremonial preparations that Americans, to the great boredom of any foreigners present, consider necessary at such occasions and without which nothing can be accomplished. A person especially selected and paid for this purpose reads several appropriate passages from the Bible, which is followed by a long prayer and a hymn, singing being one of the favorite activities of Americans on such occasions even though it is one of their weakest points. During today's proceedings no less than four songs were offered during the intervals between five speakers. With the preliminaries finally over, President Garrison, one of the well-known fighters for the freedom of Negroes, stepped forward and spoke a few introductory words in which he reiterated the society's firm resolve never and under no conditions to compromise with the demon of slavery, no matter what the consequences may be. "Because," he said, "we know, you know, the slaveholder knows, the slave knows, and everybody in this country, in heaven and in hell knows that we are right when we stand up for the rights of every human being on this earth." Then he introduced Reverend Furness, who addressed the subject simply, fluently, and skillfully, without pastoral unctuousness but also without remarkable rhetoric.

The Nebraska Bill was mentioned in this and all subsequent speeches with the greatest indignation, and each speaker showered it with bitter, well-reasoned invective. Then, after more singing, Mr. Robert Purvis appeared,[3] a tall, slim, rather dark mulatto, whom the president introduced with the following words: "I have the pleasure to introduce to this assembly a member of the race that has been outcast in our country, a race of which a large number are still considered personal property, one who is called 'colored.' Even though he is protected in the North, Mr. Purvis would be arrested as a free colored person in Louisiana if he went there, and he would be thrown in prison for a year at hard labor, finally to be—given his freedom? No, to disappear among the mass of slaves never to emerge again as a man among men! I herewith present to you Robert Purvis of Byberry."

In this country of racial prejudice, where colored people are almost exclusively given the most menial work, a man such as this, whose role as speaker and whose education give him social standing, will be favorably received and met with interest by any European, even if his speech, as was the case here, is not particularly outstanding. In general, the speeches up to this point were pleasing enough in content and skill of presentation, but they were not distinguished by subtlety of either thought or expression—until Wendell Phillips, one of the best-known men in the struggle for the emancipation of Negroes, rose to speak, taking the place of the famous Theodore Parker, who had been announced but sent his regrets. Wendell Phillips is a born orator with an abundance of verbal dexterity and an incisive, ironic, and dialectical mind. Both dedication and enthusiasm for the cause mark his character, and they lend a certain beauty to his personality, which, though ennobled by a passionate intellect, is not particularly remarkable. His speech was long, very long, but it was not tiresome because he did not lose his focus but was swept along by a wealth of facts and ideas. He spoke with much bitterness about the government's attitude and the North's half-hearted commitment and ambivalence on the question of slavery.

"Today's Tribune," he said, "states that if the shameful Nebraska Bill is passed, the North will continue its resistance just as it has done from the beginning. O, what a terrible prophecy! It will continue as it began! On March 21 it rejected the measure by a majority of twenty votes, and today it supports it by a majority of twenty votes! The North began by letting itself be bribed and bullied; will it now continue in this vein? (A voice from the audience shouted: Yes!) There has not even been the beginning of any effective resistance! If ever we would repel a *single* offensive by the forces of slavery, if ever we would dig a grave for a *single* conspiracy against law and justice, we would cover it with green sod and engrave into the whitest of marbles the legend: The North Has Begun to Resist! But at this very moment, as we receive the news from Washington that the government has made every effort to pass the measure, do not tell me that the North will continue to resist as it has begun! What is this North? It is the guiding principle of the country; it dominates not only by its numerical majority, it dominates by its majority of wealth; it educates the country, furnishes it with teachers, and writes books for all the states. It is the North that dominates the Union, the South merely supplies it with overseers of slaves; and the true merchants of slavery literally reside in the North! We cannot blame the South for swallowing up Texas or for anything else. The South could never have swallowed Texas without first gaining the support of the North. The South exerts its power through the North, and the responsibility for slavery lies north of Dixon's line. Because the country's intellectual strength, its spirit of enterprise, its education, and its wealth reside in the North we are responsible for every act of its government."

Later, referring to Mitchel, he continued by speaking about Massachusetts, which is generally praised for its support of emancipation yet has heaped distinctions on some of its representatives who have openly voiced their support of slavery; and in the end he touched on the widespread fear that any decisive stand would cause the South to bolt, thus leading to a dissolution of the Union. "What good has the Union done us?" he shouted. "It hasn't manufactured cotton in Lowell; it has neither planted wheat in Illinois nor made the West productive nor plowed the ocean with the goods of New York merchants. No, New York's wealth does not depend on whipping slaves in South Carolina! New York can stand on its own. I maintain that the Yankee will accumulate wealth even without the Southerner whipping his slave, that the sons of the men who fought at Bunker Hill are able to maintain order in the streets of Boston even without the women on the plantations of Louisiana cringing under the lashes of the whip. A Union that was brought into being by an Adams, a Hancock, and a Jay has never required the glue of the slaves' blood!"

This speech, the high point of today's meeting, would have been sufficient in itself, but just as in English drama the comic interlude must unfailingly follow upon the tragedy, we were presented with the appearance of a Mrs. Abby Kelley Foster, who unexpectedly replaced Miss Lucy Stone, the well-known advocate of human rights, women's rights, and heaven knows what other rights, who had been announced but did not arrive. Mrs. Foster is one of those numerous American ladies who are invariably and ubiquitously at hand whenever it would be the better part of valor not to compete with the men, and I truly admired the politeness and patience with which the audience accepted the well-worn commonplaces and effusions of this emancipated woman after listening to Wendell Phillips and surely flagging in their concentration on a meeting that had continued for more than three hours. For good measure, she presented her speech with that terribly monotonous and hollow pathos as well as those studied though by no means graceful gestures that one would expect from the worst actors on the provincial stage.

Incidentally, Mitchel's defense of slavery is no particular exception; he caused such a stir among the public only because of his special status and because he contradicted himself too sharply. It is a fact, which to our shame we cannot deny, that especially many Germans—I did not have as much opportunity to gather information regarding other nationalities—go so far in their groveling flattery of America as not only to disregard the evil of slavery but to consider slavery indispensable. They even have the nerve to make the absurd claim—as I once heard it expressed by a well-educated man—that it is still an open question whether blacks did not actually belong to a particular species of apes. By making such concessions they believe they curry favor with Americans, but they merely earn contempt; for they all—"those in heaven and those in hell"—know very well what slavery is really about, even if from sheer selfishness they do not wish to admit it. They know that no enlightened European can honestly defend slavery, and they see through this gambit as do the large number of Americans who, themselves opposed to slavery, rightly recognize that most of these concessions are based on nothing more than a pursuit of position and appointment. Generally speaking, in their everyday social intercourse Americans do not like the denial of nationality that Germans are so often charged with, for in their lack of knowledge and curiosity about other nations Americans welcome new and foreign elements that differ from their own kind so long as they present themselves in mostly agreeable ways.

Starkly opposed to those German-Americans who consciously suppress their better perceptions are the violent detractors of America who, too lazy and careless to adopt the ways of a new country or to learn its language, curse and argue against everything because it is different from what they had at home. They always remind me of the peasants who refuse to accept, believe, and understand anything that their grandfathers had not already practiced and approved of. Between these two extremes are those overly submissive, easily excitable creatures who, from a lack of self-confidence and inner strength and substance, unconsciously and completely subject themselves to every aspect of America, except its language—they are, to use the technical term, "yankeefied." Still, I am of the opinion that one should not judge the Germans as harshly as they often are for the habit of adapting themselves so easily to foreign nations, because it is only the outgrowth of one of their chief virtues, namely the ability, unique among all peoples, to become part of other nations' manners and customs. What does the Englishman, the Frenchman, or the Italian—all but the educated elite, that is—care for the art, literature, history, or social conditions of other nations? With us, every half-educated person has at least a general understanding of these things. But it is infuriating nevertheless when what is considered to be cosmopolitan open-mindedness among the elite shows itself among the uneducated or half-educated masses as apery and denial of their own nationality.

* * *

Notes

1. New York, June [1854], *Morgenblatt*, 48:32:761–764.

2. The Irish revolutionist John Mitchel (1815–1875) had arrived in the United States in 1853; he edited the proslavery journal *Citizen*.

3. Robert Purvis, of Byberry, near Philadelphia, an activist in the protection of runaway slaves, was considered to be the wealthiest black man in America.

9

An Excursion to Sing Sing[1]

A Camp Meeting

When the first Methodist missionaries, sent out by Wesley, the founder of Methodism, arrived in the English colonies of America, the priests of the ruling Episcopal High Church locked them out of their churches with a determination that forced the Methodists to preach in the open air, often in forests, attracting large crowds. Today the Methodists are among the largest sects in the United States; and even though they now have churches in every village where they could meet to their heart's content, the free-air gatherings, or camp meetings, have continued and take place every year in various locations in the country and are attended by a pious flock for a week at a time.

A Negro camp meeting took place toward the end of August near Sing Sing, a few miles upstream from New York on the Hudson. While it was in progress, two competing steamboats, in addition to the normal boats, transported the pious and the curious every day from New York at bargain prices.

At the corner of the street where the boats dock there is an Irish pub with benches outside for the waiting passengers and much merriment inside. Fiddlers were scratching out jigs on mistuned violins while the guests—full-blooded Paddies either in picturesque rags looking like Murillo's youthful beggar or with the dignified aspect of Falstaff's companions—were chatting in small groups or cooling their heels by the front door. But there was a profound silence when two rather coarse looking gentlemen appeared just before departure time, one of them addressing the passengers in more or less the following manner: "Ladies and gentlemen, here's the steamboat that will take you to Sing Sing for the unheard-of, one-time-only low price of one shilling. Such an offer has never been made before!" But he had not yet finished his speech when the other cut him off: "Ladies and gentlemen, you are surely not going to patronize the railroad company's steamer! That's the boat the railroad has launched to ruin the public steamboat, which provides much better and safer service. If you patronize the railroad's steamer, there won't be any boat going within a week and you'll have to pay 27 dollars to get to Sing Sing! How can anyone ask to be taken for less than two shillings? But of course, the railroad can take you for one shilling because the company refuses to pay wages and every month they hire new people!"—"Not true," shouted the first; "everyone receives a fair wage!"—"Are you being paid your wage, George?" the other one asked. "Of course," was the answer, and both were silent for a moment to catch their breath. Then the first started in again: "I wouldn't dare get on the public steamboat; it's unsafe and has had several accidents." Now the other one yelled louder than ever: "Ladies and gentlemen, you're not going to patronize the railroad's boat, etc." And so they carried on much to the amusement of the bystanders, raging as if they would tear each other's hair out even though they could hardly contain their laughter, and no one's decision for one boat or the other was affected by this daily comedy routine.

Finally the much-expected boat arrived and the first one called: "Ladies and gentlemen, your boat has come to take you."—"And the public steamer is following in its wake!" shouted the second, running down to the pier as if determined to throw everyone into the water who dared to approach the competing vessel. The other went after him, making an end to today's spectacle; and after a few moments the two boats were gliding upstream.

A strict analyst might observe that there is no coherence between the Hudson and its banks, one being grand and mighty, the others rather lovely and charming. There may be some truth to this comment, yet there is no doubt that the river combined with its banks presents a scene of great beauty and that some consider it even superior to the Rhine. On both sides the banks form gradually rising hills of fresh green, between which the magnificent river winds its way in many curves so that the banks appear one behind the other, the most distant ones veiled in blue mist. On the New York side, the bank is covered with charming villas and cottages, peeking out from behind trees; small towns and villages like Hastings and Tarrytown show themselves with such friendly and cheerful aspects, as if they were pleased with their happy situation. The marble from a quarry on the river's edge can be easily loaded onto the Hudson Railroad running close to the water.

At dusk, after a three-hour journey, we reached Sing Sing, which is situated on the most charming of river banks. Heaven knows the origin of that Chinese name! Carriages stood ready to convey the arriving passengers to the camp. A country lane rises steeply up the bank, then continues between pleasant country homes, and after about ten minutes reaches the entrance to the camp.

A large circle of about seventy or eighty tents had been erected in the midst of a small beech grove. Most of the tents were open and brightly lit, so that we could see the black and brown figures seated at long tables for dinner. Small, flickering lights hanging from trees gave off just enough light to keep us from stumbling but did not destroy the mysterious darkness of the scene. With the eager curiosity of the traveler I approached the tents and soon heard the peculiar singing of the Methodists; I followed the direction of the sound and quickly stood facing a rather high, covered platform made of crude boards. Seated on it were six preachers, four of whom were pitch black, one a darkish mulatto, and the last one almost completely white. At the foot of the platform was a small, fenced area covered with straw, in which those who had already been moved by the spirit were kneeling. Behind them, long rows of benches were set up for the rest of the audience.

When the singing ended, one of the preachers rose and delivered a long sermon of repentance, in which he exhorted his audience to change their sinful ways, explained how much God had blessed them with this camp meeting, and described in the most striking colors the future that awaits the unrepentant sinner. But as he went along he got more and more excited, screaming and thumping himself into a passion as I had heretofore never seen it among Methodists. Finally his voice gave out and, after more singing and praying, another took his place to offer the same commonplaces in about the same manner.

I soon began to notice that without exception all of these preachers and believers indulge in repeating the same stereotype and well-worn phrases, and even the most passionate crescendo toward the end never produced anything more than the shouted repetition of the same. Shouting seems to be the chief feature—just like on the American stage—and no preacher relinquishes the platform to another until his voice gives out. But the congregation seemed entirely pleased and often responded with an "Amen!" a "Glory to God!" or a "Lord have mercy on us!" while others merely sighed and groaned, seemingly suffering the agonies of purgatory.

Perhaps two hours had gone by when one of the preachers said: "Brothers and sisters, let us now conclude our service. Do not stop singing and praying, but be alert and continue your worship in the big tent to your right. God has begun to work his ways among us. Pray that you all get religion and that this meeting will see many conversions!" "To get religion" is, so to speak, the technical term of their craft, and the preachers and believers do whatever they can to shove religion down the poor sinner's throat, so that they are not to blame if he does not "get" it.

The brothers and sisters now slowly began to move toward the designated tent, some of them carrying lanterns that cast an unsteady light on the procession. I was particularly struck by a mulatto man without legs, who was pushing himself in a small cart but evidently wanted to be one of the first to get there. The tent was brightly lit and filled with worshipers, who partly kneeled on the straw covering the ground and partly stood in a circle. The scene that was now about to begin outdid everything I have ever seen in the way of excess, grotesqueness, and ugliness.

One "exhorter" after another stepped up and whipped himself and the rest into a frenzy of weeping and screaming that seemed to have no end. It was the women in particular who tried to outdo each other in uncontrolled wildness, and their show of passion made them look like repulsive furies. One woman above all, a tall and scrawny creature wearing a calico hat pushed deep into her face and the sort of long cloak typical of lower-class women here, was inexhaustible and displayed seemingly superhuman strength and endurance. She was dark-skinned, but showed neither the deep black of the genuine Negroes nor the dark yellow of the mulattoes, but rather a kind of dusty gray; and her voice had that husky timbre which is so characteristic of colored women and, under the circumstances, comes as a relief to one's ears, for if on top of everything else one would have to endure the high, shrill, screeching voices common among white women, the noise would shatter one's ears and nerves. However, at one point, when this woman had reached a peak of ecstasy, a shrill and discordant "God almighty" came from one of the corners with such irresistibly comic effect that even the worshipers burst into laughter.

A fat Negress was especially intent on proselytizing the young women and men who had come up from New York, addressing them unceremoniously by shouting at least twenty times, "Ladies and gentlemen from New York!" A young girl lay completely prostrate on the ground, sighing and shaking as if wracked by seizures, while the others prayed for her and urged her to follow her faith: "O Lord, let her have faith!" "Help her now, right now!" "Have faith, this instant!" "Prayer is the key to heaven!" It was mostly the gray-colored woman who could be heard like this; the light-skinned preacher leaned down over her and asked in a friendly voice: "Don't you want to get up, sister?"

The level of ecstasy continued to rise; the melodies got wilder and wilder, taking on more and more the beat of popular street songs; and the frenzy reached its peak when the gray-colored woman started in with at least a hundred repetitions of the refrain, "God is my love!" Most of the worshipers were clapping their hands, others swayed back and forth or jumped up and down as if possessed; the beat got faster and faster, the general scene more and more eerie and ugly—until at last the light-skinned preacher told the congregation that it was past ten o'clock and the evening's service at an end. Everyone withdrew, the still prostrate girl was picked up and carried out, and I looked around for a place to spend the night. I found it with a gigantic Negro woman who was in her tent, brewing tea on a small stove under which a group of chickens had set up camp.

I was busy eating a piece of unpardonably bad mutton when others appeared, among them the light-skinned preacher, who had suddenly been transformed from a God-inspired evangelist into a common, everyday man much given to eating, laughing, and making small talk. He had chiseled features, and the fire in his eyes had a disgustingly sensual quality that I had already noticed earlier from a distance. When he finally got up to leave, he took on the part of the preacher again, shook my hand, and said unctuously: "My dear child, have you also come to be inspired by the Bible?" My curt reply, "No, I am a stranger, and tomorrow morning I will depart," made short shrift of his insinuating ways.

In preparation for sleeping, a curtain was drawn across the middle of the tent and straw beds were made up behind it. However, not finding the two women with whom I shared my lodgings or the much-used straw particularly inviting, I preferred to sleep on some raw boards placed across two trunks. But at a very late hour a group of the faithful, both men and women, still unable to sleep, tore through the camp as if possessed, singing hymns. My hostess and I ran after them until the parade began to bore me and I returned to my tent, where I had a good night's sleep on my two boards.

The next morning I was awakened by the hymns with which the faithful welcomed the day. I stepped out and looked at the camp in daylight. Cooking stoves were smoking behind most of the tents, other tents were filled with stores of fruit and vegetables, and a milk wagon had pulled up at the entrance to the camp. After a short while, a bell called everyone for the first meeting.

The gray-colored woman took the lead again and, on this occasion, held forth particularly on the topic of slavery and slaveholders, expressing her hope that they would soon come to a realization of their evil ways, that their food and drink should turn into gall and their beds into burning sulfur until the day they see the light. One of the preachers, an old mulatto who on the previous day had spoken only in generalities, was also in fine fettle and praised the eagerness of all the faithful, who had willingly paid for the trip by railroad or steamboat that brought them here. He also praised God's mercy, which he had experienced so often himself: "Yes," he shouted, "God has been merciful to me. I was a slave, and He set me free! He gave me the gift of a beautiful wife and loving children, for which I cannot praise Him enough. Come, get up, and show yourself, dear wife, so that the brothers and sisters may see my reason for thanking God!" Indeed, a fat Negress got up inside the fenced-in area, much to the amusement of some of the white spectators, who could barely suppress their laughter. I, too, had to bite my handkerchief; with the singing starting again at just that moment, I got up to return to Sing Sing, convinced that I had seen whatever the camp meeting had to offer in the way of comedy and originality.

I had surely seen enough of crying, screaming, sighing, and shouting people conducting themselves like lunatics, yet it did not seem to me as if I had witnessed true fanaticism—I mean the kind of fanaticism that in earlier times created martyrs, instigated religious wars, and turned naturally peaceful men into murderers. It seemed to me more like an artificial enthusiasm, a cool fervor, generated by talking each other into it until they imagine it to be real—a cold fire, so to speak; hence more innocent in its consequences but all the more objectionable and repugnant in its appearance. I do not wish to say for a moment that these people are conscious hypocrites; to the contrary, they truly believe they feel everything they say, and beyond that they are driven by a motive of which they are completely unaware.

Every human being—especially anyone with a lively imagination—longs consciously or unconsciously for something that lies outside the limitations of his daily life and that can elevate him momentarily above life's sorrows and burdens. The educated person finds it in the enjoyment of art, travel, society, and literature—things from which these poor colored people have been excluded from the start. But, since they are also unfamiliar with the entertainments, gatherings, and folk festivals with which the lower classes in Europe amuse themselves, such a camp meeting is for many the only diversion in their dreary lives. The interruption of the daily routine of work, the short journey, the outdoors, the companionship and newly found friends among their own kind, the tales and stories that surely are spun on these occasions—all of this offers stimulation and diversion that under different circumstances they might get at a theater or a circus; it helps them endure these unnatural prayer services, which would otherwise be intolerable. For which healthy human being—no matter how genuinely pious—is able to do nothing but sing, pray, and listen to sermons for an entire week, all day long, with only two hours set aside for dinner and supper!

The State Prison

Upon my return to Sing Sing I visited the "state prison" of the State of New York, which is situated below the town, on the very bank of the Hudson. To the right of the men's building is the section for women, a structure with columns resembling a villa, whose front does not have the appearance of a prison. A small cottage between them serves as a kind of guardhouse, as is suggested by the guns hanging on the walls; three old men in civilian clothes are peacefully smoking their pipes.

After I had stated the purpose of my visit, one of them accompanied me to the main building. There is no guard posted at the entrance as there would be with us, and an open door admits you to the "clerk's office," where I was asked to wait a few moments. A young, well-dressed woman, evidently of the higher middle class, entered right after me; she was accompanied by a girl, apparently her sister, and two children, one of them young enough to be carried. Giving a name, she asked to see a prisoner, which friends and family are permitted to do every three months on the first day of the month. The clerk asked what the man's sentence was, and she answered: "Life!" What must have been the dark drama that had played itself out here?

After a few moments the man who had been requested came; a young, strong man of not unpleasant appearance sat down on the sofa between the two women and put the children on his lap. Apparently, this was not their first reunion in prison, nor were they bothered by the presence of strangers; they greeted each other with more composure than I, a mere spectator, was able to command. Then I departed in the company of an old jailor who was to be my guide through the inside of the prison, leaving behind these poor victims of fateful consequences.

The prison consists of a main building and two long wings that run right up to the river. Toward the land it is surrounded by a wall but entirely open toward the water, so that the prisoners can easily reach the river on one side of the courtyard created by the two wings. This arrangement avoids any prison-like appearance: light, air, and sunshine are freely admitted without offering any possibility for escape, because the mighty river provides an insurmountable barrier. In general, I was pleased to notice the absence of all unnecessary cruelties, making this prison indeed worthy of a great republic.

The horror of solitary confinement and eternal silence that a cruelly fanatic pursuit of punishment and rehabilitation has tried to establish in Europe is completely absent here. The prisoners work in a group, are permitted to speak to each other as long as talking does not interfere with their work, and are locked into their cells only at night; these are arranged on five floors of a hundred prisoners each, with light entering through the barred doors facing the hallway.

The current number of prisoners is nine hundred. The workshops and factories are located in the side wings and the courtyard, and with the help of steam engines the prisoners produce a wide variety of objects of great perfection. In the workshops one can see felt hats, iron implements of all kinds, cabinet and lathe work, clothes, and the most splendid Brussels carpets in all stages of production, from initial manufacture and dying of the material to the finished product. Each shop has a guard who surveys the entire room from a raised platform and by his mere presence maintains general order. As all of these rooms face the courtyard, such precautions as barred windows are unnecessary, and light and air stream through the high and wide windows, which offer a scenic view of the Hudson and its far bank. Due to its open and favorable situation, the prison is an unusually healthy place: the infirmary that I visited briefly contained no more than ten to twelve patients, a very favorable ratio, given a total population of nine hundred persons.

Most of the prisoners, it must be said, are very young people, and only a few have that criminal physiognomy one would normally expect in a penitentiary; in fact, I was struck by the many handsome, good-natured, honest faces, even though this is a prison only for persons who have committed major crimes. Yet upon inquiry one finds that it is rarely a basic criminal propensity but rather a lack of restraint and control—in a word, a lack of education—that fills the jails in this country primarily with victims, mostly Irishmen.

After I had seen all the departments and workshops and my old guide, in order to "let me experience everything," had locked me up in a cell for a little while, I visited the women's prison. The women's cells are considerably larger than those of the men, which barely have room for a bed that is folded up against the wall during the day. Women's instinct for decorating their quarters to the best of their abilities, no matter how poorly, demonstrates itself even here in prison: most of the cells are decorated with small pictures, embroidery, and clippings; but crucifixes and holy pictures dominate everything, indicating that most of the occupants belong to that unfortunate nation of Ireland.

Close to the prison, on a hillside along the river bank, is the cemetery, an inviting place covered with flowers. Wooden plaques show the names of the dead—a dubious honor that many a man would rather not claim for himself.

Notes

1. *Morgenblatt*, 49:51:1212–1217 (1855).

10

Rambles Through New York[1]

A Look at the Schools
Autumn is here, people have returned from the countryside, summer vacation is over, and it is back to business for children and teachers as well as merchants and workers. The number of advertisements for schools and teachers is so large at this time of year that they take up many columns even in some of the large-format folio papers. In general, there is much din and prattle about education here, and to judge from the programs and reports from all the educational institutions, public and private schools, colleges, and academies you would think that the coming generation amounts to an entire population of well-educated people and a host of exemplary scholars. Nevertheless, the European observer cannot but notice that the kind of good, average education that is so characteristic particularly of the German upper middle class can here be found only among a relatively small minority. Quite often one is astonished here to notice the immense ignorance in regard to history, geography, and the conditions of other countries than the United States by people who are generally considered to be well informed and educated. Questions about the difference between the Germans and the Dutch or the different origins of the Prussian and the Swiss language are by no means uncommon.

On one occasion a young man who probably had never had any doubts about his own education asked me why it is that throughout Europe the days are four hours longer than here. When I asked him, with some perplexity, where he had received this information, he seemed to suspect that there was something wrong with his question and corrected himself: "No, I meant to say four hours shorter." Where people are so much in the dark about the affairs of our common home, the earth, and its relation to its central sovereign, the sun, it comes as no great surprise that many are unable to differentiate between Friedrich Wilhelm and Franz Joseph—rulers by the grace of God—and do not know whether the former is emperor or king of Austria, no matter how often they read dispatches "one week later from Europe"; they seem to be content knowing about Napoleon III, the queen of England, the sultan, and the emperor of Russia. Of course there are excellent people here as well as in the most civilized countries of Europe who encompass the world in their mind and therefore satisfy the highest European expectations, and I strongly object to the suspicion that goes hand in hand with the negativism and disparagement of the American people and circumstances in which so many Germans over here indulge. This expression of their own disgruntlement about their personal misfortune and failure has turned into an "anti-Americanism" that has become something of a literary fashion.

In generalizing about a situation, however, one can only speak of the masses, and in this respect the comparison to Germany reveals a somewhat unfavorable result for America, with the possible exception of the very lowest class of the people. In so far as I have had the opportunity to discover, there are few native-born Americans here in the North who are illiterate, though the South is characterized by the worst kind of ignorance.

But in regard to domestic education there is cause for concern that applies to all social levels. As much as one may be opposed to any form of unnecessary discipline or control, it is astonishing to see the lack of restraint with which American children grow up, and many widely traveled Europeans claim that these are the most ill-mannered children anywhere in the world. Parental authority is not very much in evidence, and the desire for independence that is here so typical of both men and women shows itself at an early age: it is not unusual to see children between nine and twelve years of age who go out shopping or visiting their friends for half a day at a time without asking permission or even informing their parents. Some pursue their instinct for making money, as for instance the ten- and eleven-year-old sons of a preacher, who started a small store in their home, where they sell coffee, tea, sugar, needles, thread, etc. Their chief customers are their parents as well as a few friends and neighbors, whom they woo as patrons by offering their merchandise for about one cent less than the other grocers. The boys give every free moment to this enterprise, and they cheerfully go to the trouble of running all over town to find the best buys at the wholesalers. Their younger sister, whom they have enlisted in their enterprise, gets a percentage for attracting customers among her friends and is payed out in sweets and candy. Educated German parents would probably look somewhat askance at such a display of business talent at such a tender age, but here people are amused and pleased that their children are so "smart."

It is a matter of far greater concern, however, that nothing is done to control the propensity for wild and rude behavior, which is a part of every person's nature and can be subdued only by education. American children are willful, hence the adults react with bestial fury and passion against any person or authority that is opposed to their inclinations and purposes. One consequence of this wild lack of restraint are the many murders that are committed throughout the states of the Union not only by that class of people commonly called riff-raff but even by people of the middle and upper middle classes. The chief motives usually are jealousy, fights about money, and political animosities, as was the case just a few weeks ago when a "stabbing affray" broke out in one of the best New York hotels between two well-to-do and well-respected men who had formerly been business partners but, because of differences over money, had gone their separate ways. More than once—and just recently in one of the western states—abolitionists have been shot down in broad daylight out of sheer political partisanship by supporters of slavery who did not know them personally; and even in Congress representatives have threatened each other with pistols. It is nothing new: the papers sensationalize the event for a few days, the investigation runs its course, the murderer is either hanged or possibly acquitted, and no one gives it another thought.

However, there is much show of Christian dismay, especially in the North, about the admittedly barbaric but at least honest custom of dueling, to the point that horror stories are told about pious ladies who, in deep moral shock, lost their minds after learning of their husbands' *successful* participation in a duel; some are even said to have welcomed death itself. In the light of these murderous deeds it strikes one as truly comical to notice the Christian indignation with which several papers recently commented on a man in Milwaukee—a German, judging from his name—who, rather than let his wife's body decay in the earth, wanted to cremate her remains according to the aesthetically preferable custom of the ancients as well as her express wish and his personal preference. He was prevented by official action from implementing this harmless and inoffensive plan. The papers could not find words enough to denounce this "hellish, heathen" horror; but all these Christian and moral voices were silent when a ten-year-old Negro boy was "duly and rightfully" hanged a short while ago in Alexandria (Louisiana) because he had killed his master in retaliation for suffering his abuse.

This description, which is not exaggerated and can be verified by reading the daily newspapers, gives an idea of the almost unlimited freedom in which the young generation is growing up. But the necessity of education normally puts a limit to this happy condition, and the promising offsprings are placed in either a fashionable private institution, if the parents are wealthy enough, or a public school. These public schools are the pride of America and, in fact, are said to excel in thoroughness and variety of instruction, so that even the poorest of the poor have an opportunity to acquire a wider knowledge than public school systems normally provide. Corporal punishment is not allowed, as it is unworthy of a free nation and people; yet such a large number of children from all classes of society make it impossible to avoid measures of coercion and correction altogether, and there are rumors about occasional uses of punishment that resemble medieval barbarities. Among other things I was told that a horrid mixture of pepper and rhubarb is forced into the mouths of particularly stubborn and unruly children, and that it is more often the female than the male teachers who resort to such insidious methods.

If they pass their examinations with distinction, the best and most gifted pupils in the public schools are entitled to enroll in the free academy, which is widely considered to be the most outstanding institution in the State of New York. Because it offers ancient and modern languages, mathematics, geometry, chemistry, three-dimensional as well as freehand drawing besides the usual subject matters, the academy offers opportunities for receiving a broad education. The handsome building, with its high ceilings, bright halls, and well-stocked library makes the very best of impressions, so that one is easily convinced that this is a place where knowledge resides. The teachers all have a professorial title, and the students graduate to be "bachelors of art." The awarding of diplomas and prizes is a public ceremony, which this year took place at Niblo's Opera House in front of a large audience consisting mostly of members of the students' families. The entire stage was occupied by teachers and students and presented a delightful scene. More than thirty young men received their diplomas, and a large number of older and younger boys were rewarded with medals. As soon as a name was read the others greeted their comrade with thundering applause and cheers. Music filled the intervals between speeches given by the graduates, and the general impression would have been completely satisfactory had it not been for the usual American lack of good taste that showed itself here in its full glory by drawing out the proceedings to a total of five hours of enervating festivities. There were no fewer than eight speeches, *each* of them—for good measure—having the same subject though the titles varied: the glory, excellence, greatness, fame and progress of the United States. Of course, nothing new or noteworthy came to light, and I felt sorry for the poor boys who wasted their energies on this much-thrashed straw only to torture themselves and fatigue the audience. But in their treatment and presentation of the well-worn subject the speakers all demonstrated that ease and grace of public speech which early training has made almost a common skill in this country.

Life in American colleges and universities is quite different from European customs. For our students life at the university brings with it a happy period of freedom after the controls exerted by schools and paternal vigilance; it is a freedom which many enjoy in its full measure only during this precious time, in which neither societal nor professional concerns obtrude upon a cheerful independence. The American, on the other hand, who until now has been permitted to do as he pleases, suddenly is confronted with rules and limitations which are among those curious extremes that are so prevalent in this country. Most universities have colleges, which are at about the same level as the middle grades of our *gymnasium*, preparing students for advanced studies in a manner that is more like school than like a university. Besides attending lectures, the students take daily "examinations," which means nothing other than that they are given a specific assignment and, the following day, are questioned by the teacher one by one like school boys. The students are obligated to live either in the university building, which is locked at a certain hour at night, or in one of the boardinghouses approved by the faculty. Merchants and inn keepers are strictly prohibited from extending credit to them. At some universities, such as Harvard College in Cambridge, no student is allowed to be seen in one of the coffee houses or any other public place; church attendance is monitored and can be excused only in case of illness.

The president, whose influence extends much beyond that of a German university rector, rules like a pedagogical autocrat, and even a small part of what he asks of the students would without fail stir up a revolt among our students. The parents of a somewhat boisterous young man had asked the president of the University of Schenectady[2] to keep an eye on him, and he had done what he could by offering moral lectures, but all was in vain. Finally the president's patience had reached its limit and, after the young man had once again committed some prank, he was asked to see the president, who first spoke of the trouble to which he had already gone on his behalf, then explained that kindness did not seem to have the desired effect, and ultimately administered as sound a thrashing as any naughty boy has ever been given in a village school. The same educational ruler once had been informed that his college students were planning to enjoy the visit of a lady who was to come to a certain window after hours to be hoisted in a basket up to the male sanctuary. Driven by a zeal for punishment and correction, he immediately hurried to the scene of the intended crime, where indeed he found the basket awaiting its precious burden. Without ado he placed himself in it, was pulled up, and appeared upstairs much to the chagrin of the students, who were prepared for anything but the sudden presence of their superior procured in this manner.

Under so much constraint, much of the attraction of university life is lost, and only a total commitment to learning will keep students in school beyond the minimum number of years. But there is no reason for doing so because, like everything else in this country, education is a high-pressure activity. A lawyer in the State of New York needs to enroll for only six months, a doctor one to two years, after which he may apprentice himself to a physician; and similar conditions exist in other fields. At the University of Virginia, however, which was founded by Jefferson in 1819 and is considered among the best, the required course of study takes longer. According to the instructions of the great, liberal author of the Declaration of Independence, any church association or influence was to be forever banned, but no one, past or present, has fully understood the broad intentions and motives of this great man. The party of bigotry denounced the "infidel," and right now the students are using their own funds to pay for a chaplain who is selected every two years from the four most widespread sects—the Episcopalians, the Baptists, the Presbyterians, and the Methodists.

If we now take a look at the education of young girls, we find a strange mixture of superficiality and pedantry. The program of any fashionable "boarding school" makes you almost dizzy with the abundance of subjects offered, and it would take at least a life time to gain even the semblance of satisfactory knowledge in all of them. There is French, German, Italian, and Spanish; almost without exception Latin and sometimes even Greek, accounting, botany, astronomy, geometry, algebra, mathematics, and philosophy; and every day one can read notices in which female educators either are sought or offer their expertise in a variety of subjects as well as Latin and mathematics. But one's own surprise at such erudition and one's embarrassed sense of ignorance soon evaporate with a closer look at things: it quickly becomes evident that the musical knowledge of such a boarding-school flower is usually limited to a few waltzes, and that only very few have that mastery of French which in Germany is an essential requisite in polite society. Indeed, I have hardly ever met an American woman who speaks French tolerably well; what I did encounter quite often—for instance, at parties when guests engage in linguistic experiments—are such edifying phrases as *"vous portez-vous bon," "comment avez-vous été,"* etc., pronounced, furthermore, with such a thick English accent that it was difficult to understand them. Pronunciation is an all but insurmountable problem for the wide English mouths that are not used to pure, sharp vowels, and only the tireless efforts of a teacher can vanquish it; but where is the time in a class of fifty or sixty female students to make each individual mouth nimble! So it happens that most of them remain in impenetrable darkness about the differences between "o," "u," "ou," and "eu," even if they suppose them to be different. The lovely sentence, "*un po plous, Mongsiou, si vu vulez,*" can serve as a brief example of French spoken the American way.

There is also much ignorance about the time it takes to learn a language, and therefore it often happens that teachers are asked in all seriousness whether they would undertake to teach some promising lad French or German in three months. Incidentally, in the inner parts of the country, outside the big cities, even this much linguistic perfection is rarely achieved because French is seldom taught even in the larger, more expensive schools. All the more attention is given to spelling exercises in English, and even in the middle grades for girls who are twelve or thirteen years old spelling drills are conducted and considered the only method for learning orthography. One can imagine how boring and mind-numbing these "spelling lessons" must be for older children (who all know how to read, of course) and praise one's lucky stars for not having had to endure them oneself. Much less careful attention is given to style, and if there are women who write a fluent, attractive, and personal style they probably did not learn it in boarding school, where writing without gross errors in spelling and grammar is considered quite satisfactory.

With all this, it is easy to foresee that male mathematicians, geometers, philosophers, and linguists are in no immediate danger of being overshadowed by women, whose education hardly presents serious competition. These abstract subjects, however, are a major problem because no matter how superficially taught they take up much time and are an ordeal for the poor children, especially the study of Latin that is often begun as early as age nine or ten: the poor little things who would much rather read the *magasin des enfants* or *Robinson Crusoe* are tortured with Virgil and the campaigns of Julius Caesar. If you dare inquire into the purpose of these subjects—which are conducive to neither social success nor domestic happiness, are commonly tossed aside upon leaving school, or if studied more carefully produce little more than a dry, pedantic knowledge that is handed from one generation to another like so much unproductive, dead capital—if you ask whether a thorough command of living languages and literatures is not preferable to Latin, the standard answer is: "It greatly improves the mind!" Of course, no one explains to what extent it really does, and ultimately you are suspected of not valuing such useful knowledge out of sheer jealousy. Thus, instead of cutting it, this "Chinese pigtail" is passed on and grows ever longer. Also, these boarding schools, which often have as many as two hundred pupils, evidently can do little or nothing toward moral development: weekly church attendance only applies a superficial gloss to the raw material. "Seats in church" are always a part of the bill for one hundred or two hundred dollars that is cheerfully handed to the parents each quarter.

Besides these fashionable private boarding schools that are open to the public, there are also convent schools—even the Jesuits have such an institution—in which, as is commonly said, students are taught not for mere appearances but for true knowledge. But curiosity must here be curbed because these schools are closed to visitors, and even the normally all-effective master key of "a correspondent for foreign papers" proves to be unsuccessful. At the Academy of the Sacred Heart, a palatial building, I did not get beyond the reception room, where I had barely time to look at a handsome steel engraving of "His Holiness Pius XII" and a hideous Christ with a thorn-crowned heart *on* rather than *in* his breast, when an old nun appeared to dismiss me peremptorily because visitors, even parents, are categorically not allowed.

I had better luck at a free school connected to a convent of merciful sisters, who gave me a friendly welcome and were very glad to show me through the building. School was just over, and the children, of whom there are no fewer than a hundred in two large halls, were singing as they marched past me, arranged two by two in an orderly line. In addition, it is a shelter for poor young women without work: they labor in a large washing and ironing shop, a main source of income for the convent. Others are put to work knitting, crocheting, and doing other tasks preparing for a Christmas bazaar. I was pleased to notice that, contrary to the normal American custom, the girls do not sleep together, but each has her own bed. The cloisters are decorated with rather poor copper engravings, hanging from small black crosses and representing scenes from the lives of the saints; in the large dormitory for the girls and in small niches and chapels there are life-size wooden pictures of the Madonna, painted and richly decorated with artificial flowers, also homemade.

It is a curious experience to leave the busy and crowded streets of New York and to find oneself suddenly in the seclusion of a convent, a contrast that is the more noticeable as there is nothing compatible in the physiognomy of the city. In Prague, Vienna, or other ancient cities, on the other hand, things harmonize because priests, pilgrims, and images of saints on all sides recall the times when the pope was the ruler of the civilized world. But with all the religious freedom that prevails and despite the many Catholic churches throughout the city, New York bears the unmistakable stamp of a Protestant city; its wide, straight streets are so contrary to Catholic romanticism that a convent looks much like an armored knight in the midst of modern society. This peaceful coexistence of the most diverse elements is one of the chief attractions of this city monster—it is the poetry of reality, of a rich and colorful life, in which pictures constantly change as in a stereoscope. As the door of the convent closes behind you, you step into the world and the outdoors again: "Click! A change of picture!"

Notes

1. *Morgenblatt*, 50:4:84–89 (1856).

2. Assing must be referring to Union College, which she visited in 1852.

11

Colored People in New York[1]

Color Prejudice in the Free North

It was twenty-eight years ago, in 1827, that slavery was abolished in the State of New York, and 40,000 black and colored people were given their freedom. This number has meanwhile increased to 50,000, of which approximately 15,000 live in the City of New York, and the question must be asked: What have been the fruits of these thirty years of freedom? What have you done, after taking this first step, to improve the intellectual and material conditions of a people whom until then you had purposely kept in deepest ignorance and degradation? What sources of knowledge and income have you opened up to the colored people? What has been done for their education?

Deep silence is the only answer to questions like these, and if you ask particular individuals they are likely to reply: the Negroes are in the worst condition of ignorance, degradation, and poverty; it is a proven fact that in their abilities they are far below white people; they would have been better off if they had remained in slavery. It is perfectly obvious that, if indeed this is the case, white people are to blame, for they have neglected to undertake the most necessary and urgent steps. But that is only the smallest part of their burden of guilt and offense against the colored people. In a country where societies are instantly established for the alleviation of every conceivable social evil nothing has been done over the years for the intellectual and material progress of the colored people, and they have been left to their own fate. To make matters worse, the free North, although not tolerating slavery, has done and continues to do everything in its power to prevent the further development of the African race by erecting a wall of prejudice separating whites and blacks—including among the latter mulattoes and all other gradations of color without distinction. This prejudice is more cruel than the most barbarous law, for laws can be defeated at any time, whereas prejudices, like the caste divisions in India, remain unshakable for centuries.

Colored people are not tolerated at any *table d'hôte* and their children not admitted to either the public schools, which are otherwise open to all local residents, or the private academies, except for one institution in McGrawville, the only one in the State of New York. All but a few who are able to hire a private tutor have to content themselves with the wretched instruction offered in schools that their own scarce means are able to support. The white churches are closed to them, and in the theater listings one can read that a part of the third balcony—the worst section in the house—is open to "decent blacks." The lowest American would consider it an unpardonable insult to be seated at the same table with a "nigger," as they contemptuously refer to any colored person. The polite term is "colored people," but any white man who entertained the idea of entering into social relations with them would be unfailingly ostracized. Even the omnibuses are closed to them, and the elegant lady or the educated gentleman who would without demurral tolerate next to them a dirty, drunk, tobacco-smoking creature, who may even be laden with market baskets, would consider it an insult to their dignity if the most decent and neatly dressed Negro were to sit down beside them. The large number of poor workers who have labored during the day in the lower part of the city often have to walk several miles in every weather, while other people get home securely and effortlessly for the paltry sum of 5 cents. A well-respected black preacher tried repeatedly to oppose this injustice,[2] which is entirely the result of prejudice, but only this summer it happened that, after he had taken his seat in an omnibus, a so-called respectable gentleman promptly left the car. Thereupon the conductor forced the colored man to get off and, when the latter refused, was assisted by a police officer. The case has been taken to court but still remains undecided.

Cases like this one, which occur every day with slight variations, do not even happen in the slaveholding South, since the early intercourse with Negroes, who, serving as nurses, servants, and playmates, usually become the children's best friends, prevents the formation of prejudice against physical proximity. In general, it is a grave mistake to charge the South with all of the Negroes' miseries, though the rapid and terrible spread of slavery in most recent times has had its influence. North and South are equally guilty. The North may have emancipated its slaves, but without great sacrifice, as neither tobacco nor cotton are planted there, and foreign immigration furnishes an overabundance of cheap servants and workers. So if the northern masses are trumpeting their opposition to slavery, they are simply indulging in noble rhetoric and ideals that are in immediate retreat as soon as they are asked to put their money where their mouths are. Is it fair to demand that Southerners, out of purely humanitarian considerations, give up such a large share of their property without any compensation? And should Northerners not assume at least half of the financial burden and take on a large public debt or something like it to bring about the emancipation of the Negroes, if they really wished to remove this mark of shame that is fundamentally and eternally in conflict with the principles of a republic and the character of a free people? If the North—where intelligence, knowledge, and enlightened thought reside—did not condone slavery, why would it permit the establishment of new slave states, the passage of the Fugitive Slave Law, and the adoption of the Nebraska Bill? Who does not know that the African slave trade—which, though forbidden, continues secretly—proceeds mainly out of New York, that every year no less than thirty-five trials are conducted in connection with it (though the discovery of violations is the exception rather than the rule), and that in most of these cases the accused get off without punishment because of a lack of evidence?

Although it is evident that, in regard to slavery, a majority in the North is about on the same level with the South, purposely keeping the Negroes down by the force of a cruel prejudice, it would be unfair and unjust not to honor and recognize the relatively small minority of people who have dedicated themselves both publicly and privately to emancipation in general as well as to the protection of fugitive slaves, the education of the colored people, and the battle against prejudice. Many have therefore seen their lives and property threatened by the anger of the mob on more than one occasion. Theodore Parker, Wendell Phillips, Gerrit Smith, Sumner, and Garrison are in the vanguard of this minority—grand and noble figures, greatly admired by all who are committed to this cause. It is noteworthy that, in regard to religion, the most outstanding fighters for abolitionism also belong to the party of enlightened free thought, who are here referred to—or rather maligned—as "infidels." The party of religious orthodoxy, on the other hand, tends to defend slavery on the grounds that it is "God's will"; or it argues—with brazen shamelessness—that slavery confers a special favor upon the Negroes with the gift of Christianity!

I have mentioned the most outstanding fighters on behalf of the colored people, but there are many others who, though less well-known, have contributed their share. Opposed to all the horrors, the slave hunters, and the bloodhounds, there are those who, with great unselfishness, make every effort to assist fugitive slaves on their way to freedom and to protect them against their owners. In this connection, I must relate a recent event that caused as much hilarity on one side as it provoked anger on the other and became the subject of a bitter war of words between the pro- and antislavery press.

Mr. Wheeler, a Virginian, recently appointed as United States ambassador to Nicaragua, stopped over in Philadelphia, accompanied by a Negro woman and her two sons, boys nine and eleven years old, who were listed in the register simply as "servants." The colored employees at the hotel where Mr. Wheeler was staying probably suspected that there was something strange about these "servants," and indeed it turned out that they were slaves and that the woman was only waiting for an opportunity to escape from her master, who was keeping an anxious eye on her. Everything remained quiet, however, until Mr. Wheeler stepped on board the New York steamboat with his "property," when suddenly Passmore Williamson, a widely respected citizen of Philadelphia, appeared in the company of several Negroes and explained to the woman point-blank that she was in a free state and therefore legally free herself. In the lively argument that ensued Wheeler asked Williamson by what right he was meddling in his affairs, whereupon Williamson replied that he merely wished to inform the woman of her rights. Wheeler asserted that she was familiar with them and did not wish to be harassed by unauthorized persons, but the woman declared that, above all, she wished to obtain her freedom. Now the ambassador tried to play on her feelings, pathetically arguing that she would forever be separated from her children in "Old Virginny," who would be lost without their "mammy." But nothing availed, and the woman answered: "As dear as her children are to her, freedom was even dearer." Then this noble Virginian asked a policeman to protect his property, but was given the cool answer that he was no "nigger catcher." The slaves were put in a cart and taken away to the cheers of the crowd. But Mr. Wheeler, unable to leave well enough alone, lodged a complaint against Williamson, who has since then—contrary to all laws and despite his offering bond—languished in jail for ten months like a murderer without the benefit of *habeas corpus*. He will no doubt be acquitted, but this illegal procedure goes to prove the influence and wrath of those supporters of slavery for whom each free Negro is an abomination.

On the other hand, the well-being of the Negroes is strongly supported by a society of women who founded an orphanage for colored children in 1836, initially with very insufficient means. On upper Fifth Avenue, among the mansions of wealthy New Yorkers, a handsome building surrounded by friendly gardens is situated near the Crystal Palace and the Croton, an impressive water main channeling the water of Lake Croton eight German miles underground to two large reservoirs surrounded by a square wall, which supply the entire city with water. More than 230 children are living at present in that house where they go to school normally until age twelve; then they are apprenticed to either farmers or crafts and trades people but remain under the continuing supervision of the institution. Some of the more gifted remain at the house and are later employed as teachers.

The whole arrangement makes a very satisfactory impression, and I was particularly pleased to notice that, as far as I could see, there is no strict enforcement of unnecessary rules and the children are given as much freedom as possible. Without exception, both the big and little ones look very happy, playing with such abandon and laughing so loudly in their playground that it cheers one's heart. I gave them much pleasure by cutting little landscapes out of paper; they all wanted to watch me and get something for themselves, so that I was soon surrounded by a large circle, a veritable sample of all shades of color: from the deepest black to the most tender white with blond hair that had no trace of African origin. It being a hot day, most of them were barefoot; their clothes were clean but in many cases patched two or three times, which stood in comical contrast to the elaborate hairstyles of many of the girls. The desire of Negro women to give their wool the semblance of long hair can already be seen among these children in the most amusing manner, and I saw coiffures quite beyond the ken of any European hair stylist. There were several who had parted their hair into untold little squares like a checker board, each of which ended in a braid as thick as the tail of a mouse and half as long. I saw others with a crown of such braids standing straight up on top of their heads and with similar contraptions. Throughout the house everything is arranged along practical lines: the children's clothes are easily made on a sewing machine; the older girls do the housework; and a resident cobbler, with the aid of eight boys, supplies the institution with shoes. The only thing I disliked was again that orthodox religious coloration that gives such an unpalatable flavor to even the best institutions over here.

From all I have said so far it is self-evident that the great mass of free colored people, most of whose older generation were born and raised in slavery, have not yet been able to reach a high level of education. Prejudice bars their way to a higher level of knowledge; they are barred once and for all from white society; and since on the whole they appear not to have that spirit of speculation and enterprise that is the basis on which even rude and ignorant people achieve wealth and reputation, one cannot be surprised to find the majority employed in subordinate and dependent positions, though it must be said that, almost without exception, their performance in these positions is excellent. Black cooks, washer women, servants, barbers, hairdressers, and coachmen are always sought after, and one often finds in warehouses and factories Negroes employed as foremen, accountants, etc. who enjoy a high level of trust, and they do credit to themselves by their loyalty, sense of responsibility, and circumspection. Others live in the countryside as farmers, and here and there one finds the exceptional well-to-do Negro who owns his own business. Their potential for intellectual development cannot be denied and would bear fruit under reasonably tolerable circumstances. Furthermore, almost without exception they are endowed with a kind and cheerful disposition, and the least Negro possesses a natural politeness and friendliness that is as far from servility as it is from importunity. Naturally inclined to be happy, they are all smiles and laughter if only they can live in modestly acceptable conditions, and I have never met a colored person whose face expressed that passion and worry, that feverish haste of chasing after profit, with which the features of white people are stamped here more than in any other country of the world.

Despite all the unfavorable conditions and difficulties, one can now and then meet colored people who, gifted with uncommon talent and enduring energy, have vaulted to a high level of education and are actively furthering the progress and welfare of their people, partly by the work of their pen, partly through their personal influence. One of the most outstanding among them is Frederick Douglass, a mulatto, who was born in Maryland, escaped from slavery at age seventeen, and is now living in Rochester (State of New York) as the editor of an antislavery sheet, "Frederick Douglass's Paper." Enjoying general respect and esteem, he is known to be an excellent speaker, and his lectures on slavery are a great success with the public. I will soon write about his autobiography that was recently published.

The Fugitive Blacksmith

Among these excellent Negroes one must certainly also mention Doctor Pennington, a Negro and also a former slave, who is fighting for the freedom and progress of the colored people as a Presbyterian preacher in New York. He has published the chief events of his life and especially the story of his escape in a pamphlet with the title "The Fugitive Blacksmith," which is fascinating and moving in its simplicity and brevity. The style is unadorned and natural, the reasoning clear and to the point, and the depictions are fresh and lively. A natural, unconscious—I am tempted to say a *wild*—poetic strain sounds throughout the little volume. Pennington is not one of those saccharine personalities in whom a soft concept of Christianity has smothered the ability to hate and, along with it, the power of love and devotion which alone provides the motive force for serving a great purpose. He speaks out with bitterness and hatred against slavery and its supporters.[3]

***

Personally, Pennington has none of the hard edge and passion that is revealed in his writing; he rather gives the impression of benevolence, friendliness, and an inviting, agreeable generosity that makes it easy to get to know him. Endowed with a cheerful temperament, he loves jokes and witticisms, and the evenings I occasionally spend with him and his family are always filled with pleasant, stimulating conversation. His wife is a friendly mulatto and his son a handsome eleven-year-old brown boy with long, glossy hair who is eagerly learning German. Yet even a colored person in his position—and from the perspective of prejudice it matters little whether he is a Negro or seven-eighth white—is inexorably excluded from white society, and I would not have had the opportunity to meet Pennington had I not plucked up my courage and introduced myself unceremoniously as the "correspondent of Mr. Cotta's *Morgenblatt*."

I do not know to what extent the Caucasian race is intellectually superior to the African, but should, in the course of time, a happy turn of events sooner or later bring about the opportunity for developing their natural endowments, which—not unlike their hot homeland—still remain unexplored and unexploited, they will undoubtedly outstrip the expectations which people here and in Europe generally have of them.

Notes

1. Manuscript (1855), Assing Papers, Deutsches Literaturarchiv, Marbach.

2. Dr. James W. C. Pennington, minister of the Shiloh Presbyterian Church in New York City and author of *The Fugitive Blacksmith* (1849), a slave narrative, had befriended Assing at about this time (1855). He and his wife Almira opened their house to her, and through them Assing gained important insights into the lives of African Americans, a subject that increasingly became the focus of her personal and journalistic interests. See the second section of this essay, below.

3. About fifteen pages of manuscript—Assing's partial translation of *The Fugitive Blacksmith*—have here been omitted.

12

American Types:
Women—Irish—Blacks—Chinese—Indians—Gypsies[1]

* * *

New York's chief attraction is the cheerful mixture of so many extremes, peculiarities, and diverse elements who live peacefully alongside each other, albeit in strict separation. Among the peculiarities most evident even at first glance are the different human races in all shades and gradations that move about pell-mell, some of them to dissolve after several generations in the general American type, some of them to continue by retaining their own characteristics. It is strange how quickly a distinct type has evolved from the descendants of the European nations that have settled America—the English, Irish, Dutch, Germans, and French—a type so distinct and well defined that anyone with an eye for such things can spot the true American among thousands, no matter whether he has strayed to the North Pole, the South Pole, or anywhere else. This is not to say that every American without exception necessarily looks the same, but millions of people who have a certain look must necessarily be Americans; and generally one can say that the differences among them are not as pronounced as they are, for example, among the Germans. On the whole, it is a handsome breed: tall and slim with regular features, among which the moderately sized but penetrating eyes and the narrow, pinched lips are particularly characteristic. They bespeak an abundance of energy and reason, but also much sobriety and lack of poetic sensibility, and at first glance one detects a generally pragmatic disposition. The majority has brown hair and is pale and thin; those sturdy figures and glowing faces one meets with so commonly in Germany are rare over here.

It is the same with the women, whose slim figures lack a certain fullness just as their regular and pretty faces lack color—a flaw that is often corrected by make-up, which is here not as frowned upon as it is in Europe for destroying the natural complexion. They are rarely graced with beautiful teeth beyond their first youth, and the countless replicas of teeth marking the homes and offices of more dentists than in any other city of the world prove that all that glitters may indeed be gold, though not a natural tooth. The immoderate enjoyment of sweets, to which women may be given more than men to chewing tobacco, is probably one of the causes of this evil. In general, beauty rarely survives the years of youth, and American women bear weaknesses and infirmities that are often suggested in their stiff and shuffling gait. The life American women live, which tends to be a long series of soft indulgences—little exercise in the open air; living in rooms with the shades pulled down and cut off from the beneficial, vitalizing influence of the sun; an excessive use of pepper and other hot spices to cover up the poor quality of cooking—all these influences have negative effects. But most harmful of all is the overuse of mercury throughout the country, which many families use in the form of calomel as a kind of household remedy against any and all illnesses, just as some people with us use lilac and camomile tea as well as cream of tartar and sal ammoniac.

The Irish appear very different from the Americans; next to the Germans and the Americans themselves, they are the largest group in New York. The misery and privations that made them flee their home country do not seem to have sapped their energy, and the heavyset, sturdy figures with their round, red faces burst with health and satisfaction. Regular features and delicate figures are rarely seen with them, and their quick and heavy movements, their boisterous behavior, are marked by a singular lack of gracefulness. Already at a distance you can recognize Paddy from his unembarrassed way of treating everyone alike, from his loud shouting and his particular, inimitably comical dialect, which in its full glory is almost incomprehensible even to Americans. Two or three Irish servant girls working in the kitchen make a noise that can penetrate to the parlor, and it is exacerbated by the visitors they frequently receive. They do not care for accepting authority, resent any infringement on their liberties, and are experts at running the kitchen by a despotic constitution. Usually the worst victims of their regime, as elsewhere, are the poor Negroes, who are all but subjugated by them. Himself subjugated in his home country, the Irishman is happy to find others, who here are seen as worse than he, whom he can treat like dogs, and on whom he can take out his own suffering. Although basically generous and harmless, he immediately adopts all American prejudices, despises the "nigger," and absolutely refuses to sit at the same table with him.

Like all Europeans, Paddy is much given to pleasure, contrary to the sober Americans, and as soon as a few of them gather at an inn or some place like it they find an old fiddle and begin to dance to their heart's content even in the smallest room and the most stifling heat. On Sundays they are almost the only ones besides the Germans and the French who go out for amusement in the city. The women can be recognized by their baroquely colorful clothing, their bright silk shawls, their calico dresses, or the cotton gloves they wear with silk dresses. If fortune fails to smile upon him, the Irish immigrant does not hesitate long before turning to begging, and the number of Irishmen who wander from house to house for this purpose is immense, many among them those half-starved, ragged figures who seem to be on the verge of being overcome by misery. The German, on the other hand, will do his utmost to obtain work and, in the worst case, would rather try his fortune with a box full of penny items or a hurdy-gurdy, playing day in and day out the familiar melodies of German suffering at home and abroad.

On several previous occasions, I have written about the colored people, the most numerous of the groups mentioned so far, and all I will add here is that the good impression they have made on me from the beginning has not only proven to be correct but increased on further acquaintance. It would be hard to find another people that has been so oppressed, mistreated, and trampled upon, so excluded from all the benefits of education, and so harshly kept in ignorance, yet possesses so much natural tact, decency, and dignified courtesy. Recently I had another experience of meeting blacks among themselves at an evening party given on the ground floor of his church for Dr. Pennington, whom I have mentioned earlier. Because there are neither wealthy nor educated Negroes in New York, the guests all had to be of the working class: washer women, cooks, seamstresses, waiters, painters, barbers, hairdressers, and the general category of house servants made up a gathering of well over a hundred people. Imagine how noisy, wild, and boisterous such an event would have been among Americans or Germans, let alone Irishmen, of this class, what low humor would be the cause of their amusement. Yet it would be impossible to blame them, for they would be behaving according to their level of education.

But how sedate, proper, and tactful the behavior of these "darkies" was! No loud word, no improper joke gave away that one was actually not in the most select, best educated society, and the friendly, natural courtesy with which people treated each other would have done honor to the most fashionable salon. Even the clothes were more tasteful and presented fewer of those ridiculously inappropriate color combinations so common among that class of people. A casual cheerfulness dominated the event, and friendly, dark faces glowed with happiness while everyone listened attentively to the meager sound of an ill-tuned piano accompanying two young girls who sang fragments of popular melodies with equally meager voices. The featured event, however, did not begin until after supper. After the tables had been pushed aside, the company marched through the room two by two, singing "Old Folks at Home," "Lily Dale," "If a Body Meets a Body, Coming Through the Rye," and similar songs as a chorus. This entertainment seemed to please everyone greatly, and it was carried on for hours with unflagging endurance, so that it was finally three o'clock before they parted.

Except for two reporters of newspapers, who never miss any event of note, two English families were the only white people there, and at first I was seated next to them. But after a while I took the liberty of mixing among the darkies to become acquainted with them. It did seem to embarrass them a little, but soon they overcame their reticence, and we were chatting amiably. A handsome young mulatto from Pennsylvania was introduced to me who spoke the local version of German—a mixture of every known South German dialect—without the trace of an English accent. It is impossible to convey how funny such an encounter with a blackened Swabian or Darmstadter is, and one is tempted to repeat the question that a German farmer once asked when he was addressed in German by a Negro: "How's life treating you so far away from home, countryman, and what made you so black?"

Who are those other dark-colored figures whom one encounters particularly in the busy streets of the lower part of the city, where they sell cigars, candy, and tea from behind small stands? Their skin is somewhat lighter than that of the mulattoes, but their prominent cheekbones, the slanted, narrow slit-eyes do not suggest any relationship with the African but unmistakably reveal the Mongolian race. Their clothes, too, though very simple and not particularly conspicuous, differ from the usual: long, wide trousers that reveal just enough of the feet to show white socks and crude shoes; a long, wide, gray or blue linen jacket; and a high, black cap without visor. If the cap is removed, you can see a long, well-braided pigtail wound around the head—the Chinaman's essential, never-changing emblem and badge of honor. Since the desire for emigration and the gold fever have gripped the inhabitants of the Celestial Empire and they have been pouring by the thousands into California, a sizeable number of Chinese—it is said 2,000—have gathered in New York. Some engage in the trade mentioned above; some paint pictures, fans, and porcelain in that well-known, tasteless manner; some manufacture jumping jacks, while others have chosen the less strenuous occupation of begging.

The Chinese beggar, cowering on some front stoop with his face averted and covered by both hands as if ashamed of his misery, exudes such bottomless despair that it is impossible not to feel pity and empathy for the poor devil's hopeless situation. It seems that not only poverty gnaws at him but his longing for the fields of rice and tea, the pagodas, and the imperial beauties of small feet; but then one begins to notice that this display of misfortune and despair is simply a trick or standard etiquette among Chinese beggars, for the show of despair never varies from one to another. Many Chinese are also employed by the tea merchants in order to attract customers by their appearance.

Their features are mostly rough and ungainly as if carved in wood, and there is not much difference between them and the life-size figures drinking a cup of tea or smoking a pipe that are painted on the outside of some stores. Unfortunately I have not yet been able to explore their living quarters in the lower part of the city near the Battery, where they prepare their traditional fare of rice, rotten eggs, fried rats, and other such native delicacies. Three years ago, a kind of Chinese acting company presented a pantomime of Chinese life, including samples of songs that could hardly be rivaled in ugliness and lack of taste. I was absent from New York at that time and therefore unable to partake of this artistic pleasure, but an acquaintance told me that the music was sufficient to prove how thoroughly their taste, their feelings, and their inclinations differ from ours—in short, that it was once and for all impossible for any sympathy to develop between them and us. "If it were simply a matter of wild noise," he said, "it would suggest nothing more than pure barbarism; but no, there is a certain order, rhythm, and melody that so much violates our laws of music—a rising melody where we would expect a falling passage and *vice versa*—that the wildest chaos would strike us as less offensive." These Chinese stayed at the Hotel Shakespeare, a well-known inn largely preferred by Germans; and being such a novelty, they were at first regarded with much curiosity but soon became generally despised for their dirty, slovenly ways and their contempt for European manners. In the end, a cry of outrage rang through the hotel when they were seen in hot weather walking about their wide-open rooms all day in nothing but their birthday suits: the proprietor had no recourse but to put the sons of the Celestial Empire out of their earthly home and under the open sky.

The variety and differences in customs and manners in the different parts of Germany have often been pointed out in comparison to the United States. Over there, you need to travel only a few miles from one town to another, or just walk from one village to the next, to notice a different style of architecture, different costumes, a different dialect, and a different way of life: how distinct the customs, furnishings, and clothes of the farmers! how great the differences between Austrians and Westphalians, between villages in Swabia and in Holstein! nothing is the same, and how charming this diversity! But in this big country you find, with minor modifications, the same people, costumes, cities, towns, and houses, and a truly distinct difference appears only between the slaveholding South and the free North. New York is representative of the latter, and its fashions, customs, and way of life are busily copied, all the way to the frontier as circumstances permit, so that the provincial farmer in Sheboygan, Wisconsin, is much the same as the farmer in New York State, except for a somewhat rougher exterior. In New York City, on the other hand, the great differences among the races and nations are all the more pronounced and appear like groups of different species of trees in a forest rather than like leaves on a flower.

To show the reader literally an example of the peculiar growths of the forest primeval, we turn again to the lower part of the city, a little below the park and gardens surrounding City Hall, where we encounter a few strange figures that have never been seen in Germany. They are mostly short and squat, their skin color as dark as that of a mulatto, with whom they otherwise share no facial resemblance, however: prominent cheek bones; narrow slit-eyes; a noticeably low forehead that looks as if hidden under glossy black hair and a large, round hat; the whole figure almost completely covered by a wool blanket which serves as an overcoat. They look sad and depressed and seem to approach the passer-by only with a shy reluctance to offer for sale colorfully embroidered shoes, bags, or satchels. They understand little English or at least wish to give that impression; at any rate, I did not succeed in getting an answer from them, which is quite different from the Negro, who befriends the white man without reservation if one only approaches him in a friendly manner. The Indians distrust the palefaces, who drove them from their native forests, robbed them of everything, again and again broke all treaties with them, and, by way of compensation, gave them the area between the Arkansas and the Red River as well as a few settlements in the Northwest. I would not have had the opportunity to meet them, had it not been for a fortunate coincidence. Despite all the persecutions, cruelties, and betrayals that have been inflicted on the Indians in general, no one feels prejudiced against or an aversion to the individual Indian, as they do against the Negro; to the contrary, they are sought after for their qualities, and people are not averse to entering into marriage with them, in so far as the Indians themselves are disposed to do so, which is not always the case. In fact, I have met people who proudly claim their descent from some famous chief.

By coincidence I met such a half-breed, who lives with his family on a farm in Chapequaw, not far from New York, where he buys and sells real estate besides running his farm. Although half European on his father's side, this man, who calls himself Mr. Cooper, has the unmistakable traces of Indian blood in skin color and facial features, but in his behavior he proves to be a simple, friendly, kind, and generous man without the stamp of any particular nationality. The rest of his family, however, appears all the stranger, and to visit the farm at Chapequaw is to enter into a whole new atmosphere. After a ride of several miles on the Harlem Railroad, you have to walk inland for about three quarters of an hour until you reach—despite the proximity to New York—the most charming wilderness imaginable. You pass through a magnificent forest, between hills and rocks, and arrive at a cheerful house, which, though built on a small scale and looking almost like a toy with its tiny windows, nevertheless contains many rooms and always presents itself hospitably to friends and acquaintances. Now and then you meet people who, suffering from one kind of illness or another, are seeking Mrs. Cooper's Indian medical treatment, for she is a real squaw, the daughter of a Chippewa chief named Powell, practicing medicine as many women do. It is self-evident that a people with no knowledge of the outside world and its products would use only native plants; and because of their constant observation and direct experience of nature it is no wonder—in fact, there can be no doubt—that they are able to cure many illnesses with the simplest remedies and that they cause less harm than many a quack because they frown upon any use of metals. But fraud and humbug have become pervasive here, too, so that there are now many ignoramuses who have elevated Indian medical practices to a kind of theory, deprecating modern medicine in general and arguing that native herbs can be effective against all illnesses that occur within the region where these plants grow. Perhaps these people apprentice themselves for a few weeks to some old Indian woman, or claim they did, before they display some dried roots and plants in their window and, relying on the public's gullibility, merrily proceed on their cheating ways under the assumed title of an "Indian doctor."

Because the real Indians are much better company, let us return to Mrs. Cooper's hospitable house, where the family has completely adopted the American way of life and almost without exception speak only English among themselves. Only the wife's mother, an oddly brown Sibylla, seems to have adopted the strange new ways merely on the surface; using her native language, she remembers her wigwam in the West and the Great Sprit, Manitou, whom the family has long since abandoned for the trinity. Now and then she moves without a sound, like the shadow of one of the departed, without betraying any awareness of her surroundings. Two children—Falathea, a girl eleven years old, and Ociola, a somewhat younger boy—are all but white in color, though their features bear all the peculiarities of the Indian race, in the girl's case not exactly to the advantage of beauty.

The strangest appearance in the family, however, is the wife's sister; although she converted to Chistianity at age ten and was educated in a New England school, she steadfastly clings to her Indian heritage. When I first met her in New York at an American family's home, she wore over her white skirt a red silk tunic bordered by a yellow ribbon with rows of small glass beads as are often used in embroidery; she also wore a short-sleeved yellow silk jacket with red trim and beads over long white sleeves. Several rows of large glass beads, embroidered moccasins, and a red bow in her glossy black hair complete her dress, to which she adds a red shawl and a large round hat when she goes out. Such a getup would be enough to cause an uproar in a small German town, and even here, where people are more used to that sort of thing, it is so conspicuous that they stop in the street or crane their necks out the window.

This strange creature, who was christened Mary but goes by her Indian name Yochplefileila—meaning "light"—seemed to have taken a fancy to me and told me much about the life, the customs, and the beliefs of the Indians; she did so with such natural eloquence, using so many strange and unusual images that her narrative sometimes was elevated to poetry but sometimes also struck me as descending into false fancy. Speaking of her father, Chief Powell, who had traveled in Europe and gained much new understanding, she said: "His mind was broken like a net of light." Like the ancients, the Indians believe that the planets alternately exert their own special influence—a kind of dominance—over the world, and that there is a mysterious correspondence among them, humans, and plants. "The sun," she said, "is hot and dry and corresponds to pepper, ginger, and cinnamon. Venus, on the other hand, is cool and moist, and cabbage, peaches, and melons grow under it. The earth is moist and hot, and her dominance brings forth radishes and other hot and moist plants. The moon is simply moist; it is the body that interacts with water. Mars, however, is cold and dry and makes spruce, fir, and pine grow. Jupiter, hotter than the sun, in fact the hottest and driest of the planets, brings forth red and white pepper and all the other hot spices. Saturn, finally, is cold and dry in the highest degree, so cold and dry that only poisonous plants and snakes can grow under it."

Before we parted, I asked her whether she would write down a few lines, with which I intended to please a collector of manuscripts. She was perfectly willing, but to my great surprise this princess of the wilderness proved to be less literate than an eight-year-old child, in spite of her attendance at an English-speaking school. She went about her task and preparations like a German farmer who is asked to sign his name. First she asked for lined paper, as otherwise it would be impossible for her to write in straight lines; then the children playing in the room were commanded to be perfectly still; and then she expressed her embarrassment at not knowing what to write. I suggested that she choose something from what she had just told me about the planets, but after more than half an hour's hard work, with me spelling out each word for her—though unable to prevent her spelling "door" with only one "o"—she managed to put together a few words about the rising sun.

The reason for this strange discrepancy seems to me that Yochplefileila, after having been converted by the pious people in whose hands she found herself at that time, was so coddled, spoiled, and placed on a pedestal as a successful convert that not much thought was given to instruction. This must have encouraged her to be so satisfied and pleased with her Indian origin that it did not occur to her to strive for more. Like so many of our famous Europeans, she belongs in the category of self-conscious originals: instead of clinging with the naiveté of a true child of nature to her Indian appearance, manner of speech, and cultural traditions—though they are a natural part of her—she knows that her peculiarities give her a certain notoriety.

Last autumn, one of the most peculiar and mysterious tribes of people sent its delegates, a large band of English gypsies, to these shores; they set up camp on the other side of the Hudson, near Hoboken. I met several of the families in a small forest, where they camped out in tents, and the sight reawakened in me for a moment the old romantic feelings belonging to a time when I was enthralled with fairy tales about Indian maidens and magic rings. The construction of the tents, which were made from wool blankets spread over poles, reminded me of Indian wigwams. Crawling into one of them, I found an entire family—husband, wife, children, dogs, and birds—sitting around a large fire, on which they had probably just cooked their evening meal. The smoke escaped through an opening that had been left at the peak of the tent. Inside a nearby tent that stood half open in front, a brown octogenarian woman crouched in front of the fire, and a man and several boys lay stretched out in a corner, while the wife—the old woman's daughter—was occupied washing out a large kettle. The younger woman, a curious looking creature with black, piercing eyes and a red cloth wrapped around her head, offered to read my hand. She took me aside and, after I had removed my glove, she said . . . .

When she was finished, she said: "I could tell you a lot more, but for that I would need a good bit more money in hand." I excused myself with lacking the necessary change, upon which she cleverly suggested I might give her my earrings. I thanked her with a smile for such a bargain and preferred to ask her about her own situation and plans, to which, however, I received not much of a response. Like most repressed and barely tolerated races, the gypsies are mistrustful, and even my question about how many of them had come over was answered in several quarters only with the comment, "Oh, a good deal!" Their wagons, guarded by dogs, stood at some distance: they are traveling homes equipped with chimneys and look much like Levrasse's wagon that Eugene Sue describes so vividly in his otherwise remarkably poor *Martin l'enfant trouvé*.[2] The gypsies' preference for loud, fantastic clothing could be seen in the widespread use of bright red trim or cuffs or the fragment of a shawl for a sash or mantilla. The entire camp, set in the shade of green trees, was as picturesque a sight as one may ever have dreamed about while reading a novel: romance and poetry in rags.

Notes

1. *Morgenblatt*, 50:17:407–408; 50:18:431–432; and 50:19:453–456 (1856).

2. Eugène Sue (1804–1857) wrote popular and sensational novels about the Paris underworld and slum life.

13

Preface to the German Translation of *My Bondage and My Freedom*[1]

Were this life story fiction, artistic invention, one would have to deplore that it was not published a few years earlier, before the interest in such narratives had been exhausted by the almost countless representations of slave life that now, since the publication of the famous *Uncle Tom,* have developed into a whole new branch of literature. Yet the present work is not an invention but a true history, a series of naked, unadorned, terrible facts that are far more effective, moving, and convincing for those who can stand the truth than any work of fiction, because they represent reality and all of its consequences. Instead of an imagined hero, it is the author himself who is at the center of this narrative: he actually lived these experiences, and he is now living among us, one of America's famous men. He belongs to that oppressed race—the pariahs of American society—who, because of a decision by the United States Supreme Court last year,[2] are forever barred from becoming citizens of their own country and have no rights that any white person is bound to respect. It is the whole human being—the noble self, the passionate, spirited, gifted, and dynamic man, with his burning love of freedom and the virtuosity of his implacable hatred of slavery and slave masters—who steps from these pages in his irresistible attractiveness and distinction to meet the reader. In the northern United States his autobiography was an overwhelming success, far beyond all expectations. Since 1855, the year when it first appeared, no fewer than 20,000 copies have been issued, even though slavery is the subject of countless daily discussions and controversies in all the papers, causing the reading public to pay attention only to the most outstanding and significant writings on this subject.

The story of the author's life is the most faithful expression of his individuality and therefore needs no further explanation. The reader will get to know all his qualities in the course of this book, except for his brilliance as an orator, which is the basis of his current renown. In this country of great orators Frederick Douglass is one of the greatest. Perfect mastery of the subject, incisive and brilliant logic, and controlled moderation despite all passion are his hallmark. He often soars to tragic heights but then illuminates his subject with brilliant flashes of wit, speaks to the listener's heart, or provides comic relief with a joke. Everything is fresh, original, and compelling, and all these attributes are underscored by a perfect mastery of language and by so mellifluous, sonorous, flexible a voice speaking to the heart as I have ever heard. His abundant intellect and originality are evident in the fact that, even while all the great speakers of this country have also been exploiting the subject, he has been treating it for seventeen years without becoming repetitious or stale. The circumstances that served him well at his first appearance—a time when a fugitive slave was rarely seen on the platform and he had the advantage of novelty—no longer obtain; nevertheless, his success and his influence are still rising. In every town and village of the northern United States the mere announcement of his name is enough to fill the halls to the last remaining seat. Although he addresses it every year, I have even seen the demanding public of New York thrilled and swept away by him as if a new apostle had revealed to them for the first time a truth that had lain unspoken in everyone's heart.

Two years ago, I first became acquainted with Frederick Douglass on a visit to Rochester, and I present the following excerpt from the sketch I wrote after that first meeting.[3] All I have to add is that that first positive impression has only been confirmed and strengthened upon further acquaintance.

"At first I went to meet Frederick Douglass in his newspaper office, which is marked by a sign in large letters above the entrance: THE NORTH STAR OFFICE. It refers to the familiar symbol among fugitive slaves, who often have the north star as their only guide as they flee and are transported by the hundreds on the so-called underground railroad from Rochester to Canada. As I did not find him there, I went to his home, about a half hour outside the city. The handsome villa, surrounded by a large garden, is situated on a hill overlooking a charming landscape. Douglass is a rather light mulatto of unusually tall, slender, and powerful stature. His features are striking: the prominently domed forehead with a peculiarly deep cleft at the base of the nose, an aquiline nose, and the narrow, beautifully carved lips betray more of his white than his black origin. The thick hair, here and there with touches of gray, is frizzy and unruly but not woolly. His whole appearance, stamped by past storms and struggles, bespeaks great energy and will power that shuns no obstacle and has been the sole source of his success in reaching his present prominence in the face of all odds. One can easily see how, when little more than a boy, he stood up to his master (who wanted to beat him) and actually cowed him—as he relates in his autobiography; or, when working in the shipyard at Baltimore and finding that the white workers refused to tolerate him, he lifted up his most ardent opponent and tossed him into the water. Despite all the vicissitudes, his whole being expresses a richly endowed, original, happily mature nature. Everything about him is fresh, genuine, true, and good. Endowed with an exceptional talent for conversation, he knows how to inspire and elevate others, and in conversation proves to be cheerful, animated, witty, and knowledgeable. Glowing with passion for the cause to which he has dedicated his life, he is far too wide-ranging in his interests as not to engage other worthy causes with energy. We touched upon a wide variety of things—large and small, general and personal—in the course of our conversation, and everywhere I encountered understanding and sympathy.—Douglass's wife is completely black, and his five children, therefore, have more of the traits of the Negro than he."

If Frederick Douglass were white, with his talent, endurance, and energy he would have had a brilliant career and achieved some distinguished position despite his humble origins. But as a mulatto—even though he is a famous man whose speeches attract large and eager crowds, whose importance and influence no one can gainsay, a man who belongs to the true elite of society, a man of intellect, personal amiability, and the purest character—he is excluded from any public office and from what is generally called good society. All the greater is the respect and love he enjoys among the friends of the emancipation of the slaves. It is no exaggeration of his accomplishments and the influence of his personality to attribute to him much of the change in public opinion in favor of the colored population that has occurred in the North for a number of years and is making slow but noticeable progress.

May this biography contribute to heighten the interest in the representatives and the cause of a race that, under a so-called republican form of government, has been subjected to a system of oppression whose cruelty has hardly been paralleled in the history of all peoples and countries.

Notes

1. Frederick Douglass, *Sclaverei und Freiheit* (Hamburg: Hoffmann & Campe, 1860): ix–xiv. Assing first met Douglass in 1856 when she traveled to Rochester to get his approval and cooperation for her planned translation of *My Bondage and My Freedom*. Although she wrote the Preface in the summer of 1858 and it was not published until 1860, it appears in the present volume under 1856 because in it Assing quotes a substantial passage from a piece, now lost, that she had written shortly after her first meeting with Douglass (see n. 3, below).

2. The Dred Scott case of 1857.

3. Assing's account of her first visit to the Douglass home in Rochester in 1856 did not appear in the *Morgenblatt* nor apparently in any other publication. This is one of several references by Assing throughout these essays and reports indicating that she had little control over and not always accurate knowledge about which of her submissions to Cotta's paper were actually printed. See Essay 19, n. 2.

14

The Presidential Election and Slavery[1]

The whole country is looking forward in feverish excitement to November 4, the day on which the future president will be elected, and the excitement grows with every passing day. The presidential election is always an important event, but never before has it been a matter of principle determining the future of several states and many thousands of individuals. Indeed, it can be said that this is the most significant moment since the Declaration of Independence. Slavery is the motive power of all contests, the central point of politics: the presidential election must determine, at least indirectly, whether slavery will spread or be contained.

Any European reading the American papers must get dizzy with all the different names of political parties and the factions connected with them. There are Whigs, Democrats, Hard Shells, Soft Shells, Know-Nothings, Americans, North Americans, Republicans (also called Black-and-Yellows), Black Republicans, Negro Worshipers, and God knows what else! All of these are only subdivisions of the two large parties, the Democrats and the Republicans, the former being the defenders and the latter the opponents of slavery, yet neither having anything to do with what in Europe one associates with the words "democrats" and "republicans." It is possible for them to come to terms on any issue, but never on the question of slavery: it is the focal point of all party hatred, all hostility, and all passion.

The Know-Nothings, the died-in-the-wool Americans or Nativists, who had considerable notoriety for a while and would like to close the country to all foreigners, also constitute a fairly sizable party. Yet, even though in last year's state elections they succeeded in gaining a majority here and there, they can generally be described as a faction that is in decline. Because the American people know full well that they are indebted to immigration, that immigrants have settled large parts of the Northwest, and that they make an important contribution to the growth of the country, the people's common sense is opposed to one-sided nativist arrogance, which would like to build a Chinese Wall around the most hospitable country in the world. It is particularly laughable because, if this argument is taken to its logical conclusion, all Americans are immigrants, and only the poor Indians who have been driven from their homelands are fully entitled to call themselves Americans.

At any rate, Frémont, the candidate of the Republicans, is in every respect an honorable, hard-working man. Some have tried in vain to discover stains on his record, and only the lie that he is a Catholic may succeed in causing consternation among the ignorant masses. In a nation where the majority clings to a rigid—I am tempted to say fossilized—Protestantism, hundreds of thousands shudder in pious dismay at the mere suggestion that someone is a Catholic. But since this strategy has begun to wear off, Frémont's enemies, in the absence of better ammunition, have invented the fairy tale that he is a Jew. His accomplishments in the conquest and exploration of California, which proved his courage, endurance, and energy, and are the basis of his popular name "the Pathfinder," give him the status of a modern hero; and his romantic, poetic relationship to his wife as well as his handsome, noble appearance lend him the most brilliant image of any presidential candidate since the days of the heroes of the American Revolution.

On the Democratic side we have Buchanan (also called "Old Buck"), an old, used-up bachelor and desiccated civil servant whose life and accomplishments show no moment of distinction; at seventy, his age alone makes him unsuitable for the presidency. By law, the president has to be at least thirty-five years old, but I believe that it should be amended so as to disallow anyone over fifty-five. The world belongs to the young, not to old age, because only youth has the courage, enterprise, and energy for which experience, cunning, and shrewdness are poor substitutes. Frémont, who is now forty-four years old, represents youth, the present, and a better generation that will gradually replace the slaveholders and their followers.

Without actually having seen an American presidential election, no one can imagine the bustle and activity in the larger cities, especially New York. Votes are solicited on all trains and steamships; wherever a political club is holding a meeting huge flags bearing the candidates' names are strung from one side of the street to the other; torchlight parades are held in the evenings; and daily rallies attract the best party orators, who crisscross the country to address the people. Even the children take sides, and one evening I saw a ten-year-old boy standing on a pump delivering a lively speech to a crowd of his fellows, whom he addressed as "Boys of New York!" Recently Senator Wilson gave an excellent speech before the New York Trade Council, and Banks, the Speaker of the House of Representatives in the last Congress, spoke on behalf of Frémont to a large crowd from the steps of the Mercantile Exchange.[2] His address was a masterpiece of persuasiveness, elegance, and intelligent command of the subject. Presenting irrefutable reasons and numbers, he proved that business interests must be irreconcilably opposed to the extension of slavery and that the material well-being of the North urgently requires its restriction. Although the passionate abolitionist and friend of the Negro must have been cool to his argument opposing any intervention against slavery where it has traditionally existed and setting limits only to its extension, such a pronouncement must be seen in a different light, not only because an audience consisting mostly of merchants is least likely to be swayed by philanthropic considerations, but because outspoken, passionate abolitionists are generally regarded as muddle-headed idealists.

Thousands of voters who support the Republicans on limiting the extension of slavery would immediately switch to the Democrats if they suspected any radical abolitionist principle at work, and I am convinced that Frémont, Banks, Chase (the governor of Ohio), and many another dedicated Republican warrior are at heart better abolitionists than they are willing to admit to the mass of people whose votes they seek. Those who believe that the general public can be swayed by anything other than material advantages are flattering themselves with illusions. The free laborer is opposed to the admission of new slave states only because it would disadvantage him, and any sympathy for an oppressed race plays an insignificant and incidental part, even if it is in everyone's mouth. Many a man who today is fighting valiantly for the Republicans would get up and leave under protest should a Negro have the audacity to sit next to him at a *table d'hôte* or in a theater. Meanwhile one has to be satisfied with whatever good is being done, and, without questioning people's motives too closely, hope for a better future.

A few days ago the German Republicans held a huge mass meeting at the Academy of Music, the new opera house. The large hall holding about four thousand spectators was overflowing long before the start, and people soon crowded the hallways and spilled out into the street to catch a word or a glimpse of the proceedings. Hecker, who had left behind his remote western home for this purpose, was the hero of the evening.[3] He gave a grandly successful speech, proving his reputation as a popular speaker and arousing general enthusiasm. It is, incidentally, a shameful matter of fact that many Germans here are loyal Democrats who are outspoken in their support of slavery, and that others take a thoroughly passive attitude. I have met many men who consider themselves highly educated but are not ashamed to admit that the question of slavery is of no concern to them. If you investigate the reasons for this attitude, it turns out that some are motivated by the narrowest egoism, such as having a business relationship with the South, while the mass of people, with a simplistic faith in the printed word, let themselves be persuaded by the New York *Staatszeitung*, the German proslavery paper, that the Republicans are secret Know-Nothings who, if they came to power, would smilingly cut the throats of the immigrants who voted for them. Yet another group—and a sizable one—is so much in the dark that they believe "Democracy" has the same meaning as in Europe; in their ignorant innocence, without understanding that over here the thing is connected with slavery, and perhaps even believing that they are supporting the party of freedom, they strengthen the party of slavery by their votes. If you try to convert these people by telling them that because extension is detrimental to free labor they need to support the Republicans for their own advantage, they say with dumb, good-humored laughter: "Well, things will turn out all right!" As a mere mortal, you can in the end not even be surprised at having wasted your powder on stupidity, for against it even the gods are powerless.

I have to report on another Republican mass meeting, one held by the New York Trade Council also at the Academy of Music. Wilson, Banks, and Hale[4] had been announced as speakers, even though none of them was actually present in New York at the time—an innocent instance of humbug as it is practiced daily on such occasions here for attracting a larger audience. At the entrance they sold very handsome daguerreotypes of Frémont, all set in a pretty frame, for two shillings— barely ten silver groschen. It was a stormy evening with much rain, but the house was packed to the rafters, presenting an impressive sight. Flags displaying the seal of the United States waved on stage; on one side a banner depicting a raised arm with an axe bore the words: "We Strike for Freedom!" And on the other side a yet larger one with the same picture and the inscription: "Laborers Central Republican

Union of the County and City of New York." Such a mass meeting of a great and sovereign people is a grand and elevating spectacle, and I believe that the effort on the part of some of my reporting compatriots to describe such demonstrations as petty pranks and comedies intended to throw dust in the eyes of the ignorant masses is based on nothing other than a hate-filled, anti-American desire to belittle everything here or perhaps on an absolute inability to acknowledge grandeur when they see it.

After the band had played "Hail Columbia" and some other pieces and Chauncey Shaffer, an excellent New York attorney, had been elected president, he gave an introductory speech that, though not brilliant, was simple, to the point, and well received. He was followed by a Mr. Jenckes from Rhode Island,[5] who gave such a tedious analysis and explanation of generally familiar issues and presented them in such a deadly monotone that the audience soon lost all patience and started to stir and scrape in a manner that goes with a theatrical flop. Some shouted "Enough! Get to the end!" while others called for George Law, who had also been announced.[6] But all for naught. The speaker, apparently wishing to set a good example of patience, continued with imperturbable composure, like a clock having to wind down slowly, and in the same monotonous style; his subject seemed to inspire him as little as the audience's restlessness impressed him. Squirming in his chair, the president cast significant glances in his direction—without success. At last, the general noise rose to the common shout of more than a thousand voices: "George Law!" The orchestra started playing, and its strains finally brought Mr. Jenckes's speech to a halt.

Suddenly in the midst of this hubbub there appeared a procession of the Rocky Mountain Club, a Republican organization, marching with its banner through the hall up to the orchestra, where it was received with a loud hurrah. After this interruption, the president announced a performance by the glee club, which soon presented itself on stage in the form of four gentlemen who sang a song of many verses, all of them ending with the timid refrain: "Wait a little longer!" It is strange how this people, so magnificent in its political institutions, its inventions, and its enterprises, is so lacking in skill and taste in anything related to the arts. If, as surely would have been the case on such an occasion in Europe, the audience could have joined a full choir, it would have been an impressive performance; but these four gentlemen with their chamber voices were really too insignificant. The Americans generally look comical enough whenever they open their mouths for song, and this whole performance made me think of a lion or a bear trying to do a dog's tricks. But the audience seemed not to be bothered by any of this: with infinite patience they listened to seven or eight renditions of the "Wait a little longer!" until finally the much-expected George Law made his appearance to thundering applause.

This man, a true child of the people, once was a mason but has accumulated great wealth through successful enterprises, so that today he owns at least a million. He is gigantic in stature, and all of his dimensions are big enough for two of his kind. His large face seems to be rudely carved, reminding one of a wooden statue of an enormous St. Christopher. He is a special favorite of the people, who always welcome him with cheers, and they treat him as we would a famous comedian, whose mere appearance causes people to laugh; and whenever George Law gets up to speak it is like a scene out of a comedy. It is hard to imagine a worse speaker anywhere in the United States. Unable to speak two consecutive sentences, he gets stuck at every turn and, besides, cannot rid himself of those comical errors that are so typical of the lowest classes.

He stepped up slowly and with grave solemnity, both hands buried in his pockets, and began approximately as follows: "Fellow citizens! We are assembled here tonight at the request of the North Americans (pulling one hand from his pocket, he pauses to think and then puts it back again) to support the election of Colonel Frémont. (Hurrah!) We should look over the past and take council with each other—(a long pause)—to see what measures we can take to oppose the evils that threaten our country. (He casts a benevolent look around, then continues with uncertainty.) The matter that we thought had been laid to rest in 1850 has again been called into question. (Much clearing of throats; the audience breaks out in laughter.) And the question now seems to—(long pause)—threaten to swallow all other interests and destroy the liberty—(coughing; he stops to think for a moment, then scratches his nose: roaring laughter)—that is ours and for which our fathers fought the revolution. (Bravo! Bravo!) In the various states of this Union the legislative power of the states exists to pass only such laws as do not conflict with the Constitution and the power of the general government. (This being somewhat obscure, again much coughing.) I think"—(pause; having scratched his nose, he puts his hand back into his pocket; roaring laughter).

George Law (with much feeling): "Never mind, gentlemen! It will all work out in the end!" (Continuing laughter.) The president: "I hope that the audience will conduct itself as orderly as possible!" The phrase, "as possible," starts the laughter again, during which George Law is rattling his keys in his pocket. With silence finally restored, he continues and eventually concludes with the comment: "The Southerners threaten that, if we elect Frémont, they will march on Washington and steal the Archives and plunder the Treasury—(pause: he smugly puts his hands in his pockets)—and I believe they will wish to carry off the public buildings as well because they will need them after having gotten everything else. (Laughter.) There is a conspiracy against us, as dark, as bold, and as cold-blooded as Catiline's in Rome. (Hands disappear in pockets.) Six million people in the South, slaveholders and slaves, want to fight fourteen million free men in the North. (Scratches his nose; uproarious laughter.) I am not astonished at your laughter, gentlemen; it is surely a distressing matter, but (gravely) things are going to change soon. The election is near, and it is up to us to stop the evils that weigh on our country: we can elect John Frémont!" (Thunderous ovation.)

Amidst laughter and applause, George Law withdrew and the singing gentlemen appeared to offer the Frémont-Marseillaise, which is set to the tune of the French hymn to liberty and has the refrain: "Free speech, free press, free soil, free men, Frémont and victory!" He sat down after just a few fiery, powerful remarks, barely enough to whet one's appetite. A Mr. Noble, from Wisconsin, was the next speaker, a young man with interesting, pronounced features, whose witty and humorous cracks cascaded like fireworks on his opponents. The only thing that bothered me was his evident habit of talking down to his audience instead of raising them to his level.

The last speaker was Galusha A. Grow, a member of Congress from Pennsylvania[7]; a handsome man of noble character, he spoke with a quiet, earnest passion that was much appreciated mostly by the more educated part of the audience. Toward the end of his speech he stressed Frémont's personal qualities and then closed with these remarks: "His fame is indissolubly connected with the Pacific shores of our continent as are the rocks and mountains. When he and his soldiers were caught in a snow storm during their last military expedition, forcing them to eke out their lives by eating the horses and mules that had been killed, he proved such fortitude that, as president, he will need no other counsel but that of his own heart and mind. As they sat there by the campfire facing death itself, Frémont commanded his little troupe of adventurers to stay and endure as best they could while he would look for help. There was neither village nor town within eighty miles, and the snow lay five to six feet deep. But he left nevertheless, and by his strength of body and character he saved them from an all but certain grave and returned them to life. Today this man stands before the American people as their chosen standard-bearer in the great battle for freedom. As Washington felt it his duty to take charge of the Revolutionary Army, so it is his obligation to lead the freedom fighters to victory on the third day of November."

Notes

1. New York, November 1 [1856], *Morgenblatt*, 50:49:1173–1176.

2. Henry Wilson (1812–1875), senator from Massachusetts (1855–1873), was an outspoken opponent of slavery, a supporter of the Free Soil party, a founder of the Republican party, and vice president under U.S. Grant (1873–1875). Nathaniel Prentiss Banks (1816–1894), a representative from Massachusetts, was elected speaker of the House in 1856 after a bitter contest with a proslavery South Carolinian.

3. Friedrich Hecker (1811–1881) immigrated from Germany in 1849 after the failure of the revolution of 1848. He settled in St. Louis and later served as a colonel in the Union army.

4. John Parker Hale (1806–1873) was elected senator from New Hampshire in 1846. He was the first specifically antislavery senator, became the Free Soil party's presidential candidate in 1852, and served as senator until 1865.

5. Thomas Allen Jenckes (1818–1875), a Providence lawyer, served in the House of Representatives (1863–1871).

6. George Law (1806–1881), a self-made railroad and steamship entrepreneur, was a prominent Know-Nothing politician in 1855. Denied the position of candidate for the presidency, he supported the Republican candidate, John C. Frémont, in 1856.

7. Galusha Aaron Grow (1822–1907), first elected as a Free Soil Democrat from Connecticut in 1850, became a Republican and served as speaker of the House in his last term (1861–1863).

15

The Election—Art and Industry Exposition—Women's Rights[1]

The storms of the presidential election have passed; Buchanan has been elected, the battle lost. Having won its last victory, the party of slavery will be in power for another four years, and we can expect more egregious excesses. Perhaps in another year or two Kansas will be a slave state. Tacitly but unmistakably this election placed a stamp of approval on all the horrors perpetrated by the Missouri gangs in Kansas; the voters have conceded the point that there is no injustice in shooting and scalping people whose only crime was their desire to become a free state. With this election, Kansas has been subjected to the curse of slavery, and those of its citizens who resist this destiny have been declared traitors and rebels. In fact, this election has rejected the constitutionally sound restriction of slavery and thereby determined that slavery and freedom are equal and equally consonant with the spirit of a republic. This deed amounts to a decision that it is a crime to regard the degradation of an entire race to the status of cattle or merchandise as an injustice, but the consequences will soon follow.

While these are the results of the election of November 4, one can state with more than mere optimism—in fact one can be reasonably sure—that the party of slavery has won its last victory: despite the apparent power it wields at the moment, this victory is at bottom nothing but a defeat in spirit. Considering the fact that a party which is no more than a year old and holds no power was beaten by only a very slight margin by the oldest party in America with its one hundred thousand government employees and its eighty million dollars in expenditures, the outcome has to be seen as a remarkable victory. Furthermore, Frémont actually had a majority of several hundred thousand votes, and no effort by the opposition would have been able to beat him had it not been for the laws of the southern states. According to these, the slaves—who in every other respect are excluded from all human and civil rights—are counted as human beings only when it suits the advantage of their owners: in matters of voting, five slaves equal three free persons, so that the 300,000 slaveholders of the South may cast two million votes besides their own. Thus this abused and vilified race unwittingly helps to forge the chains that have kept it in bondage for centuries, even as the free colored people of the North are eligible to vote only if they can prove ownership of 250 dollars of property on which they have paid taxes.

As was expected, the Know-Nothings played no role in the election and, according to reports, won only in Maryland, even though they had high hopes at first of succeeding in several northern and southern states. One of the most humorous situations in this regard occurred in Boston. Major Perley Poore, a Know-Nothing candidate for Congress, was so convinced of his party's victory in Massachusetts that he made a wager with a Frémont candidate, Colonel Burbank, according to which the loser would be obliged to personally deliver to the winner a large barrel full of apples on a wheelbarrow. Frémont won the state by a huge majority, and Major Poore actually took the apples on a cart over 36 miles from West Newbury to Boston, where he presented them in the presence of a large throng of people. The occasion called for speeches and a large dinner. The major was on his strange errand for three and a half days and gave a humorous account of it in the *Boston-Journal*. Generally, the State of Massachusetts has covered itself with glory in these recent battles, as has been its wont in matters of conscience since the War of Independence. The enthusiastic reception given to Charles Sumner on the day before the election, upon his first return to Boston after being wounded by Brooks six months earlier,[2] is among the grandest, most inspiring moments in the serious drama of current events. Sumner's speech on that occasion is equal to the most beautiful and polished performances in this field; it brilliantly refutes the allegation made here and there that his powers of reasoning had suffered as a result of an injury to his brain. Quite to the contrary, they shone as brightly as ever, even though his physical strength was still much diminished.

The American people have an abundance of excellent orators, perhaps more than any other nation. Many of them inspire passion and enthusiasm through the power of their mind and incisive opinions, but Sumner possesses an artistic perfection that gives his speeches, regardless of content, lasting beauty. In their perfect harmony and poetry they breathe the noble spirit of the classics and are in the best tradition of English prose style. Every person of plain sensibility is likely to be inspired by Sumner's speeches, but only the educated few can fully appreciate their full range of meaning. Were he to write history, he would be to America what Lamartine is to France.

* * *

The art and industrial exposition currently presented at the Crystal Palace is as interesting in detail as it is generally representative. The practical utilitarianism of the Americans is revealed in almost every object and has produced some excellent results. Although there is no dearth of luxury items—opulent furniture, pianos, glassware, porcelains, silver, and articles of clothing—their number is relatively small, and they have often been seen elsewhere in even greater abundance and ostentation. Perhaps the only useless toy is a scale model of New York that has been faithfully carved in wood: every house occupies its proper place, and not the least little alley has been overlooked. The person who worked for more than fifteen years to produce it has demonstrated a level of patience and skill worthy of a nobler object. Several California houses that can easily be taken down, transported, and reassembled also look like toys but are very practical and functional. Their white exterior paint and green window shades give them a charming and friendly appearance, and they are furnished to satisfy the needs of a small family. They are two stories high, and each floor consists of a neat little room, a cabinet, closets, and other storage space.

Yankee ingenuity at its best, however, can be seen in the section on mechanics and engines, where wheels are whirring, steam engines are pounding, and new products can be seen at every turn. Here is a machine for polishing marble that transforms a raw piece of marble into a gleaming slab within moments; there is a saw mill turning chunks of wood above into small pieces below; an insignificant looking machine produces ropes and rolls them up into huge balls; a steam laundry has been set up in a small house; a mechanically improved mill is churning noisily over here, a pump is laboring over there, and elsewhere a steam-powered loom is producing fifty yards of linen per day, which is immediately turned into any number of products by a host of sewing machines that, though operated by hand, seem to be driven by steam. Here is a man printing address cards, there is another producing a sweeper that can clean the dirtiest carpet in minutes without spreading dust, and over there are the safety locks sounding their alarm bells as soon as an unauthorized person touches them.

The agricultural implements are no less interesting. There are thrashing machines doing the work of several people in an incredibly short time; also sowing machines, harrows, long rows of plows—delicate little things, charmingly painted either red or green, looking about as much like a German farmer's plow as a peasant on the stage resembles a true German husbandman. Upon closer inspection, however, you notice that the shear is incomparably stronger, can dig deeper into the soil, and is better suited for terrain in which the large German plow would inevitably break. A technician might have much to say on this topic, but the advantages of the American model are clearly evident even to the uninitiated eye. When Horace Greeley, the bright editor of the New York *Tribune*, visited the Paris Exposition he wondered about the European plows and thought that especially the Spanish and Norwegian models deserved a special patent for general unsuitability.

In the nearby display of agricultural products I particularly noticed the giant ears of corn as well as the large pumpkins and squashes among the vegetables; the grapes, pears, and melons had a scent so inviting that it all but defeated their purpose of serving as display only; but the small number of flowers compared poorly to the lavish show many a small German town would have arranged on such an occasion. America is still too preoccupied with the practical aspects of life to indulge in such decorative arts as the arrangement of flowers.

Finally, one must mention a branch of industry which is so brilliantly represented here that it borders on the realm of art: the daguerreotype with its close relatives, the ambrotype and the photograph, have been developed to a high level of accomplishment. In this section one can also find the work of the German blacksmith who, without any sort of artistic training, has used his hammer to make a life-size copper statue of Washington: despite a certain stiffness, the figure shows considerable talent.

All in all, this exposition presents an accurate and characteristic picture of America and its people in their daily activities, and in this context even the plaster cast of Thorwaldsen's "Christ and the Apostles"—left over from an earlier exhibit—is not entirely out of place. Similarly, Kiss's "Amazons" and "The Hunter's Pursuit of the Bear" by a French artist represent the life of the pioneers in the distant West beyond the Rocky Mountains. The poetic truth of this accident is more to the point than any arrangement the organizer of the exposition might have contemplated.

The "women's rights convention," a gathering of the fighters for female emancipation, was held a few days ago. Just as in Germany and generally in Europe, the mere suggestion of this issue has brought out many determined opponents who have ridiculed the whole affair and described the emancipated woman as a creature who visits saloons in men's clothes, perhaps even smokes tobacco and reduces her husband to the status of the henpecked species. It has to be said that because some of the more eccentric steps taken here as well as in Europe have had unfortunate results, the movement and its most respected representatives had to pay a price for the mishaps. However, the big difference between the European and the American propagandists for emancipation is that over there the concept is represented almost entirely by dreamy—albeit smart—men and women of exceeding youth, guaranteeing failure from the start, whereas here many eminent, experienced, and widely respected men have rallied to the cause of female emancipation. Wendell Phillips, the great advocate of Negro emancipation; Horace Greeley, whom I like to call a fanatic for the vindication of human rights without regard to either race or color, one of the few American newspapermen whose enemies have never succeeded in casting the least shadow of venality or corruption over a long journalistic career; and Horace Mann, the president of Antioch College in Ohio: they are all spirited supporters of those women whose own private lives are beyond reproach. American emancipationists, furthermore, have a great advantage over their European counterparts in that their ranks consist of representatives of a wide range of religious groups, whereas in Europe the question of emancipation was instigated only by the most decided freethinkers, leaving the great mass of people in opposition. Over here, orthodox Christians and atheists, Quakers and Methodists —among them the Rev. Antoinette Brown, a Methodist preacher—ministers of many different sects are united in peace, and therefore no one can refuse to espouse the rights of women out of fear for being seen as a heretic.

I noticed many Quaker women in the audience, which during the morning session consisted mostly of earnest, mature women speaking warmly in support of the cause; they were motivated by neither a desire for public acclaim nor any other extravagant motive. One of the most outstanding advocates of women's rights who has often spoken in public is Lucretia Mott; she sat on the speaker's platform dressed, as usual, in the traditional gray costume of the Quakers.[3] Lucy Stone Blackwell,[4] presiding over the meeting, effectively erased the poor impression she had made upon me at an antislavery meeting some time ago. Her appearance does not elevate her above the average, but she soon reveals an ability for clear thinking, logical argument, and quick repartee that makes insignificant and mediocre men— who most jealously guard their privileges—feel intensely uncomfortable. She was dressed in simple, tasteful moiré, just as all of the ladies who got up to speak showed taste, some even elegance, in their dresses; and not one of them demonstrated those absurdities of appearance of which the opposition likes to accuse them.

None of the goals and purposes of their organization—except their demand for the right to vote—would offend a fair-minded man. Who, for instance, could support a law providing that in case a husband dies intestate his widow not only receives a mere third of his estate but has to be satisfied with a third of the property she brought into the marriage, with the remainder of their property going to his relatives? Or that in such a case the responsibility for the children's education does not remain with the mother but goes to a guardian? Or that women are paid so much less than men for doing the same work—a male teacher charging 500 dollars, while a woman receives only 200; a farmhand receiving twelve to twenty dollars a month, while a female servant doing work in the farmhouse that is no less important and requires just as much time and effort gets only four to five dollars? As for the women's right to vote, it is argued that because they are as much subject to the laws as are the men, because they bear as many burdens, pay taxes, and must abide by all civil obligations they should have the right to participate in electing those who make the laws. As Lucy Stone said, it is a right that women already enjoy in Nova Scotia and New Brunswick, where they vote in parliamentary elections; yet—she added—children continue to be born there and dinners are prepared, no less than elsewhere.

A Rev. Mr. Higginson praised American women in a lively speech, remarking in particular on the superior intellectual independence and education of the women of Massachusetts. He told of a traveler who averred that he always knew with certainty the moment he entered the State of Massachusetts. "It is not," he said, "because the people speak through their noses, not because everything is cleaner there than in other places, but because the women speak their minds." The next speaker was Mrs. Ernestine Rose,[5] an elegant German-Polish lady with long locks and the traces of bygone beauty. She had just returned from a voyage to Europe and warmly praised the education, firm convictions, and independence of English and French women, especially remarking on their frank recognition of the advantages of other nations.

The discussion became lively when a young man in the audience turned to Mr. Higginson with the question whether he believed women's rights had their basis in nature or in scripture. Upon Higginson's comment that he thought they were based on God's eternal laws, the young man got ready for a long reply, and all eyes were of course fixed on him. Since only a few could hear him from his seat, however, he was repeatedly but politely urged by Lucy Stone, Mr. Higginson, and several members of the audience to step up to the platform, but evidently he felt that even such a slight concession to the rules of etiquette would compromise his rights. All he said had been said many times before, and his references to the Bible were so awkward that an old Quaker woman in her eighties shouted: "You cite the word but miss the spirit!" But Mr. Higginson's reply was exactly to the point. He said among other things that there are many wild tribes who do not know that two times two equals four; yet this does not mean that two times two equals four is not natural, as the opposition would like to argue when they say that everything based in natural law must be evident among the most uncivilized and wildest humans—which is certainly not the case with women's rights.

Wendell Phillips did not say much on this occasion, but what he said was, as usual, brilliant and triumphant. He demanded that a wider field of opportunity be opened up for women to test their abilities. "Goethe said," he concluded, "that if you plant an oak tree in a flower pot either the oak will wither or the pot must burst. What we are witnessing is that women are confined and restricted: either they will wither or the vessel must burst. Let it burst! Open a larger sphere of activity for women, and they will want to strive for higher knowledge. A good part of men's faith in women suffers damage from the ongoing necessity to support their helpless daughters."

Notes

1. New York, December, [1856], *Morgenblatt*, 51:1:22–24 and 51:2:46–48 (1857).

2. Brooks had assaulted Sumner on the floor of the Senate in May, two days after Sumner's speech, "The Crime Against Kansas."

3. Lucretia Mott (1793–1880), a lecturer on temperance, peace, the rights of labor, and the abolition of slavery, became an advocate of women's rights after women were denied seats as delegates to the World Anti-Slavery Convention in London in 1840. With Elizabeth Cady Stanton she organized the first women's rights convention in Seneca Falls, New York (1848).

4. Lucy Stone Blackwell (1818–1893), a lecturer on women's rights, was also actively engaged in the antislavery movement. She later founded the *Woman's Journal*, the official organ of the National American Woman's Suffrage Association.

5. Ernestine Potowski Rose (1810–1892), daughter of an orthodox Jewish rabbi, was a social reformer and activist. She met Robert Dale Owen in England in the early 1830s and married William E. Rose in 1836, the year she arrived in New York. She lectured widely on religion, free schools, abolition, and women's rights and campaigned for the married women's property bill in New York State.

16

Kansas and the Extension of Slavery[1]

. . . here and there it is asserted with certainty that some of his followers[2] are changing their support to the Democrats and would vote for Buchanan, the proslavery candidate *par excellence*, to beat the Republicans. If such an alliance were to come into being, thousands of foreigners, especially Germans, who have in the past voted for the Democrats out of ignorance, lack of conscience, or selfish reasons, would surely change their allegiance *en masse*. Those among them who do not care whether blacks in the South are or are not whipped or whether hitherto sacrosanct territories will come under the curse of slavery are vehemently opposed to a government that would like to exclude all foreigners from public office and make the acquisition of citizenship subject to a twenty-year residency requirement.

The one faction that presents a danger to human rights, free labor, and the progress of the nation as a whole are the Democrats, who control almost the entire South and unfortunately also much of the North. They were founded by the great Jefferson, one of the most illustrious and freethinking individuals ever to have breathed the air of this country. At his time, they were the party of true progress; in fact its supporters were the declared enemies of slavery, truly radical abolitionists on the model of their founder, whose heart was aglow with a passion for liberty and human welfare without regard to differences in color. In the course of time, however, the Democrats have distanced themselves more and more from his ideas, so that today they stand in stark contrast to Jefferson and only the name remains the same. If Jefferson with his views and principles were to rise from the dead, it would undoubtedly require extraordinary good fortune for him to escape being torn to pieces by his dear compatriots in Virginia and South Carolina.

Besides holding stubbornly to the continuation of slavery where it already exists, the Democratic party is driven by the relentless desire to gain ever more territory for this curse that threatens the white population, not to speak of the crime it perpetrates upon blacks. It is the cause of coarseness, ignorance, and poverty throughout the South, and its continuing spread is proven by the annulment of the Missouri Compromise, by the adoption of the Nebraska Bill, and particularly by the crimes against Kansas, which is being forced to accept slavery. These events clearly show that the party of the South has gained ever more power over the North in the course of just a few years. It was not until 1820 that the party of slavery arose as a mighty power, gaining the admission of Missouri as a slave state into the Union after heated battles in Congress, which ended with the eternal banishment of slavery in the entire remainder of the Missouri Territory west of the Mississippi and north of 36°30' of latitude. This agreement, which was the condition for Missouri's admission as a slave state and had been proposed and supported by the party of slavery in the first place, was at that time seen by both parties as a victory achieved by proslavery propaganda. In exchange for the loss they sustained in Missouri, the friends of freedom received only the expectation of future free states in an area that was then nothing but an immense wilderness populated by a few Indian tribes.

However, due to the hydra-like growth of the slaveholders' influence and contrary to all principles of loyalty, legality, and responsibility, the agreement was revoked when, after more than thirty-three years of peace during which the South had been enjoying the fruits of its acquisition, it became necessary to establish some form of government in that by now sparsely settled territory: at the request of Senator Douglas—the disgraceful representative in Congress from the free state of Illinois—the vast territories of Nebraska and Kansas were opened to slavery again. It all happened under the pretense that Congress had no right to intervene in the matter of slavery in any of the states and territories and that its determination was entirely dependent on the decision and the free will of the inhabitants; but it soon became an open secret that Kansas was to be a slave state, even though a large number of settlers from the northern and western free states had established themselves there. Thus, every person with a grain of justice and humanity was outraged at that unparalleled crime committed against Kansas. On November 29, 1854, the day on which elections for Congress and the future of the territory were to be held, a gang of more than a thousand Missourians crossed into Kansas. As next-door neighbors they had a strong interest in turning Kansas into a slave state, since they would otherwise be totally surrounded by free states and confronted with massive waves of escape from the ranks of their slaves. This gang terrorized, in fact killed, the unarmed inhabitants, absconded with the ballot boxes, and managed to elect by brutal force a legislative assembly consisting of the scum of the slavery party, which immediately passed a constitution that one is tempted to call the horror-system of slavery. Among other things it contains a paragraph dealing with punishment for any tampering with slave property: "Any free person who supports a rebellion or insurrection of slaves, free Negroes, or mulattoes, or who participates in it, supplies it with weapons, or commits any action to advance such a rebellion or insurrection, shall be put to death."

Furthermore, anyone persuading a slave to escape, assisting in his escape, or hiding or lodging escaped slaves is guilty of a felony and will be punished with at least five years' imprisonment at hard labor; the same fate awaits anyone writing, printing, or speaking against slavery or distributing any such writing. And finally it says: "No one who is in principle opposed to holding slaves or who fails to recognize the right to hold slaves in this territory shall serve as a juror in any trial concerning any violation of any paragraph of this act."

The abused and mistreated people of Kansas asked President Pierce for protection and assistance, but evidently without success: the president, who is the willing tool of the party of slavery and the worthy representative of the most pitiful elements of the North, not only turned a deaf ear, but finally sent troops only to make common cause with the Missouri gangs against the unfortunate population. Some of the most valiant antislavery men in Congress—like Seward, Wilson, and the glorious Sumner, in a speech that is among the best of all times past and present

—made every effort to admit Kansas into the Union as a free state, but in vain! The opposition was too strong, and the Missourians, reinforced by similar gangs from South Carolina, repeated their raids, murdered the population, laid waste to the towns and cities, destroyed property—in short, committed atrocities of every kind in an area that has been devastated for the past two years. Only the election of a Republican president can put an end to this devastation; and that ray of hope has been the cause of unbridled wrath among southerners, who fear that in the end they will be deprived of what they believed to be their certain booty. Every day brings news from the South that in the event of Frémont's election the slavery states will secede from the Union, a threat that reminds one of spoiled children who, when they cannot get their own way, withdraw into a corner griping that they won't play, but if left alone soon wish to rejoin. Their clique is headed by Keitt, Brooks[3] (the most worthless creature throughout the land, whose treacherous attack on Sumner has elevated him to the hero of his clique and made him the object of scorn among all those who are not entirely uncivilized), and Henry A. Wise, the governor of Virginia, who—not unlike a Don Quixote of slavery with a small troupe of Sancho Panzas—declared that he would move on Washington to take over the Archives and the Treasury if Frémont were elected. This ranting pack is trampling the Constitution—the political Bible of every American—into the mud and declaring it a fraud. A publication recently issued in the South states explicitly:

> The situation of the laborer as the slave of the individual rather than the slave of society would be much improved. . . . Free society is bankrupt, and a society that is not free must replace it. . . . Free society is a miscarriage, and slavery is the healthy, perfect, and natural condition to which it unconsciously aspires. . . . Our Negroes not only enjoy better material conditions than free laborers, but their moral condition is also superior. . . . Slavery for both blacks and whites is just and necessary. Men are not born with equal rights. Instead, the truth must be spoken that some are born with saddles on their backs and some with boots and spurs to ride the others for their benefit. . . . Life and liberty are not unalienable; the Declaration of Independence is fundamentally wrong and a lie. . . . We have come to the point that we are sickened by everything that is preceded by the word 'free,' the entire catalogue from free farmers, free labor, free will, and free men to free children and free schools.

Such evidence, appearing in more than just one place, speaks for itself and needs no further commentary: it is clear proof of a society demoralized by the curse of slavery. Of course, there are illustrious exceptions even on that side, as for instance a Cassius Clay who, though a citizen of a slaveholding state (Kentucky), is one of the most brilliant speakers in the Republican ranks.[4] It is also common knowledge that when Atchison,[5] one of the leaders of the gangs which devastated Kansas, returned to Missouri after his expedition, a delegation of inhabitants from his hometown demanded that he settle elsewhere because the citizens would not tolerate his presence. But these are, after all, exceptions, and the most famous representatives of the South are characterized by a combination of coarseness, depravity, meanness, and excess, compared to which any good qualities are all but invisible. Europe and the American North have judged and branded Brooks, but South Carolina has branded itself not only by tolerating him in its midst but by reelecting him, celebrating him, praising him in public—yes, even by bestowing upon him trophies, whips, and canes with the inscription, "Hit him again!" on public occasions attended by many ladies. Judged and branded by their own conduct are also Keitt, Toombs,[6] and Douglas (who conceived the Nebraska Bill): they were present at the time of the treacherous attack and not only watched in silence but forcibly restrained those who had come to assist the prostrate and unconscious Sumner. Their actions make them look like a den of murderers! By contrast, the Republican opponents of slavery, the leaders as well as the large masses, provide the supreme satisfaction of spotless purity that even the lies and slander of their opponents have failed to sully.

Notes

1. Manuscript (1856), Assing Papers, Deutsches Literarturarchiv, Marbach.

2. In the opening portion of this essay, no longer extant, Assing is presumably referring to Millard Fillmore (1800–1874); during his presidency (1850–1853) he identified himself with the Whig party but became a presidential candidate of the Know-Nothing party in 1856.

3. Laurence M. Keitt (1824–1864) and Preston S. Brooks (1819–1857), representatives from South Carolina, were involved in the attack on Senator Charles Sumner of Massachusetts on May 22, 1856. After an unsuccessful effort to expel Brooks from the House, he resigned but was immediately reelected.

4. Cassius Marcellus Clay (1810–1903), the son of a Kentucky slaveholder, was the publisher of the Louisville *Examiner* and a strong advocate of emancipation.

5. David Rice Atchison (1807–1886) was a Democratic senator from Missouri (1843–1855). A rabid slavery advocate and participant in raids on Kansas, he lent his name to Atchison, Kansas, then the center of the proslavery forces.

6. Robert A. Toombs (1810–1885) served three terms as a Whig representative in the House (1845–1853) and then represented Georgia as a Democrat in the U.S. Senate.

17

Wendell Phillips—A "Gift Enterprise"[1]

* * *

Wendell Phillips, the famous antislavery agitator, disunionist, and one of the great orators of this country, gave a lecture "On the Philosophy of Reform" a few days ago, and despite the pouring rain the cream of society attended. His speech was truly a work of art, and after only a few words one felt elevated high above all quotidian pettiness and everyday concerns to that ideal position that the speaker himself occupies. The artistic serenity that goes hand in hand with passion, the mastery of the subject, the incisive logic, the sparks of intellect and wit that brilliantly illuminate the matter at hand, the sonorous voice and the entire manner of speech that give even the rough English language fine mellifluence, but mostly the deeply resonating convictions and idealism that are at the center of Wendell Phillips's being—they are all irresistible and fill the listener with affection and respect. Many consider him unattractive, and in so far as a tall, angular figure, sparse light blond hair revealing a premature patch of considerable baldness in the middle, and something less than regular features can lay no claim to beauty, one cannot argue the point; but as soon as he warms to his subject, he seems to be transfigured by the fire of intellect: his shining eyes emit lightning; the mouth gives a hint of playful satire, suggesting an unexpected gracefulness; and one is surprised to notice that Wendell Phillips is a man of beauty.

In his lecture he considered the question who causes progress, and he proved that it is neither the people, as some seem to believe, nor governments or the press; it is not the clergy, who simply flatter the masses, nor scholars or the moneyed interests. Instead, he argued, progressive ideas are the province of individual intellectuals, who are usually decried as fanatics during their lifetime, and whose ideas become popular only after they have suffered martyrdom for them. The man who erects a memorial to someone who was ridiculed and ostracized by an earlier generation would no less ridicule and ostracize another for presenting his ideas of progress today. Wendell Phillips is himself a fanatic of progress, to which he refers as the second part of the Declaration of Independence: he is a fanatic of the idea as well as of the commitment to progress. Totally committed to it, he has never compromised with existing conditions, rejects any political ambitions for himself, even though his brilliant gifts would surely bring him the greatest success, and is satisfied with living the life of a Boston lawyer. Indifferent to the judgment of the masses, he does not care whether a majority of millions opposes him today and frankly states his view that the abolition of slavery can be accomplished only by the dissolution of the Union—a view that, in the eyes of the majority of good citizens, amounts to nothing less than blasphemy.

After having spent several years on the soil of this country one gets used to all sorts of things and no longer wonders about events that in Germany would cause people a shudder of amazement. Yet one is momentarily dumbstruck reading about a clever speculator called Perham, who conducted a so-called "gift enterprise" (an evasive euphemism for a lottery, which is prohibited by law) in which not only a farm, several clocks, jewelry, silverware, and pianos were offered but a "well-known marriageable young gentleman" with a fortune of 50,000 dollars and a "beautiful young and marriageable lady" with a fortune of 25,000 dollars, besides a large number of smaller prizes down to pictures and trinkets for six cents a piece. Each chance costs one dollar, which also entitles the purchaser to gain free admission for himself and three other persons of his choice to the panorama that is also part of Perham's business. Whoever wins the lady has the choice of being paid 50,000 dollars. However, to prevent any possibility of fraud, if he decides in favor of the lady, he is obligated to marry her in the Crystal Palace in the presence of all other lottery winners. The sale of chances has been enormous, and in order to lend his enterprise respectability, Perham has obtained the patronage of an alderman of the City of New York, who is also to act as something of a master of ceremonies. One would think of the whole thing as a mystification, if it were not a well-known fact throughout the city. Indeed, a few days ago the news spread that the lady could be seen in the Chinese Rooms, a hall on Broadway that is normally used for concerts and exhibitions. Already an hour and a half before the appointed time the curious were crowding each other, listening impatiently to the introductory strains played by some unknown artist on the piano, when in fact Alderman Briggs appeared in the company of a 167-pound person—sporting black curls, heavy make-up, and gaudy jewelry—whom he introduced to the audience as the "prize lady." There are things happening in this country that we Germans dare not dream of.

Notes

1. New York, February [1857], *Morgenblatt*, 51:15:356.

18

Hoboken[1]

Across the Hudson from New York, on the western bank of the river, lies Hoboken, New Jersey. The river is here more than half a German mile wide, but the connecting power of steam has made Hoboken a suburb of New York. Four ferries, about as big as Rhine steamers but of different construction, are constantly in motion and take you to the other side in ten minutes, providing in winter the comfort of well-heated deck cabins. The glorious, magnificent river, with New York and its port almost hidden behind a sea of ships' masts on one side and the range of hills rising on the New Jersey side, offers a grand view that loses nothing of its charm even on daily acquaintance: large and small vessels of all kinds offer an always changing and lively prospect. A great variety of ships pass in front of us: from the giant ocean steamer, just arriving with the latest news from Europe and saluting the New World with volleys from its cannons, to the sleek clipper ship, whose long hull sliced through the waters of the Indian Ocean off the shores of Australia, to the winsome river boat and the little nutshell of a dinghy that, rocked by the waves, looks like a creature of the depth rolling in its element. Even on the hottest days a cooling breeze wafts across the water, and when in summer the country glows in the colors of 41 degrees latitude the whole scene radiates a wondrous, cheerful joy unfamiliar to a person from northern climes. It is a delight to stand on the foredeck of the ferry, where the splash of a wave occasionally reaches you when the water is rough, and to face the hot but refreshing southwest wind that seems to carry the scent of the virgin forest from deep inside the continent. In winter, however, when the river is covered with ice floe, the ship often shakes from crashing into the massive pieces of ice, which at times block its passage entirely, causing it to backtrack in order to force a passage with the mighty power of an icebreaker. The normal ten-minute passage has on occasion been extended to more than two hours under such conditions, and it has even happened that the wheels froze and could not be started for six hours. Yet there is no danger, and when seen from inside the warm cabin such a spectacle has its delights.

But the terrible snowstorm of January 18 and 19, during which dozens of smaller and larger vessels were wrecked along the coast, was of a different order. In Germany no one can imagine the force of an American snowstorm: when the icy northwest gale whips up clouds of snow and drives them into your face it feels as if a thousand knives were slashing you. Only a man of steel, tempered by the horrors of the northern winter, is able to withstand the onslaught for any length of time, and woe to the wanderer who is caught by surprise out in the open field! During those fateful days, the ferries had to cancel their night runs, and in the morning, when the storm was blowing at its worst and the air was filled with a fine snow that was covering everything, all traffic nearly came to a standstill; only a boat here and there attempted the crossing. Some of the old and conscientious business people who had never missed a day of work because of the weather did not stir from the place by the warm stove and marked the day in their calendars.

Although Hoboken was incorporated as a town some years ago, it still has the looks of a country village. In many places the houses are not set up in blocks but are separated by rows and copses of trees; balconies and front yards give them the friendly appearance of villas, and the noise of business in New York does not penetrate this far. To the west lies a range of hills whose green tops form a charming frame. In the woods at the end of the town one can still meet a few scattered Indians during the summer, and along the riverbank runs a path—called "Elysian Fields"—with the river on one side and a tree-covered rock formation on the other. Abundant fresh vegetation fills the air with delightful scents. The whole place and its environment give the impression of peace, happiness, and unspoiled nature that act like a balm after the dust and noise of New York streets. Tastefully designed houses with such modern comforts as gas and water lines do their part in making this a pleasant place to live. However, Americans do not consider Hoboken fashionable, perhaps not even quite genteel; at best, small storekeepers choose to live there because of the low rents.

The French and the Germans, on the other hand, like Hoboken so much that it is sometimes seen as one of New York's German sections, although it is part of the State of New Jersey. A large number of wealthy German merchants doing business in New York maintain only their counting rooms there but live in Hoboken. Between eight and nine in the morning and after business hours in the evening the ferries are crowded. And in the early hours of the day you also notice many housewives and cooks who do their shopping in the New York market; and on Saturday, the chief market day of the week, long rows of baskets block the way like barricades. In the evening hours the ferry has a less businesslike appearance, as it is filled with pleasure seekers who, after a day's work and a good meal, are on their way to parties, concerts, lectures, and theaters in New York. With the ease and cheapness of transportation offered by ferries, buses, and railroads, the cost of one cent and the distance of about one German mile (including the width of the river) that one has to pass to get to one's destination are no obstacles. Even bad weather, as measured by German standards, does not deter people who have to attend to some business, because conditions in the morning are rarely consistent with those in the evening; and nothing but the horrors of an American winter will stop people from following through with an accepted invitation, with paid tickets, or with a general desire for amusement. Hence, the ferry is never unoccupied even late at night, and a crowded ferry is almost a sure sign of a symphonic concert, a new opera, or the performance by a famous actor.

The inhabitants of Hoboken also have their own sources of entertainment. Especially the Germans have their societies which—were it not for the fact that the proximity to New York lends them a somewhat broader and more cosmopolitan coloration—are almost to a tee like the clubs and places of amusement so typical of every German country town. One of them engages in amateur theater, with respectable businessmen striving every month to be dramatic artists and succeeding at least in presenting a sampling of German dialects. The sharp "sp" and "st" from Hanover, Hamburg, and Holstein; the soft "b" and "d" and the sing-song from Saxony; and the characteristic "j" of the Berliners mingle as happily as the costumes of all times and nations in one and the same play, even of one and the same individual—just as I once saw Garrick in *Dr. Robin* wearing an old Spanish costume, in contrast to which this man of genius also sported his usual stiff collar and cravat.[2]

Another society, mostly consisting of young Americans, presents itself as having a more serious purpose: the "Baconian Literary Debating Club" poses literary and general questions for debate by the members at a subsequent meeting. It offers young men the opportunity to practice public speaking, and many who would otherwise not read a single line beyond their account books and newspapers gain the advantage of preparing themselves thoroughly on some literary or historical subject that they must either attack or defend in debate. The members write for a newspaper that, though never published, is read aloud every month. If luck would have it that a few really gifted young men were to come together in this way, such a club could become the source of an energetic intellectual life; however, it seems that—with the exception of a few talented and bright individuals—of all the people of the State of New Jersey the dullest of the dull, the shallowest of the shallow, the most philistine of the philistines (this creature does exist here, too, although the English language has no fitting expression for it[3]) have come together here. From the outset, they oppose any sort of progressive change, and the debates, to which persons who are not members are admitted as an audience, produce marvels of silliness, ignorance, mental blindness, and twists of logical thinking. For example, during one debate on the question whether works of nature are superior to works of art or *vice versa*, a speaker cited Tom Thumb as an instance of natural beauty—and thereby achieved victory! Perhaps only the general awkwardness of speech and deficiency of expression are equal to the vapidity of the content. Rarely have I heard Americans speak so poorly: the first speaker lisps, the second speaks through his nose, the third stammers, and the fourth speaks so softly that he cannot be heard. Nonetheless, the society has an exaggerated sense of its own dignity: it engages in mighty battles over the appointment of its officers as if the future welfare of the entire United States were at stake; it solemnly establishes committees of one to determine the need for a new doorknob; and it generally seems to take the longest possible time to accomplish nothing.

The little town undergoes a profound change on Sundays, provided the weather is not too bad. Thanks to the temperance law with which the State of New Jersey is blessed—at least on paper—Hoboken has such a large number of beer gardens, inns, and saloons with and without musical entertainment that it takes the population of a large city to fill them all. Starting early in the morning, overcrowded ferries arrive, depositing literally a rush of Irish servants, German craftsmen and other honorable citizens, and Frenchmen of all stripes seeking respite from the week's hard work or the week's loafing as far away as possible from the yawning quiet of

Sundays in New York. They amble along the "Elysian Fields" by the river as if marching in a procession, crowd into the beer gardens, and seem to have such a wonderfully good time while the Americans are attending church that one is reminded of Sundays in Germany and is overcome by nostalgia for the old home country.

Notes

1. New York, May [1857], *Morgenblatt*, 51:25:598–600.

2. It is unclear to which actor and play Assing is here referring, since it cannot be the famous English actor David Garrick, who died in 1779.

3. Apparently Assing had never heard the term "philistine" used in English in the same sense as it is common in German: a person with no interest in culture.

19

Meeting of the Antislavery Societies: Frederick Douglass[1]

* * *

The annual meetings of several philanthropic societies—some active and beneficial, others inactive and useless—took place as usual during the first two weeks of May, the season of rains, winds, and thunderstorms. And, as usual, the only truly interesting meetings attracting a larger audience were those of the antislavery societies with their brilliant speakers. The lion of this season was Frederick Douglass, this excellent mulatto whom I have mentioned repeatedly in my reports.[2] Having hitherto known this talented, brilliant man only from his writings and from personal intercourse, I heard him for the first time as a public speaker, which gave me an appreciation of his great and general importance. Among the many great orators in this country he is one of the greatest, a compliment that even Sumner—an unquestioned authority—has paid him. He combines fiery passion with complete command of his subject and an admirably appropriate moderation; his perfect command of language gives weight and expression to the wealth of his ideas. Douglass is always concise, to the point, logical, and wide-ranging; often he rises to a genuinely tragic pathos, deeply moving the hearts of his audience, then he captivates them with bright flashes of humor and wit and entertains them with jokes. Withal, his entire being emanates such a refreshing originality and natural modesty that his listeners give him their undivided sympathy and warm affection. All of these virtues are enhanced by his skillful presentation and his rich, sonorous, and well-modulated voice that fills the largest hall without the least effort. When Douglass steps onto the platform, one might think he is suffering from nervous shyness: he begins softly and with hesitation; but he soon masters this momentary weakness and unfolds the irresistible power of his oratory. After his first speech at this year's convention in New York, another mulatto, Charles Lenox Remond,[3] challenged him to a debate on the question whether or not the Constitution sanctions slavery—a point of controversy that has caused much excitement among abolitionists.

I have to take this opportunity to make the point that although the abolitionists are in complete agreement about their goal, the abolition of slavery, they are split into two unfriendly factions in regard to the means by which this is to be accomplished. One faction, represented by the American Anti-Slavery Society and Garrison, its founder, argues that the Constitution sanctions slavery and is, therefore, "a covenant with death and an agreement with hell." They see a solution only in an overthrow of the Constitution and a dissolution of the Union—the North's violent separation from the South. Despite the talent of so many of its valiant fighters—Wendell Phillips, Quincy,[4] and others—they will never gain the support of the broad mass of the people, who are loyal to the Constitution and the

Union. Opposed to them are the National Abolitionists, who defend the Constitution in word and spirit against the charge that it is proslavery; in their view, any tendency toward dissolving the Union is cowardly because it can only result in an exacerbation of the slaves' condition in the South. Douglass, who once had been an eager adherent of the Garrisonian theory, later became a supporter of the other view, thus bringing down on his head the most extreme enmity of his former collaborators. Remond never fails to avail himself of every opportunity to attack this whole tendency, particularly Douglass, as well as the Constitution with more bitterness and passion than logic. The debate continued over two evenings in front of a very large audience mostly consisting of whites, with Douglass displaying such power of mind, wit, and humor as to devastate his opponent, who, probably sensing his own weakness, often became so ill-mannered and rude that one wished Douglass might confront a worthier opponent.

It is painful to think what high positions such a man would hold, if only his skin were a few shades lighter. As it is, although he is one of the very best, although he belongs to the true intellectual aristocracy, although he enjoys fame and reputation throughout the nation, and although he is gifted with a great mind and prodigious talent, with a commitment to action, personal generosity, and a spotless character—so-called society shuns him because he is a "nigger."

* * *

Notes

1. New York, June [1857], *Morgenblatt*, 51:29:695–696 and 51:30:718–720.

2. Assing's remark here suggests that she had written about Douglass on several earlier occasions since her first meeting with him in 1856, and that her comments had been published in the *Morgenblatt*; however, no previous issues of the paper contain any such material. See Essay 13, n. 1 and n. 3.

3. Charles Lenox Remond (1810–1873) was the first black lecturer appointed by the Massachusetts Anti-Slavery Society; he represented the American Anti-Slavery Society at the World's Anti-Slavery Congress in London in 1840. In the 1850s he became a radical advocate of slave revolts and of armed confrontation with the South.

4. Edmund Quincy (1808–1877), a Bostonian, was associated with William Lloyd Garrison in editing the abolitionist journal *Non-Resistance* and generally contributed to the antislavery press.

20

The Money Crisis—Antislavery Movements[1]

To provide an adequate description of the current situation in New York one would need to combine the expertise of an experienced businessman with the gift of a novelist. The financial crisis is the one and only topic of conversation: it affects thousands of people's existence; rich and poor feel its consequences; and it leaves no one untouched. Nobody has ever experienced such a shortage of money, and nobody knows how it will end. Many different causes have led to the present situation, and businessmen have just as many different explanations. One thing, however, is certain: for many years business activity has been based almost entirely on credit, and total capital has stood in disproportion to the circulation of money and the value of goods; hence, when the failure of several banks caused the erosion of credit, the whole structure was doomed to collapse. One company after another failed, pulling down others; two railroad companies, the Illinois Central and the Erie Railroad, declared insolvency, thereby precipitating a panic that destroyed whatever courage and confidence remained. In Wall Street, where the stock exchange is located, distraught crowds surged like waves and caused such a throng that an uninformed observer might have mistaken it for a revolution. People started rushing the banks, believing that their savings would be lost unless they withdrew them immediately; and this rush, which would have been difficult for the banks to handle even in the best of times, in turn fueled the general panic. With breathless attention everyone kept an eye on payments, as impassive employees counted out one pile of gold after another to the point of exhaustion and the collapse of no fewer than eighteen banks in a single day. The remaining banks then agreed to stay open but to suspend all cash withdrawals. Although all bills issued by municipal banks are guaranteed by the state and thus cannot lose their value even if the banks fail, the panic was so great that many people would not take anything less than actual gold and silver. This caused another kind of speculation: so-called "exchange brokers" set up business on many street corners eager to cash the bills workers had received as wages, collecting ten cents on the dollar even for the most secure bills while bemoaning their own imminent ruin.

The same large crowds were mobbing the savings banks, where the working classes tend to keep their money. Oral and written notifications that there was no danger, but that people's impatience imperiled their own security, went unheeded. "Everyone for himself" seemed to be the word of the day, and the chaos was so great that police officers had to be called in to secure the bank buildings. Finally they brought in some Catholic clerics because a majority of the service and working class is Irish and lets itself be guided by the priests: there was some hope that the clerical influence would have a better effect than the ideas and rational representations by others. For several days, therefore, one could encounter a few holy padres inside each bank doing their best to calm down and enlighten the people. But the circumstances themselves accomplished far more: after everyone had received the full amount of his treasure and had kept it for a night under his pillow stuffed in a wool sock or a nightcap, the majority regained their sense of confidence. Also, being afraid that their money would be stolen from them at home, they redeposited it within the next few days.

Many of the larger factories have closed as a result of the somber mood and the general pessimism, and within a few weeks 20,000 people have become unemployed. They have no prospects of finding work in the immediate future, and that drives them into the clutches of crime and depravity. This bodes ill for the upcoming winter, and both philanthropists and politicians are wracking their brains in vain to find a solution for the calamity. No wonder that incidents of robbery, which last winter made the city such an unsafe place, have started again and will soon increase despite the strict sentences recently imposed by some of the judges who have condemned cutthroats and robbers to up to twenty years and even to life in prison. It would be good to apply some of this strictness to the major criminals who murder, steal, and cheat not out of hunger but from sheer brutality, viciousness, and greed. However, this is where one notices the dark side of the American system of justice: partisanship and corruption tend to turn the best laws into empty words. If some poor devil—especially someone who is black—is charged with murder, he is often sentenced on insufficient evidence and executed with a haste which shows that no one is much concerned about committing judicial murder. Yet, someone like Brooks,[2] the depraved tool of the forces of slavery, not only got off all but scot-free after his treacherous assault on Sumner but was reelected by the worthy voters of South Carolina and continued to desecrate the halls of the Capitol with his presence until death interfered with the judicial obligations of his fellow members of Congress. And a man by the name of Herbert, who, in the presence of several witnesses, had shot and killed a servant with virtually no provocation in a fit of animal rage, was acquitted by his friends in court.

* * *

Among the opponents of slavery a new group has been formed with the goal to work against slavery by compensating slave holders for each slave who is released. Gerrit Smith,[3] the friend and benefactor of the Negroes and generally the protector of the oppressed and persecuted, is at the head of those who champion this cause; their first meeting, the "National Compensation Convention," was held this summer in Ohio. Gerrit Smith explains the idea of compensation in part by arguing that the North, because of its relations with the South and its own support of slavery, is an accomplice and therefore obligated to share with the South the burden of abolition; he also says that such an offer would convince the South of the North's good intentions. But this point of view has been met with the most determined opposition on the part of genuine and active abolitionists. They counter with the argument that compensation amounts to a recognition of the legality of slavery, since one can compensate an owner for his lawful property but not a thief for his unlawful booty. At best, they say, the North may grant compensation at a later time, after antislavery forces have gained the upper hand and will write the laws for the South—as one might offer sustenance to a defeated, humiliated enemy. At the present time, however, with the slavery power controlling the country, such a suggestion is entirely premature and will be derided by the South. The very idea of approaching slaveholders with friendly and conciliatory intentions offends the deepest convictions of every abolitionist. It is not enough to assume an impersonal attitude and to argue that hate must be directed against a principle, not against individuals. Who but the slaveholders represent the principle of slavery? Who but the slaveholders try to maintain that principle in the face of opposition from the entire civilized world? How can one oppose the principle without fighting them? Who is to blame for giving them their power but the weakness, the cowardice, the indulgence of the North?—Frederick Douglass, the celebrated fighter for the freedom of his race, has argued these points with the full force of his mind, the brilliance of his rhetoric, and the fire of his convictions.

A convention of a very different sort will also take place in Cleveland within the next few days. Another group of abolitionists, the disunionists led by Garrison, Theodore Parker, and Wendell Phillips, will meet to discuss the separation of the North from the South, which they see as the only means to achieve the abolition of slavery. There will be no dearth of brilliant speeches and mental fireworks, but the more one recognizes the blazing lights of these men, the more one is compelled to regret the enmity and spite with which most of that group attack their natural allies, who differ from them only in the means they choose for reaching a common goal. They accomplish nothing but their own isolation and the diminution of their own power.

* * *

Notes

1. New York, October [1857], *Morgenblatt*, 51:48:1168–1170.

2. See Essay 16, n. 3.

3. A radical abolitionist, Gerrit Smith (1797–1874) founded the Liberty party in New York in 1840 and was its candidate for governor; after serving one term in Congress (1853–1854), he ran again unsuccessfully for governor on the Anti-Slavery ticket. Much of his life and vast fortune was dedicated to philanthropy. Assing visited him in 1859 and wrote about her impressions (see Essay 41).

21

A Negro Colony in Canada[1]

One of the most interesting places a traveler in North America can visit is a colony of *free* Negroes in Buxton, Canada. About nine years ago, the Rev. William King, an Irishman and Presbyterian minister who had lived in Louisiana, took his slaves to Canada and set them free. Before his departure, his small number of house slaves had grown to fifteen as a result of his marriage. Not satisfied with his act of emancipation and inspired by the wish to find out whether the free Negro was capable of supporting himself as a farmer and of improving his moral and social condition, Mr. King became the head of an association that acquired on very favorable terms a large piece of land which the government had originally set aside for members of the clergy. The land, measuring six by three miles, was surveyed, laid out in a grid of avenues, and divided into fifty-acre lots, each fronting on one of the avenues. The price per acre, including the cost of surveying, came to two dollars. Level and thickly covered by oak, beech, elm, maple, and white walnut, the area was rich in deep, black loam. This was the place on which the great experiment with the Negroes was to be conducted.

Each settler was given a farm, not as a present but as private property, for which he had to pay the purchasing price plus interest in ten annual installments. In addition, he obligated himself to build a house on his property within a specified time and according to specified plans, and he had to acquire the necessary tools for home and farm without receiving any assistance for the support of his family. Only after having satisfied these conditions and having paid in full for his land, each settler would become the legal owner of his share. The colony was also provided with a free school building, teachers, and a church made of wood, in which Mr. King officiated, welcoming everyone and starting a Sunday school. This was the basic plan of the Elgin Association at Buxton, which now, seven years after its beginning, consists of two hundred families and eight hundred persons.

Buxton is about thirty miles southwest of Chatham and three miles from Lake Erie. Our coachman was the son of a hot-tempered Irishman, but his Quaker education provided his impulsive and sanguine character with a delightful disposition. For the first seven miles the road presented a magnificent prospect: it was bordered by virgin forest that had been purchased in large sections for speculative purposes. As we left the highway at the turnoff for Buxton, the road deteriorated and was full of holes that would make it impassable in bad weather, but on either side of it stood well-kept farm houses. Along the way I saw a number of black settlers, some in long wagons packed with men and women, some in one- or two-horse carriages, and once a Negro woman with a boy of eleven or twelve on horseback. They all seemed to be on the way to a meeting at a Methodist church. As we got closer to the colony, we saw more people and a lot of small houses that turned out to be the center of the village. Asking for the Reverend's house, we were shown the way to the small church nearby.

Mr. King's home is a long log house with a high, steep roof and external shutters; a covered porch extends across the entire front. The interior is divided into a number of rooms that serve the owner for an office, a living and dining room, etc., one leading into another. It is all very simple but neat and substantial. The little church, the school, and the post office that I have mentioned are nearby, all made of raw wood; at some distance from them are a steam-driven saw mill, a brickyard, a blacksmith's, carpenter's, and cobbler's shop, as well as the town's general store. Fortunately we found Rev. King at home and free to meet us; he is a man of medium height, sturdy frame, and intelligent, friendly mien. He explained to us that the colony now consists of 200 families, all of whom own the house they live in. A total of 1,025 acres had so far been cleared and fenced, and an additional 200 acres would be ready for planting in the spring. Of the fenced fields, 354 acres were planted in corn, promising a better than normal yield; 200 acres in wheat, 70 in oats, 80 in potatoes, and 120 in such vegetables as beans, peas, and turnips. The settlement owns 200 cows, 80 oxen, 300 pigs, and 52 horses; efforts at raising sheep, of which we saw only a few, were not successful.

At present, Buxton has two schools, one for boys and one for girls; the latter offers not only basic instruction in knowledge and needlework but also higher education. The enrollment in both schools combined amounts to 140. In order to make the colony self-supporting, instruction will henceforth no longer be free. Saturday classes, which are open to all, have an enrollment of 112.

Mr. King is one of the directors of the Elgin Association and has charge of its worldly affairs; but his function is only advisory because the colonists are quite independent as long as they comply with the regulations regarding houses and fences. He is also a missionary of the Presbyterian Church of Canada, and in that capacity he conducts services at the local mission church. Although the majority of Negroes are members of the Baptist and Methodist sects, many attend his sermons, which always draw a large crowd. One-quarter of the blacks attend no church at all, and no one exerts pressure on them. Intoxicating liquors are neither made nor consumed in the settlement; drunkenness does not exist; and only once since the beginning of the colony was it necessary to punish someone for violating the law. Until now, there has been no out-of-wedlock birth, and general morality and social improvement throughout the community are advancing.

Most of the settlers are fugitive slaves and one-third of pure African origin. If Mr. King's testimony is correct, the proportion of blacks is much greater here than in the rest of the province. Those who had previous experience in agriculture and some capital to start with have succeeded exceptionally well; during the same time and under the same conditions, they have cleared more land and made more improvements than the vast majority of white settlers. Those who lacked both skills and money fared worse, but even they have either made regular and timely payments or, if given extra time, invested their funds in land so that they can pay later. Many have already paid off their debts and received titles to their properties;

others will do so next year, and Mr. King assures us that at the end of ten years everyone will own his property.

The Canadian government assisted in the development of two European settlements, one a colony of Highlanders at Notowosaga, north of Toronto, the other one at Ramsey near Brookville, consisting of Irish, English, and Scottish emigrants. Although the settlers received aid in the form of supplies, tools, etc., both settlements failed. Twenty or thirty of the Highlanders and their families have remained, but all the others left; the former began to succeed as soon as the government stopped its support. Mr. King attributes the greater success of the Buxton settlement partly to the fact that the Negroes had better skills than the Europeans and therefore were better able to cope with the difficulties of clearing a heavily forested area, and partly to the fact that the Buxton colony had to be self-sufficient. The Negroes fully understood that they had to depend entirely on themselves, that there would be no advances in money, food, or clothing. This challenged their pride and self-reliance, and they worked with more energy than is normally expected of them.

Three of the fifteen slaves Mr. King brought with him have died, but their Canadian-born children have taken their place. Nine are still living in Buxton; one is married in Chatham; two—mother and daughter—are living in Detroit but will soon return to Buxton. Because of his age, an old man of 65 years received some support in building his cabin and clearing the woods. He married a woman of his own age and has been able to support her without assistance. We saw his house, his garden, and his corn field, all of which are in fine condition.

Accompanied by Mr. King and our companion from Chatham, we strolled through the settlement. Of course, the place was not a true Utopia, and neither were the cabins anything like the white-painted houses of a New England village. Everything looked new, raw, and crude. Next to the road you could still see sky-high trees with trunks two to four feet thick, half chopped through, and denuded of all branches. The road was nothing but a straight line through the forest with roots protruding everywhere and with the clearings and habitations of the settlers scattered on both sides; the cabins, made of crudely fashioned planks, are set at the prescribed distance from the road and surrounded by a vegetable patch. Yet there was not a total lack of decoration: some of the arched openings above the entrances were decked out with fresh vines, and here and there were gardens with luxurious flower beds showing bright red poppies against the dark forest primeval.

We stepped inside the cabin of a slave who had left Kentucky only two years earlier and got married since his arrival here. The cabin was smaller than required but arranged in a way that permitted future expansion. Inside we found a woman and a herd of children who, although belonging to other members of the family, had been taken in by this couple. Several chairs, a table, a large crate, a stove, and implements of various kinds made up the furnishings. The family's dinner, pork and potatoes, was still on the stove, and ears of corn were frying in another container filled with fresh fat. The husband was still at work in the brickyard.

Another house we visited belonged to a man who had escaped from Missouri fourteen years ago. He had been living in the settlement for six years, had fenced and cultivated twenty-four acres, and cleared another six. He had paid four installments, owned a wagon, a team of oxen, a mare, and two foals. Of his four children, the oldest, a fourteen-year-old boy, was reading Virgil (probably without useful purpose). As the day was warm, the smaller children were dressed lightly as they would be anywhere, their legs, feet, and arms bare—and with openings in the material that had not been planned by any tailor. We found that the house was furnished with a rocking chair and a wide, new sofa, besides the usual bed, bed sheets, chairs, table, etc. When we asked for a glass of water, it was brought in a clean mug on a saucer.

Even more comfortable was a house occupied by one of the first settlers. It was more spacious and had a garlanded entrance, a hallway at the center, and a room to each side. The walls were hung with several noticeable pictures, there was a sofa, and a rug lay on the floor. One thing all of these cabins had in common was the enormous brick fireplace occupying the most conspicuous part of the wall on one side of the room; like the chimney, it showed traces of the hot flames flickering there during the winter.

We saw only a small part of the settlement that had not yet been cultivated, we were told. We could not extend our visit in spite of Mr. King's warm invitation, but we left Buxton convinced *that the colony is a clear and convincing argument against the assertion made by the friends of slavery that the black race is incapable of learning.*

Notes

1. *Die Gartenlaube* (1857), 687–689. Although there is some evidence that Assing wrote for such other German publications as *Die Gartenlaube, Jahreszeiten,* and *Westermanns Monatshefte* in addition to her regular reports appearing in Cotta's *Morgenblatt*, only this piece and the two accounts of her transatlantic voyage in August and September 1852 (see Essays 1 and 2) have so far been positively identified as coming from her pen. According to Maria Diedrich, Assing's biographer, it is possible that Assing visited the Elgin Association at Buxton in the company of Frederick Douglass.

22

The Mayoral Election—A Fugitive Slave[1]

Fernando Wood has been beaten![2] A tempestuous time has come to an end with the municipal election. The mayor's position was the focal point of interest for all parties and made everyone intensely curious about the outcome. This is not a victory for either the Democrats or the Republicans or the Know-Nothings, but rather a triumph of the rule of law over caprice, of order over anarchy and mob rule. Fernando Wood, the incumbent, ran for the third time—an almost unbelievable audacity in light of his previous behavior, to say nothing of his generally poor administration, during which both crime and dirt in the streets reached new heights. His rebellion last summer against the state, which set off several bloody street battles, is still fresh in everyone's memory. But beyond that, the fraud and theft he committed during his career as a businessman are proven facts known throughout the city, for which he would have been sentenced to prison by any honest court had not his friends' legal maneuvers succeeded in terminating the trial.

One would suppose that under such circumstances he would have been abandoned by his followers, but nothing of the sort occurred. It is undeniable that it casts no favorable light upon a city when a large segment of its population is so disregardful of the most basic requirements of justice. Not that I would wish to say that everything is done according to the best of conscience even in the most civilized European nations, or that everyone in high office there might not be better secured in some other place. But there is at least a certain regard for external decencies, and people would be reluctant to damage their own party by giving support to a proven criminal.

In spite of the spirit of party loyalty, however, the situation here made the better kind of Democrats decide to turn away from Wood, and as the election approached he must have sensed that in comparison to earlier years his chances had diminished. He seemed willing to pay any price for gaining a large following and therefore threw himself into the arms of the worst rabble, the mob who had always considered him their special patron and who are more numerous and brutish in New York than in any other city on earth. Workers who had lost their employment as a result of the money crisis rallied almost daily in the public squares and, after listening to speeches, marched on City Hall to demand that the mayor hire them for public work. He gave them ample promises and assurances of sympathy, playing the role of the popular hero, but because public opinion had concluded that these demonstrations were nothing more than a farce financed by the mayor, the intended effect misfired. The die was finally cast when, in a moment of hubris, he issued a manifesto for the workers in which he called for a kind of crusade of the poor against the rich, asserting that private ownership of property amounted to theft—

which is certainly a fact in his own case, although he neglected to apply it to himself.

In the eyes of property owners he had become guilty of the worst of crimes, so that the more respectable Democrats—the party that had backed him in the past—put up a candidate of their own, someone whom the Republicans and the Know-Nothings could also support so as to avoid strengthening the enemy by splitting the opposition. Many of his most enthusiastic former supporters made it a point to state publicly that they would not vote for him, and when several of them were made vice presidents at a meeting arranged by Wood's followers, as has been customary, they announced the following day that this had happened in their absence and without their knowledge or agreement. The election process itself was more peaceful than it had been for many years and in the end produced a majority of about 3,500 votes for Tiemann, the opposition candidate. It is actually a small majority considering the large size of the city and can be explained only because the entire Irish rabble, a terrible crowd that is mainly responsible for the dangers lurking in the streets, is still the mainstay of Wood's power. But the end result remains the same, and now one can look with hope and expectations to a change in the city's government.

There are still complaints about the shortage of money, but orderly conditions have replaced the panic of a few weeks ago; new interests are emerging without danger of being quashed for their untimely irrelevance. People dare again to seek amusements: the theaters fill up, and crowds trample each other at the Italian Opera to hear and admire Formes, who has recently begun to display his artistry on this side of the ocean.[3] Even art exhibits draw full houses, testifying to the growing interest among Americans for painting and sculpture.

* * *

One of those events that casts an unremitting light on the darkest of American institutions—an event that has become rather common since the passage of the Fugitive Slave Law—caused great excitement in recent days in the otherwise so quiet and monotonous city of Brooklyn. Suddenly a rumor was spreading that a fugitive slave was forcibly kept hidden somewhere in the city to be returned to his master. Efforts to obtain information and to conduct searches remained fruitless until the whole matter became public and it was revealed that a young mulatto had arrived in New York a few days before on a steamer from Savannah. He is nearly white and had got on board without causing the least suspicion. Only as the ship was approaching New York did one of the passengers recognize him as the slave of a planter near Savannah and report him to the captain, who took immediate steps to have the fugitive arrested upon arrival in New York.

When the ship reached the pier, two men appeared, seized and shackled him, and took him in a cart to the house of a grocer in Brooklyn. The captain and the grocer had agreed to keep the fugitive under guard until the captain could take him on his return voyage and hand him over to his master. The two henchmen now worked as prison guards at night and were relieved by two other scoundrels during the day. Everything was done so quietly that rumors did not begin to spread until shortly before the ship's departure, when a philanthropic gentleman requested a stay of *habeas corpus* for the fugitive from a judge at one of the city courts. The decree was issued and handed to the two officials charged with its execution; they proceeded to the designated house and indeed discovered the prisoner. His keepers did not offer any resistance but changed their tune, assuming an air of embarrassment, which strengthened the officials' suspicion that the "property" for which they had been dispatched was being illegally detained. They immediately seized it and brought it before Judge Culver,[4] who quickly issued a release.

It is not known what has become of the fugitive; however, it is certain that the "property" has disappeared without a trace, and well-informed people suspect that the underground railroad had an additional passenger for Canada that day. The grocer and his cohorts have meanwhile been accused of abduction and can flatter themselves with the prospect of several years imprisonment. This altogether satisfactory conclusion, however, cannot be attributed to the laws *per se*, but solely to the antislavery disposition of the judge. A loyal Democrat in his place might just as well have kept the man in custody to have him returned to his master.

* * *

Notes

1. New York, December [1857], *Morgenblatt*, 52:4:93–96 (1858).

2. Fernando Wood (1812–1881), a pro-South Democrat and a major Tammany Hall figure, served several terms in Congress and as mayor of New York.

3. Karl Johann Formes (1816–1889) was a German opera singer who sang with the Royal Italian Opera of London (1852–1857) and made his first American tour in 1857. He died in San Francisco.

4. See Essay 28, n. 2.

23

The Kansas Controversy—Lola Montez—Public Lectures[1]

The financial crisis is over, and while other countries are still bleeding from the wounds inflicted, trade, speculation, business, industry, and fraud are once again turning their wheels here. The life of this monstrous metropolis is thriving, pulsing, pushing, and clamoring in all its bright and dark, grand and mean, magnificent and beggarly, irresistible and repulsive, perfectly pure and disgracefully filthy manifestations—but always offering inexhaustible, inspiring material for an interested observer, like a lode where the gold digger finds ever richer veins the deeper he mines. But the nation's eyes are mostly focused on Washington, where the Kansas question has become the burning issue pushing aside all other concerns.

This territory is now to be admitted to the Union with its own constitution, and the people of Kansas have, by an overwhelming majority of their votes, taken a stand against slavery, despite all the trickery and force used against them, despite the pressures of the government, despite the fraud and deceit in the election: they demand to be admitted as a free state. As they had done before on such occasions, "border-ruffians" from Missouri tried in vain to take control of the ballot boxes, and they voted repeatedly under assumed names in different communities, even though they were not entitled to cast a single vote. Their cheating was so flagrant that in one precinct of barely a hundred inhabitants they produced several thousand votes, which were later proven to have been based on names literally copied from the Cincinnati city directory. In another district they simply included in the voting lists the names of all famous Americans—names like Frémont, Seward, Sumner, Horace Greeley, Edwin Forrest, even James Buchanan. Nothing availed, and the simple truth has remained self-evident.

Yet, the South, which sees each increase in the number of free states as a decrease in its own power, has decided that Kansas must be a slave state. And the president, who has been at the beck and call of the slavery party from the start, is moving heaven and earth to force the admission of Kansas as a slave state. Throughout the country, tension and excitement have reached a fever pitch: the fire-eaters of the South are threatening again to secede from the Union unless they get their way; the people of Kansas, on the other hand, are determined to fight against the desecration of their soil by taking up arms against slavery, if necessary; and all the truly outstanding men in Congress, both Democrats and Republicans, are fighting the oppression of Kansas with the power of oratory.

In recent days, one of the sessions of the House of Representatives lasted all night, and it happened again that a died-in-the-wool fire-eater from South Carolina named Keitt, who took a more than passive part in the attack on Sumner almost two years ago, physically assaulted Representative Grow of Pennsylvania, an excellent speaker and outstanding opponent of slavery. Grow, however, was able to resist the attack by leveling his opponent. Several others took sides in the fray so that it was difficult to reestablish order. This incident shows again the essential difference between the two warring factions: the calm self-control and moderation on the part of Grow, who, though superior in strength, simply defended himself against his opponent without taking revenge, stand in stark contrast to the meanspirited, uncouth, violent brutality of the slaveholder—a contrast almost as stark as that between freedom and slavery.

* * *

Since the beginning of the new year, public lectures have started up again; for the educated public they are preeminent among the various entertainments of the winter season. I do not know whether it is generally known in Germany that Lola Montez,[2] apparently having abandoned the ballet, has tried to establish herself as a lecturer. Already last year she offered a lecture on "Beautiful Women" that drew large crowds. Recently she left the United States to return to Europe, but she came back on one of the next steamers, and a few days ago she was advertised as repeating her earlier lecture here. Long before the beginning, the church was filled to the last seat (the German reader may wonder about any connection between Lola Montez and a church, but there is nothing strange about it here, since many churches are used as public halls), and the audience was expecting her with more eagerness and impatience than most other speakers may flatter themselves to elicit.

There is much controversy about the actual age of this famous magician, but whatever it may be, one thing is certain: if she is no longer in the bloom of first youth, hers is the glow of youth's second being, which at times and for some tastes has an even greater fascination. The fire in her eyes, the lure of her smile, the graceful suppleness of her appearance amply compensate for whatever she may lack in conventional beauty; and one does not have to be a man to understand this whole "Lola-commotion," especially because everything about her bears the stamp of intelligence and talent. Her appearance and gestures still rather strongly betray the theater, and her costume—a richly embroidered, short, white dress—was not altogether appropriate for either the season or the occasion. But it suited her and, besides, had the advantage that those sitting to either side of the platform could spy the daintiest little foot that has ever been too vain to hide beneath the folds of a fashionable long robe.

Her lecture contained, strictly speaking, nothing either important or new: the influential power of beauty, the concepts of beauty among different nations, and the desperate striving to maintain beauty often by the strangest and most irrational means—all are such commonplaces that nothing much remains to be said. But Lola Montez treated her topic with such evident good humor, freshness, and wit, she seasoned it with so much zest and imagination, that she was amusing and fascinating from beginning to end. The audience expressed its gratification with loud applause and unanimous curtain calls—quite unusual for occasions like this one—which Lola acknowledged with the aplomb of the stage. There is not much to criticize: her voice, though not disagreeable, is perhaps pitched too high; her body movements are too pronounced, recalling more than necessary both ballet and pantomime. But a peculiar gracefulness easily helps to ignore these shortcomings, and heaven knows how she acquired an English accent with which even the strictest splitter of hairs cannot find fault.

It is a peculiar thing, this aura of personality: to those who know something of character, personality is more revealing than all the descriptions and judgments of others put together; hence, this notorious beauty impressed me as being not only much better than her reputation but perhaps even superior to many of those virtuous souls who unctuously cross themselves whenever her name is mentioned. Although her appearance may suggest a certain brashness and forwardness, she has none of that viciousness that surrounds each of her victims with an aura of notoriety. Without doubt, Lola Montez has come in contact with all manner of viciousness and evil in her wild and colorful life, and that may place some of her notorious actions in a more forgiving light. "Use every man after his own desert, and who shall scape the whipping?" Hamlet says; and if Lola Montez has dealt so many whippings, perhaps she only gave people their deserts.

Lola Montez is, of course, a unique phenomenon that cannot be dealt with in generalities either here or abroad; but it can be generally stated that public lectures are a measure of the intellectual level of a society's educated members. The subject the lecturer chooses, the degree of knowledge and education that he assumes his audience possesses, and the reception he is given are usually reliable indicators. The enormous sensation that Everett, a respected lecturer and scholar,[3] has caused with his lecture on Washington reveals (besides the lecturer's own fame) the public's somewhat arrogantly patriotic worship of their national hero, who was little more than a noble mediocrity, albeit a man of faultless character, unswerving republicanism, and many personal, civic, and political virtues. Everett gave his lecture about two years ago throughout the country, drawing large crowds in every town and village, and this past winter was able to repeat it with equal success in some of the same places, including New York. Yet, although himself a New Englander who has abased himself with his declared loyalty to the South, Everett is careful not to mention or allude to Washington's express condemnation of slavery, presumably so as not to "hurt the South's feelings," as the saying goes—in plain English: not to lose the South's dollars.

The popularity of all lectures dealing with questions of general knowledge, ethnology, and a social or political nature suggest an intellectual flexibility, curiosity, and openness that is typical of the American race, even though I believe the extent and the consequences of this quality have hitherto not been sufficiently emphasized in German writings about America. The educated American knows and feels that the Old World is far ahead of the New in learning and art and social manners, and he is intellectually nimble and receptive enough to learn as much from the Old World as opportunity permits. One area, however, generally continues to be a realm of darkness that enlightened American thinking has been unable to penetrate: in matters of religion, an inflexible and irrational orthodoxy is still locked in combat against progress. A more liberal tendency that occasionally rises against it is so feeble a reflection of the light spreading in Germany that I can hardly call it a dawn. Pious prejudices are still so entrenched that a furor arose last year when a Unitarian minister, Dr. Bellows, spoke in defense of the theater and dared to aver that it was not an institution harmful to morals and manners but had—or was intended to have—an educational and uplifting influence. While his remarks were happily applauded on one side, an uproar of horror sounded from the place of darkness, and many a reverend preacher rose against the alleged blasphemer. Dr. Bellows, who has since become something of a popular celebrity, is currently offering lectures on the maladies of society; they are as liberal and thoughtful as the American public will tolerate and have been met with much interest.

* * *

Notes

1. New York, February [1857], *Morgenblatt*, 52:13:307–311.

2. Lola Montez (1818?–1861), whose original name was Marie Gilbert, was an Irish woman claiming Spanish descent; she became a dancer, whose affairs with Franz Liszt, Alexandre Dumas (*père*), and King Ludwig I of Bavaria gave her international notoriety.

3. After a distinguished career as professor and president of Harvard, as a member of Congress, as governor of Massachusetts, and as ambassador to England, Edward Everett (1794–1865) was elected to the U.S. Senate from Massachusetts in 1852, but he resigned in 1854, embarrassed by his old-line Whig attitude of compromise on slavery.

24

Revivals—Women's Rights—Female Dress Reform—Women and Work[1]

It is well known that every educated European over here is critical of the dominance of religious sects: it is the cause of hypocrisy and stupidity and retards intellectual progress. But what is one to say when looking at the conditions that prevailed half a year ago and compares them to what is today in plain view! A kind of religious craze has seized the minds of the lower and middle classes; everywhere one can hear and read about "religious revivals," and there are reports from all states and towns about conversions, inspirations, and other phenomena. In New York, the whole fraud started innocently enough with the announcement of a daily hour of prayer in the center of the business district of the lower city. Pretty soon there was a second, and now after three months there is hardly a street without its "prayer meeting." In so far as they are conducted in churches, they commonly take place in the basement; in other places two or three rooms have been prepared for that purpose, with a blackboard on the wall reminding those present that nobody is allowed to speak more than five minutes to let everyone have his turn.

Many of the gatherings are very crowded, and no one who is not already familiar with such matters in this country from personal experience can have any notion of the screaming, shouting, howling, rolling, jumping, and hopping that takes place, let alone of the nonsense that comes to light. Prayer meetings are conducted even in the side rooms of some local business establishments, and the salesmen outdo each other shouting and howling until some customer arrives to interrupt the proceedings. As always when it comes to making noise, the Methodists are out in front; then come the Baptists and a few other sects; but the enlightened Unitarians and Universalists and even the Congregationalists and some of the better educated ministers keep their distance and try to avoid the excitement that has already cost several people their sanity. Nevertheless, one should not conclude that all of these people are fanatics: there may be some, but for the majority it is nothing but an artificially stimulated excitement that is mostly due to ignorance, the need to imitate others, and a dearth of higher intellectual interests.

In the eyes of the objective, unprejudiced observer, the whole phenomenon, which has suddenly sprung up like a mushroom for no good reason, resembles those medieval epidemics in which the population of entire regions and provinces, who believed that they were possessed by the devil, screamed, ranted, and raved until they lay in convulsions. It is a well-known fact that the eastern states experienced a good deal of such devilish mischief in earlier times, and the modern "religious revivals" are but a new form, a new epidemic, that will sooner or later run its course.

Some time ago, the question of the emancipation of women came up in Europe—also in Germany—only to disappear again like a shooting star. For a short while it had been something of a literary powder keg and was used by its opponents as a catchall for everything that then was considered incendiary, illegal, and revolutionary. All in all, it was only a literary and theoretical movement, and I do not know that any attempt was ever made to put the theory into practice. Somewhat later the same movement got underway over here. Everything that had been vague and uncertain there took on more concrete forms here. Women themselves took charge of matters, and they knew exactly what they wanted: recently a large number of women in Massachusetts formally submitted a petition to the legislature for the right to vote. They are basing their appeal on the principle—well recognized since the outbreak of the War of Independence—that taxation without representation is an injustice, and that, therefore, they have the same right as men to vote in public elections. Meanwhile, a commission has been charged with studying and weighing the petition, and Wendell Phillips, the great antislavery speaker, has appeared as their attorney.

Whether they will be successful seems more than doubtful at the present moment; but whatever the outcome, the seriousness with which the petition is being considered shows how differently the question is viewed here than on the other side of the ocean. Imagine what would happen if the women of any German state were to turn with their appeal to the legislative chamber or to some governmental ministry! Here, on the other hand, where the population consists of the most diverse elements, where all sorts of religious sects coexist side by side, tolerance is the first condition of peaceful coexistence and, for the most part, is actually practiced. Hence, people are more disposed to making allowance for any sort of endeavor as long as it does not directly violate the social order; they do not consider it their obligation to suppress everything only because they do not approve of it.

The women organizations, representing the rights of women, conduct their annual meetings ("conventions for women's rights") in any one of the larger cities. They gave the first general impulse, and such excellent men as Emerson, Gerrit Smith, Horace Greeley (the editor of the *Tribune*), Horace Mann, Higginson, and—as already mentioned—Wendell Phillips have become their ardent supporters. They address themselves primarily to the discrepancy in wages paid to women and to men for the same work as well as the exclusion of women from many branches of employment for which they are by all reasonable measures well qualified. Also, many laws and regulations still contain injustices in regard to inheritance, guardianship, and similar situations that infringe on women's natural rights. In general, what is at stake is opening a larger sphere of knowledge for women and consequently for women's activities.

All this is so indisputable and convincing that it should be a simple matter of course in any educated and civilized society; indeed, I yet have to meet a truly educated and unbiased man over here who does not sympathize with these goals up to a point. The vigorous, angry opposition, which does exist, comes without exception from men whose entire position of authority over women rests on nothing more than the privileges they presently enjoy: dismantle the privileges, and their authority crumbles. Women of the most disparate views are actively engaged in these efforts: strictly orthodox Quaker women join with freethinkers as well as with members of the Puritan churches—so long as they can all agree on the rights of women.

In terms of these goals, one can certainly support the emancipation movement of American women; in fact, not a single voice of consequence has been raised in opposition to it. But that is not the end of it. The evil demon of exaggeration, which has ruined many a good cause, has here too been up to its wonted mischief, causing excesses that, although superficial and unimportant, have been harmful because they have provided a basis for vicious efforts to ridicule the entire question of emancipation at every turn.

For many who generally sympathize with the cause, the franchise has become a problematic issue. Not without some justification have they argued that women in general have not yet reached a level of education where they can form well-founded, independent political opinions. Swayed by the influence of men, their votes would be but echoes of men's votes; and those women with sufficient understanding and judgment to form independent opinions will always have adequate opportunity to exert their influence. Granting all of this, it is nevertheless humiliating for women of excellent education, who are equal to well-informed men in their knowledge of the country and its condition, to be excluded for incompetence. It is a humiliation for them to see that the most ignorant, uneducated men—Germans who can hardly understand a word of English, or Irishmen who generally are incapable of reading a word in writing or print—are entitled as proud citizens of a democracy to cast their votes only because they have lived for five years in this country, which they may have observed only from some dark corner of a workshop or a saloon.

Several women's rights advocates have actually taken a stand in opposition by refusing to pay their taxes, and it was recently reported that steps had been taken to seize Lucy Stone's property. Harriet Hunt, the Boston physician,[2] does pay her taxes, but never without protest—a procedure that she has repeated every year for about a decade and that has since become a mere formality to which no one pays any attention.

Dress reform, another cause advanced by the women's rights advocates, is one of the exaggerations and excesses with which they have done damage to themselves and their movement. If some of the thoughtful women had individually made a few changes in their clothing appropriate for particular places and conditions—shortened their dresses by a few inches or replaced a gaudy hat with something more sensible—nobody would have been exercised. To the contrary, it would probably have been welcomed as a praiseworthy example of independence. But to make such a trivial, indifferent issue the subject of several conventions to which delegates traveled from all quarters was not only petty and thoughtless but generally seen as an effort to gain attention. The mistresses of fashion, like their most humble imitators, do as they please without making much of a public ado, at most consulting their dressmakers; but women who aspire to being above the masses and want to be like men call conventions and give speeches in which they offer social and moral reasons for the advantages of Bloomers and the evils of conventional clothing!

It is astonishing that so many otherwise intelligent and thoughtful women did not sense that this misstep had become so much identified with the Bloomer costume that almost all of the early reformers have long since returned to wearing long dresses. Incidentally, I find Bloomers repulsive: unbecoming even for young and pretty women, they are completely ridiculous when dignified mothers verging on the age of Methuselah vie with their children strutting about in panties and short skirts.

The advocates of women's rights, of course, are not satisfied extending the sphere of women's activities to encompass merely mechanical skills or such work as requires no particular intelligence or abilities. Rather, they demand means and ways for getting the highest scholarly and artistic training so as to obtain positions that are now exclusively occupied by men, and as far as conditions permit, many have already set an example. Among them are physicians, public speakers, and preachers. Naturally, their accomplishments have become the measure of their abilities, and it has now become fairly evident that, despite their great dedication and even when seen from the most sympathetic point of view, very few of these women represent the highest level of that natural or acquired ability of which women are capable.

Lucy Stone Blackwell, the president of the conventions, frequently appears as a speaker, and I have often listened to her not understanding why, of all possible fields of endeavor, she has chosen the platform; any speaker would have to perform at an exceptionally distinguished level to get any notice at all in a country of so many outstanding orators. Lucy Stone does not say anything that has not been said before and offers nothing but commonplaces, which her monotonous delivery makes the more tiresome. There is no trace of originality or genius, and her appearance is that of a solid middle-class woman. Just as Harriet Hunt has been paying her taxes under protest, Lucy Stone married about three years ago protesting against the institution of marriage in its present bourgeois form. I have already had occasion to describe Harriet Hunt's appearance, but I cannot pass judgment on her abilities as a physician. As a person she is both honorable and respected, her character is stamped by a genuine forthrightness; but her writings and speeches, though often true and to the point, have a breadth and verbosity that hardly make one ask for more.

In Europe, a female preacher would be considered even more peculiar than a female physician, such as the Reverend Antoinette Brown.[3] Here, too, the unusual must be accepted for the lack of intelligence and talent. In the tiresome monotone of a turning mill wheel she rehearses with slow and tedious complacency to everyone's disgust and annoyance all the commonplaces that have been spouted by a hundred thousand male mediocrities. I had the best intentions to listen to her attentively, but after the first quarter of an hour I realized that it was absolutely impossible. What is one to focus one's thoughts on, when nothing thought-provoking is being offered? Before long, the words sounded like mere noise, and even the comforting thought that this boredom would not last forever availed nothing—so that it is easy to guess what happened next. Reverend Antoinette Brown is a young woman of twenty-eight or twenty-nine and not unattractive in appearance. Like Lucy Stone, she has also been married for three years to a Mr. Blackwell, who, as I found out, cleans the house and cares for the child while his wife, who is not employed by any one particular church, travels about appearing as a guest preacher.

Lucretia Mott, a Quaker woman, makes an excellent impression; regardless of her advanced age she actively participates in every important movement with unusual intellectual vigor. I had the opportunity to hear her at one of the annual antislavery meetings, where she got into a lively exchange with Theodore Parker and made her case with skillful logic. Her entire personality suggests an impressive, energetic, active woman; but even she becomes intolerable when she makes the pulpit her platform—which happens quite often. Whatever originality of thought there may be is drowned in a flood of words that no one can tolerate who has not from the start abandoned all hope of brevity and succinctness.

More attractive, more outstanding, and more to my liking than any of those I have mentioned so far is Ernestine Rose, a Polish woman who has been living here for more than twenty years. To make her mark, she has no need for extravagance nor does she need to occupy any profession unusual for women; and although she takes an active role in the conventions, she tactfully avoids any appearance of eccentricity. Her opinions are based on a clear, liberal conception of all things and are not hemmed in by tradition. The speeches she has given at women's meetings and other occasions reveal a broadly educated, independent, and lucid mind; nothing is murky, nebulous, or illogical. Her knowledge of two continents has broadened her horizon; experience and understanding have matured her opinions. If the advocates of women's rights counted many women like Ernestine Rose in their number, their baroque appearance would soon give way to more substantial accomplishments than any refusal to pay taxes or any penchant for sermonizing can ever achieve.

* * *

Notes

1. New York, March [1858], *Morgenblatt*, 52:16:382–384 and 52:17:404–406. For some of Assing's earlier comments on women activists, see Essay 15.

2. Harriot Hunt (1805–1875), who started practicing general hygiene and hydrotherapy in Boston in 1835, founded the Ladies' Physiological Society in 1843. She was twice refused admission to the Harvard School of Medicine, in 1847 and 1850. Active in the temperance, antislavery, and women's suffrage movements, she

published her autobiography, *Glances and Glimpses,* in 1856.

3. Antoinette Brown (1825–1921), a graduate of Oberlin College, was the pastor of the Congregational Church in South Butler, New York (1852–1854). Active in abolition, temperance, and women's rights, she was refused permission to speak at the World's Temperance Convention in New York (1853). She married Dr. Samuel C. Blackwell in 1856 and was the author of numerous books.

25

Feeding the Poor—Penny Boardinghouses—Emigration Ships[1]

* * *

Last autumn, after large numbers of workers had lost their income because of the financial crisis and everyone was apprehensive about the coming of winter, a wealthy plumber by the name of Farmer used his own money to found an institution where all poor people who had signed up were given a free meal twice a day, at noon and in the evening. Its doors opened on November 1, and they remained open until springtime when gradually more normal conditions alleviated the most urgent needs. The demand was, of course, very great and would surely have been greater if every person in need had known about it. Every day saw at least a thousand applicants and some days more than two thousand; during one week the number climbed to nearly fifteen thousand.

In Ludlow Street, east of the Bowery and not far from what is called Little Germany, a banner has been drawn across the street stating in large letters: "Farmer's free dining saloon. Plenty to eat and nothing to pay." You step into a large hallway on the ground floor, which looks as if a butcher formerly may have had his shop here, where several servant maids are busy at two kitchen stoves. At my first visit I arrived when dinner was not being served, but the long table was covered with a snow-white, neatly ironed tablecloth that apparently had just been taken from the linen closet; plates and bowls of high-quality white stoneware had been set. Two large hams and a bowl of cold fish stood like trophies at the center. While I was speaking with the warden, who showed me the books with the daily entries of the number of guests and the quantities of goods consumed, an old Irish woman, a genuine product of the Emerald Isle, appeared with her children and asked for food. The warden told her in the friendliest manner that the dinner hour was over and she would have to come back in the evening. However, she was not to be turned away and became even more importunate; in the end, when she found that nothing availed, she exploded in curses and maledictions, stamping her feet and causing such a row that people in the street stopped to look and the warden told her that he would have her unceremoniously removed. I was a little taken aback over this new way of demanding gifts of charity and asked if scenes like this are common. "O yes," was the reply, "it happens every day and we are quite used to it."

A few days later I arrived during the dinner hour and found a colorful crowd of hungry humanity of all ages and all shapes—in the patched clothes of the respectable poor as well as in the rags of the hopeless, incurable beggar. Eight to ten persons would be told to stand at the table at the same time, each to be served a large bowl of soup—with meat, white beans, and vegetables—and a piece of fresh, white bread. The soup looked good and strong, and the bread, which I tasted myself, was of the best quality. Strangely enough, however, an old blanket covered the table instead of the snow-white tablecloth, which evidently was used only for show between meals.

In spite of all the palliative measures and despite the unusually mild winter, people have literally died of starvation in New York during the past few months. Poverty is generally as great as—if not greater than—in Paris or London. The three most populated districts alone contain close to 450 shelters—or, rather, dens—where the poor and homeless who have no other lodging can spend the night for a price between three, six, and twelve cents. It has been calculated that in this way, the poorest of the poor pay a total of 264,000 dollars. One look into those dens reveals an abyss of misery and depravity consistent with the mysteries of any large city.

The three-cent lodgings are usually in basements: a scant fire, a pile of kindling, the remnants of a chair, or at most a table of untold age is all that is available for the comfort of the guests. Light is normally admitted only through the door and can find its proper admittance only when someone happens to steal the bundle of kindling that covers the broken window panes. The quality of the air can be easily imagined. In the six-cent lodgings the bedsteads also consist of wood shavings, straw, and old rags. Some look like the forecastles of British ships, except they are not painted white. Some have hammocks, but between and underneath them are regions of darkness whose exploration requires the courage of an adventurer. Usually the twelve-cent lodgings have a somewhat better coat of paint, and the bedsheets are changed every six weeks; four persons are stuffed into a bed, and there are five to six such beds to each room, which under normal conditions would be expected to house two people.

For convenience, many of these places also have saloons. A horrible murder was committed two years ago in one of these dens, called "The Gate." It has the following inscription above the door:

> This gate hangs well,
> And hinders none;
> Refresh and pay,
> And travel on.

Gambling is an important sideline in some of these holes; though the stakes are low they are sufficient to have the same deplorable influence as regular gambling houses. Guests who have neither cash nor any other possessions that the host can take as security are unceremoniously put out at midnight. Many immigrants have spent the first few weeks after their arrival in such dark holes, receiving their first impressions of American hospitality and the American way of life.

The suffering and indignities to which emigrants are exposed while crossing the sea were again the topic of discussion at the recent meeting of the Emigration Commission. For some time they had been aware of the conspicuous mortality rate on board the Hamburg packet ships when compared to those coming from Bremen,

Havre, and Antwerp. The recent arrival of the "Howard" from Hamburg—which lost 38 of 286 passengers during a 96-day crossing—caused a flood of rumors and speculations that were fully borne out by the sworn testimony of several passengers as published in the English and German press. Things came to light that were as bad as the horrors of a slave ship. The ship was to sail from Hamburg on November 1, but did not get there until the ninth, causing the unloading and loading to take place simultaneously in great haste. There was no time for cleaning the steerage although so much dirt had accumulated that the passengers themselves were forced to remove it before they could use their berths; the first fumigation occurred only after the ship had been at sea for two weeks.

Only half of the food to which the passengers had a contractual right was distributed, and some items not at all; and contrary to all rules and rights those who were sick had to buy the wine that was their due from the captain. No one attended to them, and there was a complete lack of medicines because, according to the captain's statement, the pharmacy had been knocked over at the beginning of the voyage. But the most serious and damaging problem was the dearth of fresh drinking water. The law states that drinking water may only be taken from the official Hamburg waterworks, but in order to reduce the rather considerable cost, ships are usually supplied from the Elbe river, and its water is so dirty even at its best that no one in Hamburg considers it safe for drinking. After only a short time it spoils and is then as detrimental to good health as it is offensive to the taste. Even this disgusting liquid lasted only fifty days; after that they stopped the distribution of drinking water, using distilled sea water for cooking. Surprisingly, there were no more deaths from that time on, and now it is assumed that the poisonous water had been the chief cause of the mortality.

This shortage of good drinking water is one of the worst tortures that passengers on the Hamburg ships must endure. When I came over I had to suffer my share of this problem, and I remember very well the intense pleasure I felt upon arrival when I refreshed myself with water, after having for six weeks poured down the disagreeable stuff while holding my nose. The prevailing immorality on emigrant ships has often been mentioned—the documents I have before me are no exception—with the captains themselves not infrequently setting a bad example. These are all facts, the proof of which I hold in my hands, facts that recur year after year and are known to everyone over here. But what is the use of writing and speaking about it as long as in Europe nothing is done to stop it once and for all?

Notes

1. New York, April [1858], *Morgenblatt*, 52:21:498–501.

26

Opera—Musard's Orchestra—A Rogues' Gallery—Barnum[1]

* * *

An unusually early and lovely spring, which is a rarity in this climate, has arrived after a few cold days that followed a mild winter; the last social events of the winter season, balls and concerts, almost looked like gas flames in bright sunlight. The Italian opera is still in full swing, having had a brilliant season with the help of Formes and LaGrange.[2] For the first time the public got to see *The Huguenots*,[3] and even with prices for orchestra seats having been raised to two dollars, the performances were sold out and enthusiastically received. As much as Formes and LaGrange excelled in the leading parts, the overall performance of the opera did not measure up to its presentation on the best stages of Europe, and one is loath to see them drop many a pretty ensemble—favorites that one misses like good friends. Fig's *Leonora*, the work of one of the staff writers at the *Tribune* and the second opera composed by an American, as I learned on this occasion, was recently performed but only to achieve a certain *succès d'estime*. The whole work, I understand, consists of little more than allusions and it lacks originality.

At present, Musard and his orchestra are playing concerts that have been touted in advance with all the humbug that can still make an impression in this land of humbug, and no pains have been spared to puff the whole thing. Twenty-five Negroes in elegant liveries distribute refreshments and fans, which, instead of being made of traditional palm leaves with at least a semblance of poetic value, are cut out of colored cardboard covered with advertisements from emporiums and all kinds of other stalls and shops. Everything has been done to dress things up, yet the success has been as mediocre as the performances themselves, with the exception of a few solos and orchestra pieces that are not played by Musard's Orchestra but by excellent artists such as Thalberg, Vieuxtemps,[4] or the orchestra of the Academy of Music. Musard appears to have misjudged the public and failed to consider that in a city with a tradition of Italian opera and philharmonic concerts the audience is not so naive in its tastes as one might suppose; it demands something better than worn-out waltzes and cheap effects that can generally be had without artistic rendition. For instance, they present a railroad run that imitates the clanking of wheels and the thunder of the engine, or an animal show that tries to render as faithfully as possible the mooing of cows, the bleating of goats and sheep, and the grunting of pigs. For this purpose, Musard employs all sorts of peculiar and unusual instruments, probably of his own design, which actually produce such an uproar that you would like to cover your ears and run away.

The public that goes to listen to the Academy of Music, among them a great many Europeans, is not satisfied with someone like Musard. The large majority who know and demand nothing better—among them many who in every other respect are very well educated—find more satisfying entertainment at the minstrel shows. I recently witnessed a humorous instance of this phenomenon at the house of the editor of one of the best newspapers in the country, that is to say in a place of exemplary education and literary sophistication. The Hutchinsons were present, a family that has been touring the country for several years giving concerts for 25 cents admission, much like Austrian and alpine singers at home. Five or six strange-looking gentlemen—with long, flowing hair (that was supposed to give them the appearance of geniuses) and immense, fabulous collars—appeared with as many equally strange-looking ladies, their wives and sisters. One of them played the violin and was rather badly accompanied on the piano by a German; the rest sang heartily, with neither art nor method nor as well as many of the untrained singers whom one can hear so often in our public parks. At best, they were good enough that one might wish to listen to a few numbers; yet, we were forced to listen to their efforts with hardly any break, making any kind of sensible conversation impossible all evening.

Looking at the assembled society, however, provided for some compensation: almost everyone—particularly the editor-in-chief—was listening with a degree of reverence that almost bordered on ecstasy. None of them seemed to have the least inkling that this sort of music was not on the same level as a Beethoven symphony played by the philharmonic orchestra. I had just been discussing this phenomenon with an acquaintance, and we had just exchanged remarks about this naive lack of judgment, when a gaunt old lady, the true type of a New England Puritan, came up to me and said in rapturous tones: "That is true music, ain't it?" This perfect proof of what we had just talked about was quite humorous.

A daguerreotypist is presenting a gallery of photographic portraits of famous men, representing the individuals in such perfection that one can compare them only to the very best ink drawings. The ease and speed with which photographs are taken make it possible to prepare thousands of cheap copies, just like copper etchings or lithographs. Instead of illustrating the works of an author with his lithograph portrait or a steel engraving, it will be cheaper in the future to adorn it with a photograph. This reminds me of a gallery of a very different kind, where individuals are shown for a quite opposite purpose—that is, not for reasons of fame. The New York rogues gallery is a curiosity without parallel.

As soon as a thief or otherwise notorious individual has been arrested by the police, they take and file his daguerreotype in a studio in the Tombs specially equipped for that purpose. If someone has been robbed and has by chance seen the thief, he goes to the "property clerk," who is in charge of the collection of loot taken from the thieves and also functions as the inspector of this gallery, to look for his friend among the pictures. Should one of these characters escape or commit another unlawful act elsewhere, his picture is sent to the police at the new scene of crime. Barnum, the father of humbug, has prepared a copy of this charming collection and placed it in his museum next to the portraits of famous patriots, where every visitor can enjoy them.

Barnum's museum, by the way, is one of the most worthwhile and entertaining places typical of New York. Behind its magnificent name, "American Museum," it displays a collection of all kinds of playful sense and nonsense to please children of all ages. One is tempted to call it an oversized toy store, and the palace of the Prince of Pallagonia shrinks into insignificance next to it. The large five-story building is located in the liveliest part of the city on Broadway, down at the park and the corner of Chatham Street. Streaming flags and gushing music betray its location from a distance, and for 25 cents one is admitted to the inner sanctum. Since Barnum collects indiscriminately whatever appeals to his fancy, there is always something of interest to be seen, but it is mixed helter-skelter with the silliest trash.

A lindworm made of leather is displayed next to beautiful aquariums—large containers of water in which fish, sea plants, and shellfish exist in their native element, representing in miniature the life of the ocean. A flag pierced by bullets is supposed to have served in the War of Independence, and the Declaration of Independence itself is presented to a flock of stuffed birds surrounding it. Jenny Lind and Pope Leo X meet among butterflies and beetles. A piece of lace, supposed to have been worn by Marie Antoinette, seems to have been dropped accidentally among corals, where it is joined by a peculiarly carved statue of Christ, between whose feet one can discover an old-fashioned pair of candle snuffers. Next to a few pictures of Herculaneum, a few mediocre etchings and lithographs of Parisian buildings are exhibited, evidently clipped from the *Guide des voyageurs*. In the Chinese collection, one of the richest sections of the museum where one meets waxen mandarins with long braids and beauties with tiny feet in different postures, a glass cabinet contains "the living skeleton" of Tom Thumb, a giant, and other monstrosities all faithfully reproduced in wax.

Living curiosities of this sort are also included: an albino woman, a bearded boy, a few dwarves or other peculiar representatives of the human species. Several abominable peepshows, presented as panoramas, offer lessons in geography. An important element is a theater presenting several shows a day and occasionally offering some excellent farces. The top floor houses the animal show: a giraffe, a few bear cubs, racoons, ostriches, and last but not least the famous "happy family" in a large cage—a variety of animals that are by nature hostile but here exist in peace and harmony. A rat is sleeping between the paws of a cat, while a mouse has chosen the cat's back for its bed; pigeons are playing with an owl; a rooster is teasing a fox; dogs are going from one to another giving signs of recognition and friendship. The secret of this taming of wild instincts is clear enough because it is well known that animals who have become used to each other from their earliest youth easily make friends, especially if they get—as they do here—such an abundance of food that hunger can never gain the upper hand. Most visitors do not understand this but believe that Barnum has made a special discovery in the world of animals. Hence, much more amusing than the "happy family" itself is the large circle of big and little children crowding around the cage, beaming with pleasure, gaping at the miracle, completely incapable of finding out what makes such a thing possible.

As everyone knows, it was Barnum who had the unheard-of idea a few years ago to present a "baby show," modeled on the usual cattle shows, and to offer a prize for the largest and strongest child of, I believe, one year. This enterprise also met with great success: more than two hundred women arrived with their children and willingly presented themselves to the public for two days with their children on their laps, and all of New York came running and crowding into Barnum's museum as if they had never before seen little children.

Notes

1. New York, May [1858], *Morgenblatt*, 52:23:551–552 and 52:24:570–572.

2. For Formes, see Essay 22, n. 3; Anna De LaGrange (1825–1905) was a French coloratura soprano.

3. *Les Huguenots*, an opera by Giacomo Meyerbeer, was first produced in Paris in 1836.

4. Sigismond Thalberg (1812–1871), a Swiss pianist and composer, became known for his piano fantasies on operatic themes, with a preference for Italian composers, especially Rossini. Henri Vieuxtemps (1820–1881), a Belgian violinist, first toured America in 1843–1844; in 1857–1858 he returned for a series of concerts with Thalberg.

27

Kansas—Anniversaries[1]

The prospect for a quick and favorable solution to the Kansas situation has faded again. The shameless venality and corruption of the northern Democrats has led to new complications and difficulties, which, though they finally cannot prevent the admission of Kansas as a free state, have put it off to the distant future. Meanwhile, the people of Kansas have made known their determination to resist, if necessary by force of arms, the despised Lecompton Constitution.[2] Whether things will reach that point remains to be seen, but there is no doubt the president will try to force the admission of Kansas as a slave state by every possible means. That's what is called popular sovereignty in this great slaveholding republic!

The annual conventions of the societies for all sorts of good and bad purposes, which always take place in New York during the second week of May, were as usual accompanied by almost ceaseless downpours. Everyone is so used to it by now that they are not deterred from attending, expecting to be soaked to the skin several times during "anniversary week," and often one can see the convention halls filled to the last seat while the rain is coming down in torrents. This year, among all the groups it was the American Tract Society that stood out for everything that is bad. It has never accomplished anything good through the dissemination of its fatuous tracts, and no sensible person would ever expect anything reasonable and useful to come from that quarter. However, many of the pious sheep that make up its supporters suddenly did feel jolted from their heaven when this society, which is composed of the most respectable and influential preachers of all sects as well as other "promoters of religion," decided after a stormy meeting not to mention slavery in any of its tracts and not to permit any condemnation of either the principle or the practice of slavery, so as not to impede the society's work in the South. A cowardly, hypocritical, servile, greedy priesthood has revealed its true nature in all its uselessness and pitifulness. The sins and depravities of the poor and their most innocent pleasures are still condemned and allowed to be the subject of tedious treatises: drinking brandy, smoking, dancing, or breaking the blue laws can be bemoaned and judged or represented as the devil's temptations; but the country's shame and undoing, the crimes of the respectable, influential, church-going southern rulers may—heaven be helped—not be subjected to any criticism; no one may offend them because they might withdraw their support and benevolence.

Of all the conventions, that held by the American Anti-Slavery Society was, as usual, the most outstanding and interesting. If ever a good purpose united bright talents and noble hearts, capable of devotion and enthusiasm, in the pursuit of a common goal, it has happened in this society, which was founded by William Lloyd Garrison more than twenty years ago. At that time, abolitionism was far less popular than now, even in the North; it required courage and self-denial to commit oneself publicly, especially men who, by virtue of their great talent, had every political opportunity open to them, had they been willing to coast with the current. Garrison, Wendell Phillips, and Theodore Parker each have more moral fortitude and strength of conviction than half a Congress of northern and southern Democrats. In the first session this year, Garrison aimed some sharp blows at the infatuation with religious awakening, causing the audience to erupt in a storm of opposition. There was angry hissing, and ministers and laymen rose to contradict the heretical abolitionist, but he parried their thrusts with ease and proved succinctly that in spite of all the wringing of hands and rolling of eyes not a single slave had been emancipated, the number of crimes had not abated, and no good had issued from the womb of the entire party of piety.

The Women's Rights Convention, which held its meetings during the same week, drew a larger audience than I have ever seen on such an occasion. This movement, too, is beginning to find a wider and more general popularity, and I would not be surprised at all if Europe were to realize some tangible results from the changes that have occurred in ideas and attitudes over the past several years. The sessions were most interesting. As I already had occasion to mention earlier, many of the best, most distinguished men are the chief actors in the defense of women's rights and are now in the vanguard of the movement. Garrison, Wendell Phillips, and Higginson are the most noted representatives, and their brilliant speeches took the place of those well-meaning but feeble effusions by women who, though ill-prepared for the platform, have been the usual fare at these events.

For the first time, I saw George Curtis, the anonymous but well-known author of the famous "Potiphar Papers," that biting and witty satire of American upstarts, the so-called "codfish aristocracy." His appearance has something peculiarly attractive: a sovereign and exceptional mind has placed its stamp on it; his lecture is warm and lively but controlled by a noble serenity; his voice is beautiful and flexible, the impression he makes both significant and lasting. Ernestine Rose, this impressive woman whom I have mentioned earlier,[3] equal to any man in eloquence, logic, and originality of thought, spoke several times gracefully and impressively. Her opposite was a Miss Jane Lydia Jenkins,[4] one of those female reverends who, lacking any other occupation or talent, now and then endanger the country with their boring sermons. She read a long and tedious address with a high-pitched, monotonous voice, tiring her audience, and she presented a veritable patchwork quilt of commonplaces that revealed not a single spark of original thought.

During the same week, the Negroes of New York gathered to protest the many injustices, interferences with, and violations of their natural rights to which they are subjected daily. One of the busiest municipal streetcars does not tolerate colored people of any shade to use the interior of the cars; at best, they are permitted to stand on the front platform next to the driver. On several occasions fights have broken out, during which men and even women who had dared to seat themselves inside the cars despite this barbaric restriction were forcefully ejected. As a result, there have been lawsuits going back twenty years; but, as may be expected considering the generally prevailing prejudice against blacks, these have almost in every instance been decided in favor of the streetcar companies. Meanwhile, all other companies had gradually removed this restriction and opened their cars to everyone, regardless of color; only one company stubbornly refused and, a few years ago, put in service special cars for Negroes, which were marked in large letters, "Colored People Allowed in This Car," thus, to the shame of the nation, giving a flagrant illustration of the freedom and equality of which its people like to boast. Setting aside the barbaric cruelty of this practice, these so-called "crow cars" are of little practical use because they run only six times a day in a neighborhood with heavy traffic, where the other streetcars come every three to five minutes.

Rather than try to seek remedy and recompense through costly and pointless court proceedings as has been done in the past, wasting nearly ten thousand dollars, the colored people now intend to join in employing all lawful means to stop this horrid restriction. I am more than doubtful that they will have any success whatever, but it was for this reason that they have called a meeting, which was attended by a large, mostly white audience that filled the church to the last seat. However, it was not the announced purpose of the gathering that brought out the crowd, for even among the decided foes of slavery there are only few who would rise with lively interest on behalf of the free Negroes of the North; and whether blacks are allowed to ride in the cars on Sixth Avenue is, for most, a matter of such indifference that they would not bestir themselves. The magnet exerting such a powerful force was Frederick Douglass, who had agreed to appear. This excellent speaker knows how to electrify and captivate an audience. Something like a personal relationship develops between him and his listeners and elicits their undivided sympathy, letting them experience the magic of amiability that wins the heart of everyone who is fortunate enough to meet this vibrant and noble man.

At the present time there is little hope for the Negroes to come into the enjoyment of any of those rights of which they have been deprived. The Democracy is avenging itself for its latest defeats wherever it can, making defenseless and vulnerable blacks its target. The shameful decision by the Supreme Court in Washington, according to which Negroes cannot be citizens of the United States and have no rights that any white person is obligated to respect,[5] is bearing fruit in the most outrageous injustices, and all Democratic offices seem to make a point of giving it the broadest application. One of the more recent instances of harassment is the refusal to issue passports to colored people for traveling abroad; and in many other ways as many impediments as possible are thrown in their way on all conceivable occasions.

There is an accomplished and well-respected colored dentist in Boston, Dr. Rock,[6] who wishes to visit France to restore his poor health. Although he knew that the government would not issue him a regular passport, he was aware that some time ago it had provided several colored people with a kind of written document of protection; he therefore turned to Senator Wilson to obtain such a document. Wilson submitted the petition to Secretary of State Cass, who replied that the government did not issue any papers other than regular passports, which, constituting official documentation of the bearer's citizenship, had never been issued to any colored persons by the present administration. This was an unadulterated lie, as many facts have since shown, but Dr. Rock had to accept it as the truth. He now turned to a high-level official of the port of Boston, but was told that he was authorized to issue papers only to American seamen. In the end, he did receive a passport from the municipal authorities, but when he applied for a visa from the French consul, he was notified that, according to instructions, visas could be given only for passports issued by the government in Washington. Now Dr. Rock, much like a refugee without a regular passport, is forced to rely on the rather uncertain hospitality of the French government.

The Oregon Territory has recently applied for admission to the Union as a free state with a constitution that would not tolerate the presence of colored people within its boundaries, and it will of course be admitted. A few months ago in New York, a poor Negro was shot down without any provocation in broad daylight by a few vagabonds just for the fun of it. It is known who the perpetrators are, who, far from denying the deed, boast of it; but even though they have been charged, the courts of law do not find it necessary to undertake steps for their punishment—because a Negro has no rights that any white person is obligated to respect!

Notes

1. New York, June [1858], *Morgenblatt*, 52:27:641–644.

2. Named after the small town on the Kansas River where it was formulated, the proslavery Lecompton Constitution of 1857 was ratified in an election that offered a choice only between limited and unlimited slavery and was therefore boycotted by antislavery voters; it was rejected in an election the following year.

3. For Rose, see Essay 15, n. 5.

4. Little is known about Lydia Jenkins, but she was a minister active in the women's rights movement; in 1853 she was variously introduced as being from either Geneva, New York, or Waterloo, New York.

5. The Dred Scott decision of 1857.

6. John Sweat Rock (1825–1866) had practiced dentistry in Philadelphia, then received an M.D. degree from the American Medical College there in 1852, and became a practicing physician in Boston, where he was active in the antislavery movement and in the campaign to desegregate the Boston public schools. In 1861 he was admitted to the Massachusetts bar as a lawyer; during the Civil War he recruited African Americans for the famous Fifty-fourth Massachusetts Infantry Regiment and worked for equal pay for black soldiers.

28

An Excommunication—Slavery and the Germans[1]

In Europe, even in Germany, there are still a few out-of-the-way, primitive areas where, in spite of the railroad and the newspapers, the sunshine of education and enlightened thought has penetrated only slowly and incompletely, where the power of old prejudices and base customs presents a barrier against the most necessary and salutary innovations that is difficult to overcome. Throughout the civilized world these old, forsaken places, where ignorance and narrowness have long been entrenched, are regarded as custodians of the remains of the Middle Ages, as curiosities, and as remnants of a past that is fortunately gone and forgotten. It was a time that is still poetically and picturesquely represented in the ruins of old castles, the dilapidated dens of robber barons, and the legends connected with them, all of which lend a poetic aura to the most unedifying, most barbaric of historical periods. Should there still be disciples of the actual Middle Ages—the raw, naked, barbaric Middle Ages—they don't exist in the old, aristocratic Europe with its dark remnants of the past, but they do in the young, democratic America, the land where progress is driven by steam. Although America has neither a pope nor an established redeeming church, there is a hierarchy that has the power to excommunicate all those who are still within its reach.

In recent days, New York was surprised by the news that a well-known man, Judge Culver of Williamsburg (which is separated by only a narrow inlet from this metropolis),[2] has been formally and solemnly ousted from the Baptist church. An excommunication in the nineteenth century was something of a jolt, even for those who are normally all too eager to make allowances for the church's high-handed ways, and the ostensible reason for the ejection, "immoral conduct," was met by believers and nonbelievers alike with indignation. Culver's improper relationship with two ladies, whose names were mercilessly publicized on this occasion, was the cause given by church representatives after a pretense of an investigation, at which the accused had not even been present. Like a bolt of lightning it struck the peace and quiet of thousands of honorable and well-respected church members, who were horrified at the thought of having their own illicit affairs of the heart exposed. "If the church were to exert so much control over the life of each of its members," it was generally said, "the churches of New York would soon be empty; for can any man—including elders and preachers—withstand such trial by fire?"

Upon closer inquiry it became clear that this appearance of moral fervor was merely the cover for an entirely different motive, and that the issue at the center of American politics—slavery—is the real reason behind these actions. It so happens that Culver is an abolitionist who has been guilty of the abhorrent crime of repeatedly and frankly expressing his condemnation of slavery within the church itself. The cowardice and cunning of this church are unparalleled, except perhaps for some of the other churches in this land of piety. Too cowardly to risk offending the party in power by tolerating an ardent opponent in its own ranks, the church is also too cowardly to confess its own wickedness and thus resorts to a scandal: making false accusations of transgressions that, according to testimony, occurred more than four years ago without ever giving offense to anyone. There was something awesome about the wrath of the popes in the Middle Ages; they did not hesitate to hurl their sentences of excommunication at emperors and kings, and the lowliest priest had the courage, based on the authority of his superiors, to challenge the worldly powers. But the slaveholding church, currying favor with the slave owners, proves its courage and spirit of revenge by acting against individuals who cannot damage either its influence or its financial interests.

Another kind of primitive medieval behavior, here referred to as "rowdyism," has for some time made New Orleans, much like Rome in the twelfth century, the scene of crimes against public safety. The Know-Nothings are the party in power there, and in order to control all public offices and insure success at the polls, they employed hordes of the most depraved rabble, veritable gangs of thieves and assassins—as the former mayor of New York, Fernando Wood, used to do—and bought their votes with complete impunity. As a result, crime has increased in New Orleans at a rate unparalleled even here in New York, where one is used to such things. Not a day went by without assaults and murders, yet no one was apprehended because the police, who knew the perpetrators all too well, had no desire to identify them. Finally, just as in California some time ago, the citizens themselves formed a committee of vigilance for the protection of life and property; as they took control of the armory and other public buildings and set up barricades in the streets, New Orleans was in a complete state of war for several days.

Oddly enough, it was the quiet citizenry, the owners of property, who had to resort to revolution to throw off the yoke of mob rule. Negotiations were conducted with the mayor for turning over a large number of the most dangerous criminals who had hitherto been under his special protection, and for several days it looked as if law and order would prevail. However, the recent municipal elections returned the Know-Nothings to power, and any attempt to take the city out of the control of the mob—an effort that, had it been successful, would have been praised as an act of pure patriotism—is now being treated as an attack by a gang of criminals. The members of the committee of vigilance have been arrested, the Know-Nothings are back in power, and the happy *status quo* has been reestablished for the time being.

While the last several years have been generally marked by the disquieting dominance of the party of slavery, there are some welcome signs that a number of western and southwestern states, under the prevailing influence of the German settlers, may throw off the curse of slavery in the not too distant future. One of these states is Texas, which the slaveholders have hitherto considered safe because of its geographic location and agricultural products. But one can now see that the German immigrants, who are successfully and without detriment to their health growing cotton and tobacco in spite of all the assertions that only Negroes are equal to the task, are so dominant that at least three of the four states into which this large territory is expected to be divided will join the Union as free states. Furthermore, Missouri, where the party of emancipation won a victory in St. Louis, promises soon to be a free state, as I mentioned on an earlier occasion; it is a development due in large part to the increasing German influence.

German businessmen, craftsmen, and workers are an important element in St. Louis, already numbering nearly 75,000; and German farmers and vintners have established themselves on the sunny hills and fertile valleys of the interior, which the American pioneer considered too remote and therefore neglected in favor of the rich river banks. In village after newly established village German is spoken all year. In several districts, German justices of the peace hold office; there are German newspapers; local ordinances, posters, and school books are in German; and it is the Germans who achieve the best yields from the soil. Slavery disappears in the face of German industry because the slaveholder cannot compete with it, and whether he likes it or not, he must sell his exhausted land to the foreign intruders and emigrate to the South. Also, slaves are becoming too costly to be profitably used in agriculture. The price of a strong Negro in Missouri is currently about 1,200 dollars: considering the capital investment alone, without counting expenses for food and clothing, this amounts to at least 120 dollars a year—regardless of possible loss due to escape and the completely understandable, so-called laziness of the slave. (He has a propensity to work carelessly as there is no reason in the world for him to exert himself more than necessary for the benefit of his enemy and oppressor.) The most industrious, hard-working, and skilled German laborer, on the other hand, costs barely a hundred dollars per year. Under these circumstances it is no wonder that the new settlers, Americans as well as Germans, despise slavery, and that the old slave owners are glad to be rid of such costly workers and either hire free laborers or leave for parts more to their liking.

Some of the earlier settlers, no doubt, let themselves be persuaded to become slaveholders against their better conscience and even against their preference, by the generally prevalent conditions and by the particular difficulty of obtaining free laborers; but they would now happily rid themselves of this curse. This explains the fact that several former slave owners are now among the leadership of the party of emancipation, even though the chief cause of the progress emancipation has made is definitely to be found in the advance of free labor. Viticulture plays an important part in all of this because it is a branch of agriculture that could never be done by slaves; it could never blossom in a slaveholding society. No one in the slavery states knows anything about the care and attention that are required, about the selection of grapes appropriate for a particular climate and soil, about the necessity for experimentation in this country, or about the specific skill essential for making wine. The easygoing manner, the carelessness, the laziness, the lack of understanding and knowledge that are so evident in southern agriculture are insurmountable obstacles to a successful culture of vineyards.

However, Missouri, a country in every way richly blessed by nature, is perfectly suited for growing wine. The rocky hills of the interior, which the American settlers left aside because they thought the land was not arable, now yield a richer harvest in the hands of the Germans than the most fertile banks of the rivers so eagerly sought by the Americans. To this day, these hills and slopes are being sold to the settlers at relatively low, almost insignificant cost, attracting more and more German immigrants every year. German vintners are already making up whole villages, and they are, both by inclination and circumstances, naturally opposed to slavery. As good democrats (in the German, not the American sense of the word) they hate the aristocracy of the slaveholders, and as good free laborers they cherish freedom and work, despising tyranny, laziness, and any unproductive waste of time. In Hermann, one of these villages of vintners, there were, according to a German living in Missouri who provided me with this information, only three so-called Buchanan Democrats among 1,200 residents; the rest voted for antislavery candidates. The same is true of the other wine-growing towns to such a degree that the orthodox defenders of slavery consider it a kind of public nuisance of which they would like to rid themselves if it were only possible.

In my reports I have often mentioned the goals and achievements of the most outstanding abolitionists; now, for a change, I will introduce the reader to an apostle of slavery, who so far has plied his trade only in the South but has given the newspapers of the North much material for the most amusing articles. This worthy is called Reverend Brownlow,[3] and he is so convinced of the beneficent and salutary influence of slavery that, inspired by the generous wish to share this blessing with all of mankind, he wishes to undertake a kind of crusade through the North to preach to the poor infidels the gospel of the "peculiar institution." So naive is this Reverend Brownlow that he believes we here in the North are as much in the dark about the conditions in the South as people there generally are about the North, and that we are only waiting for him to enlighten us. So as to make his arguments the more acute and convincing, Reverend Brownlow has announced he will bring with him, by way of a living illustration of the abounding bliss of slavery, Alf, a Negro belonging to him, who is supposed to be prepared to discuss this subject alongside his master with anyone. It remains to be seen whether Alf, for the purpose of giving a more convincing demonstration of this bliss, will also present a pair of handcuffs, a ball and chain, and a whip. At any rate, Reverend Brownlow is paying the highest compliment to the tolerance of the North by presuming that he will be able to conduct his crusade unhindered and without danger of having to endure the martyrdom of an occasional beating, such as is the unavoidable fate in the South of anyone under the mere suspicion of abolitionism.

A perfect example of southern tolerance is the treatment given to the book dealer Strickland, who had to leave Mobile because he had a copy of the life of Frederick Douglass in his shop; even his wife was made to leave town when she returned several months later to settle her husband's affairs. Despite Reverend Brownlow's assurances, as well as those of other southern heroes, regarding the enviable happiness of the slaves, the underground railroad has never transported as many passengers as it is doing now, which seems to prove that slaves, different from other human beings, have a peculiar passion for escaping from the place where they receive the best treatment. One might almost suspect that Reverend Brownlow fears such tendencies in his slave Alf; at any rate, he has not yet begun the trip that has been touted in the papers for the past several months.

* * *

Notes

1. New York, June [1858], *Morgenblatt*, 52:31:738–740.

2. Erastus Dean Culver (1806–1889) served in Congress (1845–1847) and, upon moving to Brooklyn in 1855, was elected judge of the city court, a position he held for six years.

3. William Gannaway Brownlow (1805–1877), a Methodist minister and newspaper editor from Knoxville, Tennessee, was an outspoken slavery advocate as well as a committed Unionist who was imprisoned during the Confederacy. He later supported Lincoln's emancipation policy and was elected governor of Tennessee in 1865.

29

Malcontents—Indians—James Monroe—A Marylander Without Slaves[1]

* * *

A so-called free convention of reformers was held last month in Rutland, Vermont, causing much talk. All those who dislike current conditions, malcontents of all persuasions, were represented, but it soon became evident that the reasonable reformers, the abolitionists and the opponents of religious antirationalism, were not represented by their most outstanding spokesmen. Those whom one may call the reform riff-raff, the spiritualists and the proponents of free love, who have lately achieved considerable notoriety and actually founded a settlement in Ohio, took over the proceedings and managed to pass a resolution recognizing the actual existence of ghosts. One of the mediums at the convention, a Miss Temple, presented a long, memorized speech full of grammatical errors, but she was finally silenced by the comment that if ghosts wish to take part in the convention they would have to adhere to the same time limits allotted to humans. There were thundering orations against marriage and in favor of free love, delivered mostly by Mrs. Branch, one of the leaders among the propagandists of free love, but she was logically and succinctly opposed by a Mr. Tiffany. He stated frankly that the expression "free love" could not mean anything other than complete promiscuity, and that the evils attributed to marriage were not inherent but due to the general state of social corruption. William Goodell, an honest but ineffective abolitionist mostly known for the length and tediousness of his speeches, was irritated with the audience's usual impatience and lack of respect for his lucubrations and with being kept to the same time limit despite his objections. Other speakers got into verbal spats, and a few Shakers presented their nonsense. For comic effect, the citizens of Rutland were seized with such a panic of piety that they conducted special prayer meetings to prevent heaven's wrath against such godlessness.

New York recently had the honor of being host to twelve Indian chieftains from Minnesota, who, with their interpreter, spent a few days in the city on their way to Washington, where they were to conduct negotiations with the government. Truly handsome Indians, they were by our standards repulsive creatures with big noses, high cheekbones, and foreheads so low that their hair, which they brush forward rather than backward as we do, almost touched the bridge of the nose. Like women, some of them had plaited their hair into several long, dangling braids; another one carried two stiff feathers like horns on both sides of his head; blankets, moccasins, tomahawks, and calumets—in short, the whole finery of Indian aristocracy could be seen at its best. Even in New York, where Indians are among the many figures one encounters daily, the chiefs' appearance in the streets caused quite a stir.

A favorite popular entertainment was offered to the public a few days before the Fourth of July with one of those ceremonial funeral processions that people invent over here if no famous person has the good sense to die. After many years of resting in peace, the remains of President Monroe were exhumed in one of New York's cemeteries to be transported to his place of birth in Virginia, where of course a similar public display was made of his reinterment. Thanks to the legendary incompetence of the local councilmen and aldermen, the entire ceremony turned out to be a meager and wretched affair, which is unlikely to trouble President Monroe's eternal rest. Unfortunately, however, this funereal comedy has cost the life of a still living person. The grandson of the famed Alexander Hamilton, a young man of twenty-three who was in the regiment escorting the coffin on the steamer to Virginia, mysteriously disappeared during reembarcation, and his body was later found floating in the water. The whole event is rather suspicious and has caused many rumors.

Although not among the most unusual events in that region, a recent occurrence in Maryland, causing much excitement, is too characteristic of the conditions in the states south of the Mason-Dixon line to ignore. A very respectable Maryland farmer by the name of Bowers, who does not own any slaves but tills his own fields, had brought on himself the wrath of his slaveholding neighbors by freely expressing his antislavery opinions. Because an unusually large number of slaves had escaped from their owners for several years, he was accused of aiding and conspiring with them. Some of the slaves, caught in their attempt to flee, had been coerced by threats and by promises of not selling them to the deep South (which is the common fate of unsuccessful fugitives) to testify that Bowers had issued them false passes. On that basis Bowers was indicted, but there was no evidence against him, particularly because in the slavery states the testimony of a black against a white person is insufficient to find him guilty. Thus Bowers was acquitted, which so enraged the southern knighthood that they decided to take things into their own hands. Wearing masks and disguises, about thirty slave owners lay in ambush near Bowers' house, and at midnight they lured him out under the pretense that a passing traveler whose carriage had broken down needed his assistance. He had hardly taken a few steps when he was seized, dragged into a nearby forest, stripped naked, and tarred and feathered in true lynching fashion; whereupon he was forced to promise that he would leave the state.

This reprehensible deed, however, did not find the approbation of the majority of people in that area. Hearing his cries for help, Bowers' wife rushed to the scene and, although threatened and mistreated by the roughnecks, she was not intimidated and even succeeded in tearing off a few masks and thus recognizing some of the men. They have meanwhile been indicted and had to post bail. Nearly all of the population without slaves in that region side with Bowers and are highly indignant about his mistreatment. The two parties have since then engaged in several fights, with the slave owners shamefully succumbing and getting their due reward at the hands of their opponents. This situation brought about a large gathering of the local slave owners to confer on the measures necessary to insure the safety of human property. A Mr. Pearce, one of the senators of the state of Maryland in Congress,[2] who has been particularly active in his concern over this matter, played an especially prominent role. He bitterly complained about the losses slave owners suffer as a result of runaway slaves and was most astonished that someone might take offense at this manner of administering justice or might wish to return the favor. The final resolution endorsed the treatment Bowers was given, and all those present pledged to protect his assailants against violence of any kind. But it remains to be seen whether those who do not own slaves, by far outnumbering the slave owners, will be intimidated by this show of resolve.

Notes

1. New York, August [1858], *Morgenblatt*, 52:37:886–888.

2. James Alfred Pearce (1805–1862) was a member of Congress (1835–1843) and served in the Senate (1843–1862).

30

A Captured Slave Ship—Retreat of Reverend Brownlow[1]

* * *

An event that has caused much excitement throughout the country is the capture of the *Putnam*, a slave ship with 314 slaves aboard, by the American naval vessel *Dolphin*. This is the first instance of the American navy seizing a slave ship since the African slave trade was declared piracy, even though thousands of Negroes are annually unloaded in Cuba virtually under the very eyes of American vessels. It is an extraordinary event, almost made to order. Not a sense of humanity and justice but the wish not to be blamed by the entire world—not to mention the recent conflict with England over the right to search and the disgraceful role played in it by the American government—made it appear necessary to seize a slave ship at long last. Until now these pirates of human flesh using American ships and flying the American flag were too cunning for our watchfulness and too swift for our slowness; but suddenly a slave ship is slow and an American vessel sufficiently swift to cause a miracle. Four hundred and fifty-five Negroes had originally been put on board in Africa, and during the voyage 141 of them died of the horrors that have so often been described; 25 more have died since their arrival. The disembarkation of 314 Negroes in Charleston inflamed Southern greed: half a million dollars worth of human flesh, fortuitously washed ashore was too great a temptation for the abstemiousness of the slave drivers. The public and the press began to argue loudly and openly that it would be the height of folly and waste to send the Negroes back to Africa, as demanded by law. "We need them everywhere," they shouted; "our planters need them, our craftsmen need them, our railroads need them, our untilled fields need them, and it would be a disgrace for us and our institutions if they were to be forcefully taken from us." The disgrace, however, is inevitable, for despite all the shouting the attorney general of South Carolina has declared that only the government of the United States can decide the fate of the Negroes; and the inhabitants of South Carolina have to live with the annoyance of having the expected booty disappear from before their very eyes and seeing it returned to Africa. Townsend, the captain of the *Putnam*, has been sent to Boston, his hometown, for an inquiry. According to the law, the crime he has committed is punishable by hanging at the gallows, and this case is as simple and self-evident as it can be; yet it would be strange if an American court were not to find extenuating circumstances. The proceedings against the rest of the crew will take place in Charleston; hence, they will certainly receive lenient treatment, and the comedy will end with a general acquittal.

Reverend Brownlow of Tennessee, who, as I reported earlier,[2] had announced a great crusade through the North in defense of slavery, has encountered in

Reverend Abraham Peyne of Philadelphia an opponent who has accepted his challenge to a public debate. It recently took place in that city, and, though wielding all the blunt and crude weapons of the slaveholding rabble, our bold champion of slavery was so severely trounced by his opponent—who is not even among the best speakers—that he declared at the end of the debate the people of the North did not sufficiently appreciate his reasoning. Instead of proceeding with his loudly proclaimed intention to visit all the cities of the North, he quickly returned to Tennessee, forswearing further discussion of this subject with any Northerner.

Notes

1. New York, October [1858], *Morgenblatt*, 52:45:1072–1075.

2. See Essay 28.

31

Revivals and Spiritualism[1]

* * *

As one might have expected, the "religious awakening" has disappeared as quickly as it sprung up. Like other epidemics that for a short time devastate an area and then move on, this dark cloud has passed over without leaving many visible traces. Only a few churches are continuing the daily hours of prayer until the shortage of visitors will sooner or later bring them to a blessed end. However, another excess of our time, spiritualism, has established itself and achieved the status of a kind of civil right. Its advocates have developed it into a formal system, a kind of natural philosophy, which would not be any more irrational and illogical than many another system of philosophy, were it not for its superstitious belief in ghosts. It is amazing that many otherwise rational people, who are much too well educated to follow any orthodox religious sect, are passionate supporters of spiritualism, swear by clairvoyants and other mediums, and are eager proselytizers. An astonishing number of books have been written on this subject, presenting, among a rational thought here and there, the most fantastic nonsense. A spiritualist once showed me among other things a book with a woodcut representing in a most edifying and instructive fashion the connection between the alleged world of ghosts and our own world: a long rope, held by various airborne creatures and hanging down into a house, where it was tied to a table surrounded by a company of ladies and gentlemen forming a so-called magnetic chain.

Sometimes it is really difficult to determine where honest stupidity, madness, and self-deception end and where fraud begins. One of the most recent conversions to which the spiritualists point with great pride is that of John Pierpont of Boston, a well-respected poet and historian, who was a Unitarian minister for most of his life but suddenly, at age seventy-three, has accepted spiritualism.[2] On his visit to New York, he related his experiences every day to a congregation of believers and told them the story of his conversion. He took great pains to show his audience that spiritualism and Christianity are completely compatible, and he tried to prove and explain the alleged miracles of the Bible in spiritualist terms. With evident relish, he brought up all the hackneyed stories of ghosts breaking tables, of invisible hands playing instruments, and of mediums who professed to read a person's character by merely touching his handwriting. No one doubted that the old man was perfectly honest and sincerely believed in telling the truth, but for the objective observer it was annoying and depressing to see a man with such intellectual advantages and with the respect and admiration of thousands live to become the willing victim of the crudest fraud in old age.

Notes

1. New York, November [1858], *Morgenblatt*, 52:48:1150–1152.

2. John Pierpont (1785–1866), a Unitarian minister and reformer, was the author of *Airs of Palestine and Other Poems* (1840) and *The Anti-Slavery Poems of John Pierpont* (1843). Minister of the Hollis Street Church in Boston (1819–1845), he was ousted for his controversial and freethinking views.

32

State and Congressional Elections—Slavery[1]

After several weeks of stormy weather, the wind has died down and a brighter sun is shining in the skies of politics than for many a year. State and congressional elections have just been completed with the result that the government and its party of slavery have been thoroughly routed in all but a few of the free states. Neither strenuous efforts on the part of the antislavery advocates nor the most convincing arguments by the best speakers could have done more to effect this spectacular exposure of the corruption of the Democratic party as well as its successful destruction than President Buchanan's actions in the course of the past year. If ever a man has been guilty of murdering himself and his party, he is foremost in the ranks of the suicidal. Even in the border states of the South, especially in Missouri and Maryland, a spirit of opposition to slavery is stirring among the whites who do not own slaves. It is based on neither a love for humanity nor a sense of justice but rather on selfishness, for the interests of the white laborer are all too obviously compromised by the competition of slave labor. White laborers are finally beginning to understand their own advantage, and since selfishness rules the masses, it is the most powerful and persuasive argument. They no longer feel obliged to be the spies, the jailers, and the bloodhounds for the slaveholders; at the same time, as information about the states of the North Star continues to spread among the slaves, there seem to be more and more opportunities for escape. The so-called underground railroad reaches well into Maryland, and the daily loss suffered by slaveholders from the escape of their slaves has fanned their long-standing excitement into flames of wrath that make them fight to the death in defense of their "peculiar institution."

Because juries, which usually are made up of people without slaves, do not always protect or acquit slaveholders for their reprehensible deeds inflicted on alleged abolitionists, the slave owners of the Eastern Shore of Maryland have found it necessary to call a convention to confer about better means of protecting their so-called property. What particularly concerns them is that the perpetrators of the crimes against Bowers, a Quaker, are likely to be severely punished.[2] The convention took place a few days ago, but in spite of their bragging words the worthy knights of the South seemed reluctant to fight the nonslaveholding part of the population, turning their wrath instead against the helpless class of free colored people. They accused them of fomenting among the slaves a general discontent with their fortunate condition and of helping them to escape—as if the passionate longing for freedom and the consciousness of the right to freedom were not a fully developed idea in the mind and a deeply rooted passion in the heart of every slave in the Georgia rice fields and the sugar plantations of Alabama even without any intervention by abolitionists.

The free colored people of Maryland number almost 80,000, and many of them are closely related to the so-called aristocracy, because regardless of all the alleged color prejudice there are few slave owners who do not have one or more colored children. It is this class of people at which the greed of the slave owners is aimed: they have devised a plan that is so barbaric, cruel, and dastardly that its mere mention would cause a common cry of indignation in any civilized country. They decided unanimously to submit to the next legislature a proposal to end "free negrodom," as they call it, giving those 80,000 colored people the choice between becoming slaves or leaving the state. The question now is what the legislature will do: will the representatives of a population of 500,000 be so abject and dishonorable to violate all laws of humanity and justice and act even against their own self-interest by becoming the willing serfs and tools of 16,000 little tyrants?

* * *

Notes

1. New York, November [1858], *Morgenblatt*, 52:52:1240–1242.

2. See Essay 29.

33

New Efforts to Colonize the Negroes[1]

* * *

In addition to the already existing Colonization Society, whose purpose it is to settle Liberia with black emigrants, there is now a new society, "The African Colonization Society," for the colonization of Yoruba in the interior of Africa. Both Negroes and whites are in the leadership of this organization. They praise Yoruba's climate, which is well suited for growing cotton. It is quite possible that hard-working, skilled workers will be able to make a living there, but the members of this society are greatly in error when they say that their plan will contribute anything at all to the abolition of slavery. Quite to the contrary, the abolitionist movement will only be weakened by losing people who would otherwise dedicate their abilities and energies more effectively to the emancipation and progress of the colored race in the United States. Liberia has already done great damage in this regard, in that men who would have exerted a significant influence here have done little or nothing over there toward the progress of their people. That has been the exact purpose of the first and still existing colonization society—an organization that has counted among its members many slaveholders and had its origin not in a humanitarian or altruistic concern for the black race but in serving the interests of the slaveholders. Its goal has never been the intellectual, moral, and social uplift of the Negroes but the removal of the free colored people, who have always been a thorn in the flesh of the slaveholders. They hate and fear the educated, skilled, and capable among the colored people with a special passion, and since they cannot harm them in any other fashion, they do everything possible to get them to emigrate and thereby to eliminate them as a threat to the "peculiar institution." As soon as a colored person distinguishes himself intellectually or practically, thereby proving baseless any idea that Negroes are a primitive and ignorant race, every effort is made to persuade him that in Africa—or, heaven knows, some other country—he can achieve greater things and have greater latitude for his actions.

The members of the new colonization society argue that slavery will vanish if only the price of cotton can be forced down so far that its production becomes uneconomical, and they believe that this can be achieved by growing cotton in Yoruba. But that is also a mistake because slave owners do not use their slaves only for growing cotton; they also employ them in the production of corn, rice, tobacco, hemp, and sugar. Should cotton not yield enough profit, the slaveholders would not run away from their slaves, as the colonizationists would like to believe, but occupy them with some other kind of labor. Incidentally, the whole colonization scheme is not well received among the Negroes themselves. The simpler classes among them, the uneducated and ignorant, are by nature loyal to the soil they till; and those who are informed and think for themselves are definitely opposed because they are perceptive enough to see that the enterprise is a failure in respect to the abolition of slavery. Frederick Douglass, the famous colored orator, is one of the most outspoken opponents of this project. Even its supporters, despite their attacks on him, cannot deny that this excellent man, on the basis of his work and his personality, has achieved more for the abolition movement and in the fight against color prejudice than all those who have emigrated to Liberia.

Meanwhile the southern states threaten more seriously than ever with reintroducing the African slave trade, and there are even rumors that a ship's load of Negroes recently arrived in Georgia. A similarly disgraceful and criminal kind of slave trade is secretly being conducted out of New York, as became evident in a recent case that happened to be uncovered. An intelligent colored youth was accosted in the harbor by a so-called runner, who told him such tales of the pleasures of a sailor's life that he persuaded the boy to try a short voyage on board a ship that was about to sail for Liverpool. The runner took him to an office where he was signed on. Meanwhile, his mother had received a note for half of his wages, but when she went to cash it, it was discovered to be a forgery and payment was declined. The mother immediately became suspicious and turned to the mayor. He called in the harbor police and they boarded the vessel. The whole crew was ordered to appear on deck, and it turned out that all but the captain and the helmsmen were colored boys. None of them had employment papers, and the ship turned out not to be bound for Liverpool but to leave for Mobile the following day, where the boys were surely to be sold as slaves. The sergeant of the harbor police said on this occasion that he has often seen ships with black crews depart for southern ports and that none of those blacks has ever returned. There is nothing one can add to such horrors but to ask in vain: "How much more, how much more of this?"

* * *

Notes

1. New York, December [1858], *Morgenblatt*, 53:5:115–118 (1859).

34

Democrats Congratulated[1]

* * *

Among the official and semiofficial notabilities who had to endure the gauntlet of well-wishers at a New Year's reception were two of the chief Democrats: Orr, the current Speaker of the House of Representatives, and Senator Douglas, the author of the Nebraska Bill[2]—who is not to be confused with the famous colored orator, Frederick Douglass, whom I have frequently mentioned before. This procedure, by which the city proves its hospitality to some person of political note, is one of the most exhausting ceremonies that go with public office. Several days prior to the event the papers carry notices that New York has decided to offer the honorable Such-and-such the city's greetings and that he is requested to appear in City Hall on December 30 or 31 (New Year's Day being already filled with such ceremonies) to receive the good wishes of his friends. One or more representatives of the city (the mayor or the aldermen) then receive and address the person so honored, whereupon the whole lot of so-called political friends parades past—all those who are dreaming of a public appointment and hope to have it come within reach through the influence of some important man, and all those charming hangers-on who, like street urchins, are present wherever they can shout their hurrahs. One after another clutches the dignitary's hand, shaking it ponderously and vigorously; they exchange an endless series of "How do you do?" and "Very glad to see you!" and then they move on to make room for the next person in line. At best, a dinner follows the reception and, later in the evening, a serenade, which obliges the honored guest to give a speech from a balcony or a window.

Orr, from South Carolina, belongs to the party of the so-called Southern "fire-eaters," who immediately threaten with the dissolution of the Union whenever the North makes the slightest attempt to put an end to the South's presumptuousness and tyranny. For this reason he has little or no support even among northern Democrats; he finds no sympathizers among them, and the formal reception turned out to be so unimpressive that even the Democratic press had nothing special to report. It is a different matter with Douglas, the true representative of the northern Democrats at this time and generally and openly mentioned as the candidate for the presidency at the next election. There is no doubt that Douglas is a man of impressive intellect. He is a keen observer of political conditions and their consequences and cleverly uses them for his own political purposes. As a speaker he knows how to be persuasive and make his audience accept ideas, in which he himself does not believe. His reasoning, logic, and strategy are brilliant, but he fails to arouse people's passions because he lacks enthusiasm, warmth, and conviction. One never can predict what position he will take because it depends largely on the turn of events. No matter how far he will go, Douglas will never have more than passing distinction—in so far as distinction rests on honesty, firmness of conviction, and a broad humanity. He is not a man of noble character; his only purpose is to satisfy his ambition. If, unlike so many others, he is not susceptible to the lure of money or the promise of office, it is not because of his sense of honesty but due to his correct understanding that he can achieve his goal more safely being incorruptible than by means of these crude devices. Despite all assertions to the contrary, bribery has always undermined the political careers of those who tried to build them on such shaky foundations.

With Douglas, intelligence and calculation take the place of geniality. He is fundamentally contemptuous of people in general and considers them only good enough to serve as rungs on the ladder of his ambition. While it is part of his politics to woo the crude and common elements of the sovereign masses by appealing to their color prejudice, greed, vanity, and selfishness, the very sovereign rabble whose favor he is seeking hardly realizes that he treats them with the same contempt as he has for the "niggers" he never fails to mention with scornful purpose in his speeches. He would not hesitate for a moment to kick his dear friends and fellow citizens if by doing so he could benefit himself. Withal, it cannot be denied that "the little giant"—as Douglas is often called because of his small and unremarkable appearance—is currently enjoying great popularity among Democrats in the North. He is their man because he personifies their own cold heartlessness and greed, their selfishness, their calculating "smartness."

I must take this occasion to guard against the possibility that I may be suspected of attacking what in Europe is meant by a "democrat." Originally the word had the same meaning over here, but it has become debased and now refers to a member of a party that, while freely throwing around such terms as "popular sovereignty" and "liberty and equality," cancels out both liberty and equality by adding "for whites only." It is the party not of "democracy" but of a "slavocracy" that tramples liberty and human rights, grinding them into the dust. Unfortunately one has to admit that many Germans living here—even those belonging to the so-called educated class—are not beneath calling themselves "democrats" and, much to the disgrace of their home country, defend slavery, talk vaguely of the Negroes' lack of intelligence (though they may never have talked with any of them), and at election time vote for the "cotton ticket." Perhaps one may excuse the American who maintains a prejudice with which he was born and brought up or who succumbs to the temptations of appointment to lucrative office, which is enough to cause the fall of anyone lacking strength of character. Such temptations, however, do not exist for the foreigner, or they occur only in such rare situations that they can be discounted. He knows very well that any shameless concessions he makes in this respect carry no reward; he must forswear all principles of law, justice, and humanity with which he was brought up and purposely assume a kind of dastardly demeanor that, repugnant to all fair-minded observers, is rooted in an abyss of meanness and brutality.

I am not speaking of those innocent, irrational persons who, lacking the courage of independent thought and opinion, simply repeat the ideas they hear from others or read in the *Newyorker Staatszeitung*. I am referring to the kind who pride themselves on their education and knowledge and try to rationalize their contemptible views on physiological, economic, and social grounds. But it must be said that these excesses on the part of the German population are the exception; wherever Germans are numerous enough to exert political influence—as in Missouri and other western states—they strongly oppose all excesses and encroachments of the "slavocracy."

* * *

Notes

1. New York, January [1859], *Morgenblatt*, 53:9:214–216.

2. James L. Orr (1822–1873), a vocal secessionist from South Carolina, was a member of Congress (1849–1859) and speaker of the House (1857–1859). Stephen A. Douglas (1813–1861), senator from Illinois, was the principal architect of the Kansas-Nebraska Act (1854).

35

Cuba—Public Lectures—Mount Vernon— Buying a Slave's Freedom[1]

The project of purchasing or possibly conquering Cuba has already been heard of and commented on in Europe. Of all the ridiculous farces that have ever been staged by men in office at the expense of the military this is one of the most ridiculous and farcical. Anyone with a passing familiarity of the situation knows that the present excitement is all about a project that, for the moment at least, is as utopian as a plan for conquering the moon. A close observer will find that the originators and passionate supporters of this intended armed robbery are as unable to look each other honestly in the eye as were the Roman augurs at the time when the old gods with all their omens, oracles, and attendant tricks had become discredited. Everyone knows that Spain has not the least intention of agreeing to such a deal and, in fact, regards the mere mention of it as an insult; and it is also well known that England and France would immediately stop any attempted crusade by the knights of the South. The truth behind this grandiose scheme of humbug is nothing other than a request for an appropriation of 30 million dollars by Congress for the putative purpose of easing the negotiations with Spain—in other words, to bribe the Spanish minister—which our most honorable president, however, may use for internal bribes and other praiseworthy purposes, such as the support and encouragement of proslavery propaganda. Meanwhile, the scheme for conquering Cuba will be used as bait during the election and at other occasions, playing on the patriotic vanities and acquisitive instincts of the ignorant masses.

Some members of the southern knighthood from the sugar and cotton states who grew up under the blessings of the "peculiar institution" are as limited in their understanding of present conditions as the French nobility of the *ancien régime* was at the outbreak of the French Revolution. They are probably alone in accepting the farce at face value: blissfully convinced of the invincibility of the United States, they consider the occupation of Cuba a distinct possibility even in the face of England's and France's opposition. The general ignorance and lack of familiarity with European languages (even French) among these honorable knights of the whip, who occupy virtually all ambassadorial positions under the current administration, is chiefly responsible for bringing American education into disrepute abroad, which, given the quality of such representatives, is only too well founded. Meanwhile, a member of Congress from the North was moved to state that among all the envoys representing the United States, the ambassador to the English throne is the only one capable of communicating in the local language.

The current season in New York could be called the season of public lectures. Scholarly, literary, and social clubs are offering lectures, for which they hire the best speakers far and wide. For as little as 25 cents admission they are open to all, but the number of organizations that offer either single lectures or courses of six to eight lectures with their own speakers is even greater. There is no subject of general interest that is not discussed at one or the other of these lectures. History, literature, personalities, art, political and social questions are introduced and often presented by able men with so much intelligence and skill that one can say without exaggeration that these lectures are the place where the intellectual life and the progressive development of the nation are finding their expression. One of the most outstanding and attractive lectures offered throughout the season—in fact, one of the best I have ever heard—was Wendell Phillips's on Toussaint l'Ouverture. It was a lively and accurate account of the great man and, at the same time, a brilliant vindication of the black race, which has found in Wendell Phillips its greatest and noblest defender. He combines the most accomplished style of oratory with the most passionate enthusiasm for a cause for whose sake he has resisted all temptations of political life and easy popularity. The impression he gives on the platform is something wonderful. The fire of commitment and conviction that transforms his being and glows in every word is joined with the utmost external serenity, appearing even mightier and more powerful because of the contrast. Without any trace of histrionic pathos, without the least gesticulation, even without as much as a gesture of his hands, he spoke for a full hour without either manuscript or outline in front of him; yet he never misspoke or stumbled, and no repetition of the same sentence disturbed the harmony of his lecture.

Another kind of lectures that have become very fashionable this winter are the readings of Shakespearean plays. Fanny Kemble (now Mrs. Butler), the daughter of the famous Charles Kemble, who withdrew into private life many years ago, offered her readings again to the public during the previous winter season and was so successful that she presented another cycle this year. However, anyone who has seen Shakespeare's plays on the best German stages and still has a clear memory of the brilliant performances of those great artists cannot be satisfied with Fanny Kemble's renderings of these immortal works. It is all but impossible to find a solution for so difficult a task. If an actor succeeds in fully rendering only *one* of Shakespeare's characters in the course of an evening, it is as much as anyone could wish or expect; it usually requires the complete engagement of the artist's creative and physical powers. Thus, it seems inevitable that a nuanced representation of characters must suffer when even a talented actor has to carry the burden by himself. To make matters worse, Fanny Kemble brings to her task so much exaggerated pathos, so much cheap showmanship, affectation, and mannerism—in short, so much of the stereotypical stage manner that has been sweeping the English stage for a long time—that the naturalness and humanity of Shakespeare's characters are largely lost: instead of real human beings with feelings, we see crazed and raving figures. With the American public, whose theater is still on a low level of development, whose understanding of the arts is just beginning, and whose judgment in these matters still lacks confidence, such an aberration of taste has its admirers. In fact, Fanny Kemble was very popular—it is said that she earned 7,000 dollars with her lectures during the past two winter seasons—and so many copied her act that "Shakespeare readings" are now all the rage. Lyrical, epic, and even prose works are exploited for this purpose, more for the profit and edification of the presenter than of the audience. For the entertainment of the orthodox, someone has been found who will every Sunday offer for public consumption—and for his own profit—readings of religious poems and similar soul-saving concoctions.

For some time there has been much talk and concern about a "Mount Vernon Association," for the collection of voluntary contributions from the American people to establish a fund large enough to buy Mount Vernon, Washington's residence and place of burial, from its present owner, John Washington, a distant relative of the general, and make it the property of the nation. Balls, concerts, dinners, and lectures are therefore held for the benefit of the Mount Vernon Fund, and those in search of entertainment can dance, eat, and amuse themselves with the satisfying feeling of having contributed to an important national project. The only one who will reap a benefit from the purchase of Mount Vernon, however, is said John Washington, a good-for-nothing slaveholder in financial straits, who has made a name for himself by the rewards he has advertised in southern papers for catching his fugitive slaves. This flirtation with the memory and the bones of Washington, disagreeable as it is in principle, would be tolerable if those who are supporting the plan most eagerly and are trying to focus attention on themselves were to demonstrate at least the basic beliefs and opinions of the noble, although hardly ingenious, man. In light of the corruption and the undisguised mockery of the principle of liberty and equality that tend to turn the Declaration of Independence into nothing but a paper lie, this entire Washington and Mount Vernon game appears little more than a disgusting and sophisticated act of hypocrisy. In light of the efforts that are made for the extension and the eternal continuation of slavery, which have recently even taken the form of southerners in Congress moving the reactivation of the African slave trade, it is a cheap attempt to buy out our obligations to the living.

The call for purchasing the freedom of the Negro Bob Butt and his family stands in sharp contrast to this worship of dead relics. In 1855, during an unusually virulent outbreak of yellow fever, Butt performed a significant service to the inhabitants of Portsmouth, Virginia. As doctors, nurses, and others attending to the dead perished in large numbers, as people died in the streets and their bodies remained till the next day, as there were no more coffins for the dead, Butt showed unparalleled activity and endurance as a grave digger. Tirelessly and without himself succumbing to the infection, he worked day and night, accomplishing more by himself than all of his white helpers put together. They died one after the other, while he buried more than a thousand victims of the epidemic. At that time it became known that the inhabitants of Portsmouth wanted to purchase his freedom, but three years have gone by without success in collecting the necessary amount. His master gave him "generous" permission to travel to Philadelphia on his word of honor to attend the official burial of the doctors and nurses who had left Philadelphia to assist with the Portsmouth epidemic but became its victims, which proves that there is always more money available for the dead than for the living—especially if they happen to be black. An appeal for funds was made on that occasion, but even now the collection is proceeding slowly with only small amounts; and if Bob Butt and his family ever obtain their freedom, it will be due not so much to his fellow citizens at home as to the gifts from abolitionists of the North.

* * *

Notes

1. New York, February [1859], *Morgenblatt*, 53:14:332–335.

36

A Fashionable Preacher[1]

* * *

As often happens, the last thing one gets to know lies just around the corner; so it was that I recently heard my first lecture by the famous Henry Ward Beecher, the brother of Harriet Beecher Stowe and one of the celebrities of New York, or rather Brooklyn, where he is employed as a preacher at one of the most fashionable churches, gathering around him crowds of admirers every Sunday. By reputation Beecher is one of the great orators of this country, yet I did not find him more than one of those celebrities who lose their aura and shrink down to mere mediocrity if they are examined in the light of objective criticism. Beecher is not a man who dominates and reforms his times and environment, as his admirers claim; quite to the contrary, he is their product because he accommodates himself to them, makes concessions, and carefully avoids confronting them too harshly. He knows that his influence and success depend on the masses and therefore pulls every conceivable lever to gain the applause of the many-headed monster. He knows that pointless piety or impractical orthodoxy are tiresome and do not trigger popularity with today's public. He therefore dispenses moral aphorisms and rules of conduct, attempting to harmonize religion and common sense; in that, he seems successful, as he does not lower himself to the point where the two essentially conflict with each other.

Beecher knows the intellectual lethargy of the masses; he knows that they hate nothing more than to be shaken out of their mental torpor and asked to think for themselves. Thus he manages to offer his ideas attractively and tidily wrapped and packaged so that one can comfortably accept them without danger of being challenged by some unpleasant truth forcing one into irksome reflection. It is no wonder, then, that Beecher is at bottom a man of the general run of people, especially since he is clever enough to make religion amusing by peppering his sermons and speeches with anecdotes and jokes that, although mostly rather elementary, never fail to elicit hearty laughter. He uses language with great skill; but he falls short of being a great orator by lacking naturalness and simplicity. His craving for applause seduces him into cheap showmanship of the kind one finds all too much on the stage. He changes from a normal conversational tone to shouting pathos and back again without the least relevance to the substance. If one speaks quietly of a cup of coffee, why go into ecstasy about the accompanying piece of cake?

Beecher's appearance is neither noble nor attractive; besides a certain sensuousness, it somehow expresses a material rather than a higher kind of intelligence. His malleability in respect to the inclinations and prejudices of the masses was demonstrated particularly during the time of the "religious awakening." Although himself far too enlightened not to recognize this nonsense for what it was, he not only conducted meetings himself, but preached against Theodore Parker, who—in a very different manner—openly and decisively analyzed the deplorable state of affairs and condemned its hypocrisy, unconcerned about public opinion.

There is no gainsaying the fact that Beecher's method is very effective and productive of a rich harvest for himself: he nicely supports moderate reform, and it has made him a wealthy man. A pew of four or five seats costs as much as renting an elegant apartment in Germany, and each of his weekly lectures during the winter brings him one hundred dollars. One has to concede, however, that in regard to slavery Beecher has not been guilty of compromise, and he has done much good. On the other hand, it is evident that in a free state and a decidedly abolitionist parish it does not take much heroism or self-denial to be an abolitionist.

* * *

Notes

1. New York, April [1859], *Morgenblatt*, 53:22:526–528.

37

Anniversaries[1]

***

The "anniversaries" of all benevolent and not so benevolent associations, regularly taking place during the second week of May, are over; as usual, they were the occasion of a few good speeches and a lot of drivel. Most conspicuous among all those that is bad and disgraceful was again the American Tract Society, an organization in which the worst hypocrites, toadies, lickspittles, and mystifiers of the entire country fraternize in order to circulate their silly and tasteless little tracts that serve no other purpose than to stultify the people. I mentioned a year ago that this excellent society had followed Tartuffe's council and made an arrangement with heaven when it resolved to condemn all the little errors and sins that man is heir to as well as some of his innocent pleasures, but prudently refrained from any criticism of slavery so as not to offend its Christian benefactors in the South and to keep them from withdrawing their dues—the ill-gotten gains of slave labor.

That procedure had caused a good deal of comment in the North at the time, and those who still had an iota of faith in the honesty of these professional religionists were anxiously awaiting this year's discussions. Indeed, a few men of conscience rose to support a petition that the society condemn the African slave trade, which has recently sprung up again in the deepest South. They also recommended that the society award prizes for the best tracts written in opposition to the renewed slave trade, which the law may define as a capital crime but all relevant government agencies quietly protect and promote. But the mere attempt of the first among the opponents of slavery to be heard caused such a tumultuous outbreak of rage on the part of this most honorable and blessed gathering that you might have thought you were at a brawl in an Irish bar that would soon lead to punching and stabbing. The pious gentlemen were, indeed, on the brink of fisticuffs, and screaming, yelling, stamping, and hissing drowned out every effort by the antislavery group. Only after much resistance and persistent demands from the audience were they permitted to present their petitions. However, the eminent leaders of the organization immediately took the occasion to outdo themselves in praise of the beneficent influence of slavery in the South and to deny the members any right to give instructions to the executive committee. In the end, the previous year's resolutions were readopted for the current year by a large majority so that the pious Christians of the South would not have to fear any rough treatment from this quarter.

When all is said and done, one should be glad for this outcome, since it is self-evident how effective tracts are likely to be in fighting the slave trade; such edifying spectacles, on the other hand, provide a brilliant demonstration of the doings of the party of orthodoxy and duly discredit its efforts and purposes.

Notes

1. New York, May [1859], *Morgenblatt*, 53:25:593–596.

38

Slave Trade—Hatred of America[1]

Two years ago, when the Supreme Court of the United States proclaimed its famous, hitherto unheard-of decision that Negroes have no rights that any white person is obliged to respect,[2] our noble president, the obedient servant and supporter of the "slavocracy," was intent on using every fraudulent and violent measure to force slavery on the unwilling people of Kansas. Even at that time there were prophets who predicted that the reintroduction of the African slave trade would be the point of culmination in a chain of despicable and criminal acts with which the ruling party has built itself a lasting monument of shame for present and future generations. However, even the opponents of the present system ridiculed them as visionaries, fanatics, prophets of doom, and pessimists, pointing out that it would be impossible to get such a measure passed by Congress, since the representatives of the free states—regardless of party affiliation—and even the slaveholders of the middle states (Maryland, Virginia, Kentucky, and Tennessee) would all vote against it. But in this country of lyncherdom and vigilantism the consent of Congress was dispensable. At the very time when southern legislatures are discussing the question whether the reintroduction of the African slave trade would be legitimate and desirable, it is carried on by enterprising individuals, contrary to all laws and under the very eyes of southern state governments, as openly as off the slave coast of Africa.

Since the African slave trade became illegal, the southern slave market has been exclusively supplied by the rich slaveholders of the middle states who breed slaves especially for this purpose. With rising sugar, rice, and cotton production the demand for field hands has increased every year, yet the domestic slave population has not grown correspondingly. Hence, prices for slaves have gone up so steeply during the last few years that a strong Negro man brings on average at least one thousand and usually eleven or twelve hundred dollars. This explains why pious slave breeders from Virginia and Maryland scream in moral indignation about the possibility of having heathen barbarians get a share of the business, thereby depressing the price of human property by as much as three quarters. Under these conditions the ownership of slaves has become a privilege of the wealthy few.

Just as the northerner aspires to property, so the southerner covets in particular the ownership of slaves, which he considers the only true source of status, influence, and respectability, differentiating the man of social standing from the "poor white trash." The possibility of buying Negroes for three or four hundred dollars is, therefore, sufficient to drive the majority of southerners to the point of madness and, in the pursuit of this goal, to make them flaunt all laws and punishments. A few months ago, the yacht *Wanderer,* with a cargo of more than three hundred Negroes, docked in the harbor of Savannah (Georgia). They were unloaded and immediately distributed to the interior of the country—not of course without the knowledge and permission of the government, since it is obvious that three hundred Negroes from Africa cannot be smuggled ashore like a small casket of jewels and that the entire operation could be managed only by a conspiracy between local and federal government officials. Nevertheless it proved impossible to stop rumors from reaching the public and to keep the press around the country from taking on this issue and spreading it everywhere.

For better or for worse, it was necessary to keep up enough of a pretense of legality to launch a nominal investigation into the matter, making sure, however, not to consider the imported Negroes themselves as irrefutable evidence. A few of them, who were found in the possession of a slave trader and subsequently arrested by some honest official doing his duty in spite of all suggestions to the contrary, were released for some transparent reason and returned to the person in question. But the yacht, which bore the undeniable signs of having served its nefarious purpose, was not so easily disposed of. It was sold at public auction, an occasion that once again brought out a general atmosphere strongly supportive of the slave trade. When Charles Lamar, who is generally considered to be the owner and operator of the yacht and has been repeatedly engaged in the slave trade with Cuba, appeared as one of the potential purchasers, all the others who had expressed an interest immediately withdrew, leaving the vessel to him at about one-tenth of its worth. Only one person dared to bid against him—it is said for reasons of personal enmity—thereby driving up the price by a small amount, which so incensed Lamar that he struck down his opponent with a single blow before anyone in the crowd could intervene.

Corrie, the captain of the slave ship, was treated with even greater consideration. Although trading in slaves is legally equivalent to piracy, which is punishable by death, the grand jury said in its report that it was unwilling to indict so exemplary a citizen whose actions were prompted only by his concern for the public welfare. Afterwards, however, they realized that they had not done their man a favor because, having been initially arrested in South Carolina, he was subject to being tried there if Georgia did nothing to satisfy the letter of the law. Thus they petitioned to reconsider the decision and actually handed up an indictment, which will of course be followed by a sham trial and an acquittal.

Captain Townsend of the slave ship *Echo*, who was caught red-handed (as I reported earlier), had to be taken from Boston, where he would not have received such gentle treatment, to Charleston because that is where he was put on shore after his arrest. This change of venue to a southern court that had already acquitted the crew of the *Echo* guaranteed that the captain would go unpunished, and indeed he was acquitted just a few days ago. In light of the tangible and persuasive evidence this may seem strange, but there is probably no judge throughout the South who would not be inventive and shameless enough to discover some saving legal loophole in such cases. The clever judge—Marvin is His Honor's name—finding that the fully certified papers did not conclusively establish that the ship was the property of an American citizen, promptly dismissed the case.

Such acquittals prove once and for all that the laws against the slave trade will never be effective under present conditions in the South. A society for the general "encouragement" of this pretty enterprise has already sprung up; its members are offering prizes for Negroes imported from Africa, and a few days ago it was reported that in Texas a ship's load of them was offered for sale.

Considering the totality of circumstances as they present themselves right now, it is difficult to see how an improvement in the situation might be brought about without some crisis—some violent revolt—were it not that in recent years the true core of the people of the North had decidedly declared themselves opposed to the prevailing evils and already begun the battle against them: the hopeless degradation and corruption of the entire South; the venality, selfishness, and injustice with which almost all classes of society have been more or less infected; the daily increase in crimes; and the religious hypocrisy of thousands of priests of all sects who are driven by selfishness in their efforts to curtail light, knowledge, and humanitarianism—in short, to snuff out all those elements that would put an end to their influence. These healthy elements are undeniably at work, and only a blind, one-sided hatred of America would try to argue them away.

I must take this occasion to comment on that savage, bitter hatred of America which has appeared in the columns of many a German newspaper trying to represent this entire continent as nothing better than a den of murderers. Instead of being based on actual circumstances—as unpleasant as they may be—these accounts derive from personal misfortunes. All the dark sides are put together to make a somber picture, and the painter, who has the best intentions of offering an accurate description, is unaware that discouragement and pessimism resulting from disappointed expectations have prevented him from seeing the brighter side of things. It is a fact proven almost daily that the ability to become completely assimilated into a new part of the world and to become fluent in its language diminishes more and more with advancing age. Many a witty, educated man who held a position of honor and respect in Germany finds himself over here, perhaps against his personal inclination, driven by the storms of politics or other unfortunate conditions, confronted with the problem of finding new paths at a mature age. His mind no longer has the elasticity of youth necessary for adapting to new conditions, leaving the past behind, and finding new employment. Because he cannot find anything here, neither in the material nor in the intellectual sphere, that might compensate him for what he left behind, he instinctively blames the country and its people rather than himself for his disgruntlement, thus falling into truly ridiculous extremes.

I have a friend, rational and intelligent with the exception of this particular point, who composed his hate-filled articles for the benefit of the German press in one of the most exclusively German corners of New York. His knowledge of American conditions was entirely derived from books, newspapers, and his own observations of life in the streets. He had never tried to acquaint himself with social life, which he claimed was too tiresome and, furthermore, would have required of him the effort to become fluent in English, which he did not think worth his while.

He also refused to listen to some of the acclaimed public speakers, visit meetings or institutions dedicated to scientific, artistic, or benevolent purposes, or generally get to know any aspect of particular American conditions from personal observation. According to him, he could get all that from books and papers. For many years he lived in a dark, stuffy street in the lower part of the city, occupying a room in an exclusively German hotel used mostly by immigrants of better means.

As he is a sociable person with a ready treasure of entertaining and amusing stories, many guests would gather around him, and the new arrivals would praise their good fortune to have met a man whose experience and knowledge of the country they believed to be of great service to them. Every night they would discuss the dark and bright sides of American conditions, and my friend delighted in painting such a picture of horror and mayhem—telling all the cases of poisoning, murder, robbery, fraud, bribery, railroad accidents, and steamboat explosions that had occurred in the course of the year—that his poor listeners could neither see nor hear straight: a rowdy was crouching on every street corner; everyone brushing them in passing was a pickpocket; they could not buy anything without being duped and cheated; if they took a railroad, chances were ten to one that they would be either killed or maimed or at least loose their luggage, not to mention having to pay twice the regular fare. If anyone dared to raise some doubts, he would take a newspaper and read to them the reports of all the accidents and crimes that had happened in recent days in the entire United States from Maine to New Orleans, from the Atlantic coast to California. The people hardly ventured outside the hotel and believed it to be a special favor of heaven not to be murdered or robbed on their first walks in New York.

His talent in painting these pictures of horror was such that more than one individual who had come here well equipped to begin a successful life panicked and took the next steamer back to Germany without ever trying his luck. Preferring the vicissitudes and the expense of the voyage, they thanked their lucky stars for having seen no more than the downtown German hotel, the *Newyorker Staatszeitung*, and the well-meaning gentleman whose counsel saved them from perdition.

* * *

Notes

1. New York, June [1859], *Morgenblatt*, 53:28:671–672 and 53:29:693–695.

2. The Dred Scott case of 1857.

39

A Visit with Gerrit Smith[1]

Gerrit Smith is one of the most outstanding among the determined abolitionists who will not brook any compromise with slavery and will not take cowardly satisfaction in its restriction to the states where it already exists. They believe the health of the country depends on the unconditional eradication of slavery. He belongs to the side calling itself the "National Abolitionists," who abide by the Constitution and believe that neither the letter nor the spirit of the Constitution contain any justification of slavery. The "Disunionists," on the other hand, claim that the Constitution and the Union are the very foundation on which slavery is built.

Gerrit Smith's whole life has been dedicated to the cause of Negro emancipation. A descendant of one of the wealthiest families of Dutch settlers, he belongs to the old New York aristocracy, in so far as there is such a thing. Born into slave ownership, he had every opportunity to learn about—and to learn to despise—the horrors that are inherent in even the so-called "mildest" form of slavery. Among all those who write and speak out against slavery, he is one of the few who have actually purchased the freedom of slaves. Generosity and benevolence are among the most visible characteristics of this excellent man; they define his true greatness and, in happy combination with his great wealth, provide him the means with which to realize his humane ideas and plans. He has made gifts of many acres of land to poor workmen, both white and black, and donated a thousand dollars a month to the free-soil settlers in Kansas who had been robbed and plundered by the Missouri gangs. The antislavery society of which he is the president has received six thousand dollars from him over two years. One case that is a particularly good illustration of his active benevolence is of sufficient interest even for the German reader to be repeated here.

About one and a half years ago, a few miles distant from Peterboro, Gerrit Smith's hometown near the center of New York State, an eighty-year-old man was found in his own barn with all the signs of having been murdered. Gerrit Smith later proved the possibility that the old man had fallen while trying to hitch up his horse, that he had gotten tangled in the harness and been killed by the animal as it was kicking wildly trying to get free. Although money and other objects were found untouched, the local people were immediately convinced that a murder had occurred, and their suspicion just as quickly focused on a poor German laborer, the last person to be seen in the company of the deceased, with whom he had daily intercourse sawing wood and doing other occasional chores. Traces of blood supposedly adhering to his axe seemed to prove the crime, and the fact that he had cut off the tails of his coat was equally suspicious. All this seemed so compelling and conclusive that the man was arrested and charged; and that was the situation when it came to Gerrit Smith's attention.

Learning that the accused hardly understood a word of English and had no one nearby with whom he could speak, Smith decided to look him up, believing that his own limited knowledge of German might be of some use. Even on first sight the man made a favorable impression, which on later visits grew into a conviction of his innocence, persuading Smith to take the case. At his own expense he brought in witnesses from other towns whose testimony he considered important, and even though he had not argued a case in court for many years, he assumed the role of defense attorney. Yet the general public was so convinced that only this man could be the murderer that despite Gerrit Smith's appearance, which should have weighed heavily in favor of the accused, the jury could not agree on a verdict and a new jury had to be called. Gerrit Smith spoke again, pointing to the contradictions in the witnesses' testimony and proving that the accused could not possibly in the time given (about twenty minutes) have committed the murder, let alone washed and ironed his clothes. He also showed that the accused often suffered from nose bleeds, which may have caused the traces of blood on his axe, and that the coattails, having been found among his belongings, had been cut only to repair the upper part of the coat. Finally he had the satisfaction to see his charge acquitted, although no one doubted a guilty verdict. Smith took him home to Peterboro, gave him a house to live in, and has been employing him ever since on one of his farms.

In 1853–1854 Gerrit Smith was a member of Congress and fought steadfastly against slavery among all the half-hearted compromisers. His speeches, which have been collected in a published volume, are distinguished by clarity of logical argument and polished, effective style. Their basic tenor is a genuine, true humanitarianism pervading them like a warm breeze, a humanitarianism without the least trace of that narrow local chauvinism which displays itself throughout the world as patriotism. Among all the members of Congress, few, if any, are his equal in knowledge of the laws and conditions of this country. However, the hustle and bustle of Washington did not suit him, and at the end of the term he informed his constituents that he had decided to withdraw into private life.

This past summer I made Gerrit Smith's acquaintance at the house of my friend Frederick Douglass, the excellent and famous mulatto whom I have mentioned earlier in these writings. Holding the highest esteem and warm friendship for Douglass, Smith visited him on his way through Rochester. His tall, strong figure of above average height lends him an imposing presence; his features are noble and regular. His fresh and healthy complexion as well as his supple and lively movements make him appear younger than his sixty-two years despite a long gray beard. His voice, an unusually deep, sonorous bass, must have a mighty effect in large halls filled with listeners. A meeting under circumstances where common sympathies and convictions brought us together was the beginning of a more intense relationship than is normally the case under other conditions, and he invited me to visit Peterboro on my way back to New York.

In Canastoga, the station where one gets off the train, several ladies approached me, one of them in Bloomers, introducing herself as Mrs. Miller, Gerrit Smith's daughter. In Germany one associates this style of clothing with the idea of an emancipated woman in the most spiteful sense of the term: a person who insists on casually smoking cigars, does not know how to ply a sewing needle, is relentlessly forward, respects nothing, and above all has to attract attention. Americans are more tolerant and do not take offense when women who cannot be charged by even the most hairsplitting moral judge wear the short Bloomer costume in order to spare themselves the inconvenience caused by long, wide dresses, especially in the country. They can move much better on unpaved roads and in the mountains, though at the cost of beauty and elegance, concepts from which we are at present unable to free ourselves. If, incidentally, grace and charm are capable of improving one's clothes, Mrs. Miller can surely reconcile anyone to the Bloomer costume.

Peterboro lies at a ten miles' distance from the railroad in the midst of lovely hills that offer the prettiest views along the way. The state of New York is generally rich in natural beauty, which in its wealth and variety in a relatively small area can hardly be matched. From the Bay of New York and the Hudson, with its magnificent shores beaming happily in the southern sun, to the serenity of Lake George, which is almost comparable to the Italian and Swiss lakes, all the way to the romantic wilderness of the northern parts around Lake Champlain and the former Fort Ticonderoga; from the garden-like, fertile fields of western New York and the picturesque views in the Catskills to the giant Niagara, which in a class by itself is the culmination of all—what contrasts, what variety, what beauty!

Surrounded by old trees and bounteous gardens as one finds them only in the older, well-established areas, Gerrit Smith's palatial house is animated by the most generous hospitality, as it is home not only to a large family of children, grandchildren, and other family members but to a large circle of guests. Mrs. Smith, still an attractive woman with traces of her former beauty, radiates that friendliness that comes from the heart and shines like a sunbeam in anyone who possesses it; the sons, nieces, and grandchildren glory in their easygoing youth and vitality. An agreeable sense of enjoying life energizes the whole house, and the freethinking German visitor is bothered only by a certain aura of religious orthodoxy that unfortunately infects even the best of men over here. Good taste and a sense of comfort and beauty are tempered by what I would call a republican simplicity, which stands in agreeable contrast to the exaggerated luxury of New York's social upstarts. Gold paint, liveries, expensive furniture, or the impertinently costly chinaware of the moneyed aristocracy are nowhere to be seen, though everything that serves to enhance comfort and convenience is done to perfection.

Among the guests was Mrs. Sarah Grimké from South Carolina, one of the most outstanding women who were active in the early antislavery movements, a former Quaker who still wears the gray dress and the close-fitting cap of the "Friends." I also found a cheerful and talkative, plump little woman of about fifty who was full of genial talk, which she generally accompanied with happy laughter. The others addressed her only as "the Doctor," and indeed she has been living for more than twenty years as a practicing physician in Boston. Harriot Kezia Hunt, M.D., who is also mentioned in Fredrika Bremer's tedious book about America,[2] has told the story of her life in a book with the title, *Glances and Glimpses: Or,*

Fifty Years Social, Including Twenty Years Professional Life. Besides many of its good and thoughtful ideas, it contains far too much religious orthodoxy and too many long-winded details to have a claim on literary value.

The boys had set up a gymnastic circus, where they offered a performance to the assembled group, a hurdy-gurdy providing the music in place of an orchestra. It was a pleasure to see these healthy boys in athletic suits showing off their figures as they climbed the poles like acrobats, dangled from their feet, and then rode their horses with the style of skilled horsemen.

The next day, Mr. and Mrs. Miller took their guests in several carriages on an excursion to the falls of the Chittenango, a name that in the Indian language applies to any river flowing north, while "Chinango" is the word for rivers flowing south. The scenery along the way is charming and varied, and the falls, which are similar to Niagara in height, though not in width and water volume, are among the most beautiful and picturesque in this country that is so rich in magnificent waterfalls. Lying in the grass at the bottom of the falls, we spent a happy day. The boys played with snakes and lizards that were abundant in the damp ravine, and they climbed with the litheness of cats up various parts of the rock that forms the falls, appearing barefoot and in shirt sleeves now under the falls, now next to them, as if suspended from the rock. On the way back, a Yankee born and bred in Boston sang for me our own classical song, *"Was kommt da von der Höh?"*—like a real German student. As I have often noticed among so-called Yankees, he was completely familiar not only with German nonsense but with the better works of German literature.

Returning home rather late, I met Wilhelm Zecher, the alleged murderer, with his wife and children. Gerrit Smith had invited him to let him enjoy the pleasure of speaking German with someone. I found a young man as innocent, open, and harmless as a child, with all of a child's inexperience. After talking with him for only two minutes you are totally convinced of his good and solid, plain German character. Coming from the lower middle class, he was a hat maker in Frankfurt, and after the first ten minutes I knew his whole life story. To make sure I would learn every detail, he asked me to read a letter from his parents that he had brought with him. It seems incomprehensible that such a man, whose physiognomy and entire character speak more plainly than any language, would ever be the object of suspicion, and that without Gerrit Smith's intervention a judicial murder would surely have occurred.

He seemed thoroughly delighted to have a little German chat for the first time in years, and even though it was late and the children began to fuss, he could not bring himself to take leave, seemingly having something on his mind that he did not dare to mention. Only after Gerrit Smith urged him to speak freely, he asked me very solemnly to promise that if I ever returned to Peterboro I should let him know. After having given him my pledge, husband and wife left in good spirits.

Notes

1. Manuscript (1859), Assing Papers, Deutsches Literaturarchiv, Marbach.

2. Fredrika Bremer's book, *The Homes of the New World: Impressions of America* (1853), was written in Swedish but appeared in English translation the same year. For Harriot Hunt, see Essay 24, n. 2.

40

Frederick Douglass[1]

* * *

Among those who fled the dusty streets of New York during the past summer was your correspondent, who had sought the quiet of the countryside, determined to find a place hitherto unknown to any German journalist or member of the literary guild. It was the house belonging to Frederick Douglass, the famous colored orator, who lives with his family in the country near Rochester. American color prejudice is the demon that surrounds this house like a Chinese Wall, which only the initiates—that is, the most determined and dedicated abolitionists—dare to scale, even though the owner is universally known and celebrated.

Situated on a hill about half an hour from the town and surrounded by an extensive garden, this house has a singularly poetic appearance and, in a way, is like an island, a small separate world, where those who have the courage to defy disgraceful prejudice find a rich intellectual life and are received with great kindness, generosity, and a rather un-American heartfelt warmth. The isolation from the rest of the world, therefore, is part of its attractions rather than a deficit, and one could believe to have been transported back into the times of magicians and fairies, when a traveler might suddenly find himself inside a magic mountain, a moated castle, or some charmed garden. Intercourse with the inhabitants would make time fly so incredibly fast that, upon returning to the quotidian world, the traveler would realize that he had spent a century instead of a month inside the magic circle. In our own enlightened age, however, the daily newspapers prevent such happy forgetfulness. Also, every now and then guests appear in this modern magic castle who underscore with dramatic vividness a less than ideal but very American part of reality. They are passengers on the underground railroad, fugitive slaves, who avail themselves of Frederick Douglass's hospitality for one night on the way out of slavery to freedom and then proceed to Canada the following day.

One day, there also appeared a son of John Brown, the famous guerilla leader who, once a wealthy New York farmer, has in recent years made it his life's goal to fight the forces of slavery. More than anyone else he has helped to save Kansas from their clutches, so that it will most likely petition the next Congress for admission to the Union as a free state. The son, who is no less dedicated and enthusiastic than his father, had not long ago forcefully freed a fugitive slave and, being pursued by a United States marshal, was prepared for a surprise at any moment. He was determined to offer the utmost resistance and for that purpose carried with him a whole arsenal of pistols, revolvers, and daggers. To obey the despicable and shameless laws for turning over fugitive slaves would be to violate all basic laws of human decency; their existence creates a situation that would be an impossibility in any civilized country, and it places the most noble and humanitarian individuals on the same level with lawless rebels and rioters.

* * *

Notes

1. New York, November [1859], *Morgenblatt*, 53:51:1223–1224.

41

The Insurrection at Harpers Ferry[1]

The whole country was resting in profound peace and quiet, when in the morning hours of October 17 the magnetic wires began carrying the incredible news in all directions that an insurrection against slavery had taken place at Harpers Ferry, a small Virginia town not far from the Maryland line, a region of general stagnation. Abolitionists from the North were alleged to be the instigators and leaders of the revolt. Widespread rumors about the extent and spread of the revolt were crisscrossing the country. The only known fact was that in the evening of October 16 a number of armed men—several hundred, it was said—had suddenly seized the United States arsenal near Harpers Ferry, taken many prisoners among the local population, and taken command of the place. Everything happened under cover of darkness so quietly and quickly that the inhabitants did not notice until the next morning what had occurred. The entire South was struck with unspeakable horror. Slaveholders, like tyrants everywhere, always tremble for their safety, and everyone felt the knife at his throat. In Washington, the government was trembling along with the citizens, and the president immediately ordered all available military forces with cannons and howitzers to the place of the disturbance. Mounted police were put in place at the edge of the town and on bridges to sound the alarm at any suspicious sign. Throughout the night patrols combed the town, searching all colored persons they encountered for hidden weapons.

Early the next morning a steamboat brought Governor Henry Wise of Virginia, who told the mayor that he was in the process of placing himself at the head of a column of militia to march to the scene of the battle. Meanwhile, however, the military force sent by the president had arrived at Harpers Ferry. The conspirators had entrenched themselves in the arsenal and were desperately resisting the assault of the soldiers, who succeeded in taking the building only after several hours of battle and bloodshed on both sides. The soldiers and inhabitants now saw to their astonishment that the enemy—who had held the town hostage for a day and a half, thrown the whole country into a panic, and taken nearly seventy prisoners—was made up of no more than nineteen men, fourteen whites and five Negroes. Most of them had been killed by fire during the assault, the rest—with the exception of two—were wounded, so that only six men could be taken prisoner, one of whom has since died from his injuries. The leader, who, though wounded, was captured, turned out to be John Brown, the hero of Kansas, known throughout the country as "Old Brown." Because of his implacable hatred of slavery and his spotless character he is as respected among abolitionists as he is hated and feared by the slaveholders and all who support slavery.

This remarkable man, now sixty-three years old but still retaining the full fire and force of youth, was born in the state of New York, where he used to live as a wealthy farmer. He had no fewer than twenty-two children, of whom only a small number are still alive, however. Several years ago he left Pennsylvania to settle in the territory of Kansas. He has always been an implacable foe of slavery from the beginning, yet his abolitionism has been connected with a religious fanaticism that is an outstanding aspect of his character. He sees himself as the chosen tool of providence to free the colored population of the United States from the yoke of slavery. He has always shown himself to be of noble, unselfish, and honest character, unsullied by the least blemish. Yet he has a will of iron, an unparalleled decisiveness, quickness of mind, and personal courage. Anyone who has ever been near him is thoroughly convinced that he has never felt fear and that it would be difficult to meet a human being exceeding him in cold-blooded boldness.

When, as a result of President Buchanan's efforts and those of the inhabitants of Missouri to turn the territory of Kansas into a slave state against the will of its population, war was raging within its boundaries, Brown got involved in the most dangerous and seemingly desperate ventures. He demonstrated a courage that cannot be eclipsed by the most splendid deeds of the distant or more recent past. He became the object of the cruelest persecutions at the hands of the Missourians who devastated Kansas, and the man who had hitherto lived there as a peaceful farmer, whose efforts had been directed at finding a lawful way to make Kansas a free state, turned into a terrible avenger against the misdeeds perpetrated against him and the other settlers. One of his sons fell into the hands of a gang of Missourians on a country road and was killed by them in cold blood. Another of his sons, just because of his antislavery views, was captured and dragged off to jail, laden with heavy chains, having to walk in front of his enemies' horses for many miles from his home. The cruelties he had to suffer drove him insane, and soon thereafter he died of nervous fever. His house in Osawatomie was burned down, as was his father's; even the women did not escape the worst kind of abuse, and at one point a price was put on John Brown's head. It is easy to imagine that he became embittered as a result of these shameful deeds and that henceforth he would conduct total war against those who support slavery.

Once, at a gathering of these ruffians, a committee of five was formed; they went to inform him that he would have to leave the territory within three days and that at the end of that period they would return with a sufficient force and hang him if he was still there. Brown thanked them for this warning and quietly added: "You won't see me here again, gentlemen." Before the next morning dawned, the five members of the delegation had disappeared from this world. Better than anyone else, Brown knew that they would live up to their word, so he beat them to it.

Another time, Pate, the infamous leader of a horde of thirty-three Missourians, invaded Kansas.[2] He had dared to conceive the plan to capture "Old Brown" and take him in triumph back to Missouri but was afraid he might not succeed in finding him. However, they found their man all too soon. He approached Pate with sixteen men of his own and after a short fight, in which a few men were killed, the entire gang—with the exception of two—surrendered. Those two got away thanks to the speed of their horses.

On another occasion, a force of 320 men and two cannons left Missouri for Kansas and unexpectedly attacked Osawatomie. Brown barely had time enough to escape with thirty men into a forest on the banks of the Osage when the entire force of the enemy moved in on him. His unshakable self-confidence never gave way in the face of being so heavily outnumbered; not giving his enemy time to begin the hostilities, he quickly deployed his men and had them maintain a constant barrage of fire. Though the Missourians returned the fire, they did not know their enemy's strength, dared not enter the forest, and therefore did little damage. The result was that sixty to seventy Missourians were killed, while Brown lost only two of his men and successfully led the rest through the woods to a shallow place and across the river to safety. Later he himself launched attacks on Missouri, abducted slaves along the border, and succeeded in getting them to Canada despite dangers and difficulties. Stern and implacable like death itself, if necessary, he was never guilty of needless cruelty; to the contrary, he often proved his innate kindness and humanity.

As brave and cool-headed as Brown showed himself in battle, as inventive and subtle he was in planning strategies and attacks for freeing imprisoned friends. A peaceful inhabitant of Kansas, Dr. Day, was forcefully removed to Missouri by a gang of Missourians allegedly because he was suspected of having aided in the escape of a slave, but more likely because of his well-known abolitionist sympathies. For a long time he had to suffer in jail, then he was found guilty in a sham trial and sentenced to fifty years in prison. After a few days he was to be moved from St. Joseph, where he had hitherto been kept, to the state penitentiary in Jefferson City, when one stormy night the warden was awakened by a loud knock. He came to the window and saw two men leading a third, whose hands were bound. They told him that they had just caught a horse thief and demanded to have him placed in jail overnight. The warden admitted them and asked them several questions to make sure there was sufficient reason for jailing the alleged thief. Their answers seemed satisfactory and he led them upstairs into the interior of the jail, opened a heavy grate door, and ordered the prisoner to step in. The latter refused and declared that he would not be locked up with "niggers." The warden calmed his fears on this point, telling him that there were no niggers here, when one of the other men asked whether the "abolitionist Day" was here. "You mean Dr. Day," said the warden. "It is he whom we have come to set free," another one shouted. The alleged thief cast off his fetters and all three pointed their revolvers at the warden and told him that any resistance would be futile. Dr. Day was set free, and before they all left the jail they explained that the building would be watched and anyone who dared leave it before daybreak or sound the alarm would have to pay with his life. With that they and seven others who had come with them and waited in an antechamber left, and they reached Kansas soil before dawn. Ten citizens of Kansas had successfully done the work of freedom, and Brown had been their leader.

When Kansas had finally won its freedom and been cleansed of Missouri gangs, "Old Brown" vanished from public view, and only his allies knew that Isaac

Smith, a former inspector of coal mines, had rented a farm early last summer near Harpers Ferry with the intention—as he told people in the neighborhood—of prospecting for ore in the nearby mountains. Two sons—both of whom were killed during the capture of the arsenal—accompanied him, and over time nineteen more determined men, most of them friends from Kansas, joined him. Large shipments of arms were sent undetected to the farm, enough to fully arm at least fifteen hundred men. The original plan called for a kind of guerilla war, for which the mountains covering all of Virginia would offer the most suitable terrain. Never wanting to engage the army in open battle, Brown intended to launch raids as he had done in Kansas, abduct masses of slaves from the plantations, and on occasion raid and capture the slaveholders themselves at night so as to have them purchase their freedom by freeing one or two of their slaves. Brown hoped that the slaves of Virginia would rally to his side in a great mass as soon as they received news of the presence of his force and that the revolt would gradually spread throughout the state.

Such a war could actually have been fought successfully for a long time, and it is incomprehensible how folly and blindness could misguide a man, who had proven himself so levelheaded with all his boldness, to shut himself up in the arsenal, a place from which there was no escape and against which a military force of any size could be deployed within hours. His companions seem to have understood the situation, but his influence over them was so great that they were ready to follow him at any time and under any circumstances, even though—as in this case—they faced certain death. Only three escaped: instead of participating in the venture against the arsenal they abducted nearly thirty slaves from several plantations. Bill Cook, their leader, having been recognized by some worthless characters in Philadelphia, has meanwhile been arrested, and extradited to Virginia.[3]

John Brown began his venture so recklessly and heedlessly that his eventual destruction was inevitable; yet he has proven his quiet courage—even his greatness—since he has been in prison. The entire Democratic party has been moving heaven and earth to profit politically from this event and to paint the Republicans as the real perpetrators of the conspiracy, the most outstanding Republican members of Congress as the secret leaders or at least co-conspirators. That is why during the first hours after the arsenal was taken Democratic members of Congress and other politicians crowded into the room where the wounded man was lying and beset him with questions about anyone who might also be guilty. They hoped that physical pain, fear of death, and awareness of his desperate situation had weakened him and would force confessions from him. However, Brown resolutely declared that there were no others besides those who had been captured with him, that he was the sole source of the conspiracy, and that he had been inspired only by his hatred of slavery and his sympathy for the oppressed. Stevens, the only white man besides Brown who survived to be arrested even though badly wounded, is just as unflinching and determined.[4]

Some southern papers cannot but express their admiration for these men's heroism, even as they condemn the deed itself. What a contrast to the slaveholders and their party! While a ridiculous ado is being made about the bravery of the soldiers who—many hundreds against nineteen—finally took five prisoners after several hours of fighting, and while Governor Wise, with his typical boastfulness, congratulated the soldiers who accompanied him—though they were not even accorded the safe role of spectators during the entire operation, since the arsenal had already been taken by the time they arrived—the whole state of Virginia is nonetheless trembling before these five prisoners and wounded men. There is fear of a slave insurrection and of a forceful attempt to free the prisoners; hence, an investigation is being hurried along that does not even have the semblance of impartiality. Brown requested that an attorney from the North be sent for, but that would have delayed things too much for the slave breeders. They did not even give the prisoners sufficient time to recuperate from their wounds, and eight days after their capture they were dragged to the trial, in chains and on their mattresses, by eighty men of the militia. The prosecutor requested that the court appoint an attorney for Brown, but he declined decisively, stating that since they had already decided to shed his blood they should proceed to kill him without further formalities rather than stage the farce of a sham trial. It was only with great difficulty that he finally let himself be persuaded to accept the designated attorney.

The newspapers of Virginia are forbidden to publish the proceedings, and no one is permitted to speak with Brown because they fear that each of his words would throw an igniting spark among the slaves. The dungeon keepers have been instructed to shoot the prisoners instantly if any attempt is made to set them free. It is a foregone conclusion that all will be found guilty and that none will escape death, for in the South all crimes are forgiven except any sin violating the holy spirit of slavery. Yet John Brown has launched no other assault against slavery than Governor Wise had proposed before the presidential election of 1856 for saving the sacred institution in the event of Frémont's election: he proclaimed publicly that in such an event he would take over the arsenal and the gold deposits at Harpers Ferry and thence march straight on Washington. The slaveholders will rejoice in the execution of John Brown and his companions, but history will record their names among the noblest and most unselfish martyrs who have given their lives for the cause of freedom.

Notes

1. Manuscript (October, 1859), Assing Papers, Deutsches Literaturarchiv, Marbach.

2. Henry Clay Pate (1832–1864), a captain in the Missouri militia, commanded a group of Missouri raiders in the battle of Black Jack, Kansas, in 1856.

3. Evidently this is someone other than John E. Cook, who was one of Brown's co-conspirators (see Essay 43, n. 2).

4. Aaron D. Stevens, a native of Connecticut, first met Brown in 1856.

42

The Aftermath of John Brown's Trial[1]

As could have been predicted with all but mathematical certainty, the sham trial of the noble, heroic John Brown and his companions has ended in a guilty verdict of all prisoners. The only exception is Stevens,[2] who has been handed over to federal authorities to give them an opportunity to proceed against any possible co-conspirators in the North. To make sure that none of the accused would, by some legal sleight of hand, escape the vengeance of the slavocracy—which would find satisfaction only with the victims' death—each of the accused had been charged with three separate capital crimes: high treason, inciting the slaves to revolt against their masters, and finally murder. Every conceivable escape was thus cut off from the start, and the entire judicial proceeding was a work of hatred and revenge instead of an impartial investigation. Judge and jury were determined in advance to find the accused guilty and quash every possible opportunity for them to offer evidence of mitigating circumstances. The attorneys for Brown and his companions, who had come from the North, petitioned for a brief stay in the proceedings to familiarize themselves with Virginia law and the facts of the case. However, their request was denied out of hand so that they, tired and rumpled, had to devote the first several nights after their arrival to the most necessary preliminary studies, causing one of them to collapse from exhaustion.

The entire proceeding was dominated by a tone of incivility, barbarism, and spitefulness that seems impossible in this century and among a people that has prided itself so much on its civilization. The very spectacle of this Virginia courtroom is representative of the process and has to astonish anyone who has ever had the opportunity to observe the quiet dignity of a European trial. The judge, the lawyers, and the jury are lying, sitting, and hanging in their seats in the most unbelievable postures, placing their feet on tables, desks, and the backs of chairs, chewing tobacco, and reading newspapers. The spectators are cracking nuts, throwing the shells at each other, and from time to time engage in crude jokes, curses, and threats aimed at the prisoners. Such brutality would be outrageous under any circumstances, but it is totally contemptible when directed at men, two of whom—Brown and Stevens—are unable to stand because of their wounds and have to be brought to court on their mattresses. It is even doubtful whether the latter will be able to do his executioners the favor of surviving long enough so as not to spoil the pleasure the population of Virginia will take in seeing him hang next to his companions.

Throughout the trial all of the prisoners have maintained the same unshakable firmness and dignity, and all efforts at getting additional information from them have remained unsuccessful. Brown has received the correspondents of the newspapers in prison as well as many other official and unofficial visitors; all of them, whether friend or foe, are attracted by his strange and unusual force of personality. The enthusiasm for his cause and the probity that has marked his entire character win over everyone who comes near him, and after seeing him no one is surprised by his companions' blind faith and dedication.

Charlestown still looks like a town under siege: patrols comb the streets day and night, arresting everyone who is unable to prove his legitimate business. Strangers without such proof are not tolerated in the city and are also constantly in danger of being insulted and abused by the rabble. Immediately after the end of the trial, one of the northern lawyers was even told that he no longer had any business staying in Charlestown and that the public agencies could no longer guarantee his safety. An illustrator for a New York paper who had been sent by his editor to draw the portraits of the main actors in the agitation in and around the trial was met by the same fate. He fulfilled his assignment with utmost conscientiousness, causing the wrath of a number of honorable gentlemen, who spat fire and swore revenge because the worthless abolitionist had the cheek to draw their nasty faces as they were, not as they might be.

Even though most of Brown's companions have been killed and the rest are in prison, all of Virginia is trembling in the conviction that an army of disguised abolitionists is hiding throughout the state and that another army is on its way from the North to storm the jail, to free John Brown, and to cause havoc everywhere. A few days ago a fire broke out in the vicinity, destroying several barns and Negro cabins; panic seized the population because no one failed to see in this the realization of all their fears. In great haste every available military force was ordered to Charlestown to repel the enemy, which, however, has remained invisible even through a magnifying glass. It is not simply the fear of a possible attempt at freeing Brown that has caused all this excitement but also the horror of the fact that such a revolt could take place anywhere, the discovery that there may be people in the North who are not satisfied with opposing slavery only in word, and the dim realization that a country which was capable of producing twenty-two such heroes not only can but will eventually spawn as many thousands. A bolt of lightning has stirred the people of Virginia and the whole South out of its placidity by revealing the abyss into which it has to fall sooner or later if it continues to be blinded by prejudice and to build its future on the existence and extension of slavery.

While the South is divided between fear and anger, the North demonstrates the deepest sympathy for Brown. Though there is much criticism, it concerns only the manner in which he executed his plan because he himself thereby foiled its success, and one regrets that he was not more fortunate. The public is being asked to make contributions for the support of his family, and the response has been such that many thousands of dollars will surely be collected. The entire Democracy, with the president and Governor Wise at the top, cannot prevent Brown's celebration as a martyr. Maria Child, the author,[3] offered to tend to his wounds in prison and had already obtained Governor Wise's consent, but Brown himself declined the offer on the grounds that he was sufficiently recovered to do without further care; he asked her to devote her sympathy and help to his family. Only the church criticizes and condemns, as one would expect, because uncompromising abolitionism that will do everything to obtain the freedom of slaves is naturally far too harsh and eccentric for the entire orthodox camp. Even the most steadfast among them are still far too accepting of all existing institutions to go beyond a so-called passive resistance, which is really no resistance at all.

On the other hand, it goes without saying that the Democrats were moving heaven and earth to exploit John Brown's raid on Virginia during the recent elections in New York, attacking the Republicans and painting them as instigators and co-conspirators. The *New York Herald* in particular made itself laughable in its eagerness to demand that the government should without further ado arrest and prosecute all of the most conspicuous Republican leaders who had ever openly taken a firm abolitionist stand. In order to give weight to its agitation and slander, the paper presented letters of one Colonel Forbes that were supposed to contain proof of these allegations.[4] Forbes, an Englishman, is a political adventurer who, as has now been revealed, is at any time ready to serve any well-paying master no matter what party or cause he may represent. He claims to have served under Garibaldi in Italy in 1848 and to have come to America as a refugee in 1849 after the restoration. A few years ago he made the acquaintance of John Brown, who was already at that time involved in plans to free the slaves, and was able to gain his confidence to the extent that Brown not only revealed to him all of his plans but appointed him to a leading position in his future army.

Such schemes for the future, however, did not suit someone like Forbes, whose entire ambition for the present and the future was exclusively focused on money. Heaven knows by what tricks and pitiful stories about the suffering his family had to endure in Paris he succeeded in gaining the sympathy of Brown and his wealthy friends that he received nine hundred dollars for future services. Yet Forbes pressed his demands ever more forcefully and vehemently, and when, of course, they were not satisfied he threatened to make revelations, which—it now turns out—he actually did make to the government. But he did not receive the wages of his treason because they either took him for a fraud or preferred to let the conspiracy erupt. Then the miserable creature vanished until, following the events at Harpers Ferry, he sold his story to the *Herald* trying to prove that he had earlier revealed John Brown's plans to a number of the leading Republican members of Congress and other party leaders—among them Senator Hale and Horace Greeley[5]—who therefore are at least guilty of passive co-conspiracy.

The *Herald* believed that it had dealt the Republicans a decisive blow, yet the results proved that all of its intrigues were for naught since the worthless creature, who has now revealed himself to be a traitor, has played too pitiful a part to cause much damage as an enemy. Since he cannot provide actual proof, the "No" from those who have been implicated—all of whom forcefully decline any knowledge—has far greater weight than his boasting. In spite of all the agitation, nobody doubts that next year's elections will result in a Republican president. It is, however, sufficiently possible that Forbes did actually make these revelations, and it would be natural that those who received them—feeling nothing but sympathy for a venture that people who hold the cause of the slaves close to their hearts would wish the best of success—either gave money in support or at least kept silent, as would be the duty of every honest and unequivocal opponent of slavery.

As one observes how Hale, Greeley, and even Giddings,[6] who has shown himself in Congress as one of the staunchest abolitionists, are anxiously trying to cleanse themselves of any suspicion of co-conspiracy, one man has stood up to acknowledge frankly his participation in the conspiracy, even though the consequences for him are more dangerous and pernicious than for most others. It is the famous orator Frederick Douglass. Immediately following the events at Harpers Ferry he was identified as one of the secret leaders of the conspiracy, and only by his hasty flight to Canada did he escape the clutches of the United States marshals,[7] those henchmen of a government that, on a mere command of the president, can arrest any citizen in any state without first obtaining the permission of that state's authorities. In Rochester, surrounding his apartment, and in Syracuse, where he was to give a lecture on that fateful day, the hunters of men sat in ambush to carry him to Virginia and to certain death. The slavocracy would not have let such prey escape them: he is a man whom they hate with particular fervor because of his revelations about the slavery system and the slaves' lives and because his great gifts are the best proof against all assertions about the intellectual inferiority of the colored race. From Canada, Frederick Douglass published a letter, a magnificent, brilliant manifesto dictated by that implacable hatred of slavery and that dedication to liberating the oppressed which knows no consequences, no matter how devastating their effect on his life.[8] At present Douglass is on his way to England, which he is about to enter for the second time as a refugee. Whether and when he can return, and whether his effectiveness as an orator will not be at an end, only time will tell.

Notes

1. Manuscript (November, 1859), Assing Papers, Deutsches Literaturarchiv, Marbach.

2. See Essay 41, n. 4.

3. Lydia Maria Child (1802–1880), an ardent abolitionist and prolific writer on antislavery subjects, was the editor of the *National Anti-Slavery Standard* (1841–1849).

4. Hugh Forbes had met Brown in 1857 and was hired as a drillmaster and military tactician to train Brown's company.

5. John Parker Hale (1806–1873) from New Hampshire was the first specifically antislavery U.S. senator (1846–1865); Horace Greeley (1811–1872) was editor of the famous and influential *New York Tribune* (1841–1872).

6. Joshua R. Giddings (1795–1864), a forceful antislavery politician from Ohio, served as a member of Congress (1838–1859).

7. Returning from a clandestine meeting with Brown in Pennsylvania just prior to the raid on Harpers Ferry, Douglass moved quickly to evade possible arrest and briefly stayed in Hoboken with Assing, who helped him proceed to Rochester via a circuitous route.

8. As Maria Diedrich, Assing's biographer, has pointed out, Douglass's letter of October 31 to the Rochester *Democrat and Observer* strikes quite a different note than is suggested here by Assing's sentence. Whereas Assing, she writes, apotheosized Douglass "as John Brown's only legitimate heir and as the revolutionary upon whose survival the nation's hope for moral regeneration rested," Douglass made it plain that he had never given his consent to Brown's raid on Harpers Ferry.

43

John Brown's Execution and Its Consequences[1]

John Brown and his companions have become martyrs for their conviction, their dedication, and their love of freedom. The men who stirred up the entire Union and caused panic in the South are dead. The 2nd of December was the day of death for a hero whose name will be engraved together with the noblest and bravest in the annals of history. Virginia could not breathe easy as long as this man had breath; she trembled in fear and anger at the thought that he might escape her vengeance.

Never before, perhaps, have so many precautionary measures been taken against six helpless prisoners as in this case. All of Virginia was in something of an undeclared state of war, and all of Charlestown resembled an encampment: on the day of the execution Governor Wise had deployed no fewer than three thousand men representing all branches of military service. No stranger was admitted without either special identification or absolute proof of essential business. Everybody else was immediately arrested and taken out of state; this fate befell even persons from the North who had been living in Virginia for many years, were generally known there, and had never run afoul of the law. Military escorts were placed on trains, and for several days the movement of people was completely halted because the government had seized the railroads for the transportation of soldiers. At night no one dared step out of his house for fear of being shot because the soldiers in their eagerness kept shooting at anyone who did not immediately respond to their "Who's there?" No distinction was being made between bipeds and quadrupeds, putting cows and pigs in imminent danger, and it is remarkable that no one was killed as a result of misunderstandings. Well-known local citizens, loyal slave owners, and government officials were arrested by eager recruits who did not know them; they had to prove their identity before being released.

The insanity reached its peak with rumors coming from all sides about armed gangs that were supposed to have been seen or smelled gathering near the border to liberate John Brown and his companions by force. Whether these rumors were invented by some practical joker to heighten the fears of the population or whether they sprang from the people's overheated imagination remains unclear. It is certain, however, that Governor Wise, who has proven himself to be a veritable Don Quixote of slavery in his reaction to all events since John Brown's raid on Virginia, believed every rumor and made himself ridiculous by sending off letters, asking the president for military assistance and recommending vigilance to the governors of Ohio and Pennsylvania.

While the population of an entire state was close to lunacy, the man who had been the cause of it maintained until the end a heroic calm and steadfastness which even his sworn enemies were forced from the start to admire in him. He calmly put his affairs in order, wrote his family and friends, and conversed freely with all who came to visit him. Though he was religious to the point of being a fanatic, as I mentioned on an earlier occasion, he rebuffed all efforts by the clergy of Virginia, explaining that their God was not his, but that he would consider it the highest privilege to be accompanied on his way to the scaffold not by a preacher but by a good slave mother and her little Negro children.

His wife had requested Governor Wise in advance and had received his permission to be given her husband's body after the execution; she had also been permitted to visit her husband on the preceding day. She asked for the favor of spending the last night with him; however, the representative of the Virginia slavocracy denied her this sad satisfaction. Four hours was all they were granted for their last farewell. When Brown was told this news, he replied proudly and decisively: "Oh, I don't ask favors of the State of Virginia; let them do what they believe they have to do!" His unhappy wife had already arrived at Harpers Ferry in the morning of November 30, but was retained in custody until the afternoon of the following day. Several of her friends—two gentlemen and a lady, who had accompanied her from Philadelphia—were forced to stay behind despite Governor Wise's earlier promises that they would be allowed to travel freely. One cannot easily fathom what concerns would prompt the knights of Virginia to deny a lady the company of her friends. But after all the instances of cowardice that have daily occurred in Virginia for two months, after all the shots fired at animals, shadows, and milestones, it is no wonder that the mighty military force assembled in Charlestown was too afraid of two men and a woman from the North to let them come near. A military escort accompanied Mrs. Brown to Charlestown, and after many unnecessary formalities and after being searched by the warden's wife—because the executioners suspected that she might bring her husband poison or a weapon so that he could deprive them of their prey by taking his own life—she was finally led into her husband's prison.

Reading the reports based on the warden's comments is to witness the most moving tragedy. Brown and his wife both displayed admirable strength and self-control; and while one can understand this attitude in the old hero himself, who died in the conviction that his death would be the most effective means to achieve the freedom of the slaves, it is more remarkable and admirable than comprehensible in the woman. Only for a few minutes at the beginning did they stand in silent embrace, and when the woman later seemed overcome by her suffering he gave her courage by saying in a friendly tone: "Be calm, Mary; be calm and show how strong you are!" It is told that she straightened herself as if electrified and controlled her emotions. They spoke about their affairs until orders arrived after two or three hours from the commanding officer to end the meeting. A short farewell, and the warden led Mrs. Brown away. A military escort accompanied her back to Harpers Ferry where her husband's body was turned over to her the following afternoon.

The next day the entire military force was deployed in a circle around the gallows at a distance of fifty feet because Virginia was still trembling in fear of an invasion from the North. In fact, two cannons were trained on the scaffold, and a proclamation by the governor recommended that, for reasons of personal safety, all spectators stay at a suitable distance. In all this excitement John Brown bore himself with steady calmness to the very end. His step was light and sinuous as he emerged from his prison. Seemingly cheerful, he even smiled at the assembled crowd. A black woman with a child in her arm happened to be standing near the prison gate. She belonged to that despised and oppressed race for which John Brown was about to give his life. He stood still for a moment, bent down, and tenderly kissed the child; then he climbed into the wagon and sat down on the box that contained his coffin. The prison warden sat next to him, and they conversed freely and easily.

A number of other small details have been reported, all of which suggest that this firm demeanor was not artificial or studied but the natural result of complete inner peace and fortitude. He climbed the scaffold with firm steps, took off his broad-brimmed hat with an easy movement of his shackled arm, tossed it on the platform, and looked down on the assembled crowd. John Brown was ready, but the troops first had to perform some pointless maneuvers, and it took eight to ten minutes till they had all taken their positions, John Brown standing the while with the noose around his neck and the hood covering his head. A loud grumbling at this brutality rose from the people; every moment seemed an hour until everyone was ready and the sheriff gave the signal. John Brown is dead; Virginia has slaked its thirst for vengeance.

The North was showing colors of an entirely opposite hue on that fateful day. Hardly a city that did not have a demonstration honoring the old hero. In many places cannons were fired, bells rung, memorial services and public assemblies conducted, expressing the highest praise and sympathy for Brown. Many houses displayed black crepe; in the Massachusetts legislature a petition was submitted to suspend the session for that day; and some newspapers carried black borders. In a word: it was a day of general mourning. When Mrs. Brown, accompanied by Wendell Philipps, brought her husband's body to their North Elba home in upstate New York and was passing through Pennsylvania, she was unable to prevent formal receptions in several towns and the overnight deployment of an honor guard by the coffin, despite her efforts to avoid public notice and reach her destination as quickly and quietly as possible.

The servile northern tools of slavery are no less enraged at these demonstrations than the South itself. In an effort to quell the anger of their cotton-producing benefactors they organize meetings "for the salvation of the Union," in which they curse Brown, the abolitionists, and the Republicans in general and praise Governor Wise and the South, assuring them of the unalterable loyalty and submission of the northern Democracy. At a large Brown gathering recently held in New York, where Wendell Philipps displayed his incomparable rhetorical powers in glorifying Brown, a gang of these Union saviors tried to break up the proceedings and actually created such chaos that the police had to step in and throw out and arrest a large number of demonstrators. It soon became clear that the noisiest among them were no common rowdies but for the most part well-known businessmen, who were highly indignant and chagrined when they were treated to a night in the police station like common vagrants and troublemakers. Similar efforts occurred in

Philadelphia, but they were also suppressed.

Such efforts to save the Union are usually inspired by members of the administration and wealthy merchants whose business depends on trade with the South. They are trembling for their material interests and therefore move heaven and earth to keep their lucrative customers. Meanwhile everyone, in the North as well as the South, knows the reason for such declarations of loyalty and that they in no way express the opinion of the general public.

Two weeks after Brown's execution, his companions Cook, Coppoc, Copeland, and Green were also hanged.[2] Virginia was almost deprived of half of the spectacle because Cook and Coppoc, locked away in a common cell, attempted to escape on the eve of their execution. They had fashioned a saw from an old knife and used it to cut through their chains during several nights of labor to the point where their fetters appeared outwardly solid but could be thrown off at a moment's notice. A screw from a bed served them as a chisel for loosening the mortar in the wall, allowing them to take out one stone after another until they had an opening large enough to let them through. During the day it was covered by the bed in which they slept; they hid the stones in a stove and the mortar between their bed sheets. Since the hole was located only five feet above the floor of the prison yard, they quickly reached it; yet they still had to climb over a fifteen foot wall. They solved this problem by using the gallows from which John Brown had been hanged as a ladder. When they had already reached the height of the wall and were about to jump down on the other side they were unfortunately—on the very verge of freedom—discovered by a watchman, who immediately sounded the alarm, and both of them were apprehended in the prison yard. If they had reached freedom they could have easily gained the nearby mountains where it would have been difficult to apprehend them, particularly since Cook, having lived for some years in these parts, knew every hideout.

The two Negroes, Copeland and Green, were hanged first, Cook and Coppoc an hour later. These men also proved to be calm and steadfast till the end, thus worthy of the cause for which they were put to death. They all died as heroes, and none of them showed any remorse for his part in the venture. When Coppoc and Cook were standing next to each other on the scaffold, their hoods over their eyes, Coppoc turned to Cook and held out his hand. At the same instant Cook said: "Stop! Just a moment! Where is Edwin's hand?" And once again they warmly shook hands.

For the time being the curtain has descended over the corpses of almost twenty men, five of whom became victims of the laws of the South, while the rest died during the assault on the arsenal at Harpers Ferry. Nobody, however, is blind to the fact that this is just the first act in the grand drama that sooner or later must unfold before the eyes of the world. The moral pressure is now infinitely greater than it would have been had John Brown succeeded in his venture. The heroism of these men has filled even the South with astonished admiration; at the same time, the cowardice and baseness, the brutality, crudeness, and rottenness of the slavocracy have been exposed in a stronger light, slavery has been branded with more disgrace, than all the efforts of the abolitionists have ever been able to accomplish. Men who hitherto have not dared to ponder the legality of slavery, have suddenly been torn from their lethargy. To their amazement they saw twenty men, all of the purest and most unassailable character, who personally suffered nothing from slavery and had nothing to gain from its abolition. All of them were well situated in occupations with solid incomes, many of them had only recently married, yet they were willing to leave their homes and families, risk life and liberty, to obtain freedom for people they had never met.

These events also clearly show the rottenness and hollowness of the bonds connecting the North to the South. The same man who was hanged in the South as a traitor and murderer we in the North honor as a martyr and a saint. Considering, furthermore, the hatred, animosity, and bitterness with which the two parts of the nation are facing each other; considering that they have been on display more than ever before in the few sessions that the newly convened Congress has held so far; and considering that slavery and freedom simply cannot in the long run exist side by side, one cannot be blind to the fact that a great conflict is both necessary and inevitable. This conflict can and must end in splitting the Union, and only such a split will bring about more natural and harmonious conditions.

The slavocracy understands this as clearly or even more clearly than the North and is all too well aware of its own weakness. The South knows that even the timid and passive resistance of the Republicans, who are not opposed to slavery where it has long been established but simply do not wish to permit its further extension through the creation of new slavery states, will inevitably undermine slavery and lead to its ultimate destruction. The South also knows that it cannot survive under conditions of equal rights but will be crushed by the superiority of the free states; it therefore yells and screams, demanding that the majority bow to the minority's desire for the protection, maintenance, and extension of slavery and renewing its old threat of tearing apart the Union if the South doesn't get its way.

The slave owners argue that slavery is not only legal in those states where it was established a long time ago but also in each territory under the Stars and Stripes. They absolutely deny the existence of even a square foot of land outside the free states where slavery would not be by definition legal. They also assume every slave owner's right to take his slaves into any free state and to keep them there as long as he chooses. Beyond that, they demand the abolition of all laws that forbid the African slave trade as an act of piracy because they consider such laws as a direct insult to their way of life, which depends on the slave trade and the products of slave labor. Finally, they refuse to recognize that a colored person, no matter how light his skin as a result of his aristocratic paternity, might have even the least right to freedom. In the next presidential election the South's chief demand will be that the North not only accept these principles but take an active part in their implementation.

Notes

1. Manuscript (December, 1859), Assing Papers, Deutsches Literaturarchiv, Marbach.

2. John E. Cook was a young man who had been a law clerk in Connecticut and first met Brown in 1856. The brothers Barclay and Edwin Coppoc (the name is consistently misspelled as "Coppic" in Assing's manuscript text) both participated in Brown's raid at Harpers Ferry; Barclay escaped capture, but Edwin was tried, sentenced to death, and executed. John Anthony Copeland was a free African American from North Carolina and a graduate of Oberlin College. Shields Green, a former slave, had been introduced to Brown by Frederick Douglass in Rochester in 1858.

44

Literary War of the North Against the South—The Octoroon[1]

All those living on the other side of the Atlantic who are still naive enough to believe that banishing books and persecuting their authors are the exclusive prerogative of despotic monarchies would change their views if only they could take a close look at the conditions in the South of this great republic. About eight months ago a book appeared in New York with the title *The Impending Crisis of the South* by Rowan Hinton Helper of North Carolina; it swept like wildfire through the United States and was in everyone's hand in a very short time. The crisis the South is approaching is nothing less than its complete impoverishment and entire ruin caused by the curse of slavery on that region. The book is dedicated to the six million whites in the South who do not own slaves but who are subjugated and kept in ignorance and political dependence by an aristocracy of about three hundred thousand slaveholders—a situation that is only one step above slavery. The author addresses his remarks primarily to them, the most numerous class of the South, and he calls on them to cast off a yoke that subjugates, lowers, and impoverishes them more with every day that goes by. The blow that this book delivers against the system is the most severe that slavery has been dealt in recent times.

Helper fights the enemy not primarily with reasons based on humanitarianism and justice, which have been exhausted by the abolitionists of the North and are usually modified by the selfishness of the ignorant masses to serve their own interests; rather, he argues with statistical tables and hard numbers gleaned from official documents in Washington. Confronted with the unrelenting, unarguable facts themselves by reading this book, even the dimmest of Southerners who do not hold slaves will want to join the cause of the abolitionists out of self-interest. They will learn among other things that in the year 1790, when the first census was taken, the state of New York did not have half as many inhabitants as the State of Virginia, while in 1850, just sixty years later, Virginia had a population of only a little more than one-third of that of New York. Even more surprising is the discrepancy between North and South in regard to trade, industrial products, and agriculture, despite the fact that the South was in a dominant position during the first years of independence. We learn from this book that alone the value of the hay harvest in the free states, which in 1850 was $142,138,998, exceeded not only that of the hay harvest in the slavery states but the total of their tobacco, hemp, sugar cane, and even that of the all-dominant cotton production by $3,533,275. We learn, furthermore, that the average cost of an acre of land in the northern states was $28.07, in the Northwest $11.39, in the South, on the other hand, with generally better soil, only $5.34. We also see that the real and personal property of the inhabitants of the state of New York would be sufficient to buy the total property— including the slaves—of the states of Arkansas, Delaware, Florida, Maryland,

Missouri, Mississippi, Tennessee, Texas, and the District of Columbia—and that New York would still retain a balance of 133 million dollars after this trade.

There is a similar imbalance in regard to knowledge, education, and everything having to do with them. While in 1850 there appeared 1,790 journals and newspapers in the North, the South had merely 704, all of which together had a lower circulation than the 428 papers that are printed in New York City alone. The most striking difference, however, is in the number of adults who are illiterate: although the total population of the North is more than double that of the South, and the former receives an annual infusion of many thousands of illiterate Irish immigrants, the South is still far ahead by 100,000 white adults who can neither read nor write.

It is no surprise, then, that the slavocracy is fuming about this book and has made its possession such a crime that any person who is found to have it in his possession is likely to be in danger of his life, to say nothing of the author, who might praise his good fortune for being subjected to the mockery of a trial rather than having a lynch mob string him up on the next tree. However, as is usual in these matters, the worst enemies have turned out to be better than the closest friends: all the noise, whining, and shouting of the Democrats has called the public's attention to this book and has been more effective in giving it widespread circulation than any amount of Republican praise could have accomplished. The most determined vigilance of the slave drivers cannot prevent the smuggling of thousands of copies into the South. At the bottom of innocent-looking crates of cloth, clothing, school books, agricultural implements, general tools, and a thousand other necessary and unnecessary objects with which the North supplies the South down to the last detail, lie hidden copies of *The Impending Crisis of the South*.

In general, much incendiary material reaches the South. Even though the *New York Tribune* and some other antislavery—albeit moderate—papers are no longer distributed by the postmasters of the South, the *Herald*, which is the chief organ of the northern slavery party, takes it upon itself with amusing naiveté to make sure that our dear friends of the South will not miss any news regarding antislavery efforts. Any meeting taking place in New York, in which the consequences of slavery are denounced in the most colorful language and slavery itself is opposed by the most incisive arguments, is reported; or when some outstanding abolitionist calls for a vindication of John Brown and a crusade against all slaveholders, you can be sure that the *Herald* will be the first to yell fire the next morning and reprint every word of the incendiary document in its columns for the South's edification. The service the *Herald* thus renders to the good cause through its blind anger does not go unrecognized or unappreciated; at a meeting of one of the most radical of the abolitionist groups a resolution was passed to extend the organization's profoundest gratitude for the generous dissemination of its principles and ideas.

Since the Negro question is the central issue in politics, since it is the main question compared to which all other questions pale in significance, it is no surprise that it takes center stage also in other spheres of life and events of daily living. A correspondent who wishes to describe the life of a large city and the extent to which it represents the country as a whole must be intent upon reporting with utmost fidelity to the truth and attend to the great variety of life. So when we turn our attention away from politics to literature, we notice that nothing has lately made as much of a stir as a play presenting the conflicts that the Negro question causes in all aspects of southern life. *The Octoroon*—a term applied to those who are seven parts Caucasian and one eighth African—is the title of a play that has been so popular all winter that afternoon matinées have been scheduled in addition to evening performances, which cannot accommodate the crowds. The author is Dion Boucicault, an actor. Judged from an aesthetic perspective, the play has not the least merit: even when applying a magnifying glass, one cannot detect any trace of character development, thought, or interesting plot complications. Events that are part of the daily life in the South and can be read about in the daily papers are loosely strung together; a few dramatic effects, such as a fire consuming a steamship, are arranged to keep the audience's interest—in short, a brilliant success and no less brilliant monetary rewards are the result of a few cheap tricks. However, as little value as such a work may have in the eyes of a serious critic, one cannot deny that *The Octoroon* has definitely made a positive contribution by the great impact it has had on the masses. Facts that for most people have remained distant and of little importance have suddenly been put into focus through the illusion of the stage, revealing themselves as terrible realities. That such a piece, with its strong opposition to slavery, should have such undivided success and cause not even an attempt at remonstrances by the opposition, proves that public opinion has happily made some progress. It is less than seven years ago that the rabble forced an end to the annual meeting of the Garrisonian antislavery society, and only a little later did the rabble in Philadelphia set a hall on fire in which a similar event was to take place.

Notes

1. New York, February [1860], *Morgenblatt*, 54:11:263–264.

45

Lecturers—Painting—The Cooper Institute[1]

***

Among the most notable and characteristic aspects of the winter season in New York, as well as most other major American cities, is the large number of addresses, lectures, and speeches of all kinds that are offered on a large variety of subjects. Almost every evening one has a choice of ten or twelve or more lectures, not counting the regular talks on specific subjects presented—often at no cost—by a number of institutions and organizations. It would be interesting to see a listing of all those who are full-time or part-time "lecturers" by occupation. Their number must be immense and is steadily growing, even without counting the men in political offices, members of Congress, and others who travel from time to time—such as during presidential elections—through various states to speak to the public. There are famous orators, such as Wendell Philipps, Frederick Douglass, Chapin,[2] Henry Ward Beecher, and Everett, who speak on literary, philosophical, social, or political topics. They are often engaged by lyceums or by literary and scientific societies—sometimes for one hundred dollars per lecture—and travel all winter repeating two or three lectures in larger or smaller towns, occasionally speaking at no cost about other subjects.

In addition, there are the agents, both male and female, representing anti-slavery, temperance, women's emancipation, and other societies and associations that send them out to canvass the country for new members and supporters. Many of these "lecturers," whose abilities are not brilliant enough to excite the spoiled and jaded public of the large cities, limit their activities to the smaller towns in the interior, where, without becoming famous, they at least make a decent living. I know women who out of the necessity of providing for their own income have supported themselves and their families in this manner. Anyone here can choose to become a lecturer: whoever believes he can improve his circumstances and has—or thinks he has—a sufficiently good voice, an agreeably flowing manner of speech, and a handful of reasonable ideas on any subject whatsoever may try his luck at lecturing; he may rent a church in some small town, announce the gathering, and try out his powers of speech. It is not unheard of that speakers whose names are not yet household words will go from street corner to street corner with a bag of nails and a hammer (or, in its absence, even a stone) posting their own handbills. Like in all other trades, there are many humbugs; besides the many honest lecturers who present themselves according to the best of their abilities, no matter how limited these may be, there are those who pretend to be lecturers, even though no mortal has ever heard them give a single presentation.

In New York, a corrupt German preacher annually announces a lecture, but since he knows that not even a dozen people would choose to attend, he visits all of his friends and acquaintances in advance to force admission tickets on them. At 25 cents a ticket everyone is glad to be rid of the annoying blatherer, though no one seriously intends to be at the lecture. On the evening in question, the Reverend gentleman always happens to be indisposed and unable to perform his responsibilities due to hoarseness or some other impediment.

This year's exhibit of the works of American artists is scheduled to open next month, which shows that in the realm of art there is generally much activity and evident progress. Sculpture and painting are being cultivated and are enjoying more and more popularity. "The Studio Building," a rather palatial structure containing only artists' studios, has for some time accommodated about thirty artists; walking through these studios offers an opportunity to see not only what has been produced but also works still being created and not yet seen in public. It is here that Leutze does his work; having been trained in Germany, he has become the painter of American history, although hitherto he has limited himself to scenes from the War of Independence. He has just finished another large painting, representing the battle of Princeton, in which Washington is once again the central figure.[3] The painting, of which I had earlier seen the preliminary drawing in Leutze's studio, is excellent, and the public is delighted to see its hero glorified once again. But will the public welcome with the same applause the artist who at some point in the future will be daring enough to paint the second act of the battle for freedom—the struggle between slavery and freedom—that surely and inevitably will have to be enacted?

Church, the great American landscape painter, also works here on his wonderfully beautiful and imposing representations of American scenery; but since he is not in New York at present, I could not gain entrance to his studio. However, in Gignoux's studio, I did see a charming picture, a landscape in the first flush of spring.[4] The poetry of spring is not very well known over here; it is rarely made the subject of painting, possibly in part because spring is of such short duration and often becomes less than delightful due to bad weather, and partly because the deep, rich colors of autumn present such a compelling subject. Gignoux, however, has captured the scent, the fresh and youthful charm of a sunny day in May with remarkable truth and fidelity. In comparison, a small, early painting by the same artist, showing the polar sea and the reddish-yellow winter sun at noon low on the horizon between icebergs, makes a strange impression. During the winter months, the artists of the studio building arrange a monthly evening reception, at which all completed work is exhibited; tickets are distributed to the friends of art and other preferred individuals.

Recently women have been given an opportunity to receive training as painters and graphic artists, an opportunity that hitherto had been completely lacking. A wealthy man by the name of Peter Cooper[5] has established a drawing academy for women, called "The Cooper Institute," in a building specially constructed for the benevolent purpose of offering free instruction and making it possible for women to find employment opportunities in a field that had hitherto been open only to men. For this reason, the Institute is less designed to develop female artists, of whom there will always be only a small and select group, than to offer women the opportunity to gain facility in those branches of art that can be usefully employed for industrial purposes. Toward this end, attentiveness and perseverance are sufficient, as for instance in drawing patterns, ornaments, labels, and similar objects for which there is never a lack of customers. Yet anyone is free to go beyond these limits.

The studios are located in a long series of rooms that are connected by a hallway and amply supplied with plaster models, copper etchings, and all necessary things except high-quality paintings for copying—the absence of which has been the cause of complaints. I saw a few older women working on woodcuts, an activity that must be a good source of income given the large number of illustrated newspapers. Free lectures on chemistry, mathematics, and geometry are also presented in this building. The enormous costs of the Institute are covered by the high rents that are charged for stores, stock rooms, and similar establishments located on the first floor. Among these is also one of the largest rooms, which is used for lectures and other public events and is booked almost every evening during the winter months.

***

Notes

1. New York, March [1860], *Morgenblatt*, 54:17:407–408 and 54:18:430–431.

2. The least well-known of this group of famous American orators is Edwin H. Chapin (1814–1880), a Universalist minister and pastor of the Fourth Universalist Church of New York City. He became one of the popular and successful orators of his age, speaking to ever larger audiences at different meeting halls in New York.

3. In May 1853, Assing had commented on seeing Leutze's "Washington Crossing the Delaware" (see Essay 3).

4. Frederick Edwin Church (1826–1900) was associated with the Hudson River School; Régis-François Gignoux (1816–1882), born in France, settled in New York in 1840 and was also associated with the Hudson River School.

5. Peter Cooper (1791–1883), a wealthy inventor, industrialist, and philanthropist, is primarily remembered for establishing Cooper Union for the education of the working classes.

46

Mormonism—Preparations for the Presidential Election[1]

The House of Representatives recently passed a bill prohibiting polygamy in the Utah territory, the home of the Mormons. At first glance it seems quite astounding that a country where people squawk and chatter more about morality and propriety than in any other country in the world, where they sigh and roll their eyes in tones of smugness and postures of piety about other peoples' corruption and godlessness, should publicly and legally permit the existence of an institution that conflicts so sharply with the notions, attitudes, and conditions of civilized society. However, in a country that in the name of the republic permits the existence of a kind of slavery that has no parallel in any civilized or uncivilized nation as to its cruelty, barbarism, and immorality, it should not be surprising to discover contradictions and inconsistencies at every turn. If it were not for the indirect influence of the slavery question, polygamy among the Mormons would hardly have been tolerated until now.

Since the Democrats assert that Congress has neither the right nor the authority to prohibit slavery in the territories but that the decision depends entirely on "popular sovereignty," they could hardly in the same breath recognize and make use of a right—which they have so stubbornly denied with respect to slavery—simply to suppress the lesser evil. This is particularly true because the Mormons, acting on the old principle of "I scratch your back if you scratch mine," have always been exceedingly friendly toward and tolerant of the "peculiar institution." Without the support of the Republican majority the bill would probably not have passed in the House, and it still remains to be seen whether or not the Senate will concur. Whatever its fate may be and no matter how gently the administration has handled the Mormons, Mormonism has certainly reached its peak. A few years more or less matter little, and even if the number of its adherents should increase in the immediate future, it would not guarantee more than a temporary existence.

The whole system lacks inner vitality because it is based neither on progressive ideas nor on any noble element of human nature. The entire doctrine is void of anything that might claim to be new, even if it were just a new error. Unlike the fanatics of earlier times, Joe Smith, the Yankee prophet, did evidently not believe that he was the messiah who would reveal a new truth or bring a new light to the world. With the single exception of polygamy and the belief that it is divinely sanctioned, Mormonism does not differ sufficiently from other major Christian sects to deserve the name of a new religion. It differs hardly more from them than they differ among themselves, and were it not for this one single point, Joe Smith and his "Latter-Day Saints" could have settled quietly and peacefully among other Christian sects. However, this would not have satisfied his ambitious plans: he could not expect power, influence, or fame by being the founder of a sect that did not spring from the needs of the times and therefore had no prospect of growth and achieving increasing importance. Little intelligence, genius, and education as he may have had, he did not lack savvy; and if he was a stranger to the noble motives of human nature, he was all the more familiar with its low and contemptible aspects. They were the basis of his scheme, and he hooked his followers with the bait of polygamy.

Some people like to see a parallel between Mormonism and Mohammedanism, but this view confers an unwarranted honor on the former because from their very beginnings these two religions have been based on opposing principles. No one can deny that Mohammed's appearance and teachings brought about enormous progress among his times and his people, and that their condition improved much beyond anything they had previously known. Even the idea of polygamy that is so offensive to us appears in a different light when we consider that the great prophet lived among a people whose women existed at the lowest level of education, where marriage was hardly known and promiscuity rampant. Under such circumstances, the laws restricting the number of wives a man may have to four and providing for divorce seems more like a salutary restriction than a concession. On the other hand, no one could possibly mistake the fact that in our age, in our civilization, with our ideas and our women's position in society the Mormon prophet simply appealed to the basest instincts and appetites of the crudest and most uneducated rabble. It is exclusively from this group that Mormonism recruits its supporters, and never has a halfway educated man been won over. Not even considering all other absurdities, offenses, and awkwardnesses, the complete absence of any trace of education and beauty, the prolific crudity and intellectual barrenness in the speeches and proclamations of Brigham Young and other prominent Mormon leaders would be sufficient to fill even a person of few intellectual pretensions with disgust and revulsion.

In the next few days the Democratic convention for the nomination of the next candidate for the presidency will take place. The Democratic camp is very busy, and delegates as well as all those who have an interest in the proceedings are rushing to Charleston, which has been selected as the convention site and is anticipating an economic harvest as it has never gathered before this occasion. For weeks all available rooms in hotels and private homes have been booked at prices that seem incredible by normal standards. Larger rooms go for fifteen, eighteen, even twenty dollars, small bedrooms for six to seven; and people gladly pay three or four dollars for the worst garret. It goes without saying that a thousand conjectures are made about who will be chosen to be the candidate, but as of now S. A. Douglas, the darling of the northern Democrats, has the best chances. Whoever will be it, either he or some southern fire-eater, it is certain he will have a hard fight on his hands against the ever increasing Republican element. As long as the Republicans do not make some mistake, there is reason to hope that the year 1861 will see the first Republican president installed in the White House.

***

Notes

1. New York, April [1860], *Morgenblatt*, 54:22:522–524.

47

Presidential Candidates—Anniversaries—Humboldt's Letters[1]

A time of excitement lies ahead: the campaign for the presidential election has begun. On May 18, the Republican convention, meeting in Chicago, chose Abraham Lincoln of Illinois as its presidential candidate by a large majority in a session lasting only a few days. The electric wires carried the news instantly to all corners, and as usual on such occasions fireworks and cannons were set off in the evening. The determined radical Republicans, however, feel bitterly disappointed and betrayed because they had little doubt that William Seward would be the chosen candidate. He is one of the most distinguished members of the Senate, who during his long political career has consistently proven himself to be one of the foremost and untiring defenders of liberty and progress as well as an implacable foe of slavery. An experienced statesman, an excellent speaker, a man of great talent, ability, and broad education, he, more than any other candidate, was destined to be the standard bearer of the party of progress. His defeat shamefully proves the lukewarm convictions of the masses, for whom such a man is too radical; instead, they prefer a relatively obscure person, who has not been as daring in his commitment to the fight for human rights, progress, and dignity.

The Democratic convention took place as planned in Charleston in April; but this formerly powerful party is internally so unstable and divided into so many factions that the convention adjourned after many stormy sessions to reconvene in mid-June in Baltimore. It was the slavery question that again was the cause of the dissention. Not satisfied with all the concessions that the unprincipled, cowardly northern Democrats had already made, the South demanded a platform, according to which slavery in the new territories could not even be determined by the will of the local populace but would be recognized under all circumstances as the basic legal condition protected by law, without giving the settlers any opportunity to reject the enemy. If only out of prudence, the northern delegates could not agree to this provision because such a platform would cause the loss of the few remaining Democratic supporters and bring about an inevitable defeat. The most formidable candidate of the northern Democrats and the only one who might threaten a Republican victory is Stephen Arnold Douglas; but his nomination was prevented by the furious opposition of the southern fire-eaters, who consider him a renegade and therefore hate him more bitterly than they hate Republicans and abolitionists.[2]

A third party, an extremely conservative one with a platform whose major point is the maintenance of the Union, but which in every other way hardly penetrates the surface of generalities, had its convention in Baltimore and elected John Bell from Tennessee as its candidate. However, it is all but moribund because it responds in no manner to either the demands of the North or those of the South. Next to the other two parties it is of no consequence.

Abraham Lincoln, whose supporters in the West call him "honest old Abe," is a man of the people who has reached his present position entirely through his own exertions. He was born in 1809 in Kentucky, but his family soon moved to southern Indiana, where he spent his youth under conditions of extremely hard work. All in all, he had barely six months of the most inadequate schooling, earning a living now as a field hand, now as a day laborer or riverboatman on the Wabash and the Mississippi. In his twenty-first year he went to Illinois and has lived there ever since. Here he began his career also as a field hand, then took a position as a salesman in a bookstore, and a year later volunteered his services in one of the campaigns against the Indians, rising to the rank of captain. The next step up took him into the Illinois legislature, having meanwhile studied law and become a respected and influential attorney.

In 1846 he was first elected to Congress, and in 1858 he became a candidate for the Senate together with Douglas, whose term had ended. He has the reputation of an unblemished, completely upright character; however, he seems not to have distinguished himself in terms of unusual ability or outstanding intellect. On the other hand, the horror and anger with which the Democrats have greeted his nomination may be a good sign that he can bring together the various factions and free the country from the hated yoke of slavery and its willing servants.

The anniversaries with their usual downpours and crowds of supporters are over. Among all the societies that hold their annual meetings at this time of year the antislavery groups and those for the emancipation of women are the only tolerable ones, even though the latter often become ridiculous and repulsive because of the exaggerations in which their representatives indulge. They are the only organizations in which arrogant religious orthodoxy is not the end-all and be-all, and they are represented by the most brilliant and accomplished speakers. As a conscientious reporter, I did not fail to attend several of these meetings; however, even with the best intention to recognize and be receptive to everything that was new and valuable, I do not know what to say without repeating myself because few issues emerged that had not already been dealt with *ad nauseam*. With his compelling manner of speech and his brilliant mind, Wendell Phillips is almost the only one who is still able to throw new light on old subjects and can capture a jaded audience.

While listening to the various speakers at these meetings, I could not escape the impression how superficial American life is and how quickly it therefore ceases to be a subject of discussion. For the immigrant who first experiences these large meetings and listens to all the polished speakers they always appear grand, important, and impressive. This is especially true for a German, who has not seen anything like it before because of the absence of public life in Germany and the consequent dearth of accomplished public speakers: he is swept away, enthusiastic, and uplifted. But someone like myself, who has followed the meetings for almost seven years, participated in the causes that they pursue, and thought about the issues, I cannot but notice that the speakers are so repetitive that they finally seem to be mere copies of themselves. All the little vanities, the desire to be noticed, which for some are as strong a motive as the cause itself, all the personal weaknesses and problems that remain hidden to the inexperienced eye, reveal themselves upon closer inspection. You are astonished at the limited horizon, the narrow view, the one-sided, traditional ideas, the religious orthodoxy—all of which prevent a truly broad perspective. You become impatient with listening to extended discussions of social and religious questions that have long since been agreed upon among people of education in Germany.

Far be it from me to dismiss the good influence that such organizations, especially those opposed to slavery, have had on public opinion; I am convinced that there is no better way of getting to the generally thoughtless, intellectually torpid, and prejudiced masses. For what has greater and deeper impact than the living words from the mouth of a gifted orator? Yet all the good that results from such efforts does not prevent that a person who needs no further education and information on the subjects in question is often seized by a feeling of intellectual vacuousness when he asks himself how much of what he has heard is worth remembering.

***

Humboldt's letters to Varnhagen are the talk in literary circles here as much as in Europe.[3] The reading public's expectations were aroused and its patience tested because, given the speed with which the first printings were sold out in Germany, the local German book dealers could respond to the many inquiries only with counseling patience. However, at present two reprints are being circulated, of which the first edition as well as an English translation by Friedrich Kapp are also already sold out. The enlightened and freethinking part of the public is of course rejoicing that Humboldt is one of their own, while the opposition is sore and upset just like in Germany. Of course, Americans miss many allusions to particular persons and circumstances in Prussia, but Humboldt's boldly liberal thought and his opinions about slavery and American democracy rile Democrats and the religiously orthodox sufficiently to have them vent their anger—rather amusingly—in several newspapers.

Notes

1. New York, May [1860], *Morgenblatt*, 54:26:617–619.

2. See Essay 49, n. 2.

3. *Letters of Alexander von Humboldt to Varnhagen von Ense. From 1827 to 1858. With Extracts from Varnhagen's Diaries and Letters of Varnhagen and Others to Humboldt* (trans. Friedrich Kapp; New York, 1860). The comment Assing makes here is particularly interesting in light of the fact that Karl August Varnhagen von Ense (1785–1858) was her uncle, an outspoken and active supporter of German political liberalism. Before coming to America, Assing lived for some time in her

uncle's house in Berlin together with her sister, Ludmilla, but the arrangement did not work out for Ottilie. After a family crisis, she returned to Hamburg and eventually left for America, while her sister remained with the uncle. Ludmilla edited and published her uncle's papers even though they were officially considered radical and subversive by the Prussian authorities. This volume of the correspondence between Varnhagen and Humboldt in translation contains a preface by Ludmilla Assing.

48

Election Prospects—Southern Fear—A Convention of Infidels[1]

With every passing day, the prospects are better for a glorious victory by the Republicans on November 6—a victory that will put an end to the rule of the slaveholders and the contemptible, disloyal, and cowardly northern Democrats, who for nearly eight years have steeped this land in shame and made it the object of contempt among other nations. On October 9, Pennsylvania, Ohio, and Indiana held elections for state offices, which are nearly always a reliable indicator of the results in the presidential election in those states; the Democrats suffered tremendous defeats everywhere, but mostly in Pennsylvania, which once was the bulwark of the Democrats in the North. The wealthy merchants of New York are trembling for the well-being of their clients in the South and for the profitable African slave trade, which they have been able to conduct and expand with impunity because the Democratic administration winks at their behavior: in the course of one year no fewer than fifty slave ships have departed from the port of New York. These merchants are raising enormous sums of money to purchase votes for their candidates. Particularly in the city of New York, where the scum of all nations gathers, the roughest, most ignorant, and extreme part of the Irish population are always ready to become the willing tools of the Democrats. Because they are a numerically mighty ally, bribery will flourish again this year, but it cannot succeed against the overwhelming Republican majority within the state, which declared for Frémont already in 1856. As the most populous state in the Union, New York can cast thirty-five electoral votes and is therefore the chief stronghold of the Republican party.

One of the most brilliant spectacles in some time was recently offered to the citizens of New York in the spectacular torchlight parade of the "Wide Awakes." This is the name that the members of the Republican Club have given themselves since the beginning of this year's campaign, but it is a term that cannot be translated because in German it would make little sense. The Wide Awakes have chosen a special uniform for their parade; it consists of a short leather coat and a leather cap. There had been earlier parades wherever there are Wide Awakes, but they were local, and this time it was decided to do something on a large scale and invite Wide Awakes from every part of the country. Clubs came from Connecticut, Maine, Rhode Island, New Jersey, and many towns in New York state, and on October 3, you could enjoy a magnificent torchlight parade of almost 20,000 people. In rows of sixteen, it made a veritable stream of light and was truly picturesque: every organization had its own flags, banners, emblems, and mottos, as well as its own leaders and musical bands. The parade marshals were decked out in gold embroidery, waving plumes, and glistening stars, and the uniforms shone in the most varied colors, with some companies wearing blue coats and others sporting red, yellow, black, or silver coats and caps. In the light of the torches they all presented a brilliant effect that was still heightened by the countless rockets, roman candles, and all other manner of fireworks.

It was gratifying to notice the good behavior and quiet demeanor that the Wide Awakes displayed without exception. Neither wild yells nor rowdy behavior, so common and unavoidable at all Democratic events, marred the impressive proceedings. There were none of the usual cartoons of political opponents or banners with bitter and insulting attacks that usually mar such occasions. The crowd evidently consisted of the most respectable class, the true core of the people. Some people feared that Democratic rowdies would cause serious disruptions, and indeed the Democratic gangs—the so-called Dead Rabbits and Short Boys, who make the Five Points and its environment unsafe by causing street fights—gathered and greeted the parade with hisses, threats, and curses. However, the influence of a quiet and dignified demeanor on the part of the Republicans was so great that even the rowdies were cowed, and there were only a few negligible incidents of jeers and catcalls. Only on one occasion did a dastardly coward throw a brick from a house, seriously injuring one of the torchbearers.

A large Democratic meeting took place a few days later, also involving a torchlight parade, and it was a perfect opportunity for making comparisons. A more glaring contrast would have been impossible to imagine: it was a veritable orgy of licentious freedom. Several participants in the parade tried to use rockets to set fire to a Republican flag hanging over the street, and when they approached the headquarters of the Republican clubs on Broadway they suddenly attacked the members who had innocently gathered on the sidewalk, causing such scenes of violence that the police had to step in and restore order by force. To this day the Democrats have never repudiated the elements of rowdyism and brutality that are part of their ranks, and it is incomprehensible how any person, even someone of only moderate education and civilization, would not be filled with horror and disgust—no matter what his political persuasion may be.

In sharp contrast to the happy excitement that has spread across the entire North in anticipation of imminent victory, the slavocracy of the South is paralyzed with anger: they not only foresee the inevitable end of their political power and majority but suffer from their old illness—excessive fear of an alleged slave insurrection. One might call this fear a chronic disease that, even though it doesn't manifest itself simultaneously in all parts of the country, acts like an infection moving through the body from one organ to another; it travels from slave state to slave state, never ceasing to torment them in this or that provincial corner. This past summer the panic seized Texas. Several persons were hanged, others mistreated, tarred, feathered, and driven out of the state, and a large number of Negroes were murdered without any facts having come to light. At present, the evil has emerged again in Norfolk, Virginia, and it seems to have robbed those who have fallen under its spell of all judgment and rationality: the most ridiculous and patently contrived inventions drive them to the edge of lunacy.

That is what happened in Texas, where rumor had it that the Negroes had huge amounts of strychnine with which they intended to poison the wells and thereby exterminate the entire white population. And the story that currently keeps Norfolk and its surroundings at a fever pitch is just about as plausible and believable: it is rumored that a shipload of abolitionists, probably equipped with weapons and ammunition, will soon come ashore to set the slaves free by force. A free Negro by the name of Dick Ryan is supposed to be the ringleader. If fear and panic were the only result, one might watch from a distance and rejoice in the self-inflicted and well-earned torments of the slavocracy; yet, as is invariably true in such matters, the full weight of a bad situation falls upon the those who are most helpless and oppressed—the slaves and the free Negroes. A system of terror and torture is being visited upon them that has its parallel only in the inquisition of the Middle Ages.

On the basis of the most unsubstantiated rumors masses of slaves and free Negroes alike are captured and forced by the whip to confess everything of which they are accused; and then the alleged conspirators and their collaborators are just as summarily whipped to death or hanged for having made these forced confessions. Judicial murder based on mere suspicion happens over and over again. A poor Irish working man was shot down for no other reason than that he started running away when the officers approached him; the same thing happened to a free Negro, who thought it wiser to take to his heels than to let himself be arrested for alleged arson. A thorough search is being conducted for the horrible Dick Ryan, a creature whose existence is at least as unproven as that of the sea serpent; and it is by no means implausible that some day hence some tramp will identify some poor Negro as this horrid imaginary monster and have him strung up on the next tree.

The slaveholders themselves concede that such a system of terror is necessary for maintaining slavery; nevertheless they insist that slavery is the greatest blessing for the slave as well as for his owner and the population as a whole. Even the most eager defenders of slavery in the North admit that it cannot be very agreeable to live among a people that can be put into such a state of panic at any moment by every Tom, Dick, or Harry. It must be unpleasant, they concede, to live in a society in which public order depends on a slave's confessions dictated by the lash, and where the most peaceful citizen is constantly in danger of being imprisoned, even murdered, for alleged abolitionist convictions or the mere possession of a book that is not approved in the South.

A few days ago, a meeting of freethinkers—a "Convention of Infidels"—took place here. The term "infidel" is applied to all those who are not members of any religious sect and who merrily go their way without concern for church or priesthood. Over here, religion is almost a matter of fashion among the masses and the means of securing advancement and material profit. Many thousands consider a freethinker as little better than a murderer or at least a thief. It takes a good deal of moral courage, therefore, openly to oppose the prejudices of the majority, and many would be reluctant to go so far as to show themselves in such an assembly. But in spite of the anathema a large and apparently most civil and well-educated group had gathered. Most of the speakers were older men whose furrowed brows showed signs of independent thought, having gradually freed themselves from the bonds of narrow sectarianism. Ernestine Rose, that excellent woman whom I have had occasion to mention earlier,[2] and who is always on the side of progress, participated vigorously in the proceedings.

The purpose of the meeting was to determine the most suitable measures by which the masses might be freed from the intellectual degradations of a hypocritical, unconscionable, and cowardly clergy and thereby might achieve a general advance in morality, humanitarianism, and progress. A number of resolutions were introduced to this end, causing much lively discussion. On several occasions opponents in the audience took the word, but they were heard with great patience and politeness. One of them attacked the entire convention in such terms of crude abuse that he would most likely have been thrown out of any other meeting. But he was given full opportunity to vent his anger, and as soon as he had finished, an old gentleman with long white hair and beard as well as notably sharp features and equally sharp logic so overwhelmed him that he was never heard from again. In Germany, public issues are commented on primarily through books, whereas here it is done in meetings, speeches, and debates; if this does not lead to much deep thought, it cannot be denied that many who lack patience, attention, or time for reading books of weighty content are motivated to think independently by listening to speeches they can understand.

I cannot conclude these comments without mentioning a "ratification meeting" of the German Republicans. Carl Schurz was the principal speaker of the evening and he was received with enthusiastic applause. He is one of the best orators in this country, which is the home of many accomplished speakers. A man of rich intellectual endowment, of brilliant expression, and of irresistible wit and humor, he speaks with both ease and elegance, which is all the more impressive as his whole manner of being exudes a fresh and natural demeanor. There is nothing artificial about him, no straining for effect; everything is fresh and direct and seemingly an inspiration of the moment. He analyzed and refuted the resolutions recently adopted by the German Democrats, which he dissected so thoroughly that nothing remained in the end but the name. Increasingly understanding their own position over here, the Germans are abandoning the so-called Democracy and adopting Republicanism.

Notes

1. New York, October [1860], *Morgenblatt*, 54:48:1147–1150.

2. See Essay 15, n. 5.

49

The Presidential Election—Republicans and Democrats[1]

The campaign is over. For the first time in many years the propagandists for slavery, the Democrats, have suffered a decisive defeat, and Abraham Lincoln, the candidate of the Republicans, has been elected president by an overwhelming majority. Never since the beginning of the republic has a campaign been more heated and passionate, and more than ever it has been a contest of principles—between freedom and slavery. For the Democrats it was a desperate battle, a matter of life and death; the more all prospects of success faded because of divisions within the party, the more passionate and bitter did the attacks on the Republicans become. The entire South made an effort to use its old trick of intimidation, with newspapers and speakers threatening separation from the Union if Lincoln were elected. Although they themselves did not believe in the realization of such a threat, the willing henchmen of slavery in the North put on grave expressions and predicted the inevitability of the calamity; however, the people were not taken in by this old bugbear and refused to be chased into hiding. When the October state election in Pennsylvania with its large Republican majority left no doubt about the outcome of the presidential election in that state, every rational person had to admit that the election of any one of the three remaining candidates—Bell, Douglas, or Breckenridge—was an impossibility.[2] At that point, the Democrats' last remaining hope was New York, whose thirty-three electoral votes would decide the outcome; and as certain as it was that New York City—the home of the scum of all nations thanks to the masses of rude and ignorant Irishmen—would deliver a Democratic majority, just as surely the powerful Republican majority in the state as a whole would predominate.

The Democrats did not have a shadow of hope in either the West or the East. Only New York was doubtful and therefore had in recent weeks become the stage for the Democrats' major efforts and campaign activities. Fearing for their clients in the South, a few wealthy merchants led by the house of Henry Smith and Townsend had managed through endless intrigues and primarily by means of bribes to bring about a fusion of the three anti-Republican parties, and they set off all the mines they had laid. But even if the state of New York had presented a Democratic majority, none of the three candidates would thereby have been elected to the presidency; yet Lincoln—though having more votes than any other candidate—would not have had the absolute majority over the other candidates that he needed to win the election. In such a case, which has never occurred since the beginning of the republic, the Constitution provides that the president be elected by the House of Representatives. If a majority cannot be found there either, the matter goes before the Senate, which merely has the authority to elect a vice president, who, however, can function as a president. This was the Democrats' calculated hope: they knew that a majority could not be achieved in the House and that the whole process would not have advanced by March 4, the date the president has to commence his duties; the Senate, on the other hand, has been a continuing stronghold of slavery, and it could not fail to elect Joe Lane vice president, an extreme propagandist for slavery.[3]

Such a situation would have prolonged throughout the winter the feverish excitement in which the country finds itself during a presidential election. Business activity would have largely stopped and a money crisis would have brought about an inevitable calamity, but these patriots were ready to place this burden on the people to maintain their own power. They availed themselves of every possible trick. For instance, several of the big clothing stores which earn large amounts of money from their southern customers distributed a circular to their German tailors (their principal work force) informing them that in case of a Republican victory the South would inevitably secede, which would stop all business in the North and force all tailors working for these houses out of work. Only a collective effort on the part of the Democrats could prevent such a calamity, and every tailor was urged to cast a Democratic ballot. They had counted on the ignorance and credulousness of the tailors, but the latter were not so easily scared and called a meeting to discuss appropriate action. The authors of the circular sent their emissaries to the meeting to explain in the darkest colors the consequences of a Republican victory; they also prophesied a general revolution, anarchy, and a Negro rebellion, but even these scare tactics did not hit home. As one of the tailors calmly replied: "If the slaves in the South are freed, they will soon be in need of clothes, and they will make just as good customers for us as their masters."

Immense sums of money were spent to buy votes, but what succeeded in New York City was a failure among the true people in the country. Efforts were even made to manufacture a money crisis and to drive down stocks so as to frighten the masses and push them into the Democratic ranks; but this cheap trick created nothing but outrage and rebounded on those who had tried it because everyone saw through it and understood that the health of commerce and industry depended on the conclusion of the campaign and would necessarily suffer from any prolongation of it. It soon became clear that the Democrats' game was over, but the henchmen of slavery made a final desperate gambit by deciding to use illegal votes to so inflate the Democratic majority in the city that it could challenge the Republican majority in the country. However, nowadays this is no longer as easy as it was in earlier times when Democratic thugs would roam the city in gangs to cast their votes in every district with impunity. Today, a list of eligible voters is prepared in advance for every district, and all suspicious situations are investigated; since everyone who has evidence of an illegal vote receives a $100 reward, it is no wonder that there are many close observers at each polling station. The "Wide Awakes" have distinguished themselves through excellent service and vigilance at the polls: their calm, resolute demeanor so impressed the thugs and rowdies who formerly used violence to keep many voters away from the polls that the day of the election was quieter than ever before. It passed almost without incidents—an unheard-of fact—

and the result is a Republican majority in New York State of nearly 50,000 votes.

The "Wide Awakes" turned out to be an outstanding aspect of this year's campaign. As is generally known, the Republican party is still new, having first presented itself as an independent party four years ago with Frémont as its candidate. Even though it had been growing and spreading quickly, at that time it lacked the kind of systematic organization that made the Democrats so powerful. Since then the Republicans have used their time well: throughout the North and even in some of the border states more and more Republican clubs have been springing up every day, and at the beginning of the campaign their membership presented itself as the "Wide Awakes," a well organized and impressive force. One look at them—at their meetings, their parades, or their demonstrations—sufficed to convince you that these were the representatives of the best and most educated part of the nation. It was a genuine pleasure to see all these well-educated, mostly young men in the light of their torches, dressed in colorful coats, marching in their evening parades or welcoming some celebrated speaker. Their movements had almost military elegance and precision, and in this respect they stood particularly out against the Democrats, to say nothing of the fits of rudeness, the loud brawling, and the many drunkards that inevitably accompany the presentations of the Democrats. No matter how often the "Wide Awakes" were attacked by Democratic rowdies or, more commonly, threatened with assault, they always went unarmed; and though they were perfectly capable of defending themselves, they were never the aggressor and have never been guilty of the least excess.

In no way less typical but far less attractive a figure is the so-called "fancy-man," the professional Democratic rowdy. He is in his glory during a campaign, but even during the rest of the year he works his mischief, being of a class of people that the German reader can hardly imagine. The political rowdy has widespread and absolute influence over a wide circle of his ilk; during election times he often controls more than a thousand votes, for which he is very handsomely paid. For the politician and his allies he is therefore an invaluable asset who may perform any invidious deed with impunity. He is normally a professional prizefighter or gambler, but there are also fancy-men who pursue these noble callings only for their amusement, making politics their profession. The fancy-man lives in an elegant hotel where he spares himself no luxury and mostly is at home in the "bar room." He wears the most costly linens and is dressed according to the latest fashion, and only the insider recognizes him in the street for what he is. Passionate and dissolute in the highest degree, he is also the most vicious and dangerous scrapper ready at the drop of a hat to knock or shoot down anyone who gets in his way.

It is quite common that rowdies will sink their teeth into each other in a fight and, beastlier than wild animals, bite off each other's ears and noses—a crime that is regularly listed as "mayhem" in the municipal registry of crimes. If the fancy-man is either drunk or particularly excited he beats or shoots complete strangers in the street without the least provocation, having no fear that he will be apprehended by the criminal justice system because his political patrons make sure that he remains out of sight. If perchance he should be arrested, a Democratic judge, who probably just sentenced some poor devil to several years incarceration for having stolen a gold watch, will greet him as an old friend and will let him go on the mere promise to be available for an inquest. But because such an inquest never takes place, he feels completely immune to punishment and therefore emboldened to any crime, often committing three or four murders until he reaps his own reward and is killed in some grog shop by one of his own ilk.

It is also by no means unheard of that the patronage he enjoys at the hands of the high and mighty will eventually get him an appointment to some municipal office or that he will achieve dignity and influence by becoming an alderman or a member of the Common Council. Indeed, the current president was shameless enough to appoint an individual of that kind, Isaac Rynders by name, as U.S. marshal of New York "for services rendered." He will no doubt occupy this post until the new president's inauguration will relieve all present officeholders of their governmental duties.

While Lincoln's election was greeted with shouts of joy in the free states, the South rants and raves madly. In Georgia and South Carolina the legislatures have been called into session to deliberate the question of secession from the Union. Some hotheads may be serious about this matter, but in the end all the noise will drift away like smoke. The North can manage very well without South Carolina and Georgia, but they cannot do without the North, which buys their cotton and supplies them with necessary industrial products. When all is said and done, they will find it a lot easier to chatter about secession than to carry it out. They would have to become independent states with their own army and navy, for which they lack the funds. No person of reason could seriously advise to take such a step, but the fanaticism of slavery seems to have robbed people down there of their senses and will lead them to their ruin. "Whom God chooses to destroy, He first drives into madness."

Notes

1. New York, November [1860], *Morgenblatt,* 54:52:1242–1245.

2. John Bell (1797–1869), a senator from Tennessee who supported slavery but opposed secession, was the candidate of the Constitutional Union party; Stephen A. Douglas (1813–1861), senator from Illinois, was chosen as the candidate of the northern wing of the Democrats; John C. Breckenridge (1821–1875) was vice president under James Buchanan and became the presidential candidate of the southern faction of the Democrats.

3. Joseph Lane (1801–1881) represented Oregon in the U.S. Senate; he was originally from North Carolina and served as a general in the Mexican War.

50

Developments in the Southern Part of the Union[1]

Instead of the peace and calm that usually follow a presidential election, this one seems to be merely the prelude to a series of storms that are threatening on the nearer and farther reaches of the political horizon. Led by South Carolina, the southern states are agitating so passionately for a secession from the Union that you would believe they actually mean it, were it not all too well known, on the other hand, that empty threats, posturing, and bluster are the characteristic manner of the southerners. Hence, it is still very probable that the recruiting of volunteer regiments, the firing of guns, the beating of drums, the waving of flags, and the cessation of payments all amount to little more than threats, posturing, and bluster. Of course, in speaking of the South one always refers to a handful of wealthy slaveholders who, in terms of their number, are insignificant when compared to the masses of the actual people; but in those states—primarily in South Carolina—where the worst kind of oligarchy rules under the guise of the republic they are the sole rulers, wielding power and enacting laws for their own purposes without regard to the interest and welfare of the majority. Within that clique, secession from the Union has become an article of faith: whoever opposes it is considered a renegade, and anyone aspiring to office or seeking to retain his position must, for better or for worse, go with the flow and join in the general hysteria, even if only a few hotheads truly mean what they say.

It may seem strange that Lincoln's election should be seen as sufficient reason for secession, since the president, who lacks any legislative power and has no authority over the local conditions in the separate states, can do little more than oppose the extension of slavery into the territories, being powerless to do anything about it in the states where it has been established. Yet this is not the real point but rather a mere pretext and the signal for a rebellion that, as it now becomes apparent, has long been prepared for. What is really at stake is the reintroduction of the African slave trade, a goal that the cotton states have dreamed of for a long time, knowing full well that their pet project could not be realized within the Union. Another reason is the anger with which the slave states regard the development and swift progress of the North at the same time as they witness among themselves a proportionate decline in population and wealth. They are angry that the young state of Ohio has outstripped its neighbor Kentucky; that Virginia, which at the time of the revolution looked down on New York, is now shamefully lagging behind; that Charleston with its perfect location as a major seaport is a mere village compared to Boston. Instead of seeking the cause of these conditions in slavery, they make themselves ridiculous by blaming the Union, ranting against the North's imagined infringements on their rights.

Whereas the whole movement toward secession in the South is nothing but a crusade of tyranny and oppression to establish the forces of slavery as absolute ruler, it is nevertheless carried out in the name of liberty. A foreigner unfamiliar with the situation arriving in South Carolina today would necessarily believe that here is a shackled and oppressed people that has risen against its tyrant. Everywhere in Charleston you can see symbols of liberty and hear them sing the Marseillaise and other republican songs calling for resistance against tyranny and oppression. At the same time, however, these very heroes of liberty are trembling in fear of their own slaves, and the conditions on the plantations would arouse your pity if you could pity the slaveholders who have by force brought upon themselves what they so well deserve.

Recently, I read a letter from a lady in South Carolina that describes the present situation in glaring colors. Every night the field slaves are locked into their quarters, and even the house slaves, about whose love and loyalty for their masters there has been so much talk, are being anxiously watched. They are forbidden to visit each other and kept restricted to the house as much as possible. It isn't necessary for the slaves to inquire into the reasons for these measures because they have learned so much about the abolitionists and about Lincoln from the careless talk of their masters that they believe his election will give them their freedom. Every day the plantation owners fear an uprising, and they have doubled the number of their overseers and sleep only behind locked and barricaded doors with loaded pistols under their pillows; and the women take turns watching their children. All of this amounts to the much celebrated blessings of the "peculiar institution."

The system of terror against alleged abolitionists is also continuing: since it is enough to come from the North to be counted among the undesirables, there is no end to expulsions, physical abuse, and even murders. Woe to the merchant, the physician, or the teacher from the North who might wish to force some negligent or malicious debtor to live up to his obligations! He will be denounced as an abolitionist and can be glad if he escapes across the border to the free states without injury and with only the clothes on his back. Craftsmen and workers whose expectations of better opportunities made them go to the South were officially forced to return by the same steamer by which they had arrived, and the steamship companies have given notice that for the time being they will no longer take steerage passengers.

Even if some of the southern states are in earnest and all the noise is more than a ploy to scare the North and to force it into shameful concessions for the sake of maintaining the Union, independence by one or more of the states would be beset with enormous practical difficulties that the fire-eaters are ignoring in the first flush of battle; the experiment would soon lead to countless complications and consequences. There are fiscal matters, customs regulations, and all manner of questions that would first have to be resolved. For instance, the United States has paid France fifteen million dollars for Louisiana, three million dollars to Spain for Florida, and many millions more to Texas for its claims on New Mexico, and it is more than unlikely that any one of these states would ever be willing to repay the cost of its acquisition. Furthermore, in the event of separation such states would have to establish their own army, navy and postal system which all together would cause an expense that could only be covered by taxes ruinous to the relatively small population.

Though the dismemberment of the Union would cause material losses on all sides, it seems to be the only means for ending the unnatural, volatile condition that necessarily prevails when states continue under one government despite their sharp differences in ideas, interests, institutions, customs, and inclinations—in a word, a nation where slavery and freedom are locked in irrepressible conflict. This feeling seems finally to have taken hold of the Republicans, and little as they have actually done to advance or advocate separation, they now openly express the desire that the South should finally live up to its threats so as to settle the matter once and for all.

In the free states, it would forever put an end to the business of hunting down, capturing, and returning slaves, and the politicians, the Democrats, and the Unionists of the North would have no more reason to grovel before the southern tyrants and to curry favor with them by making shameful concessions. These people are now full of apprehension, and in order to demonstrate their submissiveness to their patrons below Mason's and Dixon's line they exhaust themselves in devising the most laughable proposals for solving the current crisis peacefully. One of them suggests in all seriousness that Lincoln should resign to save the Union; another counsels the electors of the State of New York, who were elected as Republicans and are therefore morally obliged to vote for Lincoln, to cast their votes for Breckenridge, the candidate of the fire-eaters; and a third one demands that the Republicans abandon their principles regarding slavery (that is, its restriction to the states where it has been in existence and its exclusion from the territories) and offer the slave states all sorts of guarantees in this regard.

In recent days this worthy class of individuals even resorted to violence in Boston, interrupting an antislavery meeting where eminent abolitionist speakers like Garrison, Wendell Phillips, and Frederick Douglass participated in the proceedings. Among the rowdies were wealthy merchants as well some of the scum arising out of the darkest corners of the city, who had been specially hired for this occasion by these honorable men because none of the decent workers and artisans would have been willing to do the dirty work. There were tumultuous scenes like those of twenty years ago when the abolitionists were still opposed by the majority of the people, and Wendell Phillips at one point seemed to be in danger of his life out in the street.

***

Notes

1. New York, January [1861], *Morgenblatt*, 55:6:141–144.

51

The Public Crisis[1]

Ever darker and more threatening are the clouds gathering on our horizon, and events are happening so swiftly that every new month reveals a different state of affairs. The despicable rebellion of the slavery propagandists is spreading in ever widening circles. Since my last report the declaration of secession by South Carolina has become a reality, the news of which has already been carried across the ocean. Mississippi, Alabama, and Florida have followed South Carolina's suicidal example, and only an unexpected turn of events can prevent Georgia, Louisiana, and Virginia from following suit. The Democratic slavocracy has succeeded in bringing the country to the brink of civil war.

Whatever turn events may take, one thing is certain: that the South through its separation from the Union has signed its own inevitable death warrant. The peaceable citizens who constitute the middle class have long since been aware of this, but one cannot begin to grasp their dispiritedness if one has no more reliable source of information than the southern papers, which can hardly outdo each other in celebrating the enthusiasm that allegedly has gripped all parts of the population. The man of business looks at the future with horror because inevitable ruin lies ahead: credit has collapsed and general bankruptcy must follow. At first he had a vague hope that the division of the Union might be accomplished peacefully and that commerce and industry might flourish again. However, now he understands only too well that he and all those who trusted in the integrity of the political leaders have been duped and that an event has occurred which may soon draw the country into the horrors of an internal war. In several southern states cash is almost unavailable and the threat of a rise in prices is looming.

In addition, there is the constant fear of a Negro revolt, which the slaveholders have been doing their best to bring about. They have been so excessive in their angry outbursts against the Republicans and busily spreading so many lies among the people that it is no wonder if the slaves have finally come to believe what they have so often heard spoken in their presence: that immediately after his inauguration Lincoln would take his army to the South to free them all, and that Hannibal Hamlin, the future vice president, is himself a Negro—or at least a mulatto—an allegation recently voiced at a public meeting by a certain Thomas Watts, a member of Congress from Alabama.

Another scourge of the southern knighthood's own making are their allies, the "poor white trash," as the whites who do not own slaves are called in the South. It is from this group, who in their ignorance and coarseness stand hardly half a step above the slaves, that the disunionists have drawn their mercenaries with whom they expect to fight the federal government and the North; they are standing guard and patrolling the streets, attacking and occasionally even murdering Union loyalists and alleged abolitionists. The brutality, licentiousness, and violence of these savage gangs are beyond all comprehension; in South Carolina they are the governing power, leaving the original leaders of the movement quaking like the sorcerer's apprentice before the demon they have unleashed but cannot exorcize. Anarchy is already in full swing, and every day these rowdies force their entrance into peaceful houses to demand food and threaten pillage unless the owners buy their departure with heavy payments.

Incidentally, the angriest and loudest voices among those who want to dissolve the Union are in no way disinclined to benefit as long as possible from the advantages of the detested Union. Even though South Carolina has been an independent state by its own declaration for one month, it still enjoys the services of the U.S. mail, and many of the men in Congress, representing a seceded state or a state about to secede, have no qualms about occupying their seats and accepting their salaries from the government they consider the enemy. Should the dreaded Negro uprising actually erupt, it would squelch all rebellious movements more quickly and more surely than all repressive measures of the government could do, for none of the slave states has the means to fight a superior black force. At the first news of the destruction of a few plantations and the killing of some slaveholders and overseers, these very loudmouths and ruffians, who today are only too eager to curse the North, would come crawling on their knees, begging for its protection and assistance.

With this excitement dominating the country from one end to the other, politics is almost the only subject of conversation. But in other ways everything seems to be running its normal course: theaters and other places of entertainment are as busy as ever, and in everyday life there is little evidence of the alleged money crisis. Among all the theatrical events, lectures, and other entertainments of the season, however, nothing has aroused as much interest as the lectures by the famous horse trainer Rarey, who has returned from his European tour and now explains and demonstrates his famous system at Niblo's Theatre. During every performance he presents new and still untrained representatives of the equestrian species and tames them in front of the audience. The crowds are enormous, and long before the start of each show you can see the curious jostling each other at the entrance to the spacious building, which seats four thousand people and is always filled to capacity.

***

Notes

1. New York, January [1861], *Morgenblatt*, 55:9:209–211.

52

Outbreak of Hostilities—Martial Spirit[1]

A complete transformation of everything has occurred within just a few days. The events of recent weeks may have left little doubt that a peaceful settlement of the conflict between the North and the South had become less and less conceivable. In truth, only the halfhearted and fearful favored it, and only the short-sighted were unable to understand that slavery and freedom can never coexist peacefully and that any compromise must sooner or later result in an even bloodier battle. People generally realized that they have been walking on a volcano, but the longer a condition of excitement and tension continues, the more one gets used to it. As long as the flames do not shoot up in anyone's immediate proximity, everyone goes about his usual business like those who have built their houses at the foot of a lava-spewing mountain or in an area of frequent earthquakes. Although in New York and throughout the country people have been complaining about the hard times and the cessation of all business transactions, everyone has continued to work, pursued amusements, and made plans for the summer. I myself was making plans to take a trip to Haiti, in order to learn by direct encounter about the conditions in this Negro republic.[2]

But like a bolt of lightning came the news that Fort Sumter near Charleston, where Major Anderson and seventy of his men were still under siege, had been attacked by about 5,000 rebel troops; and already the next day it was reported that the forces occupying the fort had capitulated. It was a hard blow because all the papers had so often repeated the story of Fort Sumter's strength and invincibility that one was led to imagine a little Gaeta.[3] The fact that Sumter went up in flames almost like a house of cards on the second day clearly shows that all these earlier descriptions are part of that arrogant American penchant for boasting which insists on declaring everything American superior and beyond all comparison without taking the trouble to learn about the advantages and achievements of other nations.

Suddenly the terrible news came fast and thick and, together with a thousand unproven rumors, raised the excitement to incomparable heights. But just as quickly the entire North rose as one body in defense of its independence and self-determination. Immediately after the fall of Fort Sumter the citizens' militia and a force of volunteers were called up for the defense of the country and the protection of the government, and the response has been so overwhelming that soon hundreds of thousands instead of the required seventy-five thousand will be ready to do battle. All previous partisan bickering is a thing of the past: Democrats, Republicans, and Know-Nothings vie to be first. Neither fortune nor social position matters, with the upper classes being perhaps relatively most numerous. Germans are stepping forward by the thousands, and Frenchmen, Italians, Mexicans, and Cubans form their own companies. Even the Canadians, who normally do not concern themselves much with the problems of the United States, are now swept up by the general enthusiasm, and a company of six hundred men has already offered its services. The heads of many mercantile houses have offered to equip their salesmen, to pay them full salary during their absence, and to keep their positions open until their return. Others provide the government with free war materiel or offer it large amounts of money; ladies volunteer for service in hospitals and form organizations for making bandages, surgical dressing, and whatever is needed for treating the wounded.

A regiment from Massachusetts was the first to set out, and its appearance in New York on its way to Washington was greeted with a storm of enthusiasm. It seemed impossible to raise the excitement to higher levels, but the effect created by the news that this very regiment was attacked by a mob during its peaceful march through Baltimore and could proceed only after the loss of several dead and wounded beggars description. It was as if all of New York was ready to arm itself and march south to wreak vengeance. Soon afterwards it was learned that the rebels around Baltimore had burned the bridges, destroyed the railroad, and cut the telegraph wires so that this route was blocked for any additional troops. Furthermore, the North was cut off from all official news from the South and even from Washington for eight days, and it had to rely on reports of travelers who had succeeded in reaching the North by various detours. It was feared that an attack on Washington might occur at any moment, and the uncertainty added immeasurably to the confusion and the anxiety.

Since then the troops have been able to reach Washington by water across the Chesapeake Bay and via Annapolis, and a part of the railroad has been repaired, reopening a direct connection. The capital is now regarded as safe, and the general opinion prevails that a military occupation of Maryland and Virginia as well as the establishment of a military court are the only means by which peace and order can be restored and a decisive blow struck against the rebels. "Through Baltimore, not around it!" is the general hue and cry, and hundreds of thousands stand ready to open the way. Even the Democratic thugs and ruffians, who previously had stood in service to the party of slavery, are suddenly filled with the spirit of patriotism and have formed a regiment that one can only wish as an occupation force on the slaveholders.

The most contemptible role is played by those who at one time not only justified and encouraged but advocated the secession of the South, and who are now making a virtue out of necessity by supporting the government in order to avoid public disdain. James Gordon Bennett, the publisher of the *New York Herald*, is foremost among those who belong in this category. His paper used to vie with the press of the secessionist states of the South in excoriating the entire Republican party, until the day when he was visited by an angry mob that forced him to raise the American flag. He was so frightened that since then the *Herald* has been loyal, speaking in a voice that is the exact opposite of what it used to be. The same is true of other Democratic papers. A few weeks ago, Fernando Wood, currently again the mayor of New York, not only openly declared his sympathy for the rebels but called for New York City to secede from the Republican state and become an independent city; but suddenly he has become a patriot devoted to the Union and its government.

As a result of these events, life in New York has taken on a completely new aspect. All other interests have taken a back seat to the great question—the fight for the country's political institutions and integrity—which concerns everyone and gives shape and color to every phase of life. The first column of the newspaper contains only military news or news in some ways related to military preparedness. Large street signs advertise the recruiting offices of the various regiments; here you meet long lines of volunteers who have just been recruited, and there you may see the imposing and moving spectacle of a regiment marching off to war. In the large square at the Battery, the southernmost end of the city, troops perform their drills from dawn to dusk, and long rows of barracks have been erected in the park at City Hall for housing the troops from the North and the West. All the papers are issuing extra editions, and often the crowds are so thick in front of their offices that the street is nearly blocked. Here and there you can see a rope stretched across the street holding up a life-size effigy of straw or wood with a wooden mask for a face looking much like a human figure from a distance. Usually this scarecrow bears the name of Jefferson Davis on its back or a message like "The Fate of all Traitors."

The most impressive aspect, however, is the unfolding of the American flag wherever a flag can be mounted. On all public buildings, on all vessels in port, on newspaper offices, banks, hotels, theaters, over the entrances of shops, stores, and restaurants, on ferries and railroads—everywhere waves "the Stars and Stripes," the white and red stripes of the flag with its blue field set with thirty-four white stars. Even private residences are so decorated, and you can see long rows of houses where at least one and sometimes every window displays the flag. Some people show their patriotism by raising particularly large flags made of expensive, heavy silk that can cost several hundreds of dollars. At least three out of four persons you meet are wearing a tricolored cockade, and in every store you can see objects decorated in red-white-and-blue: watch bands and ties, shoes with rosettes, ladies' bonnets with ribbons and flowers; I even saw one hat draped in a complete flag. All the boys who normally sell laces, hairpins, buttons, and such objects in the streets are now trading only in cockades and bows, and they are doing better than ever before. The horses pulling the streetcars, omnibuses, and carts all bear at least one and sometimes three or four little flags on their heads, and their harness is painted in three colors; even dogs sport the flag or red-white-and-blue collars.

With all the enthusiasm that has captured the masses of people who are taking up arms, and with all the enormous amounts of money that are being generously offered, one might look forward with confidence to a quick and glorious victory over the rebellion, if only the government were as decisive and resolute as the citizens. Until now, however, it has displayed anxious hesitation and a reluctance to act decisively and forcefully, with the people openly deploring such conduct. We have reached the point where almost all the real Republicans who elected Lincoln criticize him and his cabinet for this timid policy, while some of the Democratic papers that previously attacked him most passionately have suddenly turned out to be his well-wishers. They outdo each other praising his moderate approach because they are secretly glad that their dear friends in the South have been treated so leniently.

It is this lack of action and patience that encourages the South and that has brought us to this point, because the Southerner is violent, brazen, and cocky as long as he is given no resistance; but, like all braggarts, he is—as I have said before—cowardly and easily frightened by determined opposition and forceful action. According to the latest reports, it seems that the general levying of troops in the North and the concentration of several regiments in Washington have already cooled the enthusiasm for war in the South, and it would not be altogether a surprise if at least in the border states the clamor for war were to give way to proposals for compromise. This is the most dangerous shoal, because as long as the slavocracy has not been made to feel the superior strength of the free states its excesses will continue. Only a peace that has been dictated at the point of the bayonet in either Richmond or Charleston, only a peace that will forever break the power of the slavocracy and lead to the gradual but complete eradication of the curse that is at the root of the present disaster, only such a peace will bring about lasting and beneficent consequences.

Notes

1. New York, May [1861], *Morgenblatt*, 55:23:548–550.

2. Assing had made plans to travel with Frederick Douglass to Haiti, expecting to fulfill two long-held dreams—a personal view of the "Negro republic" and being with Douglass for an extended period of time without his family and other distracting obligations.

3. A fortified town in central Italy on a high promontory in the Tyrrhenian Sea, Gaeta had been a symbol of endurance until its fall to Victor Emmanuel II in 1860–1861.

53

The War[1]

Everyone is looking with curiosity and impatience at the Union's progress in the war against the rebellious slavery propagandists of the South. You reach for the morning papers with feverish haste, hoping to find news about some important victory or troop movement only to read that since the Union occupation of Maryland everything has generally remained the same until the recent incursion into the interior of Virginia. The enthusiasm and warlike spirit of the people have not cooled but are growing ever warmer. Regiment upon regiment is being formed, millions upon millions of dollars are placed at the disposal of the government. The city is a veritable showcase of uniforms, and in the large public squares, where normally children and their nurses seek the shade, a colorful throng gathers on sunny days to watch the soldiers doing their daily drills.

The apparent slowness of the government's response to the rebellion may have its explanation in the fact that the North suddenly, unexpectedly, and without preparation found itself drawn into this war and that the commanders did not wish to take any precipitous steps until all preparations had been made and the troops had enough time to be thoroughly trained. The enemy is in a quite different situation. For more than six months he has been preparing and spoiling for war; but since the North launched its efforts of recruitment he has not done anything to let deeds follow upon words. With Washington secured and Maryland occupied, the rebels now contradict their earlier boasts, claiming they had never intended to attack the capital and are interested only in protecting their own borders. It is the old story of the fox and the sour grapes. Whether it is a matter of cowardice or a ruse of war, the objective observer feels compelled at such a moment to provide an overview of the warring parties, of the probable outcome of the present crisis, and of the future prospects in general.

Anyone who has taken the trouble over several years to understand the nature of the southern people cannot be surprised to see that hopeless corruption, demoralization, licentiousness, and brutality are the characteristic traits of the entire population of the South. If there were not a single argument to be made against slavery on philosophical and humanistic grounds, its effect on the white population as it manifests itself in the slave states would be more than sufficient to convince the world of its total infamy. Since slavery is the only institution that is markedly different in the societies of the North and the South, its influence can be confidently said to be responsible for all the depravities that have caused and sustained the present rebellion. From the very beginning of the disturbances there has not been a day without horrors like those of the dark Middle Ages, which in our own century have become an impossibility in even the least civilized nation. On the mere suspicion of abolitionism or loyalty to the Constitution and the Union, under whose flag the country has flourished for more than seventy years, men are hanged and burned alive and even women tarred and feathered. Recently a man in Arkansas was even strung up by his legs, and eight days later his body had not yet been removed.

There is no telling how many people have been driven from their communities and properties by wild bands of secessionists. Woe to the man from the North who has the temerity of wishing to collect a debt in the South! If he cherishes his life, he will have to forfeit his money forever. A recent example illustrating this system of robbery and murder are the letters of seizure, issued by Jefferson Davis in the name of the Confederacy, giving a field day to pirates and buccaneers: the confederated states will pay twenty dollars for every person killed by pirates on an American ship but twenty-five dollars for every living prisoner delivered. Since there is no reason to believe that a gang of people whose actions have violated all laws of justice and humanity will pay extra for feeding or occasionally exchanging their prisoners, this clause can only mean that Jefferson Davis will not forego the pleasure of personally seeing his victims hanged.

The North's chief advantage over these dehumanized hordes is its immense superiority in numbers. War preparations began only six weeks ago, following the fall of Fort Sumter, and already 500,000 volunteers have signed up, of whom 200,000 are already fully organized, while the remainder are ready to march at a moment's notice. It only depends on the president whether he will inform Congress in his message of July 5 that at least 400,000 men are ready to put an end to the rebellion. The North is equally superior in the substance that makes up its army: as I have mentioned earlier, it consists of the best of the American people. Although it cannot be denied that New York and other large cities send their share of tramps and vagabonds, they are nothing in relation to the masses of decent, honest people who have either lost their work due to the political upheaval or voluntarily relinquished their employment.

On the other hand, despite all the boasting and clamoring for war among every class of its citizens, the South has already had to resort to conscription. A large part of its army is said to consist of men who are still loyal to the Union in their hearts, but who have been given no other choice than to either serve the rebels or be persecuted as "abolitionist traitors." It is evident that all these forced rebels will use the first opportunity to rally around the Stars and Stripes. Thanks to slavery, there is no honorable working class in the South, and the vast majority of the army is therefore made up of the riff-raff that has nothing to lose—do-nothings, the lazy, ignorant sons of small slaveholders who consider it beneath their dignity to do an honest day's work. They are goaded on by ambitious, unscrupulous politicians who, in their anger over being deprived of their former political power, have plunged the rest into a suicidal enterprise. Knowing full well that their heads are on the block, they use every means of tyranny and prevarication to stoke the fire and excitement of the blind masses.

Also, the United States has credit resources both here and abroad, and banks and financiers vie with each other in their eagerness to lend as many millions as the situation may require. The secessionist states, on the other hand, have had to rely on forced loans that no one of good sense will support with an amount higher than required. They would be hard pressed to raise 100,000 dollars abroad, with the inevitable result that this rebellion will lead to utter self-destruction, the worst ruin that any people has ever brought upon itself. However one may think about revolutions in general, whether they are justified or unjustified in principle, it has to be admitted that no rebellion more groundless, unprincipled, and criminal than this was ever begun and instigated. The slave states have never been oppressed; under a government elected by themselves, the people have enjoyed all the rights and freedoms that a republic based on the principle of popular sovereignty can guarantee its citizens. None of their rights and freedoms was in the least threatened by Lincoln's election, but their politicians had lost the prospect of occupying the most important and lucrative offices for the next four years, thereby losing the influence they had wielded throughout the country to the detriment of the North. They had become powerless to extend the curse of slavery by force to the territories and thereby to gain additional slavery states in the future. The dumb, ignorant masses—they who have nothing to gain from slavery, whose condition of perpetual poverty and impotent ignorance is the result of slavery, and twenty of whom together do not have the means to buy the smallest Negro child—they are the blind tools pushed by their leaders into crime and ruination.

Much of the blame must be laid at the feet of the Democratic party in the North. Fearful of losing their influence and the spoils of office and also in an effort to intimidate the Republicans, they always sided with the South and encouraged the rebels by misrepresenting the masses of the North, claiming their sympathy with the South and their readiness to support it. The common reaction and complete unity of the North as a whole have destroyed these illusions with one stroke, so that the leaders of the rebellion have to confront the hopelessness of their situation and all their circumstances, to say nothing of the possibility of a slave insurrection which would raise an enemy behind their lines more formidable than all the armies of the North.

If, therefore, one can have little doubt about the ultimate victory of the North—even without indulging in false optimism—the question remains whether such a victory will bring about a lasting, truly salutary peace. The circumstances that have led to the outbreak of this rebellion at this time are accidental; however, the deeper, seminal cause existed already at the inception of the republic and has grown along with the country until it assumed its present dominance: it is the central conflict between slavery and freedom that no power in the world can resolve. It will continue until the last slave on this continent has gained his freedom. Until then it is beyond the power of the warring parties to make peace even if they would, for the principles they represent are stronger than they and will always lead to new battles. Only a devastating blow against slavery itself can assure peace for the future.

The border states have to be liberated either peacefully or by force and the others so severely restricted that slavery would become powerless and soon expire. But no matter how clear and convincing the conditions themselves speak for such a course, neither the government nor the mass of the people seem to have understood the situation. The populace simply feels outrage over the insolence, the excesses, and the treason of the South; but in their enthusiasm for the Union only one in a thousand really perceives the true source of the conflict. Thus the question of slavery recedes into the background: people fight the traitors but do not understand that ever more will rise from the earth as long as this curse upon the land is not erased. The government reveals its shortsightedness by treating the slaveholders as gently as an ally.

The rumor of a slave insurrection was recently going around in Maryland, and General Butler, the commander of the United States troops in that state offered to suppress it. It is not an isolated case. In Pensacola, several slaves took refuge at Fort Pickens in the belief that they would find protection under the Union flag. But the commander returned them in chains to their owners so that they might flog them to death. Colonel Dimmick, the commander at Fort Munroe, Virginia, is mean and cowardly enough to assure the rebels that there is not a single abolitionist under his command and that he would not tolerate any tampering with the system of slavery. The president and his cabinet act in the same spirit. John Brown, Jr., the son of the venerable martyr killed by the Virginians, having inherited his father's courage and his hatred of slavery, offered to organize several black regiments and to conduct raids with them into the rebel states, but his offer was categorically rejected by the government.

If the nation and its political leaders do not soon realize that humanitarianism and politics in the conditions of the country go hand in hand, and if they do not begin to act accordingly, they have no one to blame but themselves if the next presidential election will lead to a yet more devastating and bloody war.

Notes

1. New York, May [1861], *Morgenblatt*, 55:27:644–646.

54

War—Douglas's Death—Missouri Germans—
A Black Hero—Barnum[1]

We have been at war for several months, but the great mass of the people have not yet understood that we are not fighting against a so-called rebellion, a conspiracy of a few ambitious party leaders, but that a great, terrible, and inevitable revolution has finally broken out—a revolution whose seeds were present at the founding of the republic and whose eventual outcome will determine the fate of the country and the nation. The war between the North and the South is quite simply and irreducibly the eternal war between slavery and freedom that has been repressed and postponed by halfway measures and compromises for more than seventy years and has now erupted with all the more force. For anyone who is passingly familiar with the history of this country and can look at the facts with a sharp eye this is so clear that it seems unnecessary to make any further comment. Nevertheless, the government and the people have shunned no effort to mislead themselves and the rest of the world.

There has been much talk about saving the Union and about a conflict between North and South, and until recently many people, especially those in the merchant class, were shortsighted enough to believe in all seriousness that a peaceful solution could be found; they would have readily agreed to every craven compromise simply "to prevent the spilling of blood"—in truth, to make money. When Congress met in extraordinary session on July 4, Lincoln's message gave an elaborate explanation of the situation since the first outbreak of violence without once mentioning slavery as the true cause of the conflict. He asked Congress for authority to issue bonds for 400 million dollars and to raise a volunteer army of 500,000 so that the war against the rebels could be brought to a quick and certain conclusion—but he did so without stating that this was not just a war against disloyal slaveholders but against slavery itself.

In a word, while the South has made its intentions abundantly clear in words and deeds from the very start, the North—particularly the government—has not yet demonstrated that it is in earnest. With the exception of a few well-executed military moves in Missouri and the western part of Virginia, a long sequence of missteps, halfway measures, errors, and stupidities, all of which demonstrate how a war should not be fought, is the sum total of what has been accomplished so far. No doubt, everyone wishes to defeat the South if it could be done without abolishing slavery, the cause of the conflict. The truth is that the southerner feels the most bitter and deadly hatred against the North, an attitude he has shown at every opportunity through many acts of violence and hostility, not only since the outbreak of the war but ever since John Brown's raid into Virginia. Strangely enough, however, although attacked, betrayed, mistreated, and ground down by the haughty slavocracy, the North has not yet risen in that righteous indignation which drives a humiliated and insulted people to vindicate its rights. In truth, it seems as if the effect of many years of slavery had poisoned the nation so profoundly that only the hope of victory and the fear of defeat could now arouse it.

Whereas the South is employing every conceivable means of violence and treachery—raids from secure positions and the use of infernal machines and even poison—the North is still prating of "our fellow citizens in the South," "an unfortunate error," "spilling our brothers' blood," and "the horrors of civil war." While in the South slaves as well as free Negroes are forced to construct batteries and entrenchments for the purpose of our destruction, we categorically reject all offers to organize black regiments "so as not to offend our fellow citizens in the South." The departments of government in Washington are full of low-level officials whose treasonous conduct is an all but open secret; they use their positions to spy on the government that pays them their wages, yet they are kept in office in order "not to offend our brothers in the South." Spies and traitors who are caught in the act are released as soon as they take an oath of loyalty to the government, which they naturally break within minutes. One member of Congress submitted a proposal to abolish the hateful law requiring the return of escaped slaves, but it was not even considered. However, events are more powerful than people, and the events of the recent past will put an end to all self-delusion.

The severe defeat that our troops suffered in Virginia is casting a dark shadow over the entire North. The victorious end of the battle seemed assured when a sudden panic spread for no apparent reason and victory turned into general defeat. As usual in such situations, there is an endless search for explanations and everyone tries to put the blame on someone else. Some claim that General Patterson,[2] who was supposed to advance and cut off the enemy's expected reinforcements, kept his position and did nothing; others believe that the large number of spectators at the encounter, being suddenly seized by fear, gave the signal for a general retreat. Others again blame the newspaper correspondents for urging the government to attack before making adequate preparations. Yet another explanation insists on the incompetence of the generals who were placed in positions of responsibility, although they had no knowledge of military affairs and strategy.

The rebels' cruelty and barbarism in this unfortunate battle and their violations of all modern laws of humanity and warfare have no parallel in the annals of civilized peoples; only the monstrous effect of slavery can serve as an explanation. The dead had their noses and ears and even their heads cut off; the wounded were propped against tree trunks and were used for target practice till they died; ball games were played with human heads, hospitals set on fire, prisoners murdered. A soldier belonging to a New England regiment was observed as he dragged a wounded rebel out of the hot sunshine into the shade to give him water out of pity; but as soon as the southerner had been partly restored he shot his benefactor through the heart. Such deeds, revealing the spirit that moves the South, show the utter impossibility of concluding this conflict with halfway measures, leniency, and compromise instead of energetic, unrelenting, total war.

Death has prematurely ended the career of one of the most famous American statesmen of our times. Stephen Arnold Douglas, the head of the northern Democrats, died on June 3 in Chicago of nerve fever, not yet 48 years old. Of lowly origin and without wealth, he achieved his illustrious position as one of the most outstanding speakers in the Senate through native ability and persistence. He faithfully represented the American people. Lacking true greatness, having no principles, devoid of human warmth and respect for human dignity, cold and egotistical, he nevertheless possessed a deep understanding of the conditions of the country and the nature of its people, and he had the keenness of mind and incisive logic that made him a dangerous opponent in any debate. Boundless ambition was his chief passion and the presidency the goal of his efforts; it would have been his, had not the excessive desire to gain the favor of all parties led him into contradictions and inconsistencies ultimately resulting in failure. Douglas spoke with one tongue to the North, with another to the South, and with a third to the Senate in Washington, so that all parties eventually saw through him and rejected him. But in the present conflict he sided decisively and unmistakably with the North and the government, and at the time of his death he was well on his way to regaining his popularity. Despite his talents and the importance Douglas achieved over the last fifteen years, he had few of the qualities of human greatness that would make his death a great loss for the country.

The eagerness and determination with which the Germans are ready to defend the laws and unity of their adopted country are a silver lining on the dark cloud looming on the horizon. While the war in Virginia has not yet brought about a decisive result, with the rebels becoming stronger rather than weaker, the Germans have saved Missouri for the Union. It is the only slave state where Germans have settled in sufficient numbers to stand up as a force. In St. Louis most of the wealthiest merchants are German, and in the interior of the state Germans own farms and vineyards. As the secessionist war spread among the American population of Missouri, the treasonous governor stood at at the head of the conspiracy; he had promised Jefferson Davis that the state would secede. Missouri's economic well-being and her credit would have been utterly destroyed, perhaps a whole generation sacrificed; but hardly had the conspiratorial scheme been uncovered, when the Germans rose up as one. Volunteer regiments sprang up everywhere to protect the loyalists among the population and to defend the state. The governor and the state officials who supported him were driven out, and Missouri is now generally regarded as loyal to the Union. Colonel Siegel,[3] son-in-law of former Pastor Dülon of Bremen, has become a hero whose courage and military expertise have yielded great success. Besides him there is Colonel Börnstein, and many other Germans are known to have contributed to the good cause in more or less illustrious positions.

Despite all the efforts of the government to keep the Negroes from the scene of action and despite all the talk of the inferiority of the black race and its inability to profit from the benefits of freedom, one Negro has stirred so much interest and admiration through the courageous act that gave him his freedom that he has become a celebrity. A few weeks ago, the schooner "Waring" left New York with a valuable cargo bound for Montevideo. A few days into the voyage it was seized by one of the southern ships that endanger the American waters. The captain and the helmsman of the "Waring" were returned to New York, and five sailors of the privateer took command of the ship, keeping a passenger, two crew members, and William Tillman (the colored steward of the "Waring") as prisoners. The pirates had decided to land in Charleston, and Tillman heard the captain tell his crew that he intended to sell the "nigger" at slave auction for a profit of at least a thousand dollars.

He determined to defend his freedom at whatever cost and asked two sailors, his fellow prisoners, for assistance. One of them refused to go along; the other one, however, a German by the name of Stedding, promised to assist him in his dangerous undertaking. They waited impatiently for an opportune moment to realize their plan, but it didn't present itself until they were within fifty miles of Charleston. In the middle of the night Stedding came and told Tillman that the pirate captain and the helmsmen were fast asleep, and Tillman immediately began his perilous task. He dashed down to the cabin with a hatchet, the only weapon he had been able to obtain, split open the heads of all three with a terrifically accurate aim, and then—with Stedding's help—fed the still twitching bodies to the sharks. It was the work of just a few minutes and was executed so quietly that the other two pirates did not even wake up. They were tied up but later released in return for the promise of help in steering the ship. Having accomplished the main task, Tillman and his comrades still faced a difficult problem. They had to return to New York, but since none of them was able to steer the ship they faced calamity and destruction, to say nothing of another encounter with a privateer. However, with favorable winds and waves they finally reached New York, where Tillman joked that he returned as captain of the ship on which he had gone out as a steward.

From the sublime to the ridiculous, etc. The bloody drama turns into comedy. As soon as Barnum, the owner of the American Museum and the true father of humbug, had become aware of the excitement caused by the appearance of "the black hero," as he was called, he had the idea to turn Tillman into an object of speculation. He persuaded him and Stedding to appear in his museum so that they could receive their friends and tell their story. Thus the hero of the "Waring" is now displayed in Barnum's Museum among the wax figures, the stuffed animals, the seals, the albinos, the bearded ladies, and the other wonders of the sea and land. Admission 25 cents.

Notes

1. New York, May [1861], *Morgenblatt*, 55:27:644–646.

2. General Robert Patterson (1792–1881) was relieved of his command on July 25, 1861, after bungling an important assignment in the Shenandoah Valley.

3. The "Colonel Siegel" mentioned here is most likely Franz Sigel (1824–1902), a German-born Union officer who later became a somewhat inept general known for his ability to rally the German-American element to the Union cause. "I fight mit Sigel" was their well-known slogan. Colonel Heinrich Börnstein (1805–1892), mentioned in the following sentence, was a native of Hamburg but lived in Austria before coming to the United States in 1848; he owned and edited the *Anzeiger des Westens* in St. Louis and commanded the Second Missouri Volunteer Regiment.

55

Civil War—Frémont and the Government—A Rogues' Gallery[1]

One summer of confusion and excitement has passed, and even the most hopeful optimists are beginning to understand that the conflict and the fate of the country will not be decided by a short military campaign, but that we are in the midst of a long and ruinous war whose end no one can foresee with any confidence. People placed their hopes and expectations in the wisdom, understanding, enlightened thought, and righteousness of the present government; yet to date almost nothing has been done to justify that faith. After weeks and months of waiting and hoping for deeds and results that might cast a few rays of light on the dark canvas of the current state of affairs, one cannot deny the sorry truth that there have been no fundamental changes for the better. As I wrote several months ago: the government continues to make all sorts of efforts to suppress the rebellion of the slaveholders, but it fails to take the one measure that would surely and inevitably lead to the desired goal—the liberation of the slaves.

In almost every military engagement of significance victory has been handed to the rebels because they were attacked with insufficient force, and discontent and demoralization are the inevitable results of such mistakes. It seems that no government was ever offered more good will and dedication: money and people sprang up like mushrooms, but public confidence was just as quickly squandered and deceived. Almost everyone in the North sees the weakness, ineptitude, and irresponsibility of the administration, and many of those who, just a few months ago, were among its most enthusiastic supporters and defenders, now raise their voices in well-founded accusations.

A look at the main events of the war reveals the most depressing and dispiriting picture. Not even considering such minor accidents as the raids near Great Bethel and Vienna, where our troops became the victims of ignorant militia officers, there is hardly a bright spot, except for a few successes in West Virginia and the capture of Fort Hatteras in North Carolina, which was accomplished from the sea. Hardly had the terrible impression of the battle of Bull Run worn off, when the country began to mourn the news of another defeat in Missouri, where a large rebel force from Arkansas had swept across the border. A small army of 5,000 men under the command of the brave and capable General Lyon was cruelly sacrificed by the government to the destructive force of 30,000 rebels.[2] It is Lyon who, in conjunction with the German population, is primarily responsible for having saved Missouri from falling into secessionist hands. To the eternal disgrace of the government, Lyon himself was killed in that engagement after having loudly and repeatedly called for reinforcements—but to no avail. Washington was deaf to his pleas and left him and his comrades in a situation in which only a miracle could have saved them from perdition. Nonetheless, they accomplished feats of heroism and prevented the enemy's advance, yet not without dying for their courage. Then the town of Lexington, Missouri, after a valiant battle, was captured by the enemy and its insufficient defense force taken prisoners. In both places it was obvious that a few thousand reinforcements could have prevented defeat.

They speak of the continuation of the war, but in all honesty the North cannot claim much progress. In April, Washington was threatened by a rebel raid; in July and August there was renewed danger; and a single defeat at this time may endanger the capital once again. The first time, telegram after telegram describing the advance of the rebels was published in the papers; the same fears and the same excitement occurred after the battle of Bull Run; and it will be a wonder if autumn passes without another panic. In fact, we are still at about the same point where we were when Major Anderson was forced to abandon the shattered walls of Fort Sumter to the enemy. At least outwardly the enemy appears as proud and arrogant as he was at the beginning of the war, and if—as one hears—he suffers from lack of funds, hunger, and demoralization, none of these can be credited to the actions of the government in Washington.

One of the greatest evils, in fact the thing that blocks those who wish to crush the rebellion forcefully and effectively, is the petty rivalry and jealousy with which members of the government treat their most dependable friends and allies and systematically try to ruin them. When a European general achieves a decisive victory, he is almost smothered by praise and rewards; titles, promotions, medals, and all sorts of tokens of esteem are showered upon him. But over here they search for some excuse, some minor violation of formality, to get rid of him and to throw him to the press. There are many instances of this, and the reasons for this procedure are not difficult to explain. The cabinet consists mostly of men with long-term or short-term ambitions for the presidency; some of them are, in fact, known and declared candidates for the next election. But a general fortunate enough to gain a major victory would, of course, assume a position of such trust and affection with the people that any desire he may have for becoming president would leave all other aspirants hopelessly behind. Hence, everyone watches with an eagle's eye that no one will gain in popularity to threaten Seward, Chase, or Cameron.[3]

What proves this assertion beyond a doubt is the administration's treatment of Frémont, who two elections ago, in 1856, was the candidate of the Republicans but lost against Buchanan. Frémont then withdrew from public life until last summer when he was given the command of the Army of the West, an appointment that greatly satisfied the people, who warmly admire the shining figure of the conqueror of California. Neither the poison of jealousy nor partisan ambition could defile his spotless character. As commander of the West, Frémont was responsible for ridding Missouri of the enemy who laid waste to the southern part of the state. With an insufficient force consisting mostly of new recruits and threatened by a superior force of immeasurable size, Frémont understood that it was necessary to put an end to the halfway measures and the forbearance with which the rebellious slaveholders were being treated. On August 31, he proclaimed a state of war in Missouri and announced the confiscation of all rebel property and the liberation of all slaves. The proclamation came like a bolt of lightning striking the revolting slaveholders more forcefully and decisively than anything since the beginning of the war.

Frémont's action was certainly the most important, the most fateful, event of the summer. The approval of nearly the entire North resounded as one voice, while the rebels were seized by panic and wrath. The people as well as the press declared its conviction that in this brief and simple document the "famous trailblazer" had indeed blazed a trail out of all the current confusions and difficulties. The whole country was intensely attentive during the first few days after the proclamation had been published. It was unclear whether Frémont had acted on his own or at the behest of the government, whether the president would agree with it or not. Those who still had confidence in the antislavery tendencies of the government did not hesitate to attribute the manifesto to the wisdom and courage of the administration in Washington; others, however, basing their judgment on previous experience, predicted a categorical rejection by the president. The tension was truly painful, but it proved the great importance generally attributed to Frémont's measure. The central point at issue was whether the war against the traitors was to be fought by diplomatic finessing and dissembling or by cannons and martial resolve.

It was unfortunate for both the country and the cause of humanity that Frémont did not act with the cabinet's approval. The president thoroughly disapproved of the emancipation of the slaves, asserting that Frémont had exceeded his powers, and he referred to the letter of the law and some technical distinctions to avert the well-earned punishment that Frémont had in store for the rebels. Without any doubt, the administration would have liked to fire Frémont at a moment's notice, and a rumor to that effect was already being disseminated by telegraph to all corners of the globe. But they were afraid of the people's reaction, understanding that the reputation of the public's hero would first have to be systematically ruined, and since then he has become the subject of a barrage of attacks from the fiery furnace of calumny and animosity. It seems incredible that a government would seek to discredit one of its own generals and cross him in his plans and actions, because the consequences will inevitably have to be borne by itself and the country as a whole. Nevertheless that is what seems to be happening.

Just when Frémont needed them most, five of his best regiments, which he had taken great pains to organize, were suddenly ordered by Washington from Missouri to the Potomac, where they have been idle ever since. Many of his most competent and trusted officers have been removed to distant posts. Yet in spite of these setbacks Frémont has been remarkably effective: with the inadequate means available to him he has raised an army of 50,000 men, whom he personally took to the battlefields of southern Missouri to attack the rebels and, if necessary, pursue them across the border to Arkansas. Should he return in victory, his triumph would be complete, and the people's adoration would provide him so much support that his enemies would have to surrender at least temporarily. On the other hand, the smallest failure, a single lost battle, would provide a pretense for the government to dismiss the conqueror of California and, if possible, to block his way to all future greatness and power.

Like everywhere in the world, comedy is asserting its rightful place next to the deepest tragedy even under the current circumstances. A good joke at the expense of the secessionists has recently made the rounds here. Everyone in New York has at least heard of the rogues' gallery, a collection of daguerreotypes of all the thieves, forgers, burglars, and other such honorable personalities who have had their run-ins with the police over the years. Every individual who is a threat to public safety and has been arrested must let his face be added to this picture gallery, which is under the control of the police and helps in locating and identifying criminals. Recently someone added the pictures of Floyd, Jefferson Davis, Wise,[4] and other traitors, assuming they would here be placed in the proper company. This prompted a humorous petition to the commissioners of the metropolitan police in the *Tribune*, purportedly submitted by the criminal element of New York and signed by twenty notorious characters. In words expressing their indignation, the undersigned protested the undeserved insult to themselves: it was hard enough, they stated, for people guilty of nothing more than minor violations of private property to bear the burden of society's contempt without the humiliation of being placed in the company of traitors—traitors who had abused their positions of power and trust to plunder the public treasury and to deliver the state and its people into the hands of the enemy. The petition ran in all the papers, but it is not known to what extent this joke has caused any of the persons in question to make amends.

Notes

1. New York, October [1861], *Morgenblatt*, 55:48:1147–1149.

2. General Nathaniel Lyon (1818–1861) had been put in command of the St. Louis arsenal at the outbreak of the war. Having successfully subdued all the hostile sections of the state of Missouri by spring 1861, he was killed in the battle of Wilson's Creek in August.

3. William Henry Seward (1801–1872), an ardent antislavery advocate and senator from New York (1849–1861), was Lincoln's secretary of state; Salmon P. Chase (1808–1873), also strongly opposed to slavery as a U.S. senator and governor of Ohio, was Lincoln's secretary of the treasury; and Simon Cameron (1799–1889), a former Democrat who had turned Republican in 1856, served as secretary of war under Lincoln for less than a year (1861–1862). All three had strong presidential ambitions.

4. Besides Jefferson Davis, the reference here is to John B. Floyd (1807–1863), a Confederate general who had been secretary of war (1857–1860) in the Buchanan administration, and to Henry A. Wise (1806–1876), also a Confederate general, who, as governor of Virginia (1856–1860), had signed John Brown's death warrant.

56

War—Slavery—The Charleston Fire—An Important Document[1]

The last days and weeks of the past year were largely troubled by concerns about a war with England. Even the greatest optimists understood that the rebellion of the slaveholders is enough to require the full strength and attention of the nation. Regardless of the impossibility of facing an external enemy with the necessary force and with any expectation of victory, such a war would totally eliminate any shadow of hope that the rebellious South might be subjected. The secret secessionists in our midst knew this very well, and they tried to instigate the people's hatred and anger by means of vicious articles about England in their publications, hoping to force the government to take on a provocative posture. This time, however, the masses were not fooled, and when in response to England's peremptory demand for the release of the two commissioners Mason and Slidell (as well as their secretaries)[2] the government willingly complied, everyone breathed a sigh of relief. People do bemoan the fact that the present conditions make such ready compliance unavoidable; they are annoyed with the partisan sympathies England has shown for the southern rebels from the start; and they understand that England has violated her history and principles for the sake of this issue. But it occurs to no one to question the unpleasant necessity itself.

In earlier times, when one had driven the defenders of slavery into a corner with incontrovertible reasons, their argument of last resort was invariably that the slaves were content and happy, treated humanely, and devoted to their masters. Some silly stories were always offered as proof, about loyal slaves who had refused to accept their liberty out of pure affection for their kind masters and for the overseer's whip; or about others who, after having been freed, chose to return to slavery. And there are other such stories that, if in fact true, are only exceptions proving nothing; they are clearly contradicted by the thousands who year in and year out travel the so-called underground railroad to follow the North Star to freedom. Anyone who took the trouble to delve deeper into the situation and had the opportunity to get to know those happy, contented slaves could easily see the hollowness of these arguments. Yet a large part of the unthinking masses had accepted them as ready coinage. After all, it is so easy and comfortable to ignore or deny injustices and evils you have no wish to abolish!

Recent events, however, have put an end to these fairy tales: those happy, contented slaves who breathe nothing but love for their masters have suddenly been put in the category of ogres, mermaids, vampires, dragons, and basilisks. When our troops occupied Beaufort Island in South Carolina, the large slave population joyfully welcomed them as liberators and allies. The planters, scrambling to flee from the advancing troops, had in vain tried to persuade their slaves to follow them. Neither beatings nor shootings proved more effective than all attempts at persuasion. Even the horror stories they told of "Yankees" killing, maiming, or selling slaves to Cuba made no impression. Heaven only knows how these ignorant people knew better, despite every effort to keep them in the dark about things; all we know is that from the start they considered the Yankees their friends and saviors.

Thousands of them are coming from the interior of the state to descend on Beaufort and its neighboring islands, often under considerable risks to their lives. There they enjoy the protection provided by our cannons and bask in the glory of freedom. They demonstrated their much-praised affection and devotion to their masters by destroying their abandoned houses and smashing, rather than appropriating, the most valuable objects they found inside until the soldiers stopped them. They obviously acted out of a deep, bitter, well-founded hatred, which they were able to vent for the first time, a hatred so powerful and overwhelming that it triumphed even over the natural impulse of acquisitiveness. Many of these former pieces of personal property are now working for wages in the fortifications, the cotton fields (unless the planters had set them on fire before their flight), and wherever they can find work; the rest are selling the soldiers chickens, vegetables, and fruits that remain in abundance on the abandoned plantations.

The same conditions exist at other points of the southern coast that are in the possession of the United States. The Negroes prove to be hard-working laborers and faithful, reliable allies wherever you go, and they often provide valuable information about the movements of the enemy. Our soldiers, who are now coming into firsthand contact with slavery, which they have hitherto known only from hearsay, are developing an understanding of the curse that lies on this country and are slowly being transformed into abolitionists. I have no doubt that the people of the North, who only a year ago disrupted and shut down the meetings of the abolitionists, would now applaud the government if it had the courage to address the four million people who are its natural allies and announce the complete emancipation of all slaves.

The great fire at Charleston is an event that in quieter times would have offered journalists an unending source of descriptions and comments. Since the news reaching us from the seceded states is incomplete and much is being kept from us, reliable details about this fire are not available. But so much is certain: the fire burned for several days, and in its extent and destruction could be compared to the great conflagration of Hamburg.[3] The oldest and most important part of the city, the center of commercial life, almost all public buildings, several hotels, churches, and theaters have been leveled; many families have lost their homes, and consternation and confusion seem to reign everywhere. Most people cannot quite suppress a furtive smile of satisfaction that, of all places, the capital of South Carolina has been the scene of such destruction, for that state has always played the part of the misbegotten son, the troublemaker, in the Union.

When the colonies fought for their independence, Charleston was the home of the most committed and passionate Tories, and South Carolina joined the Union under its present constitution only reluctantly. The bait held out for winning over the state, the price for its agreement at that time, was the perfidious concession of maintaining the African slave trade until 1808. But within less than fifty years South Carolina agitated for the first time to upset the government and destroy the Union. The plan failed at that time partly because of the firmness with which President Jackson suppressed the rebellion, and partly because South Carolina was unable to find allies among the other slave states. Now, hardly thirty years later, South Carolina is again leading the rebellion. It was here that the first act of secession was passed, and for months—even years—they seized every opportunity to fan the flames of hatred throughout the South and to drive the other slave states to a point of no return. The first shot on the starving force occupying Fort Sumter was fired from Charleston, signaling a civil war whose end cannot yet be predicted with any shadow of accuracy. It can be said in truth and without exaggeration that South Carolina has always been the enemy of the Union and of all human progress, the block to all liberal democratic institutions, the supporter of despotism, and the enemy of the people.

People ask whether the fire was an accident. At this time, nobody can answer that question completely, if it can ever be answered. Rumors have it that it is the work of black and white arsonists, that there is a conspiracy of the Negroes, with weapons hidden in the slave quarters. No doubt, if these rumors are true, the facts would be kept secret, and it seems neither implausible nor surprising if something like this had actually happened. In times like these, when every day in the South is marked by violence and the whole social structure has disintegrated, the masses are seized by a kind of madness; witnessing the daily horrors drives them into a state of mental intoxication and causes them to repeat these very horrors. The events of recent times may have had this effect on the slaves, who also are driven to revenge themselves for the injustices of two centuries and will do so even without an organized conspiracy. We know that the coast of South Carolina looked as if it had been caught in a firestorm. The approach of our naval fleet had caused panic: the planters, fleeing before an enemy against whom they harbor a greater hatred than the people of the North can feel in return, in many places set fire to their own cotton fields. When in their haste to escape they failed to do so, they hid in the swamps and woods until they could return in the dark of night to start up the terrible fires. They seem to have made a vow to turn the land into a wilderness rather than let its fruits fall into the hands of the enemy.

A most interesting document that makes an important contribution to the history of the South's rebellion has just been made public. All along, many Democrats—whether due to shallowness or dishonesty—have seen the cause of the revolt in the election of a Republican president; but it is only a pretense to disguise the execution of longstanding plans. This sort of sophistry must totally collapse under the evidence of this document, because it provides incontrovertible proof that the slaveholders' conspiracy was being prepared as early as 1850. After the seizure of Port Royal by the Union army, one of the naval vessels sailed to Beaufort for the first time. Several officers went ashore to inspect some of the abandoned houses that, as mentioned before, the slaves had looted and destroyed. When they came to a place that had once been a lawyer's office, they found all the cabinets forced open and the floors covered with papers, among them a manuscript of about twelve folio pages in a green envelope marked "Cooperation Account Book. Federal Niggers." Whether this simple manuscript was the only thing worth noticing or whether it was the title that caught his eye, the officer picked it up and found to his amazement that he was holding in his hands the file of the Southern Rights Association of St. Helena, South Carolina—the seed from which the poisonous tree of secession has sprung.

We have here a short but important chapter in the annals of our history. According to it, these South Carolina men, among whom we can find the names of several of the leaders of the present rebellion, had already conspired in 1850—during Fillmore's presidency, some years before the Republican party even had a name, and a decade before it came to power—to unseat the government of the United States and to form a southern confederation. Even though in that year they were split on the question of collaborative or independent trade among the separate states, they were and have remained in agreement on the central point. They were determined to destroy the Union, and those among them who had achieved influential positions in the federal government used these to advance their own plans and to work toward their realization.

Notes

1. New York, January [1862], *Morgenblatt*, 56:7:163–166.

2. In the "Trent Affair," James Murray Mason and John Slidell, Confederate diplomats on their way to London and Paris, respectively, had left Havana on the British ship "Trent." The ship was searched by the captain of a Union vessel who arrested the diplomats and their secretaries without orders. When the British accused the Union government of violating the freedom of the seas and issued an implicit threat of war, the commissioners and their secretaries were released.

3. The great conflagration of Hamburg that destroyed large sections of the city occurred May 5–8, 1842. Assing was then a young woman in her early twenties, living with her sister in the house their parents had left them on Poolstrasse. Although the sisters and their property survived the destruction, it spurred their decision to leave Hamburg and move to Berlin.

57

Slavery and Government—Women and Slavery— Soldiers—Supplies[1]

Almost everyone you meet in the northern United States to discuss the present conditions will express the opinion that slavery in this part of the world has reached the beginning of its end. He will tell you that the indignities have reached full measure and that the chains of slavery will be broken before the clouds of war will have dissipated: all the dark stains that have marred our laws to maintain the coddled and petted monster will be expunged, and the principles of true democratic liberty will be realized from the borders of Canada to the Gulf of Mexico, from the Atlantic to the Pacific. This shows that the people are ready for the great step to be taken, the step that will determine the present and the future of the republic. No one can reasonably entertain the slightest doubt that the proclamation which would finally lift the old curse would be cheered by a vast majority in the North. In fact, every day petitions to that effect arrive in Congress, but until now no one in Congress, in the cabinet, or on the battlefield has taken a bold, decisive, courageous step toward the abolition of slavery.

On the contrary, although everyone concedes that some day slavery will have to cease and will end with the suppression of the rebellion, only a few members of Congress dare to speak out firmly in favor of such a proclamation; at best, it is suggested that the slaves of acknowledged rebels be declared free, but even on this point there has been no agreement. Because of slavery, the present condition of the country is in shambles: its wealth has been destroyed; hundreds of thousands of citizens have been torn from their occupations and forced to risk their lives for the survival of the nation and its government; countless families have been in mourning or in a state of despair; the rebellious slaveholders have been making desperate efforts to find help and support for the most despicable cause for which a country's peace has ever been disrupted. With all of this, the government in Washington seems to regard slavery as an institution more hallowed and sacrosanct than any other property right or social contract.

Every abolitionist move has until now been carefully suppressed: no one in Congress or the army who is not determined to apply himself as fully to upholding slavery as to maintaining the Union may expect to enjoy the administration's confidence and esteem. Most of our generals have done less to earn laurels in victories over the enemy than to heap shame upon themselves by returning fugitive slaves. This tender treatment of slavery can be seen everywhere. Just a few days ago there was proof of it in an event that in and of itself was of no importance but whose consequences are much talked about. The Hutchinson Brothers, well known for their performance of popular songs, had undertaken a tour of the Army of the

Potomac to entertain the soldiers. Among their songs were some of an abolitionist nature that were applauded by the soldiers but not by the commanders, who were so offended that not only was any repetition of these songs prohibited, but the Hutchinson Brothers were once and for all banned from the camp on the Potomac.

What is the secret of this submissiveness to slavery? The whole world knows that slavery alone is the cause of the rebellion, and members of Congress from the North and the West speak openly about it. However, the problem is that the president and his cabinet are most decidedly opposed to any measure that would threaten the sacred institution. The influence of the few slave states that so far have remained loyal to the Union is much greater in this regard than the express wish of the entire North. These border states are now repeating the same game that bore such disastrous fruit at the beginning of the rebellion. They constitute the dam holding back the abolitionist consciousness that has developed in the masses, which, if it were allowed to flourish, would totally extinguish this horrible rebellion. Under the guise of loyalty, these states are now building a firm bulwark of rebellion just as they did a year ago. It is out of consideration for the border states that our soldiers have to demean themselves in the dishonorable trade of slave catchers; it is for their sake that slavery continues to exist in the District of Columbia; it is because of them that the most capable men are relieved of their military positions as soon as they reveal their opposition to slavery; and it is to assuage them that the government regularly appoints successors whose views are unobjectionable.

Among those who are committed to the suppression of the rebellion one can differentiate among three different types. The first, whose numbers have most increased in recent weeks, are those who see slavery as the cause of the conflict and its abolition as the most effective means to fight the South. The second is mostly made up of many former northern Democrats who wish to see the rebellion suppressed by all means and under all conditions, but for whom the abolition of slavery is only the measure of last resort. The third group consists of those who would like to see peace and order restored but only on the condition that no limitations be placed on the slavery system. The membership of the last group comes mostly from the border states, and it is they who, in the name of an arbitrary and willful interpretation of the Constitution, try to move heaven and earth to prevent the government from taking a bold step. As long as they retain their influence there is little hope for improvement.

A general understanding of this situation and a strong discontent with the prevailing system of halfway measures have now become so widespread that they have reached even the population of Washington and stirred up a veritable revolution among them. Men like Horace Greeley, the editor of the *Tribune* who for some time has been an advocate of emancipation, as well as Cheever,[2] and even Wendell Phillips, could formerly not have spoken publicly in Washington but are now being asked by clubs and literary associations to give very well received lectures. Frémont—now before the investigating committee that is looking into his conduct in Missouri—is also greeted and welcomed by citizens and soldiers wherever he shows himself. On the other hand, McClellan, the commander of the

Grand Army of the Potomac does not enjoy such recognition.

While the feelings of the people have finally made an impression even on Washington, the actual seat of the treasonous conspiracy is located there, and many employees in many branches of government hardly bother to conceal their sympathies for the slaveholders. Congress has recently taken on this matter, and the investigating committee has just issued its report, which reveals that several hundred officials are more or less compromised, having either directly or indirectly given encouragement to the rebels. No wonder, then, that with the help of spies at the very center of things the enemy has known about all military plans and movements in advance and has been able to prepare for them!

The most fervent secessionists, the most active spies, however, can be found among women. In truth, even if there were no other argument against slavery, its demoralizing influence on white women would be enough to see it as the greatest curse weighing on the country. Manners, decency, justice, honor, and humanity are being sacrificed by these overt and covert secessionists; they do not recoil from debasement or crime. It is easier to imagine than to explain the schemes of subterfuge they use to inveigle themselves into the confidence of those they believe to have knowledge of the government's plans. Women are the carriers of treasonous correspondence, and many have been caught red-handed, their clothes literally stuffed with letters. Those who have no opportunity to do such service reveal their wrath against the North and the Union loyalists in imprecations that are commonly used only by male rowdies. In St. Louis, no officer of the Union can step into the street without being insulted by a female rabble in words and gestures that, if they were used by any man, would immediately lead to his arrest. But it would be wrong to believe that it is the lower-class wenches who carry on in this way; no, the ladies of the so-called better classes of society, the wives and daughters of the slaveholders, are the ones who try to outdo each other in this sport of impudence.

Another outrage that is perhaps even more destructive to the conduct of the war than the problem of spies, is the extraordinary influence exercised by officers of the regular army. Their envy and jealousy toward the volunteers shows itself in petty intrigues, meanspirited lies, and fierce hostilities. If an officer who is not a West Point graduate performs brilliantly in battle, he can be sure to become the target of the most passionate attacks; there is no end to the chicanery and insults until he is relieved of his command or, tired of the humiliations and abuse, he resigns. Among the volunteer officers are many Germans who had military careers at home; the combination of theoretical knowledge and experience they possess is something the products of West Point have had no opportunity to acquire in many years of peace. In such cases the anger is all the more passionate, but the addition of a stupid, self-righteous nativism does the rest. A good example is what happened to Franz Siegel,[3] to whom more than to anyone else the government is indebted for keeping the state of Missouri from joining the secessionists. From the very start of the war, Siegel demonstrated not only admirable courage and activism but also true talent, and the successes he has achieved are very remarkable, considering the difficulties with which he has had to cope.

"What can you expect of a people that has no sense of civic responsibility?" an acquaintance asked me as we were talking about the stupidities and malfeasances that characterize the most amateurish and bungling conduct of war in our times. Even if this remark is too harsh when applied to the mass of the people in the free North, it fully fits the hundreds of thousands who see the war as an opportunity for enrichment that they are using for all it is worth—the suppliers and agents who negotiate the government's purchases. Their dishonesty is so blatant, it does not pretend to masque itself in lawful conduct. Uniforms that turn to rags on the soldiers' backs in two weeks; rations that can only be thrown out; half-dead horses that barely survived the moment when they were turned over to the government: all these are proof of the patriotism with which these honorable men serve their country.

None of them has handled this branch of business with greater success than the brother-in-law of Secretary of the Navy Welles,[4] who had been asked by the latter to buy ships. With full knowledge and consent he collected a brave little profit of two and a half percent for each vessel, making him more than $70,000 in two to three months. This handsome bargain has recently been publicized and investigated by Congress. Loud voices everywhere are calling for Morgan, the patriotic ships agent, to return the money, but he has not yet made any moves. This sort of thing begins to prove to the world that this war, which is costing the nation two million dollars a day, could be fought for less than half this amount if it were only done honestly and lawfully.

Notes

1. New York, February [1862], *Morgenblatt*, 56:13:310–312.

2. Most likely George Barrell Cheever (1807–1890), an evangelical minister who took radical positions on a variety of issues, including prohibition, capital punishment, and abolition.

3. See Essay 54, n. 3.

4. Gideon Welles (1802–1878), a former Connecticut Democrat who had become a Republican over the slavery issue, served effectively as secretary of the navy in two Lincoln cabinets and under Andrew Johnson (1861–1869). His brother-in-law was probably Junius Spencer Morgan (1813–1890), a businessman and investment banker in Hartford, Boston, and London and the father of the famous financier John Pierpont Morgan.

58

Drastic Change—Southern Knighthood—Executing a Slave Trader[1]

A new era has begun in the history of our internal war. Instead of the pessimism, disgruntlement, and dark worries with which people viewed the future, hope and courage have sprung up everywhere. It is hard to say whether the brilliant victories of the Union forces in North Carolina, Kentucky, and Tennessee have brought about this change more by way of the material gains that have been made or more by means of the moral influence on the North and the South. The entire North is delighted, and even the most pessimistic prophets of doom have stopped trying to prove the "impossibility" of defeating the rebellion. The rebel leaders have *de facto* given up, even if they are not honest enough to admit it; for the time being they are still blinding their own supporters with all sorts of contradictory sophisms.

A new spirit has taken hold of the government. Instead of the politics of halfway measures, hesitations, uncertainties, concessions, and empty gestures, we now see a resolve to finish by whatever means and under whatever circumstances the most dastardly rebellion that has ever beset a nation. The public and the press are preoccupied with speculations and explanations of the cause that is at the root of this change. Some attribute it to the energy and activism of the new Secretary of War Stanton; others—without denying Stanton's achievements—point to the fact that General McClellan, until recently the sole and supreme commander of the army, is now restricted to commanding the Army of the Potomac. In this limited role he no longer has the power to block all other generals or to void, by a command to retreat, the good results of whatever determined step someone else may have taken. Perhaps he was simply driven by envy and jealousy and did not want to see that, for example, Frémont would have been able to clear the state of Missouri of all rebels in a matter of a few weeks if he had been given free reign, while McClellan himself and his enormous force have been standing idly by on the banks of the Potomac. Perhaps his evident sympathy for the representatives of slavery makes it impossible for him to hurt his former comrades, thus making him into something of a traitor himself. It is certain, at any rate, that McClellan has proven to be the best enemy that the rebels could have wished for, and that all those who have taken the side of the slaveholders and defended the "rights of the South" as long as they decently could have been the first to praise him.

It was certainly time that better people were given some freedom to act. The word among the Germans here is that our compatriot Carl Schurz, who recently returned for a while from his ambassador's post in Spain, has been much in the company of the president and is exerting his strong influence. It is generally said that one of the effects of this influence is the recent change in the administration's treatment of Frémont, who is expected to be reappointed to an important command in the West. Also, Colonel Siegel is expected to be promoted, so that one can hope that his talents will again serve his country, despite all the intrigues against him. However, people are only whispering this news about the German influence into each other's ear, as it were, and are careful not to publicize it so as not to provoke the open or latent hostility of a nasty, arrogant nativism.

February 22, Washington's Birthday, which is an annual holiday, this year became the occasion for celebrating recent Union victories. The red-white-and-blue decorated the streets, just as it signaled the beginning of war last year after the fall of Fort Sumter. Parades, meetings, speeches, dinners, and a few paltry illuminations in the evening filled a day that the masses of the people seemed to enjoy more than any other holiday since the founding of the republic. It was amusing to see large flags, enormous eagles, and other expressions of patriotism decorating the papers that only a year ago publicly supported the secessionist party. These papers had even gone so far as to call on the citizens of the North to overthrow the government and accept the constitution of the South until public outrage forced them to change their tune. The *New York Herald*, whose editorial department once waved the banner of secessionism, now displays a particularly amusing impudence in this regard—a greater indifference to anything like conscience or decency than anyone has ever dared to exhibit.

Despite presenting this appearance of patriotism, these champions of conscience betray their real party loyalties at every turn: now that the first victories against the secessionists have been won, they already begin to call for amnesty, cease-fire, and conciliation. It is difficult to think of more bizarre contradictions and inconsistencies than those with which these furtive friends of rebellion and slavery seek to confuse the judgment of the masses through their publications. In the same breath they tell their readers that the slaveholders are both wrong and right, that they have to be subjugated by force and won over by conciliation, and that all we need to do is fight a bloody war of extinction to live again in brotherly harmony. At least the southern rebels are not guilty of this kind of nonsense! I have before me an excerpt from a Virginia newspaper that speaks of southern defeats with all the bitterness of profound hatred and the wrath of despair; it expresses the opinion that the planters would rather kill themselves, their wives, children, and slaves, that they would rather burn down their cities and cotton crops and strew salt upon their fields than to return to the despised Union.

It was a particular irony of fate that on February 22, the same sun that illuminated the celebrations of the first great victories in the free states, where all eyes were again looking to the future with confidence, was shining in Richmond, Virginia, on the inauguration of Jefferson Davis for a six-year term as president of the so-called "Confederate States." Given the misfortunes of their present situation —attacked by sea and by land, without expectation of being recognized by any foreign power, threatened internally by the seething discontent of the masses, who were led into the rebellion with lies and false promises—their leaders must recognize this celebration as more of a farce or a funeral than the beginning of a promising future.

Brought into existence without any compelling necessity, based on no moral or human principle, resting only on the barbaric, evil system of slavery, the whole Confederacy is nothing but a painted, dressed-up corpse showing the horrors of putrefaction to even the most nearsighted spectators. As criminal and unscrupulous as this conspiracy was from its very start and long before it revealed itself in broad daylight, the treachery and viciousness of its execution are even greater. In fact, its most characteristic trait is its viciousness, which makes it different from conspiracies in the histories of other countries. There have always been honest revolutions and conspiracies, provoked by real or imagined injustices. Sometimes it was an oppressed, mistreated people who rose to burst the chains of slavery, sometimes a few ambitious men or a whole class of society felt themselves deprived of their rights and banded together for the overthrow of an established government. But there has never been a conspiracy in which *all* the leaders—excepting a few— held high and influential offices in the government or the army of the United States, which they used (some of them for many years) to work toward the overthrow of the very government they were pretending to serve.

James Buchanan, the former president, himself a product of the North and without interest in or possibility of occupying a position in the leadership of the South, encouraged the conspirators out of his own evil propensities and willfully closed his eyes to their ubiquitous treacheries. John Breckenridge, the former vice president and president of the Senate, was one of the ringleaders who hardly hesitated to take the side of the rebels after his term of office had expired. Floyd, the secretary of war, was a thief who, as much as a year before the outbreak of hostilities, arranged to have large quantities of cannons and guns moved from all the armories of the United States to the South or sold them as scrap iron to make sure that the government would be unarmed at the critical moment; in the end he stole six or seven million dollars. The secretary of the navy ordered all ships that were under the command of loyal officers to distant waters, where any order to return would reach them only after weeks or even months, leaving the government at the start of the war with a single battleship and a handful of gunboats. Large numbers of officers on land and at sea all but handed over to the enemy forts and battleships and then joined the rebels. And there are Jefferson Davis, Alexander Stephens (the vice president of the seceded states), Mason, Slidell, and many others who used their positions in Congress for many years to undermine the country, at a time when secession had already been decided and was being actively prepared.

These are the founders of the southern Confederacy and their henchmen: they constitute that honorable southern knighthood and are the ones who speak of the workingmen of the North as the "refuse of society." Their conduct of the war is just like them: cruel and barbaric when they so outnumber their enemies that they need not be afraid of the least danger, they show extreme reluctance when opposed by an equal force; in their blind anger they resort to treachery and even to poison, as they did a few days ago in Arkansas, where they poisoned the supplies they were forced to leave behind when retreating from the Union forces, causing the death of several soldiers and officers.

There was a time when the swagger of the southerners so impressed the North that their bravery was accepted at face value; in fact, many thought it impossible that the North could defeat the rebellious slavery states. But the panic spreading throughout the South over the raid by John Brown and his twenty companions already revealed the true nature of southern bravery. Several million citizens outdid each other trembling in fear, and in South Carolina they were still afraid of the heroic fanatic even after he had been safely locked away in Virginia. And what besides naked fear was it that prevented the rebels from seizing Washington last spring? The whole world, South as well as North, knew that the city was helpless and hopelessly cut off, and that even a small handful of determined adventurers could have taken it. The impression that a southern victory at that time would have made at home and abroad would have been immeasurable and overwhelming, and it would have greatly advanced the South's prospects for gaining recognition. Their leaders had bragged about it in advance and promised that it would be a great event; but they made no attempt, the opportunity passed, and to this day the history of the war has not registered a single example of the much-touted southern heroism. On the contrary, whole regiments can be seen throwing down their weapons and fleeing without a fight at the mere approach of the enemy. When Fort Donelson in Tennessee was seized, our troops took no less than fifteen thousand prisoners of war because the troops occupying the fort lacked the courage to fight it out, even though the prevailing conditions favored them.

Although for more than fifty years, since 1808, the African slave trade has been considered piracy punishable by death, more than a hundred ships a year sail from the various ports of the United States to go on slaving expeditions, and some of them are caught red-handed. But now, for the first time, the captain of a slave ship was sentenced and actually executed in New York. Nathaniel Gordon, captain of the "Erie," a notorious slaver, was a criminal of the worst kind, for whom even the most skilled defense attorney could not claim any mitigating circumstances. The investigation had revealed that the voyage on which he was captured was his fourth slavery expedition, not counting earlier ones that could not be proven. Nevertheless, a certain group of "honorable businessmen" declared their sympathy for him, and there are even those who do not hesitate to call his execution an act of murder. Under the pretense of some formal error in the proceedings, they exerted themselves to start a new investigation, and when they did not succeed they tried to persuade the president to commute the sentence. This case was not so much about the individual as about the question whether the slave trade could be continued without penalties from either New York or Boston, and the captain's execution is therefore the first blow directly aimed at the trade itself in this country.

Notes

1. New York, March [1862], *Morgenblatt*, 56:16:382–384.

59

The War—The Slavery Question—Color Prejudice[1]

The recent news that Union forces have taken New Orleans has everywhere caused the happiest excitement. New Orleans is the real capital of the South, and its occupation signals a new chapter in the history of the war. Despite the general conscription and the other forceful measures that had to be taken, the total suppression of the great conspiracy is, in the eyes of the world, only a matter of time. In spite of all the suffering the war has brought upon the country, in spite of the burden of debts and taxes that will weigh on the people for years, everyone can see that the war will be beneficial for the country—like a thunderstorm in summer that is fertile and salutary for all of nature even if lightning should kill a few persons. Anybody whose notions of humanity and justice have not been poisoned by the national epidemic of slavery must admit that the bloodiest war is preferable to the so-called peace that we "enjoyed" under the rule of the Democrats and the slave masters; he has to admit that this war must be regarded as the salvation and deliverance of the nation if—as seems to be evident now—slavery will be dealt its final blow.

Such a result would exceed the highest hopes that the most optimistic abolitionist might have had two years ago. Most people at that time knew that sooner or later war would break out between the two sides, but the general state of demoralization to which the North had sunk, because of its longstanding accommodation to slavery and its many contacts and common interests with the South, had extinguished all hope that the slaveholders, who had everything to gain from maintaining the *status quo*, would start the war on their own initiative. Even the Republicans did not wish to be suspected of abolitionism, arguing only against the extension of slavery into the territories. "No slavery beyond the existing slave states!" was their slogan; but in truth it was a concession that aroused no enthusiasm and could not lead to forceful, decisive action. It seemed too crazy, too fantastical, that the South would ever be the aggressor and would willingly give up its rights, which were protected under a mass of peculiar laws and ordinances; it would simply never have entered any rational person's mind. Even if one admitted that some individuals in the South were prepared to commit suicide, the mere assumption of the possibility that entire states would do violence to themselves without cause would have been considered too mad to deserve consideration. And even when South Carolina threatened with secession, it occurred to no one to see it as anything other than a scare tactic. In a real sense, then, we are indebted to the slaveholders for this revolution because without them it would probably not have broken out in this century. Contrary to the radical changes that have shaken other countries, this one has been instigated not by the forces of reform but by the representatives of existing social injustices.

One of the significant events, an important chapter in this conflict, is the abolition of slavery in the District of Columbia, which passed by a wide margin in both houses of Congress and received the president's signature despite the furious opposition of the delegates from the border states and the few friends they still have among the northern Democrats. The actual number of slaves freed is only about three thousand, but the impact of this measure is therefore in no way lessened, because the District of Columbia is under the immediate jurisdiction of Congress, and the existence of slavery in the capital city of the free citizens in the world's largest republic had always been a stigma on the entire nation. In earlier years, some of the determined friends of liberty in Congress had tried in vain to rectify this disgrace, but they were easily voted down by the majority party at that time, and the task remained to be done by the present revolution. The former slave owners have each received an average compensation of three hundred dollars, and this arrangement is accepted even by the most vociferous opponents of slavery because a nation which for so many years has been an accessory to injustice cannot suddenly declare that hitherto legalized private property is theft or robbery. However, slaveholders who are guilty of treason or participation in the rebellion are excluded from this benefit, and one can imagine that many who had earlier bragged about their treasonous plans and activities are now moving heaven and earth to prove their loyalty; others, who knew very well that all their efforts and oaths would not clear them, moved their slaves head over heels to Maryland or Virginia at the first news of the passage of the emancipation bill. The horrible law that had hitherto been in force in the District as well as in the slave states, denying legal status to the testimony in court of any colored person (regardless whether slave or free) unless it is supported by a white person's testimony, has now also been abolished through a clause in the emancipation bill. Hence, the colored population in the District now enjoys the same rights as they have in the free states, although many of these still have constitutions containing barbaric and inhuman laws in regard to this unfortunate race.

Meanwhile, on the island of Port Royal off South Carolina, which was taken by our troops a few months ago, Negroes, who were abandoned by their terrified masters and had thus obtained their freedom, are busily planting cotton and other crops. Reports from that region are very positive and encouraging; they convincingly contradict the silly, base, and ignorant fairy tale that the Negro will work only under duress. If these people, demoralized by slavery and mistreatments of all kinds, had actually sunk into that alleged laziness and apathy, it would not come as a surprise nor would it be an argument against them; but the energy and eagerness that they now display, according to eye witnesses, is more than one might ever have hoped or expected. Leaving out all higher considerations of morality, justice, and humanity, it is out of obvious self-interest that all liberated slaves be kept as free laborers in the same areas where they hitherto had to work without wages. Forcing them to emigrate—regardless of the cruelty of such a measure—would be like cutting off one's own right arm. Like slavery, however, its offshoot, color prejudice, has a way of blinding people to their own advantages and leads them into doing the greatest harm to themselves. It is, therefore, not surprising that the old colonization schemes are again being revived in both North and South by obtuse minds filled with prejudices; and it is not improbable that some states will implement them—but with disastrous consequences to themselves.

Among the many signs of progress heralding the approach of better times it is worth mentioning the imminent recognition by the United States of the republics of Haiti and Liberia and the establishment of diplomatic relations with them. A few days ago, the Senate passed the resolution by a large majority, and there is no doubt about subsequent approval by the House of Representatives. The glory of first submitting the bill to the Senate and supporting it with incontrovertible reasons belongs to the extraordinary Charles Sumner, that untiring fighter for freedom, justice, and progress. Although diplomatic relations with ambassadors and officials of all ranks have been entertained with states of all zones and latitudes and sizes, from the European powers down to His Majesty King Kamehameha of the Sandwich Islands, Queen Pomare, and all sorts of anthropophagi, Haiti and Liberia had no official existence despite the fact that trade with them has for some years been stronger than with Cuba—all because of the dear old American color prejudice. The opponents of the bill argued that these states would send us coal-black Negroes as ambassadors, who would then have to be received and treated the same as other members of the diplomatic corps. As powerful as this prejudice surely will remain for generations within the broad masses, it was no longer strong enough to prevent the passage of a useful and desirable measure.

***

Notes

1. New York, May [1862], *Morgenblatt*, 56:24:572–574.

60

General Hunter and the Government—Blacks—The Homestead Bill[1]

If in the midst of a profound peace a bomb were suddenly to explode in the central square of a large city, it could hardly cause more excitement than did the memorable proclamation issued in the middle of May by General Hunter, the commander of the Union forces in the South. It is a badly written but brief, pointed, and clear document in which the general states that Georgia, South Carolina, and Florida—all of which have deliberately rebelled against the United States—are in a condition of war; and then he adds that since the laws of war and slavery are incompatible, all slaves in the aforementioned states are herewith forever granted their freedom. For anyone who seriously wants to put an end to this despicable rebellion the political wisdom of this proclamation—to say nothing of the moral issue involved—is too self-evident to require any further explanation. Its military necessity was underscored by the news that the slaveholders, in a desperate effort to win or at least continue their struggle, are forcing their slaves to perform military service and are deploying them in constructing entrenchments in the most dangerous and exposed places.

If all commanders in all of the rebel states were to implement measures such as General Hunter's, the war would soon be over and the problem of slavery eliminated. But the history of the past year and a half shows that generals and government officials have treated the slaveholders with such timidity and consideration that truly dedicated abolitionists are unlikely to begin celebrating this much-desired event. The first question that presented itself was whether Hunter issued his proclamation with the president's knowledge and approval, or whether he dared take this important step on his own responsibility. If he made his own decision, will the president, who has often shown his narrowness and his dependence on the prejudices of those surrounding him, not distance himself from Hunter as he did earlier in a similar case involving Frémont? Will he destroy the salutary effect of Hunter's proclamation by some clever modification to show the relentless rebels that he is more interested in maintaining slavery than in suppressing the rebellion?

The news that the president learned about the proclamation only from the newspapers and was unprepared for and completely surprised by it did not exactly help to lay such suspicions to rest. In fact, a few days later a presidential proclamation put an end to all illusory hopes and expectations. It stated with great emphasis that Hunter, having taken this step without the knowledge or approval of the administration, had exceeded his authority and declared his proclamation null and void. In the second part of his notification the president refers to his message to Congress, in which he recommended the gradual emancipation of the slaves, and he begs the southern states with a certain sentimental pathos—even going so far as to plead with them—to take the hand that he is holding out to them.

The tone of the document is as repulsive as its content, and it is of a piece with the timid conservatism the president has displayed in regard to slavery since his first day in office. But of the many millions of people who have read the president's proclamation, perhaps only half believe in the president's and his cabinet's truthfulness in this matter or trust his assurances. It seems all too unlikely that a commander in such a responsible position would take such a fateful step on his own and jeopardize his own position by risking the administration's disapproval, especially someone who had hitherto not shown himself to be a passionate opponent of slavery and could look at Frémont as a warning that lesser infringements of the so-called rights of the slaveholders could result in becoming the target of hostility, intrigues, and lies on the government's part.

Under these circumstances it seems plausible that General Hunter's emancipation proclamation was authorized by the administration, but that the president and the cabinet lost courage and issued a cowardly denial once they heard the furious clamor of the secret and public friends of the rebels and saw the pressure exerted by the representatives of the border states. However that may be, despite the lack of a sense of justice throughout the nation and despite the president's own dislike for sudden and complete emancipation, slavery is doomed on this continent. Thanks to the South's implacable hatred and thanks to the blindness of its citizens' refusal to accept the dishonorable compromises with which the North had intended to purchase a miserable semblance of peace a year and a half ago, slavery will be destroyed by the inexorable course of events.

One important sign of progress in this regard is a letter from the governor of Massachusetts, John Andrews. It is an answer to the president's call for an additional 100,000 volunteers, of whom Massachusetts is expected to furnish three or four regiments. The governor clearly expresses his view that if these men will have to fight the South they would consider this added claim on their patriotism a very heavy burden because they would confront an enemy who does not abide by any law of modern warfare, uses every means of trickery and force against them, and even deploys slaves as soldiers and in support units against them, while the Massachusetts men are forced to respect the so-called rights of the slaveholders. If, on the other hand, the president would support General Hunter and legally recognize the equal right to patriotic action by all men, including blacks—if, in other words, he would permit Negroes to participate in battle—the roads would soon be flooded with the masses who wish to answer the president's call.

In some of the northern states, New York among them, black regiments are being formed, and several representatives have submitted to Congress petitions to arm the slaves who seek their freedom under the banner of the Union forces. Such a measure will soon become a necessity because of the question of what is to become of our soldiers in New Orleans or on the coast of South Carolina once the unhealthy season of the year begins. The white northerner will soon succumb to it, whereas a few black regiments could confidently stand up against it as well as against the enemy. Regardless of the lack of encouragement that the Negroes have so far been given by the government and by many generals—yes, even despite the shameful return of fugitive slaves that occurred until Congress decided to stop it— we have to be grateful for many important services they have rendered. In enemy territory, where the population either has the most intense hatred of the Union troops or is intimidated by the system of terror that reigns throughout the South, it is the Negroes who often provide the most useful information about the enemy's movements and numbers, and they have brought about many a victory and prevented many defeats.

Robert Small, a South Carolina slave, recently accomplished a heroic feat. The steamer "Planter" was in Charleston harbor, laden with a million dollars worth of cannons and ammunition for shipment to the coastal fortifications. The crew consisted entirely of slaves, and Robert Small was the pilot who was to steer the ship out of the harbor. The departure was scheduled for early morning, and it therefore aroused no suspicion when Small began to fire up the boilers the night before. He had his family come aboard, and at daybreak the steamer went merrily on its way leaving the harbor in full view of the cannons of Fort Sumter and Fort Moultrie, where no one had the least doubt that the commanding officer was on board and nothing was amiss. When the steamer approached our naval blockade, Small raised the Union flag, fired several salutes, and handed the "Planter" over as excellent booty. Congress awarded Small and his companions a third of the value of the cargo, to which they were legally entitled, so that the heroic slave is now a free and wealthy man. Even a writer of fairy tales has probably never dreamed of a more sudden change in fortune. When the result of the vote in Congress was announced, an aging representative from Kentucky, who wants to see the Union saved only by white people, became so enraged that he took his hat and left the Capitol cursing—an event over which Small will most likely not lose any sleep.

***

One of the most useful measures for the growth and well-being of the country, an act that will benefit Americans and foreigners alike, was recently passed by Congress and is now the law of the land. It is the Homestead Bill, and it provides that all uncultivated land belonging to the government will be made available to agriculture at no cost. Every American citizen or anyone who has declared his intention to become a citizen, also every head of family and anyone who has served in the present war is entitled through the Homestead Bill to cultivate and settle on a piece of land of up to 160 acres for a nominal fee of ten dollars. After fifteen years of occupation and cultivation the land will become his property without further cost. As long as ten years ago the friends of progress and the supporters of free labor tried to get this law passed by Congress. However, their efforts have been blocked by the determined and vicious opposition of the party of slaveholders and their allies. Envious of the North's progress and growth, they fear both the immense gains in immigration and wealth that the free states of the West would derive from this law and the flood of nonslaveholding land owners—the target of the southern knights' particular loathing and abhorrence—who would come and threaten the South.

Notes

1. New York, May [1862], *Morgenblatt*, 56:28:665–668.

61

The Emancipation of Slaves[1]

It often happens in life that a person who has focused all of his activities and efforts on a single, lofty goal does not feel as fully satisfied in finally reaching it as he had anticipated. He finds either that the achievement was not worth a whole life's efforts or that the sudden quiet after such strenuous activity, which had provided him with opportunities for developing his highest abilities, creates a certain vacuum in his life. The abolitionists have found themselves in a similar situation ever since the president's proclamation promising to set free all slaves residing in any southern states that will still be in rebellion against the United States on January 1, 1863. For nearly thirty years the abolitionists, individually and collectively, have been dedicating all their talent and strength to one great cause—the overthrow of slavery—and they have done so without regard to persecutions and animosities that they have had to endure from the very start to the present moment. Some of them have foregone brilliant careers so as to maintain their independence and to be free of any consideration of public favor and approval. Until the outbreak of war, not many of them entertained any hope that they would live to see the day on which the sun would rise to shine on a population of free human beings; yet everyone was convinced that if he were to be so favored it would be a day of the greatest satisfaction and fulfillment.

This day now seems to be only a few months off. The slaveholders and their friends in the North are furious, while the abolitionists, instead of celebrating, are looking at each other doubtfully. They are skeptical not because the value of the thing itself appears diminished to them on close view but because of the doubt—hanging over them like a black cloud—that this proclamation was indeed intended to bring about the unconditional abolition of slavery; they fear that instead of being given the solid gold of complete emancipation they might be paid in paper notes of dubious value. The president's proclamation, if fully implemented, would indeed put an end to slavery in the rebellious states and force the border states to accept the government's offer to emancipate their slaves with appropriate compensation, since slavery in the middle states alone, with free states both to the north and to the south, would be an impossibility. However, it seems highly implausible that this measure will ever be completely implemented.

The difficulty of proceeding resolutely in states which until now have been almost solidly in southern hands is self-evident. But the greater problem is that even in those places of the South where the Union flag is flying much of the work of liberation will necessarily have to be done not by the friends of emancipation but by its enemies. With few exceptions, the generals, who rule with almost unlimited power in those parts of the rebellious states that are under the control of Union forces, are among the most obdurate supporters of the slave system. Their views, tendencies, and antipathies agree far more with those of the slaveholders than with the opinions of the majority of the people in the free North. In fact, many of them are generally regarded as traitors, and there is a lack of will or courage to subject them to a nonpartisan inquiry.

It is a strange and amazing fact that the present administration, although elected only by the votes of the foes of slavery, has almost entirely left the conduct of the war to its most bitter and fundamental enemies and has let them benefit from its favors and emoluments. The people who remain in command are men like McClellan, who has not accomplished anything since the outbreak of the war, has never attacked the enemy, or when he did so was almost always defeated—with the possible exception of the battle at Antietam; or men like Buell, whose complete incompetence has caused a series of the most disgraceful routs. On the other hand, generals like Frémont, Hunter, and Phelps, whose abolitionist views are well known, are being persecuted and vilified; they are either relieved of their command or intentionally driven to resignation by insults and discriminations. One can say without exaggeration that a Democratic—that is, a proslavery—general will receive better treatment from the government even after the most ignominious defeat than a victorious emancipationist.

It is generally said that McClellan makes so little effort to hide his sympathies for the rebellious slaveholders that at the outbreak of the war he spoke of his regret about having to fight against Virginia and of the pleasure it would give him to attack Massachusetts instead. In almost all battles, the New England regiments—most of them from Massachusetts, the real center of abolitionism—are given the most dangerous assignments and consequently suffer the most terrible and disproportionate losses. McClellan has demonstrated his tender regard for the rebels by continuing to protect the property of the most outspoken and active secessionists even after Congress declared an end to such doings. Their owners having joined the rebel forces, these magnificent palaces were standing empty; they were protected by unwilling guardsmen, while there was a dearth of army hospitals and thousands fell victim to the typhus epidemic raging in overcrowded buildings. Fruit and vegetables were rotting in fields and gardens, while the soldiers suffered from scurvy; they even had to make do with ditch and swamp water just to keep the sacrosanct wells of the rebels untouched.

The consequence of this novel method of warfare was that the 150,000 men of the Army of the Potomac were reduced by about 30,000 in less than a year by illness alone. But McClellan remains the celebrated hero among the open and clandestine friends of the slaveholders; the honest and truly loyal general population, however, is divided only on the question whether in his sympathy for the secessionists McClellan would go so far as to spare them any real harm or whether he is the embodiment of the most pathetic incompetence. These are the people who are tired of the half-truths and halfway measures, those who do not wish to see slavery preserved at the cost of the nation's welfare and future prospects. It is perfectly clear, at any rate, that the emancipation of the slaves will not be resolutely pursued wherever it is in the hands of a McClellan or any of his numerous fellow sympathizers.

Looking at the emancipation proclamation itself, which is now the chief subject of conversation and the touchstone of loyalist sentiments, one realizes that its effectiveness will be largely destroyed because it is now a necessary measure of war rather than an act of justice and humanitarianism. It comes too late, the president having resisted for too long everything that resembles an act of emancipation in the hope that nobler motives might prevail. His hand was finally forced by desperate circumstances resulting from a series of bloody defeats in which nearly all gains of the previous six months were lost: the attack on Maryland, the threat to Pennsylvania, Ohio, and Washington. A measure that would have been regarded by the civilized world as an act of virtue, can now only be seen as a concession to the force of circumstances, which—more powerfully than the president's will— promises the complete overthrow of slavery before the thunder of the cannons has died away.

Nevertheless, the hatred aimed at Negroes is as strong as ever and has recently shown itself again in all its virulence as the government continued its efforts to expatriate free Negroes. These are nothing but concessions offered to assuage the anger of the defenders of slavery over the emancipation measure and to neutralize the naked prejudice of the Negro's enemies. As much as the southerner likes to have the Negro in his midst as a slave, he hates every free Negro, seeing him as a living argument against his cherished system of slavery, while the northerner cannot stand any colored person. That is why the offensive hue is to be removed from the country, no matter what objections are made on the grounds of humanitarianism and justice. But since they are ashamed to stand before the world or to look each other in the eye, they choose to put up a smoke screen, inventing the most absurd ethnological reasons and arguing that the presence of different races in this country is an evil, a source of unrest, and the cause of the present war.

They do not want to concede that slavery, just as it is the sole cause of this war, is also the cause of color prejudice, of negrophobia; they do not want to understand that such hatred would never have developed if Negroes had originally not been brought here as slaves but had voluntarily immigrated like the Germans, the Irish, and all the other nations. The colored people are fully aware that their own well-being is the last thing that matters in all these plans, and that the mountains of gold they are promised in Central America are nothing but false promises used to make them emigrate like obedient sheep because in this day and age no one can be so despicable as to force free people out of the country who have not been guilty of anything. As badly as they are treated here, as restricted and oppressed as they are now, the fear of unknown evils that may lurk abroad seems to outweigh their present grievances. At any rate, one does not hear much about the success of various schemes urging them to emigrate.

In an effort to get their plans launched, the colonizationists sought the support of the intelligent mulatto Frederick Douglass, hoping that their scheme would be helped by his persuasiveness and influence among the colored population, since he is their most outstanding representative. However, this excellent man, who stands above all petty racial differences and whose views are inspired by the highest human and most farsighted perspective, did not want to have any part in this enterprise. He explained his opinions about questions of race and colonization in a superbly written letter, which completely sweeps aside the whole project for anyone who is not blinded by prejudice.[2]

For many years, the American church as a whole has been notoriously known to be one of the strongest supporters of slavery. The Episcopal church has been particularly active in this praiseworthy mission, and none of its conventions has proceeded without some stormy scenes in response to any mention of slavery as a not altogether perfect institution. The slightest suggestion—perhaps in the form of a petition that the convention should censure not even slavery itself but merely the illegal African slave trade—was sufficient to arouse the majority's wrath: screaming, hissing, and banging, they would vent their anger so that you thought the honorable gentlemen would at any moment tear each other's hair out. In a society like America, where ethical concepts have been stood on their head through centuries of contact with slavery, such behavior has not damaged these gentlemen's reputation in the eyes of most so-called "respectable people"—that is, as long as the North shared in the guilt of the South. Today, however, things are seen from a different perspective. Many who have hitherto blindly subjected themselves to the authority of the church must feel their faith and respect somewhat shattered as they see many a pious father who has always been on the side of law and tradition openly excuse and defend the rebellion of the slaveholders, as is happening at the convention now being held.

Since the outbreak of the war, so much criminal and treasonous nonsense has perhaps only been voiced in the meetings of the most extreme slavery Democrats. At issue was the question what resolution the church should pass in regard to southern priests who have deliberately raised the banner of rebellion and thereby broken all connections with the church of the North. As Dr. Hawks,[3] one of the most celebrated lights of the pulpit from New York, put it: there was no use in poring over all these "petty," "dirty" little issues of the day that would get buried and swept away with this entire movement. A Mr. Reetfield[4] asked whether we would act any better if we were in the place of "our southern brethren," and he expressed his conviction that we would act worse. He confessed that he had gained a more favorable opinion of the people in the South since his travels through that section. Bishop Doane,[5] who seems to enjoy a better reputation in the church than in the world of business—you may remember when he brought financial ruin on a public school under his guidance and supervision—called upon the convention for Heaven's sake not to alienate the southern church. And several other gentlemen told touching stories about the piety and kindness of people in the South, especially Virginia.

However, a Mr. Ruggles[6] took the cake when he said that the sin committed by our southern brethren was after all not so grievous—a mere breach of contract, not a moral injustice. He tried to defend the actions of the southern church in a lengthy speech, expressing his hope that the four million slaves in the South would not soon be given their freedom. Dr. Goodwin,[7] who presented a clear, concise, and truthful account of the South's actions, was ordered to be silent and abide by the rules. Since the convention is still in progress, I cannot yet report the conclusion of their deliberations; but it can be said with certainty that a firm, thoughtful resolution cannot be expected from this community of the faithful.

Notes

1. New York, May [1862], *Morgenblatt,* 56:28:665–668.

2. Most likely, Assing is here referring to Douglass's "The President and His Speeches," *Douglass' Monthly,* September 1862.

3. Francis Lister Hawks (1798–1866) was an Episcopal clergyman, historian, and professor, who was associated with both the Church of the Mediator and Calvary Church in New York before moving to Christ Church in Baltimore because he sympathized with the South.

4. Reetfield has not been identified.

5. William Croswell Doane (1832–1913) later became the Episcopal bishop of the Albany diocese, but Assing may be confusing him with his father, Bishop George Washington Doane (1799–1859).

6. Samuel Bulkley Ruggles (1800–1881) was a prominent lawyer and a member of the General Convention of the Protestant Episcopal Church.

7. Daniel Raynes Goodwin (1811–1890), an Episcopal priest, was at various times president of Trinity College in Hartford and provost of the University of Pennsylvania.

62

Consequences of War—Congressional Elections—McClellan[1]

You get used to many things in this world, even to war—as long as you live far enough from the battle not to have to fear the loss of life and property. Were it not for the barracks in the park across from City Hall, housing soldiers who are on their way either to or from the battlefield, or for the recruiting tents with their eagles and red-white-and-blue flags in some public squares, the look of New York would never suggest that we are in the middle of a civil war that will determine the future and the very existence of the nation. The throng of the crowds on Broadway and their colorful clothes are the same as in the calmest, happiest days. Theaters and other places of entertainment are thriving, and one's everyday life shows fewer signs of restriction than it did in those earlier years of peace when decline in trade caused a monetary crisis.

True, the law of *habeas corpus*, the most important guarantee of individual liberty, has been temporarily suspended, but the loyal citizen knows that the purpose of placing this weapon in the hands of the government is not the exercise of unchecked tyranny but the apprehension of traitors and their accomplices. He therefore accepts this temporary suspension of his rights without demur, especially because it poses no personal danger for himself. Far more distasteful is the drafting of recruits that has now begun. However, because this war did not begin as an adventure but was literally forced upon us, there is little public complaint; yet people quietly use whatever tricks and conniving it takes to escape military service. All the dark prophecies of inevitable and total impoverishment and of grass growing in the streets of New York have turned out to be wrong. In general, the material conditions of the free states are far better than expected and more favorable than the secret and public friends of the South would like them to be.

Those with a clear and unbiased view of things had predicted that the blockade of the southern railroads would disrupt the operations of trains in the South to the advantage of the northern railroads, but reality has exceeded all expectations. The enormous amounts of western grain and cattle that formerly were shipped down the Mississippi by steamboat are now transported by northern railroads to northern ports, and the stocks of these railroads are soaring higher than ever. Only now that trade with the South has been completely cut off has it become clear that trade with the West is a sufficient compensation. True, the country has incurred immense debts, the people have been severely taxed, and the cost of goods from abroad has gone up by a quarter to a third due to an increase in tariffs; on the other hand, labor is in such great demand and wages are so high that even the poorer classes do not feel much pressure. We have even had the good fortune of an unusually rich harvest in all parts of the country: with grain, grass, and fruit crops outdoing each other, it seems as if nature wants to show its good will. Looking at fields, pastures, and orchards can almost provide some solace for the discouragement and pessimism over last summer's terrible defeats caused by the incompetence or treason of several Union generals.

Just as the North is only now beginning to feel its strength and independence, the South must face the gradual erosion of its hopes and expectations. At first the southerners laughed at the plans to blockade their harbors and believed they were not worth the paper on which they were written. But when reality put an end to their delusions, they predicted that the power of cotton—on which they had based all their conspiratorial calculations—would force Europe to intervene and break the blockade, that banks and businesses in the North would falter, and that people there would devour each other. But this so-called absolute power of cotton, which the South trusted so absolutely, has sunk to the level of a dethroned, devastated king. Because cotton cannot be exported or provide food, it is for the moment a useless product abandoned by the planters, who now use their slaves for growing grain and raising pigs to meet their most pressing needs and still their hunger.

This situation proves that the free states have more than enough energy, wealth, and materials to bring the war against the rebel states to a victorious conclusion. With Buell's removal from the West and McClellan's from the Potomac—unfortunately a year overdue—the government has at long last shown its desire to rid the army of all those semi-traitorous elements who sympathize with the South and have for one and a half years conducted the war in a manner that has not yet brought us a decisive advantage. Yet, one cannot deny that a threatening crisis may be looming: the results of the congressional and state elections leave no shadow of hope that the war will be conducted with full energy or that the nation will soon rid itself of the stigma of slavery. The victory of the so-called Democratic party in Pennsylvania, New York, New Jersey, Ohio, Illinois, and Indiana—the party that has always been ready to make all sorts of concessions to the slavocracy—clearly signals a reaction. It also reveals such a lack of conscience, such a total absence of any sense of honor, liberty, and independence among the masses that one despairs over the nation's future and feels the misfortune of being chained to it by circumstances.

In New York, the result of the elections was particularly shameful. It is bad enough that Horatio Seymour,[2] the elected governor, is a man who used to speak—as long as he could safely do so—of the rights of an insulted South and the excesses of the North; a man who referred to the war as unconstitutional and unprincipled; a man who would have gladly and forever opened up all territories to slavery. But what can one say about the election to Congress of Fernando Wood, the former mayor of New York, a declared secessionist, and a cheat and fraud? Every street urchin in New York knows that Fernando Wood, at the outbreak of the war, not only was on the side of the South but urged the city of New York to secede from the state—although this is a political crime in which he is joined by many accomplices here. But every street urchin also knows that a few weeks ago Fernando Wood lost a case in court that was brought against him for fraud and forgery, a case dragging for years from one court to another because he has used every means of bribery and intrigue to postpone or avert judgment.

***

As devastating as the victory of the Democrats may be, it may have salutary results. It is the natural and immediate consequence of the politics pursued by the president and his cabinet, who put the army in the hands of their political enemies so as to curry favor with the border states and the Democrats of the North. Democratic generals have sacrificed soldiers and wasted the nation's wealth, blaming the Republicans. The administration finds itself defeated and realizes that flattering its enemies and rebuffing its friends has been to no avail. You would expect that this experience would provide the impulse for new and better policies, and the first step in that direction may be McClellan's removal from his command on the Potomac, which is currently the chief topic of conversation. His supporters, including the entire party of slavery, are beside themselves with rage, and they try their very best to present him as a martyr and a victim of party animosity. But any effort at reviving a corpse could not be more hopeless than trying to claim military renown for McClellan.

Devastating official documents were released at the time of his dismissal: reports of military commissions of inquiry and a report by the commanding general Halleck,[3] who himself is a Democrat, prove beyond a doubt that—as the abolitionists and radical Republicans have long since known and said—McClellan never seriously intended to defeat the enemy; he wilfully disobeyed the orders of the president and the secretary of war to attack Richmond; and he is responsible for several of the most embarrassing losses and defeats. It is a case of the most devastating and self-inflicted personal shipwreck ever suffered by any person. The catastrophe was unavoidable, but one wonders why it did not occur much earlier. It seems beyond comprehension that pure party machinations can create an aura of accomplishment for a man who, even if he were honest, is only the embodiment of the sorriest incompetence; but the masses were completely blinded. One can understand that a general who has proven himself to be brave and capable may later make some mistakes or even turn into a traitor, and that the masses, grateful for his earlier deeds, will continue to believe in him. But McClellan has no such history: he had never seen battle, and expectations were all one had to go on. Even though his military experience consisted only of defeats, his admirers never changed their minds: they called him the Little Napoleon, ranted about a military dictatorship, and spoke about his lost battles with the reverence and admiration that a Frenchman has for names like Lodi, Arcole, and Austerlitz.[4]

Notes

1. New York, November [1862], *Morgenblatt*, 57:1:22–24 (1863).

2. Horatio Seymour (1810–1886), a Democrat from upstate New York, opposed most antislavery measures, including Lincoln's Emancipation Proclamation; he was the Democratic presidential candidate in 1868 but lost against Ulysses S. Grant.

3. Henry W. Halleck (1815–1872) had been appointed to succeed Frémont (one of Assing's heroes) in Missouri; beginning in 1862, he served as general-in-chief and as Lincoln's military adviser.

4. Lodi, in Lombardy, northern Italy; Arcole, in Venetia, northeast Italy; and Austerlitz (Slavkov), in southern Moravia, Czech Republic—all three are sites of important Napoleonic victories.

63

New Defeats—Corruption—Religious Conditions[1]

Bloody defeats have again dampened the hopes and expectations of the past weeks, and the future is shrouded in dark clouds. The cause that brought about this latest debacle—whether incompetence or unscrupulousness—is unlikely to come to light for the time being; but whatever it may be, there are always so many northern elements working against the North's interests that no misdeed can come as a surprise. Should the North be the victor in this war, should the nation emerge viable and cleansed of the stigma of slavery, it will not be the result of its inherent strength and virtue but despite its weakness, despite the treason and incompetence of its generals, despite the greed and corruption of its politicians and officials, despite the lack of principle and the indifference of the masses. Everyone knows that the existence and the future of the nation are at stake, that any temporizing, every opportunity lost, spells so much gain for the enemy and so much increase in the danger of foreign intervention. Yet there are relatively few men who will honestly and with all their might strive to do their duty to the best of their ability. Instead of unselfish patriotism, which alone can help a nation survive a crisis such as this, you meet the narrow spirit of partisanship wherever you turn.

The truly radical abolitionists understood as long as a year ago that the cause of our defeats and of the war's continuation was not the enemy's strength but our own insufficiency, dishonesty, and lack of total commitment. They expressed their convictions honestly but were shunned and vilified, and the conservatives even called them nothing less than outright traitors. But they have been brilliantly vindicated by events: over the past few weeks, in particular, one official disclosure after another has revealed a state of affairs far worse than they could then have anticipated. Accused of major dereliction of duties, three generals are at present being court-martialed; several others have also been charged and will soon be tried; and many against whom there is no direct proof are nevertheless considered traitors by public opinion. But what follows from all this? Not the kind of moral revulsion that treason and lies would normally excite among halfway decent people! The public views things with a kind of cool detachment: many try to gloss over the abominations with rationalizations, and the party friends of the stigmatized are not beneath making them into martyrs and exploiting them for political gain.

Even McClellan, to whom the country is indebted for the most embarrassing defeats and the most pointless butcheries, the man whose paper renown finally went up in smoke with the official report issued by General in Chief Halleck—even McClellan is still being praised by the northern Democrats (the secret friends of the South) and his name touted as a party slogan. The generals feud among themselves out of jealousy and party animosity; they try to inflict damage on one another without regard to the consequences. Reliable sources are spreading the word that since their hero's dismissal several of the younger officers on McClellan's staff have done their best to demoralize the army and are tireless in their opposition to Burnside, McClellan's successor. Whether McClellan knows about and condones these activities remains unclear for now—and probably forever.

This unscrupulousness and wrongdoing extends to all spheres and branches of the administration. It was recently discovered that a large part of the bombs delivered to the Army of the Potomac did not explode, a situation that caused several arrests. The system of providing medical treatment is more chaotic than would be tolerated in any other civilized country. Every day the newspapers report new and detailed outrages, demanding solutions, but nothing effective is ever the result. The hospitals are so badly equipped that one would believe we are among a semi-barbarous people; and the extent of mortality has no parallel. Anyone with injuries that prevent him from moving on his own might as well give up because hospitals and the care—or rather carelessness—of physicians and nurses will surely complete the work that the enemy's bullets failed to do. The inevitable consequence of this neglect is that epidemics of typhoid sweep through the army claiming more victims than the bloodiest battles. The physicians—whom one would normally count among the most educated and humane of men—outdo each other and all the rest in cruelty and incompetence. Lack of experience and the many years of peace, which had once been given as excuses, can no longer explain matters; nothing but the most egregious carelessness and indifference can be at the root of this unmitigated chaos. Every government official believes he is entitled to serve himself first and to use his position to get the greatest personal advantage at the public's expense.

Among the causes that have brought about this depraved condition slavery is so self-evident that only an American Democrat can have the audacity to deny its influence. Yet another cause, even more vicious than slavery because of its widespread effect on all classes of society, is the lie that is spread by a hypocritical religiosity. After a superficial glance at the United States, some European travelers see in the predominance of the churches the basis for an optimistic view of the future of the American people; but after several years of carefully observing conditions and events one cannot avoid the impression that it is precisely this element that is the largest obstacle in the development towards a healthy, ethical society. In essence, the American people are not more religious than any other; most particularly, the fanaticism that sometimes leads other nations into hatred and persecution of those who hold different beliefs is not part of their nature. The Americans are on the whole too shallow, not deeply intellectual enough, to give much thought to these matters; but social convention has given rise to the role of the church as an essential condition and a measure of respectability, social status, and gentility. A person's behavior will be judged more leniently—even if it cannot be justified on strictly moral principles—if he belongs to a fashionable church; if he and his family occupy their pew twice every Sunday, enduring the service (awake or asleep) to the end; and if at night he reads to his family the printed prayers issued by the church that he has joined for reasons of maintaining tradition, family relations, or business connections. The wealthy and fashionable belong *par excellence* to the Episcopal church, the middle and lower classes usually are Baptists and Methodists. All of them consider the more liberal Unitarians and Universalists as infidels and heretics, the latter being well represented in the North but in the orthodox South known and despised only by name. The young people grow up in this system of mindless religiosity. In no other country do children and young people enjoy so much freedom and absence of rules, yet in regard to this one single issue they have no choice but to subject themselves absolutely. Already at age five or six children are dragged to church and forced to listen to hours of preaching without understanding a word. For good measure, they may then be sent to Sunday school in the afternoon, where their heads are stuffed with equally incomprehensible Bible verses. The least complaint about this weekly torture would be seen as an instance of such unpardonable godlessness that young America soon learns to toe the line. It knows that twenty lies and a hundred cases of disobedience and naughtiness will be overlooked and that mother will make excuses for occasionally missing school and being lazy, as long as it accepts the boredom in church without fuss. The young soon learn that, in essence, it is all a matter of appearances, and that appearances are the basis for a lifetime of lies and hypocrisy.

"Look at it this way," a respectable gentleman once told me in a small circle, candidly speaking his mind about this system of appearances, even if he lacked the courage to go against prevailing attitudes. "What would happen to our churches and ministers if they were to be visited and supported only by those of true conviction and faith? We older people go to prove our respectability, perhaps also to set a good example; some go believing that they can atone for their misdeeds during the rest of the week; others go because they are used to taking their Sunday nap on the cushioned pews and under the soothing sounds of the organ; and still others go because the routine of business has so shriveled their minds that they simply would not know what to do with themselves on Sundays without the church's help in killing time. Young people go to see and be seen, to show off their new clothes, perchance to have an innocent *tête-à-tête,* or to submit to their parents' rules. But they are all happy and cheerful when it is all over, and not one in a hundred would sacrifice time or money if it were not for their secret motive."

The ministers do everything in their power to keep up this state of affairs. They know they depend on the public's good will and, for this reason, are strict only in regard to doctrinal orthodoxy, excessively accommodating and flexible in everything else. They flatter the biases and views of their patrons especially in matters of slavery and color prejudice; they do not risk unpopularity by being overly strict but gladly wink at this or that as long as nobody challenges their status and authority, the church receives its usual tithes, and the faithful are not overly stingy in the annual bidding for pews. So they weave a web of lies and they all see through it; and, one hand washing the other, they will continue for a long time to come—until, some day, a great moral revolution will bring us healthier and more natural conditions.

***

Notes

1. New York, December [1862], *Morgenblatt,* 57:5:116–118 (1863).

64

Emancipation Proclamation—Conditions in Mississippi[1]

Of all the New Year's Days that the young republic has experienced none has been anticipated with greater excitement and expectation than the First of January 1863. Everyone knew that it would be a significant, consequential, perhaps decisive day for the country's future. "Will the president keep his promise and issue the Emancipation Proclamation he had promised three months ago?" That was the big question on the minds of all parties, North as well as South, in the rebel states and in those that have remained loyal. It was well known that the Democrats in the North and the semi-loyal border states had exerted themselves enormously to persuade the president to leave the thing undone. At the same time, the rebellious slaveholders and their publications tried to hide their fears by declaring the measure to be impossible, unenforceable, ridiculous, and therefore ineffective and harmless. They repeated the old fairy tale of the slaves' affection for them, but in the same breath contradicted themselves by ranting and raving, piling the usual litany of curses and maledictions on the president and the abolitionists, and giving blood-curdling accounts of slave uprisings.

The true abolitionists felt torn between fear and hope, cognizant of the president's history of aversion to any sort of strike against slavery. They were hardly able to comprehend that the great goal had come within reach through the enemy's own suicidal blindness, the goal to which many of them had dedicated all their energies and the best parts of their lives without believing that they would ever see the day of fulfillment. However, during the last week of the old year, news from reliable sources at the seat of government left no more room for doubt that the grand strike against slavery had really been decided on. The impression was deep and lasting, much greater than could have been expected. The colored people celebrated the day with public gatherings, speeches, and other festivities; cannons were fired in some cities, fires of celebration were lit, and all publicly issued papers rose in value on the stock exchange. It was evident that the people—even if they have not yet fully understood the evil of slavery or felt the moral revulsion that educated Europeans experience—welcomed its demise as the beginning of better times.

As important and fateful as this proclamation will prove to be, one has to recognize that it again reveals itself as one of those halfway measures so characteristic of this president and his advisers. Those slaves in different regions who, under the threat of arms, have been returned to an enforced loyalty but would nevertheless support the rebellion if they could do so without being punished, are excluded from this proclamation, a provision that significantly reduces its overall effect. Of course, once slavery in the rebel states has been given a mortal blow, the other states, whose main business it was to breed slaves for the southern market, have to follow suit and emancipate their slaves. But now, as the government has regained only a minuscule part of the South, it is a voluntary surrender of its advantage not to exercise its power wherever it can.

At any rate, it is very doubtful, in fact unlikely, that the Emancipation Proclamation will cause a general uprising among the slaves in the near future. Since the outbreak of the war, thousands have fled to seek freedom and entered into service with the Union armies wherever they were accepted, proving themselves to be brave, dependable soldiers. Since the beginning of the rebellion, the slaves have been treated too hypocritically, insidiously, and cruelly by the federal government and particularly by the Democratic generals, and their hopes have been too often crushed as to rise up against their masters in the expectation of protection and assistance from the Union. They also know that giving them their freedom was not a voluntary act based on humanitarianism and justice but that it was done out of necessity, even reluctance, because all other steps had proven to be fruitless. Furthermore, as for now, we cannot offer them anything but a paper proclamation to compensate not only for earlier decrees in support of slavery but for deeds of horror and outrage that have been etched into the slave's heart with his own blood.

Yes, there was a time when such an edict would have been sufficient to join the entire black race into an army of active allies; but how can the slaves forget McClellan's proclamation in which, on the mere rumor that a slave uprising had occurred in Maryland, he offered the slaveholders to suppress it "with an iron fist"? How can they forget Halleck's and Dix's orders removing all fugitive slaves from the ranks of their forces?[2] How can the slaves of Louisiana not remember their thirty companions who arrived in New Orleans, unarmed and carrying only their tools, hoping to find protection, but who instead were shot and killed in cold blood by our own troops? How can the slaves of Mississippi not remember the terrible events at Vicksburg, where three thousand of them were used for many weeks to dig a canal only to be ungratefully dismissed and kicked out of the encampment by the officers after having completed their labors? How can the slaves of Alabama forget four hundred of their companions whom General Mitchell had promised their freedom in return for their loyal services,[3] but who—upon his transfer—were turned over the very next day to their so-called owners by his successor, General Buell (who, incidentally, is suspected of treason)? The history of this war is replete with such shameful actions: they are the monuments of a moral condition that is beyond expression.

As much as the war has had a disturbing effect on all conditions of life, as heavy a burden as it has been on the whole nation, in the free states, far from the scenes of battle, people are relatively well off. Life and property are as safe as in times of peace, and everybody continues plying his trade and still has time and means for some amusements. I do not often find much so-called poetic justice in life, but in this particular case one cannot complain about its absence, for those who have engaged in rebellion are saddled with the greater burden; little as they are inclined to acknowledge their suffering, enough of it becomes known to reveal their living conditions, which no one in the North can really fathom. Almost completely cut off by water and by land from all supplies, unable to produce the most essential materials, southerners suffer to an extent that in itself would be sufficient to get them once and for all over any ideas of secession, were it not for the implacable and bitter hatred they feel against the North.

A few days ago, I spoke with an officer who is stationed with his regiment in Mississippi, and he gave me a vivid description of the local conditions. One cannot imagine a more desolate scene than the northern part of the state of Mississippi nor more unlawful conditions than those prevailing there. This becomes particularly noticeable if you venture a few miles beyond the outposts of the Union army. You will not see it when the army is on the march or when some of the companies are scouting for food and a crowd of stragglers move along the bypaths and swarm around searching every farm house, thus providing some life and activity. But if you are by yourself, without companions, you witness the widespread destruction wrought throughout the region by the guerilla war that is being fought in the Southwest. The first thing you notice is the deep silence that reigns everywhere. As you pass by long stretches of fenced fields dotted with occasional houses, you never hear the cheerful sounds of country life and work: neither the songs of workers in the fields nor the neighing of horses; neither the mooing of cows nor the bleating of sheep—none of the sounds that give life to the countryside. The cattle has long since been driven off by one or the other army. You climb a hill that offers a distant vista, but there are neither humans nor animals; the whites are probably sleeping in after the previous night's guerilla raid, and the blacks have taken off to seek "Uncle Abraham" and their freedom.

The country roads are just as quiet and desolate as the fields. You can walk on them for miles without meeting a living being. In some of the abandoned houses doors and windows are wide open and desolate emptiness looks out of each hollow frame because nothing of value remains. The traveler sometimes thinks he hears a noise or sees the movement of some creature, and he looks around him suspiciously. A squirrel jumps across his path, and he pulls out his revolver. Whereas in times of peace he is glad to meet a companion on the road, he now is frightened at every noise: a trotting horse, a breaking twig, a shuffle through fallen leaves—all are signs of danger. The guerillas are the cause of it all, and they strike terror into the local residents rather than into the Union army, on which they can inflict little damage.

The guerilla leaders believe that the dearth of cotton will bring about an imminent state of anarchy in the North. Therefore they burn the cotton, ruining the planter and preventing him from selling it to some "Yankee" who may have taken the risk of such a speculation for the sake of large profits. Because the guerillas receive no military pay but live solely on the gains of robbery, you can imagine that they do not closely question the political opinions of people whom they visit on their raids. Any way, the supporters of the Union are too few and far between in Mississippi to provide sufficient prey. Alleged loyalty to the Union is, therefore, the pretense that often hides personal enmity, jealousy, or sheer thievery, and every farmer is more fearful of his own neighbors than of the Union forces.

If you step into any of the few houses that are still occupied, you will find that the owners of large estates often are almost without any supplies and are living solely on corn. They all tell the same story: that both friendly and enemy troops have taken all their cattle, horses, cows, pigs, and grain; that their Negroes have run away and the guerillas burned their cotton. If the traveler gets into a longer conversation with such a man and gives him to understand that he is interested in buying cotton, he suddenly finds that a supply of cotton is hidden in a nearby swamp and that its owner is eager to sell it for Union money. Except for the troops, cotton traders are actually the only ones who dare to come among these people, and their business is extremely dangerous. If successful, the profits are very large; but few days pass on which one of these daredevils is not seized by the guerillas and has not only his cotton and all his cash stolen but is forced to return with hardly any clothes to cover his nakedness, with feet bare, and head uncovered.

The state of Missouri is the first slave state that is about to abolish slavery within its borders and to accept the compensation offered by the government. This triumph of freedom over slavery is largely the result of the German influence, and it is the second great victory won by the Germans in Missouri—the only slave state with a large German population. Two years ago, at the beginning of the rebellion, when the treasonous governor of the state was doing his best to pull Missouri out of the Union, it was the Germans who first rose in defense of the state, defended it against local and outside secessionists, and saved it through their loyalty and courage. It was here that Siegel, who had formerly been a school teacher in St. Louis, gained his first laurels as a chief defender of the state before assuming an even more important post in Virginia.[4]

Notes

1. New York, January [1863], *Morgenblatt,* 57:9:214–216.

2. For Halleck, see Essay 62, n. 3; John Adams Dix (1798–1879) had served as a senator from New York (1845–1849), ran on the Free Soil ticket for governor (1848), was a major general in the Union army, and later served as minister to France (1866–1869).

3. Major General Ormsby M. Mitchel (1809–1862), his name sometimes appearing also as Mitchell, was put in charge of Union forces between Huntsville and Montgomery in early 1862; he took a strong attitude against uncooperative southerners and may well have promised freedom to slaves for "loyal services."

4. See Essay 54, n. 3.

65

Humbug—Psychology—Dwarves—Behavior of Negroes in the South[1]

The war has brought about many changes, and its influence has become more or less, directly or indirectly, noticeable in almost all phases of life. One thing, however, remains untouched, resistant to all changes, forever self-renewing, rejuvenating, and taking on new forms: it is humbug, that distinctly American product, growing as profusely in its native soil as the potato prefers a foreign earth to give it full body and flavor. It is thriving today as much as in bygone days, when the Fish siblings first began moving tables, starting a national epidemic[2]; or when some years later a few calculating priests started the nonsense of a religious awakening for their own self-serving purposes, and people came from the most dubious business practices to public prayer meetings, rolling their eyes, shouting "Glory to God," and then returning to haggling and usury.

Today's humbug, which has not yet spread very far, appears under the pompous name "psychology," a term that refers to a certain magnetic condition allegedly caused by a combination of animal and mineral magnetism. While under its influence, a person is more or less controlled in his movements and sense perceptions by the will of the magnetizer. This so-called discovery or invention is nothing new, and I remember distinctly that about eleven or twelve years ago an American visiting Hamburg tried to exploit the people's longing for miracles; but he thoroughly failed because of the public's inherent common sense and was roundly ridiculed and driven out of town. For the true believers among the American audience, however, no fraud can be so crude as not to be served up with success. Germans would treat as rubbish the things that can make good money over here by anyone who knows how to do them right, as can be seen in the success of Professors Fiske and Brittan,[3] who did not go wrong in their assumption that the people of New York can be easily fooled. For several weeks they have been up to their mischief, and they still find enough people who willingly pay 25 cents admission to be made fools of.

I went to one of their first presentations. It was open exclusively to ladies, the announcement stated, to give them an opportunity to experience at first hand the influence of magnetic force without being in danger of appearing ridiculous or unmannerly in the presence of gentlemen. This baiting of curiosity had its desired effect: what extraordinary things could be expected when such caution was necessary! At the outset, the alleged Professor Brittan spoke about the "grand silent forces of nature," and how these are influenced by magnetism, which was the actual subject of the lecture. Magnetism is supposed to be the force through which one person exerts virtually unlimited power over another; it is the force through which a Van Amburgh or Martin can tame dangerous wild beasts.[4] But the audience's credulity was stretched even more by stories about "trustworthy and truthful" persons who, by sheer will power, were able to influence the dreams of others over a distance of many miles. And to be sure that these birds would be recognized by their plumage, the gentlemen announced that every individual who had ever come under their influence would be free of all future illnesses without resorting to any medical assistance.

After this promising introduction they proceeded to the experiments. Those who wanted to learn from direct experience were asked to seat themselves in the first few rows, then the so-called battery was revealed; it consisted of thick, round zinc plates into which a five-cent piece had been embedded. It was placed in someone's hand with the command to observe it carefully and silently without interruption for several minutes. A deep silence ensued, while the magnetizer walked twice among those who wanted to participate in the experiment, brushing his hand over their temples and holding their thumbs. Then the zinc plates were removed, and a few moments later the professor resumed his walk, repeated his magnetic strokes with every lady, and then requested her to shut her eyes—which was promptly done. "Now," he said, "you cannot open your eyes! No, you cannot, you cannot!" Of course, the majority, including myself, popped open their eyes, but a few, perhaps five or six, started grimacing as if they really had difficulties. The former were dismissed as incorrigibly honest or healthy; the others were taken to a platform where the humbug continued.

I do not pretend to be familiar with the depths and abysses of New York society and its modes of expression, but after all my observations and comparisons I could not fail to detect a certain undefinable something among those "psychologized ladies," as they are called in the jargon of this *métier*. I could not help but place these ladies in the category of suspicious characters, two of them clearly revealing in dress and demeanor that they belonged to a very low class of society. One of the suspicious ladies laid her hand flat on that of the magnetizer and could, it seemed, retract it only after many attempts and only with the greatest effort. Another one was unable to remain seated in her chair and was irresistibly drawn out of it, while two others were physically so shaken by his will that they could not stand on their feet but were forced to sit down.

When this farce was over, they experimented with psychologizing of the senses. The same suspicious lady who had been so cooperative throughout again assumed the leading part. She was given a glass of water, which the magnetizer changed first into honey, then into wine, then some bitter liquid that made her grimace, and finally into lemonade. After this demonstration had again been crowned with success, they performed experiments with the eye. A white handkerchief was made to appear successively green, black, and red in the eyes of the magnetized person and was finally presented to the one cooperative individual as a little black kitten, which she stroked and petted as if she held a real animal in her arms. Turning it then into a small child was not so great a leap, and, after the spell had been removed, she acted most surprised at holding in her hand someone else's pocket handkerchief.

For the ultimate clou, the magnetizer made her see the hall as suddenly empty, then dark, and finally filled only with gentlemen—and with that the entertainment came to an end. To prove that everything had been done honestly, the magnetizer gave repeated assurances that he did not know the ladies who had been so receptive and had never met them before. Upon which a woman sitting next to me, who had watched the whole proceeding with a skeptical smile, mumbled quietly in a thick German accent: "If you believe that, I've got a bridge in Brooklyn I can sell you."

The big event of the last few days, however, was an undeniably concrete truth and reality: a wedding of dwarves never seen before. Charles Stratton, whose fame, as the tiny Tom Thumb, has also spread to Europe, was wedded a few days ago to Miss Lavinia Warren, a little lady of his own stature. New York went all but crazy with pleasure over this event, especially the fashionable world. For a long time people doubted whether the rumors were true, believing that it was nothing more than a clever speculation by Barnum, the great representative of American humbug. He had exhibited the bride among the curiosities of his museum and made such a to-do about the upcoming wedding, arousing everyone's curiosity to such an extent, that he took in several thousand dollars in just a few weeks. But this time, Barnum proved to be as solid as a rock: the wedding actually took place, and New York went crazy. At Barnum's expense, one of the foremost stores made a royal wardrobe for the bride, and the ladies came in droves to admire the costly pieces in miniature.

Finally, on February 10, the appointed day, the excitement was out of control. If on that day the news of the fall of Richmond had come, I suppose the frenzy could hardly have been greater. The wedding took place in one of the fashionable churches on Broadway. Hours before, the crowds had grown enormous: windows, roofs, cornerstones, and lampposts were occupied by the curious; buses and other vehicles had to take detours along side streets; and admission tickets were bought at thirty to forty dollars. It certainly was a rare spectacle, because how often do you see four dwarves at once? A sister of the bride, somewhat smaller than she, as well as Commodore Mutt, in his full twenty-nine inch height, appeared as bridesmaid and bride's escort, giving one the feeling of belonging with the Lilliputian race. The tiny pairs were greeted with applause, and the whole ceremony was treated like public entertainment, much to the annoyance of the religiously orthodox, who expressed their outrage over Barnum's moving his museum into a church. After the couple were married, the crowds flocked to the Metropolitan Hotel to congratulate the little people.

The most positive reports about the behavior of the colored people who have been freed from slavery by the war and the Emancipation Proclamation are coming from places in the South that are under the control of the United States. Those who cultivate the land or construct canals and entrenchments under the supervision of the government are as industrious, orderly, and reliable as one might wish. The black regiments are the most useful and have proven their courage under fire during the few opportunities that they have had; they have developed a fortitude and discipline that would have done honor to the best army in the world. There is nothing really surprising in this, and it seems plausible that those who used to work under the lash for the benefit of their enemies and oppressors, will be doubly eager to work if they can do so in freedom and for themselves; and that he who fights for his own and his family's freedom and future will make a brave soldier.

Yet American-Democratic color prejudice has so long insisted on the contrary and attempted to prove it with a thousand ethnological, social, and religious sophisms that the Negro's laziness and stupidity have become a motto of the slave-Democracy. These propagandists of Negro hatred are beside themselves with anger now that success is disproving all their assertions, particularly because in the first place they did not speak from conviction but simply to advance a party line or perhaps out of genuine American hatred of the Negro. They opposed the abolition of slavery not because they really believed that the sugar crop, the cotton crop, or public safety would be endangered, but because they felt that the Negro would rise in his social position and be more equal to the white man. They did not fear that the freed slave would be lazy, but that he would be all too industrious; not that he would sink even lower, but that he would be capable of rising above his despised place; not that he would be unworthy of freedom, but that he would progress to prove all these prophecies wrong. Of course, people who have spent their entire lives proving that Negroes are like animals cannot gracefully accept the factual defeat of their arguments, and the freed slave could not have done them a greater disservice than he did by displaying all those qualities they had denied him.

As many terrible mistakes as the government of the United States has made since the beginning of the war, it is not yet too late to save the Union and to free the nation from the stigma of slavery if the government only had the moral courage and the skill to mobilize the enormous power that is at its disposal among the four million Negroes of the South. The immediate future must decide this issue.

Notes

1. New York, March [1863], *Morgenblatt,* 57:14:332–334.

2. Leah Fish (ca. 1814–1890) was the oldest of the three Fox sisters of Hydesville, New York, who started the spiritualist fad in 1848; she had been married to Bowman Fish. Kate Fox Jencken and Margaret Fox were Leah's younger sisters. Assing had written on two earlier occasions about her personal experience with séances. In June 1857 (*Morgenblatt,* 51:30:718–720), she commented on the spiritualist movement in general and gave an account of attending a performance by a Miss Laura Edmonds. The term "epidemic" in reference to spiritualism already appears in this earlier piece, as Assing explains that the continuing popularity of spiritualism, "in spite of all efforts at enlightenment," is due to the shrewd connection between religion and spiritualism: "Those who were interested in spreading the belief in ghosts were clever and calculating enough to tie their theory to existing religion, thereby assuring themselves a hold on a large part of the broad religiously orthodox masses . . ." (719). In the same piece, Assing mentions that

three years earlier she had looked into spiritualism and found it nothing but a fraud: "In vain I had made it clear that I did not want to have anything further to do with this deceptive farce [Miss Edmond's performance], having seen through the whole thing three years ago in the 'spiritual circles' of Mrs. Ann Leah Brown" (720). Returning again to the subject in February 1858 (*Morgenblatt*, 52:13:307–311), Assing once again expressed her astonishment that the silliness of spiritualism still had such a strong grasp on the popular imagination: "Although the ghostly nonsense is no longer a daylight affair, having somewhat withdrawn into darkness since the embarrassing defeat at the hands of the investigating committee in Boston, it continues to exist no less. It has, in fact, become so well established in certain circles that no single bolt of lightning will be able to shatter it; nothing but the gradual progress of enlightenment will eventually shine some light into this owl's nest" (310). In the remainder of that essay, Assing relates yet another specific encounter, this time with a Mrs. Cora Hatch, who was reputed to have advanced from simply moving tables to entering trances in which she "answered the most difficult philosophical, theological, and scientific questions with depth, thoroughness, and erudition" (310). At 15 cents admission, this was obviously a bargain, especially since other ghosts in the past had not allowed themselves to be bothered for anything less than one dollar. "Still," Assing continues in her characteristically sarcastic tone, "pity for the ghosts in reduced circumstances would hardly have made me go, especially after the experiences I had in this line some years ago; but I am of the opinion that it is more rational to overcome one's distaste and get to know the whole ghostly business from the ground up than to stay away full of contempt, leaving the field to those who, stultified by superstition, hear and see only what they and the medium wish to hear and see and then spread all those miracle stories that others accept as revelation" (310). In short, Mrs. Hatch turned out to be as much a fraud as the rest.

3. It is unclear to whom Assing is referring here. Perhaps "Fiske" is a misreading of "Fish" (see Leah Fish, n. 1., above) by the editor or compositor of the *Morgenblatt*, where many American names are misspelled throughout Assing's contributions. One would suppose that "Brittan" is a reference to Emma Hardinge Britten (1823–1899), who came from England to America in 1856 and was very active in spiritualist circles in New York at the time of Assing's writing. But Assing's subsequent reference to "gentlemen" invalidates the possibility that these "professors" were women. Hence, the identity of these two spiritualist performers remains a mystery.

4. Isaac Van Amburgh (born ca. 1805) was famous as a lion tamer both in America and Europe; Martin has not been identified.

66

American Conditions—Mob Rule[1]

It cannot be denied that the scenes of murder and arson this past summer constitute a chapter in the history of New York. Three days of mob rule are too horrible ever to be forgotten. But it would be a grave error if this terrible outbreak of mob passion would be dignified by the term popular revolt, let alone revolution, or if one were to see it as an expression of the people against a continuation of the war or against the draft. No matter how uncivilized or how blinded with prejudice the American masses may be, they are not guilty as a whole of perpetrating these scenes of horror. These events are, rather, the work of a cabal of Democratic leaders (the "copperheads"), traitors, and secret friends of secession. They have used the Irish as their tools—the Irish, who are always ready and willing when it comes to disturbing the peace, and in whose hands the whole conspiracy turned into a campaign of murder, arson, and pillage.

It was not mere coincidence but the result of collusion between the Democratic party leaders of the North and those of the South that the murder and mayhem in New York occurred almost simultaneously with the rebels' invasion of Pennsylvania and Maryland. It sounds incredible but it is true that Horatio Seymour, the governor of New York, was one of the chief ringleaders in this conspiracy, and that he had made advance preparations to deliver the city almost without a fight into the hands of the rabble, having withdrawn most of the troops. The enemy's incursion into the free states, mentioned above, which once again threatened Washington, was calculated to foment discouragement and discontent with the government. They hoped that anarchy could be turned into revolution, and that a frightened, terrified public would let itself be tempted by the governor and his allies to assume a hostile attitude against the government, thereby forcing the administration to accept a disgraceful peace that would, in fact, put the free North under the rule of the slave masters.

Hence the governor's and his followers' continual attacks on the draft as an unconstitutional, tyrannical measure that the people have every right to resist in every way; hence the appeal to the rabble's prejudices; hence the stubborn resistance to all decisive measures for putting an end to mob rule and reestablishing law and order. Hence also the outrageousness of his—the head of state's—addressing, from the steps of City Hall, those hordes as "my honorable friends," a mob that was still hot from the burning buildings they had ignited and pillaged, still red with the blood of its victims. The outrage of his promising them to use his influence for stopping the draft! Hence, finally, after order had been restored, the desperate but unsuccessful efforts on the part of the Democratic city judges to use the law of *habeas corpus* to free the jailed disturbers of the peace. The cheers for Jefferson Davis, the public expressions of sympathy for the leaders of the southern

Confederacy, and the tearing down of the Union flag wherever it was raised—all these are undeniably the actions of the party that has been the cause of all those horrors.

Fortunately, however, the conspiracy of these so-called Peace Democrats backfired on them. It is well known that the incursion into the northern states ended at Gettysburg, where the South suffered a defeat. Mob rule in New York was suppressed, and its ringleaders were remanded to the justice system. In truth, as terrible as those days were and as revolting the crimes, on the whole the consequences have been salutary: they delivered the final blow to this despicable party, which stood behind these horrors, and they opened the people's eyes to the abyss toward which the party was driving them. The instigators forgot or were too shortsighted to understand that the rabble is easily aroused but difficult to restrain. It does not seem to have occurred to them that the hordes of Irish riff-raff whom they had chosen as their tools—after having destroyed the draft offices, after killing and persecuting the poor Negroes, after pillaging their houses for whatever scant rewards they contained—would turn in their bloody and drunken rage on the houses of the wealthy white inhabitants, which would yield a far richer harvest and offer opportunities for venting the anger the poor harbor against the rich.

Thousands of people, who were blinded by prejudice and party loyalties, who year-in and year-out had followed the Democratic party through all ups and downs, and who had agitated against the abolition of slavery and against equality for Negroes, were seized by outrage and pity when they experienced under their very eyes the horrible cruelties of Negro persecution: innocent people, whose only fault was the color of their skin, being driven through the streets like wild animals, being treated with incredible cruelty, being hanged and shot down. These people turned away from the party, whose leaders had deliberately fomented these horrors. And, fearing for their own lives and property, those few who were totally demoralized by their hatred of Negroes and incapable of pity suddenly realized that an alliance with the enemies of the country and its lawful order would have serious consequences. Even the disturbers of the peace themselves are now distressed because they have to go to the penitentiary, whereas those who used them as their tools and promised them impunity are free and deny any complicity.

No doubt, public opinion has undergone a revolution, and the result of it can be seen in the outcome of the elections in Pennsylvania, Ohio, and Indiana. Last fall, the copperheads won large victories there; this year, the friends of the Union and the government have been even more triumphant. Although it will take many years and several generations until the nation will emerge from its hatred of color, it injustices, and its prejudices, all of which are the consequence of slavery, nevertheless the spirit of the nineteenth century, the spirit of progress, is too mighty to be suppressed in the long run by conspiracies and intrigues.

Belonging to the elements that are most stubbornly resistant to progress, the Irish go hand in hand with the slaveholders and are their strongest allies. Mob rule in New York was rule by the Irish. Despised and oppressed in his home country, demoralized by poverty and brandy, the Irishman brings with him the poor man's hatred of the rich and his bitterness against social order. He is glad to find in the Negro an even more despised and oppressed piece of humanity, and he expresses the dignity and equality that he enjoys over here by kicking and stepping on the Negro whenever he can. I do not believe that there is an American city with a sizable Irish population in which the rabble could not be aroused by shouting "Hang the nigger!" Such an uprising would lead to persecutions, mistreatments, and even the murder of these unfortunate pariahs of society. Also, the Irishman is a born thug who gets the greatest pleasure out of scraps and fights, and since he usually has nothing to lose, it is quite natural that he is always on the side of breaking the law and defying order.

Most crimes are committed by the Irish; they represent the majority of those in prison, and during the days of the uprising they proved that they constitute the true mob. In other words, they were cruel, determined, and brutal when no one offered resistance and they could vent their anger against helpless victims—women, children, the sick,nd the old—or against individual men they captured, committing atrocities I shudder to repeat. But they were cowards when they encountered strong and calculated resistance. When, despite all efforts to the contrary, the governor's troops finally arrived in the city, one could witness the spectacle of the riff-raff dispersing by the thousands in all directions, even before the shots of a single company had been fired. The mere presence of a small cannon, deployed before the doors of a Republican newspaper, the *New York Times*, worked like a charm and protected the whole neighborhood. In another part of the city, a gang of about twenty attacked the house of a United States government official. Being at home with only his wife, he handed her a revolver, armed himself with another, and was ready to defend himself. But the enemy was not prepared for such determination, and the whole gang turned tail and ran from the two-person army.

Such a crude, unrestrained, ignorant people represented in such large numbers would under all circumstances be a problem for any country, but the situation here is even worse because the Irish are the natural allies and indispensable supporters and tools of the Democratic party; because of their hatred for the Negro the party treats them with favoritism. The Irish decide the elections in New York through legal and illegal voting; they occupy many of the municipal offices, and without them the entire uprising would have been impossible. The true instigators— Governor Horatio Seymour, Fernando Wood, the notorious former mayor, and his brother, James Brooks, the publisher of one of the most vitriolic papers of the slavery party,[2] and others of their ilk—had of course indulged themselves long enough in attacks on the government; as the saying goes here, they had "talked treason." But with all that, they still have to maintain a certain respectable demeanor: they cannot themselves lead the arsonist hordes, kill the Negroes and string them up on lampposts, destroy orphanages and pillage the houses of alleged abolitionists. For this kind of honorable work they need henchmen who do what their leaders preach directly or indirectly, and only the Irish are suitable for this work in large numbers. Although their deeds of horror have earned them the contempt of all loyal, well-meaning citizens, and even though people look upon them with disgust, only the most unimaginable and improbable turn of events could stop their ominous influence.

The Germans stand in complete and most delightful contrast to this decadent people. They have always been respected for being peaceful, industrious citizens, who now and then may have broken the burdensome and pointless Sunday laws; but since the outbreak of the war they have been held in the highest esteem. All in all, Germans have proven their absolute loyalty and supported the government in word and deed. They were among the first who heeded the president's call to arms, and among the most competent generals are Germans like Siegel and Rosencrans (whose anglicized name cannot completely disguise the original Rosenkranz)[3]; and it is thanks to the Germans that Missouri has remained in the Union and is now on its way to becoming a free state. Efforts were underway during those days of mob rule to involve the Germans in pillage and in the persecution of Negroes. Emissaries rode on horseback through Little Germany, where the poorest and lowest classes of Germans are crowded together, asking them to join the raids, but the good sense of these people deterred them. A few contemptible individuals, of whom every society has its share, did join the gangs, but the few German names in the lists of those arrested remain almost invisible compared to the large number of Patricks, O'Donohues, O'Learys, Maloneys, etc.

The good that Germans have done, however, has so far been only the result of efforts by individuals and perhaps by local organizations; they were inspired by a common spirit, yet everyone acted on his own. In recent months this has changed: a German political organization has emerged whose main purposes are the defeat of the rebellion and the complete abolition of slavery as the only means by which the country can be saved and a permanent peace can be secured. The ablest men are in the leadership of this organization, and it may not be long until the Germans in America will not only be respected as individuals but achieve recognition and importance as a nation.

Notes

1. New York, November [1863], *Morgenblatt*, 57:50:1194–1196.

2. Assing's reference to James Brooks as Fernando Wood's brother is obviously in error. The paper that reflected the despised copperhead politics was the *New York Express*, edited by James Brooks, who was known to have instigated the mob in New York to oust the government in Washington; Wood's brother Benjamin was editor of the *New York Daily News*.

3. For Sigel, see Essay 54, n. 3. Rosencrans was probably William Starke Rosecrans (1812–1898), who had won an important victory at Corinth, Mississippi, in October 1862; however, after his defeat at Chickamauga in the fall of 1863, he was relieved by U.S. Grant and given command of the Department of Missouri.

67

Colored Troops—Cost Increases—Luxury—Worker Unrest—Bloomerism[1]

When the government, forced by necessity, decided to arm the free Negroes and the slaves in the face of American color prejudice, all the friends of the rebels—the secret as well as the openly declared friends—shouted: "But the Negroes don't want to fight!" It was a silly objection, behind which lurked the fear that the Negroes would be all too serious in battle, that they would prove to be the slaveholders' all too bitter enemy and thereby deal slavery its final blow. Success has fully confirmed these expectations. Wherever blacks have stood face to face with the enemy, they have displayed a courage and discipline that would have done honor to the best-trained white troops. Most of all, the Fifty-fourth Regiment has earned a claim to fame at Charleston, but it had to pay dearly for it with the blood of many of its best men. It happened last summer during an ill-prepared attempt to take Fort Wagner. Whereas in European warfare it is customary not to charge until a fortification has been thoroughly prepared by siege, in America one usually begins with such an attempt, is badly routed, and then starts the same foolhardiness at the next fort over again. Instead of using only experienced troops for such a dangerous attack, the Fifty-fourth, which had only been in a few minor battles, was ordered to launch the attack in the middle of the night. Heedless of all difficulties, they undertook the charge with great courage and discipline. Under heavy enemy fire, the brave black soldiers climbed the parapet of the fort, where they fought hand to hand in total darkness, and according to all reports they would have succeeded in taking the fort if one of the white regiments that was supposed to reinforce and support them had not failed to arrive and left them in the lurch, for reasons yet to be explained. So they had no other choice but to retreat after desperate combat. Their colonel, many officers, and hundreds of soldiers were killed, but that attack, though not crowned with success, is one of the most magnificent episodes of the war.[2]

In view of these facts, which everyone recognizes, and in spite of the dramatic change in public opinion toward a more favorable view of the despised colored people that this episode has brought about, the people and the government are still far from treating them even with a minimum of justice. Whereas the white soldier receives thirteen dollars a month, the black soldier gets only ten—for the same services, the same privations and efforts, and in spite of the even greater dangers that he can expect at the hands of the evil and cruel southerners. And because the ten dollars are reduced by deductions made for his clothing, this pay is in the end no more than half of what his white companion-in-arms gets. It is true that the state of Massachusetts, where the first colored regiments were formed, promised to remedy this wrong out of its own funds in case the Congress and the administration failed to make adequate provisions. But what happened is that soon after the brilliant attack on Fort Wagner they had the audacity, effrontery, and indecency to offer only ten dollars to these brave men after all. Because they were in enemy territory, far from home, subject to the whim of their officers, and cut off from the means of subsistence, it was hoped that they could be forced to accept the disgraceful offer out of necessity. But, angered by the injustice, these brave men unanimously rejected it, preferring to undergo even greater privations than are imposed by the normal conditions of war until the matter would be resolved.

With no less obvious injustice, which should not come as a surprise after such events, the army stubbornly refuses to make any colored person an officer. No matter how brave and how equal in ability and knowledge he may be compared to all the white officers, he cannot be promoted to second lieutenant—to prevent, for Heaven's sake, any offense against sensitive Democratic prejudices! This past summer, the secretary of war suggested to the famous orator Frederick Douglass, a colored man who had probably captivated him by his majestic and congenial personality, to act as a recruiting officer and to organize colored regiments in the South. The news of this appointment caused a considerable public stir and was reported in every newspaper. As far as I know, there was no word of criticism, yet the secretary of war did not have the courage to act on his own freely conceived and proposed idea. He tried to back off by means of petty excuses and intentional misunderstandings, so that Douglass, fully aware of the game that was being played, broke off the discussions completely disgusted and dismayed. But in a situation where Frederick Douglass—a man who is certainly and admittedly the most outstanding among the colored people in talent, character, and influence—cannot become a major or captain, there is no shadow of hope for all the rest.

All of this, though literally true, seems most barbaric and almost fantastic to the enlightened European. But what is one to say about the fact that Negroes, having no expectations of promotion and being denied equal pay for equal service, have until recently not even been given the same protections of life and liberty as white soldiers? Immediately after the president's proclamation calling the Negroes to arms, the southern Confederates declared that no colored soldiers falling into their hands would be considered prisoners of war and exchanged; they would be instantly hanged instead. The radical papers, especially the *New York Tribune*, which has fought tirelessly against slavery since its first appearance more than twenty years ago, urged revenge in kind as the only way to stop such barbarism, but in vain. The threats were ignored or dismissed as being nothing but threats that the rebels themselves would not dare to implement. But southern cruelty and barbarism have remained unparalleled in this century, and one could not really be surprised that Negroes, who served in the Union forces as soldiers, workers, teamsters, hostlers, and servants, were murdered, hanged, shot, butchered, or enslaved by the hundreds whenever they had the misfortune of falling into southern hands. The government never objected, the atrocities continued, and, without counting the cruelties now and then perpetrated against individuals, no fewer than six such massacres had occurred before the government took the first step to protect its defenders. Only after that attack on Fort Wagner and after the rebels had again declared their intention to hang or to sell into slavery the soldiers they had captured did the president issue a proclamation announcing reprisals. It came late and was again forced by necessity like all the measures that have until now been taken in the fight against slavery.

An immense increase in the cost of everything is one of the inevitable consequences of the war that become more noticeable every day. Since paper money is now the only means of exchange, the relative value of gold has risen by almost half; and since goods from abroad can be bought only with gold, it is self-evident that the import merchant has to pass the cost of the discount on to the customer. Add to that the high tariffs, which for silk cloth can be up to forty percent, and almost every imported item is twice as expensive as it used to be. Formerly one of the cheapest domestic products, cotton has gone up fourfold because it is so scarce; and the agricultural products of the North, though plentiful due to an excellent harvest, have similarly increased in price because labor has become more expensive since the beginning of the war, which has claimed the services of strong, able workers by the hundreds of thousands. In some branches, such as mining, there is such a dearth of laborers that coal has more than doubled in cost. Naturally, this has consequences for factories, railroads, and steamships, and therefore life in New York is now probably more expensive than in any other city of the civilized world, not even excluding London.

Yet, luxuries seem to be more rather than less evident, and you do not hear anyone complaining about hard times. Many people have suddenly made fortunes through speculation, and they are eager to show their wealth. More than ever, long lines of gleaming carriages crowd Broadway and Fifth Avenue. For those who seek work there is no dearth of opportunities, and instead of the grass growing in the streets of New York, as the South predicted at the outbreak of the war, the city is the very picture of commerce and comfort.

The last few days have been marked by unrest among the workers, whose wages have not yet been raised. Machine operators, cigar makers, bus drivers, shoemakers, and carpenters attended rallies, most of them resolving to demand a raise in wages in proportion to prices. Wherever factory owners and other employers failed to offer such raises the laborers put down their work and now seem to be resolved not to take it up again unless their demands are met. They do not wish to prevent others who are willing to work for the old wages, but they themselves plan to remain idle as long as some other work is available to them. But they make it clear that under no circumstances will they return to their former positions if the increase they demand is not given. When the streetcar drivers stopped work one day, New York was deprived of its undeniably essential rail traffic, and for much of the public it was almost as great a calamity as when the Croton waterline or the gas pipes are not functioning. Businessmen who wanted to get from their houses all the way uptown to their far distant places of business were forced either to walk or to take their chances in the overcrowded buses. Of course, in the end the railroad companies had to yield, and the following day transportation returned to normal. The whole process was very orderly, and the drivers did not return to work until all their fellow workers who had been especially targeted and fired by the companies had been reinstated into their former positions.

That most unfortunate of all classes, the poor girls who have to earn a living by sewing, have also had a meeting—not for the purpose of deciding to stop work, but to try to obtain a raise in wages without taking that extreme step, to form an association of mutual support, and to bring their plight to the public's attention. Present at the meeting were about four hundred nicely dressed and decent looking girls, who earn their living by sewing skirts, vests, trousers, shirts, tents, umbrellas, canvas boots, and corsets; as well as by stitching books and book bindings, folding papers, sorting wool, trimming hats, fashioning hoop skirts, and doing any work on the sewing machine. This occasion revealed that some of these poor creatures earn only one dollar a week, hardly any of them more than three dollars, in spite of working most strenuously eleven to sixteen hours a day. As the cheapest boarding houses for workers charge two and a half to three dollars a week for room and board, the most fortunate ones will keep 25 cents (about ten silver groschen) after the deduction of expenses. All the facts that came to light at this meeting proved that the wages for these women workers have been considerably lowered since last year, and that the manufacturers were cruel and unscrupulous enough to exploit the helpless condition of these poor girls to compensate for the higher cost of materials and other goods. In some shops it is customary to deduct 25 cents from wages if a seamstress misses one shirt button. Other heartrending revelations suggested that in no other area are fundamental changes more necessary than here.

It should be self-evident that these social issues—including the conflict between slavery and freedom that is shaking the country in its foundations and will determine the nation's future—ought to claim the attention and active involvement of every thinking and feeling person. Yet wherever you go, you meet reform-minded idealists who, lacking in ability to make a name for themselves through major accomplishments, become ridiculous in their obsession with the unimportant. Having made their appearance ten or twelve years ago and already then being thoroughly laughed at, the dress reformers recently held one of their jolly conventions. In the small town of Milton, New York, there is an establishment for the water cure whose proprietor, Dr. Jackson, has featured himself as a passionate advocate of the Bloomer costume; under his influence things have gone so far that many of the ladies in Milton actually stalk about in skimpy skirts and puny panties. Occasionally he organizes a convention at which twenty or thirty such ladies are exhibited and, in a sense, used (though they may not know it) as advertisements for his water cure. The convention hall was crowded, and because care had been taken to present only slim and well-formed figures in Bloomers the spectacle was by no means disagreeable—although any woman endowed with a somewhat remarkable *embonpoint* would, so appareled, look like a caricature.

Enthusiastic applause and loud laughter, however, resounded when the Bloomer ladies, instead of walking up the stairs from the hall to the platform, hopped and skipped upstairs one after the other, each assisted by a gentleman, probably to demonstrate the ease and freedom that this style of brief clothing permits. Several ladies and gentlemen delivered speeches regarding the advantages of the Bloomer costume as to comfort, economy, and particularly health. Some averred that merely by wearing Bloomers they had been completely relieved of such fatal illnesses as consumption and diseases of the liver. Furthermore, they severely criticized tight lacing, which was really off the subject, as lacing has little to do with the length of dresses; it is not an essential part of current clothes, and hardly requires a dress reformer to demonstrate its deleterious effects. For several centuries, physicians of all stripes have proven its harmfulness beyond a doubt. The audience was also told about a man who had succeeded in simplifying and economizing his apparel to such an extent that his entire suit was held by only two buttons and could thus be put on or taken off in less than one minute. However, this miracle of compression and inventiveness, which would have been well worth seeing, was not personally introduced, and it was left to everyone present to paint the two-button suit in the richest colors of the imagination.

These people spoke—and some of them with genuine conviction—as if they had discovered the panacea for all the world's woes. They told of persecutions and attacks they had had to endure for their dress, and because the ungrateful world seems not yet to have sufficiently matured to recognize the merits of these martyrs-of-the-cloth, they compensated one another by mutual admiration. "My charming friend Mrs. Trombridge," "My most talented friend Professor Porter," "Our invaluable and erudite Dr. Jackson," and other such addresses drenched us like an eruption of rain, and I thought that these modern reformers should most appropriately call themselves the "Mutual Admiration Society."

Notes

1. New York, November [1863], *Morgenblatt*, 57:52:1241–1244.

2. Robert Gould Shaw (1837–1863), and the famous 54th Massachusetts Regiment are memorialized in Augustus Saint-Gaudens' sculpture in the Boston Common.

68

Anniversary of the Antislavery Society[1]

At the beginning of December, the American Anti-Slavery Society, under the presidency of William Lloyd Garrison, celebrated its thirtieth anniversary in Philadelphia. It was attended by several of the founders and originating members of the society as well as other outstanding abolitionists, among them a number of celebrities, such as Henry Ward Beecher, Frederick Douglass, and Senator Wilson of Massachusetts. It was a gathering that had no parallel anywhere in the country in regard to talent, oratorical skill, moral principle, endurance, and energy in the pursuit of the one great goal. For those who were present at the time the society was founded thirty years ago the contrast between now and then must have been particularly poignant. Instead of the illustrious group of famous men who spoke today to thousands of attentive, supportive, and admiring listeners there were then sixty-three almost unknown young men and a few invited guests, who held their first meeting in a modest room. Among those guests, giving her first speech against slavery, was the Quaker woman Lucretia Mott, who is now of an advanced age and has been an active member of the society from the start. Her request to speak at that time was met with consternation and temporizing, because even if people were used to hear women speak at Quaker meetings, prejudice would not let them be seen on the podium at other public events. She was finally allowed to speak out of courtesy, and for the first time she thrilled her audience with an eloquence that has since made her famous from one end of the country to the other.

The founding of the American Anti-Slavery Society was preceded by a number of local organizations, primarily the Massachusetts society, established by William Lloyd Garrison a year earlier; and even before that, a group of women had organized a society there to serve the same purpose. Mutual agreement and commonality of purpose, however, were stronger than old-fashioned prejudice: the societies soon united, and antislavery societies have counted women among their members and given them equal access to the speaker's podium ever since that first initiative. In accordance with the basic principle of equal rights for all, the antislavery leaders have generally been ready to defend the civil and social rights of women, and it is they who have set in motion the process of change that has benefited women in the past—and is still benefiting them today.

But the founders of that earlier time were in yet another way not entirely free of prejudice. They believed that no public meeting would be effective or dignified if not some man of influence, status, and distinction presided over it. That was a major problem. Despite the progress that has been made since the start of the war, despite that fatal blow that slavery has received in the current battle, unconditional and systematic abolitionism is still not fashionable among the so-called good society; and in those earlier, less advanced times it was despised as nothing less than heresy and treasonous demagoguery. How, then, find the man who was needed? They finally turned to a well-respected man in Philadelphia who had frequently presided at public meetings, supported many benevolent organizations, and showed himself to be the friend and benefactor of all persons and good causes, including abolitionism. Nevertheless, he politely declined the request, probably because he was afraid to offend public opinion by such a daring step. But the abolitionists understood that, for the time being, they could not expect anything of a nation that had not even accepted the rudiments of civilized and humanitarian principles. They had to rely solely on their own strength and ability and not be deterred by the persecutions and attacks from the high and low Democratic rabble that tried to interrupt their meetings, assaulted their members, and threatened them with death, which they escaped only by good luck. Of the original sixty-three founders of the society forty-eight are still living; eleven of them attended the ceremony.

It is self-evident that the present crisis, which will end in the inevitable demise of slavery, is the natural, inevitable consequence of the irremediable conflict between slavery and freedom. And it is also self-evident that this crisis has more quickly come to its climax by several years because of the unparalleled suicidal blindness of the people of the South. Nevertheless, to the abolitionists belongs the credit of having first raised the question of slavery in all of its importance, having virtually forced the public's attention on it, and having persisted in the fight with untiring endurance despite all attacks and animosities. Many of those who used to go along with the unthinking crowd have thus been awakened to slavery's baneful effects and converted to different views. It is the abolitionists who first came to represent the spirit of the nineteenth century, the spirit of civilized progress, while the masses were still mired in a barbarism from which they are only now beginning to emerge; it is they who are the vanguard of the present revolution, as Montesquieu, Voltaire, and Rousseau were the vanguard of the French Revolution.

***

Notes

1. New York, January [1864], *Morgenblatt,* 58:6:140–143.

69

Effects of War on Social Conditions and on Slavery[1]

***

The certainty that the war must end with the suppression of the rebellion has become the prevalent opinion among all classes—not even excepting the majority of southern slaveholders—and the copperheads of the North hardly deny anymore that their southern friends are fighting a lost cause. Also, the abolition of slavery is now seen by most as an inevitability, but it is premature to try to fix a time by months or weeks for it to happen—as some politicians and journalists are occasionally fond of doing. Regardless of the uncertainties of war and of the resources that a half-defeated enemy still has available, there is another, no less dangerous enemy in our own ranks who will try to continue the war as long as a single armed rebel remains: having infected all classes of society, dishonesty, greed, and venality are the real problem.

The vast majority of the people want to see the rebellion ended and long for a peace based on victory; but opposed to them are the many speculators, suppliers, high and low government officials and agents, and other human vermin of whatever name who see the war as a bottomless well of wealth, giving them the power to make their baneful influence felt. The fraud and corruption that are revealed today only to be repeated tomorrow as well as the brazenness with which they are carried out have no parallel, at least not in the size of the amounts fraudulently obtained. In this regard, the Department of the Navy has almost become a legend. Everyone knows that nothing matters and nothing can be accomplished without fraud or bribery, and that care has been taken to make the government pay the highest prices. For instance, last year it became necessary to obtain a supply ship, but instead of buying one, it had to be leased for the modest sum of 350 dollars per day. In the end, after a year of this game, in which the beneficiary had made a fortune of almost 400,000 dollars, the government bought the ship for 40,000 dollars. And similar things occur in other departments: the Treasury Department, among other things, keeps an agent in Philadelphia to sell bonds in connection with the most recent public debt issue, and he receives one-eighth of one percent of each investment made.

One of the most despicable activities is now being conducted among the lower classes by the so-called recruitment agents. The government's payment of a fifteen-dollar premium for any volunteer brought into the ranks of its army is a practice whose unfortunate consequences was predictable. All those who may be sly and crafty but are not sufficiently honest and industrious to work for a living, all those who live at the expense and well-being of others, in short, all the industrial oligarchs were given *carte blanche* to practice their wiles to their hearts' content. Former emigration runners and thieves who still have a semblance of honesty because they were not caught red-handed during a break-in or with their hands in other people's pockets have now become recruitment agents, plying their trade at the expense of the poor fools they seek out as their victims. Often they are not content to collect the fifteen dollars to which they are legally entitled but succeed in extorting from some innocent youth the three hundred dollar premium that the state of New York gives to every volunteer. They get their victims drunk and in some cases use more dangerous narcotic poisons, when wine or brandy are not strong enough to overpower their prey, and deliver them into their hands. Recently, three black recruits who had just signed on were found dead with all the symptoms of heavy poisoning. At times, false representations make ignorant, illiterate individuals believe they are contracting to be hostlers, sailors, or something like it, discovering too late that they have the honor of belonging to the army of the United States.

Thus corruption permeates all levels of society, pollutes and destroys the atmosphere, and makes one look toward the future with apprehension. What in the world is to be built on the ruins of the old Union? What can be expected of a people or of lawmakers and statesmen who lack any sense of decency, whose moral sense remains in such a state of confusion that party leaders, politicians, and ministers are capable of cravenly announcing—as they recently did to maintain their popularity—that they are no abolitionists and for all the world do not intend anything more than to restrict slavery to its present boundaries? Many of them would reject any accusation of abolitionism with greater indignation than they would any imputation of thievery. The current president, whose highly praised honesty seems suspect when seen from the point of view of general morality and humanitarianism, is a typical representative of the American people. In his letter to Horace Greeley, the editor of the *Tribune*, he states that it makes no difference to him whether the Union is to be saved with or without slavery; and in his latest message to the Congress he assures us that at an earlier time he had "hoped" to suppress the rebellion without having to abolish slavery. These are significant documents that cannot be misinterpreted. It is impossible to be mistaken: only conditions and circumstances have turned this war into a crusade against slavery; not outrage against this incarnation of evil and crime but a belated understanding of its detrimental influence on the progress of the nation has made this war possible. If southerners, convinced that theirs is a lost cause, would today declare their readiness to put down their arms on the condition that slavery would be guaranteed within the existing boundaries, without a doubt the president, his cabinet, and a majority of the Congress and the people would gladly consent.

The change that is occurring in public opinion is nevertheless immense. The force of events brings about what the nation's sense of morality and justice has been unable to accomplish, and no one finally can escape its effects. It is a sign of the times in this respect that a pamphlet has recently appeared with the title "Miscegenation," in which it is argued that the intermingling of the white and the black race is an unavoidable necessity and the only means by which the ongoing degeneration of the race on this continent can be prevented. The piece is obviously well-meaning and is the product of honest conviction, but it is written with neither brilliance nor originality. The moral, physiological, and historical reasons adduced by the author have mostly been accepted by people of enlightened thought; some of his other reasons are either superfluous or lack a sound foundation. Its significance, however, lies in the fact that there is someone today who dares to champion a cause that hitherto has here been considered to be the most contemptible, offensive, disgraceful, even immoral idea that has been banished by society. A woman who may have left her husband with another man has a better prospect of being again accepted into the graces of this society than she who marries the most respectable and well educated colored man out of love, respecting all legal formalities.

As little as two years ago, any word in favor of mingling the races would have caused a unanimous outcry of shock and horror. It was the very issue on which even declared abolitionists, who called for complete civil equality for the Negro, could not overcome their prejudice. Many who treated the colored man socially as an equal and who did not hesitate to go against public opinion by showing themselves in public with him as a friend would have revolted against the thought of darkening their pure Anglo-Saxon blood by mixing it with the African. And those who had perhaps no personal objections were loath to incur the rejection and contempt of the masses. Even Wendell Phillips, one of the most courageous leaders in the struggle for the cause of the Negro, came out only last year in favor of the intermingling of the races; and Harriet Beecher Stowe, in all her descriptions of southern life and relations between the races, did not give a single instance of true love between their representatives, and yet, though rare, they do occur in spite of all prejudice and ostracism. The author of "Miscegenation," meanwhile, has not dared to publish his work under his name, thus significantly diminishing the value of his commendable service; but now that someone has made a start, the issue will not be allowed to rest.[2]

Notes

1. New York, January [1864], *Morgenblatt*, 58:11:262–264.

2. Given Assing's relationship with Frederick Douglass, these comments on miscegenation (the German text consistently reads "Miscenegation") are most revealing and interesting; however, Assing was not aware of the fact that the pamphlet, which she took to be a document of courageous outspokenness on a virtually taboo subject, was actually a fraudulent political document designed to embarrass the Republicans. As Maria Diedrich puts it in her biography of Assing, "the publication was launched by allies of the Democratic Party as part of their campaign of racist demagoguery . . . [and] fell in line with the party's attempt to implicate the Republicans. It was written by David Goodman Croly and George Wakeman, both working for the conservative *New York World*." The complete title

of the 72-page pamphlet, published in December 1863, is "Miscegenation: The Theory of the Blending of the Races Applied to the American White Man and the Negro."

70

A Negro Regiment—Radical Germans[1]

A great revolution like the one now occurring on this continent has, so to speak, its milestones—events that demonstrate the stations of the profound changes that sometimes take place within a few months. Such a milestone of the revolution was the recent departure of a regiment of colored volunteers from its encampment on some of the nearby islands and its passage through New York to the steamer that was to take the soldiers to New Orleans. In more peaceful times it would appear to an up-to-date observer, penetrating with a keen philosophical eye the future for decades to come, as if the masses were moving frighteningly slowly and even reluctantly toward the goal that they must reach sooner or later, according to the compelling logic of events. Thus it took the majority of the people and its leaders a full three years to recognize at least in part what measures were necessary to have the nation emerge victorious from the crisis it is compelled to undergo. Having once achieved this recognition, however, the nation is swept up by the current of history and irresistibly carried toward the great goal—the complete emancipation of the Negroes.

Nearly three years ago, when a group of enlightened, patriotic men who were convinced of the need to arm the colored people planned to organize a few Negro regiments, they asked the government whether it would quietly tolerate such an enterprise and close its eyes if these troops were, for instance, to march through Pennsylvania. But their request was definitively and categorically denied. No one wanted to be obliged to the hated and reviled blacks so as to feel free to continue trampling on them at will. Later, when every patriot saw that arming the Negroes was an absolute necessity, the conservatives howled, threatened to dissolve all social bonds, and set up their most cherished straw man: that all white soldiers would immediately put down their arms. The friends of slavery here and in England wailed at the horrible barbarism of the idea that the slaves should take up arms against their lawful and kind masters.

It is not yet two years ago that the president and his postmaster general, Blair,[2] were seriously and busily promoting the distasteful and impractical scheme of colonizing the entire black population of the United States somewhere in South America. And as little as eight months ago the rabble of New York chased the Negroes like wild animals through the streets of the city, hanged them, tore them apart, and set their houses on fire. But just now it was the same New York, the same Broadway, where people lined the streets in dense crowds along the sidewalks, on balconies and roofs, and came in carts to greet the soldiers with cheers, applause, flags, and bunting. It was the second such regiment to have been raised in the state of New York, and having taken on its organization, one of the local patriotic clubs handed the regiment its flag in front of the clubhouse on Union Square. To the thrilling sounds of music they marched down Broadway to Canal Street and thence to the steamer "Ericson."

The soldiers looked splendid, presented themselves nobly, and were admired by all. Many are of tall, powerful stature, and these children of the tropics inspired confidence by their strength, their endurance, and their courage. Most of them were genuine Negroes—a remarkable sight because despite all the hatred against Negroes and all the theories, amalgamation of the races is proceeding so inexorably that on a normal day you will see ten mulattoes to one true Negro. Naturally, the black population of New York was there *en masse*, most of them in their Sunday best, their dark faces beaming with pleasure seeing their brothers so honored and recognized rather than despised, mistreated, or at best tolerated as an inevitable evil. It was as if we had been transposed by magic into a Negro city. The streams of black people pouring in from all sides increased with every passing minute, forming a sea of people in the large open square. But in spite of the crowd there was perfect order: everywhere you looked people were friendly and full of good spirits; no loud or rude word and no argument disrupted the overall good feeling. A few cannon shots are being fired from the ship to welcome the soldiers; before long they get on board across the wide gangway. The wheels of the steamer are already beginning to churn. Final farewells are crossing the water in both directions and kerchiefs are flying: "*Bon voyage!* to you brave and loyal brothers-in-arms!" A few moments later, the steamer is on its course toward the hot South.

***

The German political organization is spreading and gaining in influence in a very positive way. Since the beginning of the year, it has had its own English-language paper, the weekly *German American*, which is to establish a connection between German and American radicals, as all uncompromising foes of slavery are nowadays called. The chief points in the program adopted a year ago by the Germans at their convention in Ohio are as follows: maintaining the Union in its entirety; absolute suppression of the rebellion; complete and irrevocable abolition of slavery throughout the country; and distribution of all confiscated rebel lands among the soldiers of the Union forces and the liberated Negroes. In essence, these are the same points for which Americans of the radical party are also fighting, and their papers have welcomed the Germans as powerful and desirable allies and friends. Both groups are naturally intent upon selecting a candidate who is most supportive of the principles defined in their programs—and this means that the great and brilliant Frémont may once again step into the limelight.

Notes

1. New York, March [1864], *Morgenblatt*, 58:17:406–408.

2. Montgomery Blair (1813–1883), who had settled in St. Louis as a lawyer in 1837 and was defense counsel in the famous Dred Scott case (1857), served as Lincoln's postmaster general (1861–1864); he represented the moderate Republicans and eventually had to resign from the cabinet to assuage the radicals in an election year.

71

The Presidential Election[1]

The approaching presidential election, the great periodic change to which our republic is subjected every four years, is the central issue that for the next two months raises to a fever pitch the activities, the scheming, and the intrigues of party leaders and politicians of all stripes as well as of those who are in public employment and those who seek it. The approaching election drives the interest, the wishes, and the passions of the whole nation. The candidates have been nominated: Abraham Lincoln for the Unionists, General McClellan for the Democrats; they will be engaged in one of the most heated and hard-fought campaigns that this continent has ever seen. The outcome will determine not only the fate of a political party but that of the entire country. Whether the North or the South, freedom or slavery, shall dominate and dictate the laws of the nation is the question tied to the names of the two men who have been elevated to represent the fundamental differences.

On the one side is the so-called Democracy, the party that up to the outbreak of the war had governed the country for many years in an alliance with the southern slaveholders, whom they served as willing tools in the effort to spread and secure slavery. The slaveholders' open rebellion against the United States broke with one stroke the party's dominance and left the Democrats of the North in a minority opposed to the broad masses of the people living in the loyal states. Hence the Democrats' hidden and public sympathy for the rebels, their exertions to block every measure for suppressing the rebellion, and their continual clamor that the war is barbaric, unjustified, and contrary to the spirit and the letter of the Constitution. They know that the continuation of the war will eventually result in the inevitable defeat of their southern allies and of slavery itself and diminish their own prospects for an uncertain period of time. Aware that the present moment is the last opportunity for regaining power, they are bent upon elevating one of their tools to the highest position in the country so as to achieve reunification between the two separate states. This would reestablish the hated reign of the slavocracy and provide such guarantees for slavery that its curse could not be lifted for many generations to come.

The program accepted by the Democrats during the last days of August at their convention in Chicago—the "Chicago Platform," as it is called in the American language of politics—contains not a word of condemnation or even criticism of the rebels. It conceals the fact that it was the rebels who began the war; that, like robbers, they took possession wherever they could of the ships, armories, treasuries, currency, custom houses, and fortifications belonging to the United States; that they made prisoners of the weak forces occupying the forts—all before our side had fired a single shot. This despicable program indirectly justifies the leaders of the rebellion, who argued at the time of the fall of Fort Sumter that Lincoln and the abolitionists had declared war on the South and thereby forced North Carolina and Arkansas to secede in self-defense. There is not a word suggesting that the South has done the least wrong or that the government had the least right to oppose it. The party's program is limited to accusing the government and demanding the unconditional cessation of all hostilities. Any mention of slavery, this "cornerstone of the southern Confederacy," is carefully avoided, perhaps to avoid judgment by a civilized Europe, which the South has wooed since the start of the war by arguing that slavery had nothing to do with the outbreak of hostilities. But any such mention is really unnecessary because Democrats of all persuasions are in total agreement on this point, and not a single person among them would hesitate to spread this southern blessing to the free states, if the lords of slavery demanded it and the thing itself were possible.

At first glance, the nomination of McClellan seems to contradict the purposes of the party that chose him. Condemnation of the Union and the motto that "The Union has no right to force any state to remain within it" have been the main points of the Democrats' credo ever since it has become evident that the exercise of such force would mean the abolition of slavery. Yet McClellan has served the Union as a general since the start of the war, and to the great annoyance of his supporters he was forced to resign as commander-in-chief of the Army of the Potomac almost two years ago, although he did not have to give up either the rank of major general or his salary. In other words, he was a willing instrument of the very force that is an abomination in the eyes of the peace advocates, and he even came out in support of the much-maligned draft. Upon closer inspection, however, it turns out that the contradiction is mere appearance and that McClellan is the right man for all traitors in the North and the South because even if he does not openly adhere to the theory of states' rights, he has never wavered in his support of slavery—and that is the true touchstone of Democratic orthodoxy.

True, he was the commander of the large Army of the Potomac, but he conducted the war for the purpose of protecting the slaveholders from the consequences of their own suicidal madness instead of punishing them for the treason they had committed; and his superior Union forces never seriously threatened the far weaker rebels or cut off their retreat. His conduct of the war was so gentle, so restrained and considerate, that he served the rebels far better than if he had joined their side. Some southern newspapers even claim that he had originally offered his services to the Confederacy, but the brilliant prospects and advantages apparently offered him by the rightful government persuaded him to unsheathe the sword against his political allies. When rumor had it that a slave rebellion had broken out in Maryland, he was the first among all the generals who offered to suppress it "with an iron fist"; he is said to have bragged about not having taken even the smallest steps against the rebels since the president's Emancipation Proclamation.

Personally insignificant, timid, and pretentious, McClellan is a willing tool in the hands of the traitors, who believe that his election will put them in power. They expect to place the country at Jefferson Davis's feet, to dictate the terms under which he will condescend to return to the Union, and for many future generations to grind freedom and civil liberties into the dust under the iron heel of the slavocracy. Considering the fraudulent and dishonorable position that McClellan has occupied as a general of the republic and a friend of the rebels, one cannot be surprised at his pleasure to be the candidate of a party that wants peace at any price.

The disgracefulness of the Peace Democrats can be seen most clearly in the fact that their hopes of getting into power depend entirely on the accidents and defeats that may befall the Union forces before election day because under no other circumstances would the people permit having peace imposed. These Democrats see every victory over the rebels as a stroke against them and as a calamity dampening their hopes. When the nation learned about the fall of Atlanta, which is one of the most important strategic points, it was celebrated throughout the Union by shooting off cannons and fireworks, but the Peace Democrats, or "copperheads," walked about with long faces, cursing the inconvenient victory. Their chief supporters are the Irish, without whose help they would be powerless. Crude, brutal, ignorant, given to drink, and full of hatred for the Negro, the Irish have a penchant for viciousness and violence, and they are the willing tools of the Democracy. There is no question but that the election of McClellan would result in organized mob rule, which would see to it that no speaker and no paper throughout the country would dare to speak out for liberty and other such rights. In particular, they would deal with any expression opposing the sacrosanct institution of slavery as high treason, and persecuting Negroes and hunting down slaves would become everyday spectacles.

The large Union party, on the other side, consists of many former Democrats and generally all those who do not secretly or openly side with the rebels or are so blinded by hatred of the Negro that they put the survival of slavery above the survival of national unity. It is the Unionists who represent the core of the people, and their victory can only be thwarted by unexpected military defeats and accidents before the election. Maintaining the Union through the unconditional submission of the rebels and totally abolishing slavery because it is the cause of the present civil war are the main points of the program that was adopted at the Unionist convention in Baltimore last June. Unfortunately this is where their platform stops, leaving its good points incomplete by not saying anything about total equality for the Negroes. There is nothing about civil equality, even though 100,000 colored men are currently serving on the battlefields of the nation, exposed to greater dangers than their white comrades because the "Knights of the South" do not treat them as prisoners of war but murder them in cold blood. Color prejudice—the curse that weighs on the American in general and even on the enlightened opponent of slavery—causes him to withhold the ballot from his truest friend, the always loyal and faithful colored man, even as he sees nothing wrong with letting the whole gang of ignorant and crude Irishmen cast their votes in support of traitors and enemies. In this regard, the platform reflects the attitudes of the people.

The Unionist cause, however, lacks an important element without which no party can be assured of victory: enthusiasm for its candidate. Abraham Lincoln is not the choice of the people but of office holders, politicians, and speculators—all those who want to continue to reap the benefits they have enjoyed under his administration. He was forced upon the people by political cliques with nothing less than unseemly haste. They had decided his nomination in advance, and all other candidates were excluded. Lincoln's lack of perception, education, and energy; his lukewarm commitment; his consideration for rebels and traitors in contrast to the injustice and ruthlessness with which he often treats his most loyal allies; his petty intrigues against Frémont and Secretary of the Treasury Chase as soon as he saw them as competitors—all these are incontrovertible facts that have brought on him the censure and dislike of the nation's elite. Every enlightened, educated man who truly has the nation's welfare at heart openly concedes that he would have preferred another candidate, but given the choice between McClellan and Lincoln he will of course do his best to prevent the calamity of a Democratic administration. Lacking great popularity and the ability to obtain it, Lincoln will receive the votes of all Unionists and opponents of slavery, but only because they regard him as the lesser of two evils.

Besides these two candidates there is a third, but he is only nominally in contention even though far superior to them in ability, honesty, understanding, and conscience: he is John C. Frémont. As early as the beginning of the year, after it had become clear that among party leaders Lincoln's nomination was a *fait accompli* that would be pushed through, a group of patriotic and enlightened men decided to start a coalition against Lincoln by nominating a radical candidate. For some time they had been disturbed and outraged by the administration's missteps and halfway measures. Some of the best and most distinguished men, among them Wendell Phillips, were active in this movement, which also found much support among the Germans. Frémont was thus almost unanimously chosen as their presidential candidate at a convention in Cleveland toward the end of May. Their program contains many of the same points as that of Lincoln's party: maintaining the Union, subjection of the rebels, and the abolition of slavery; but in addition, it calls for the civil equality of all colored people and the confiscation of rebel land and its distribution among the freed slaves.

Although no better candidate had been nominated for many years and the party platform deserved to be welcomed by an informed people as a sign of progress, the general conditions here are such that the whole enlightened enterprise failed. Although, as stated before, the leaders of this movement include some of the best and most distinguished men, they lack the reputation and the political status that impress and thrill the masses. They themselves realized that they were too weak to constitute even a respectable minority, let alone to get some of their candidates elected, and therefore looked about for allies on some other matters. They believed that a few minor concessions might enlist the support of the Democrats, who at that time had not yet chosen their own candidate; hence they elected John Cochrane as their vice presidential candidate, a hard-boiled, old-fashioned, unprincipled politician who has a history of belonging at one time or another to all parties, including the ultra-propagandists for slavery.[2] Frémont himself was drawn into this alliance, causing total shipwreck. Meanwhile the Democrats, trying to reestablish the old slave power, were delighted at this split among their opponents, and some of the radicals, upset by the concessions to the enemy, withdrew in disgust. This leaves Frémont isolated and without party support, and his strongest supporters face the necessity of voting for Lincoln so as not to strengthen McClellan by splitting the opposition.

Whatever party or candidate will eventually win and whatever events may occur, any person of normal insight into the situation and conditions can confidently predict that the days of the war are numbered and that both parties are firmly resolved to end the war as soon as possible. The Democrats favor a peace that will deliver the North into hands of the slaveholders; Lincoln and his cabinet, on the other hand, know all too well that the people are tired of this drawn-out war, and that their own reelection would be all but assured if they could promise an honorable peace in the near future. The recurrent rumors of ongoing peace negotiations—although repeatedly denied—are not without foundation, and there can also be no doubt that the rebels are at the point of exhaustion. They are keeping up the unequal battle only because they are hoping for victory on election day, but the house of cards that is the Confederacy will tumble with the probable defeat at the polls.

The next few months will most likely confirm this prognosis, leaving only one great question: Are we to have a peace that will forever eradicate slavery? Only such a peace will be a permanent blessing. Any other arrangement that would leave the cause of the war untouched would amount to no more than mere fraud. All the bitterness and animosity would then remain and surely lead to another bloody conflict some generations hence.

Notes

1. New York, September [1864], *Morgenblatt,* 58:43:1031–1032 and 58:44:1052–1053.

2. John Cochrane (1813–1898) had been a states-rights Democratic congressman from New York (1857–1861) who favored a conciliatory approach to the South; however, opposing secession, he supported the Union during the war. Frémont's and his opposition to Lincoln soon collapsed; they withdrew and campaigned for Lincoln.

72

The Presidential Election[1]

One of the most important and fateful days that can occur in the life of a nation has come and gone: the day of the presidential election, which determined whether this great republic will deserve this name in the future and be governed by the spirit of progress, freedom, and humanity, or whether it will be ruled by intolerable despotism—worse than that of the most absolute monarchies of the Old World—the despotism of the slave masters that goes hand in hand with barbarism, ignorance, and reaction. Lincoln on one side, McClellan on the other: both are men of mediocre talent who have not achieved historic fame by their own accomplishments but were propelled by the course of events to represent the divergent principles defining the people's choice. The people have voted and determined that they do not want to have anything to do with a peace that could only be achieved by compromises, dismemberment of the Union, and a surrender of power to the slaveholders and their allies. They have expressed their willingness to continue the war for the entire Union with all their might, their blood, and their worldly possessions until the complete suppression of the rebellion has been accomplished. Not since Monroe, who won all electoral votes except one, has a president been elected by such a large majority as Lincoln, and therefore none has been as disgracefully defeated as McClellan. Out of twenty-seven states he received the votes of only three—two slave states, Kentucky and Delaware, and only a single free state, New Jersey.

This great victory has all but made certain the abolition of slavery, because the results of the Congressional elections that took place on the same day have assured the two-thirds majority necessary for passing such a resolution. Looking back over the last few years, one has to be truly astonished at the enormous progress, the vast changes, that have been brought about by a revolution in people's thoughts and feelings. Only four years ago, a party daring to make the abolition of slavery the chief plank of its platform would have been derided as a group of half-crazy visionaries, fanatics, and demagogues by as large a majority as has now voted in favor of this measure. And as little as two years ago, the masses howled and crossed themselves when radical proponents of progress opposing slavery urged that Negroes be armed, but today we have more than 200,000 colored soldiers.

The excitement and tension before the election were unparalleled. Of course, every presidential election has its public meetings, activities by political clubs and the daily press, torchlight parades, and a flood of pamphlets, but this time all such expressions had a level of seriousness and intensity as never before. Everyone felt that it was not just about party interests, lucrative offices, and personal ambition but about the unity and the very life of the nation. At this fateful moment, the greatest victory that the army could have achieved, even the fall of Richmond itself, would have been seen only as a weight tipping the scales.

Just as on the one side the people became more optimistic and everything pointed to a happy outcome, so anger, bitterness, and spite grew among the Peace Democrats, rebel sympathizers, Negro haters, and supporters of the slave system. They knew that McClellan's election was their only trump and that its failure would spell the end of their last hope to regain power and to sway the people to pass laws for the continuation of slavery. But now, if ever, the old saying proved itself: "Whomever the gods choose to destroy they first afflict with madness." Not content to fight for an idea that conflicts with justice, liberty, and civilization and is anathema to all educated nations, the supporters of slavery adopted measures that would have killed a worthier cause. The more public opinion turned against them, the more they shouted and clamored that they alone represented the nation and its ideals, that only a fraudulent election could deprive them of victory, and that in such an event they would not bow but fight for their rights and burn down the cities of the North. Imagine the outrage that these threats caused among a people whose entire system of government rests on the principle of majority rule to which the minority must submit. The result was that many who had been loyal Democrats during their entire lives abandoned their party and voted for Lincoln.

Threats made by these so-called Democrats were the least of their reprehensible actions. One day, just before the election, a gigantic fraud was revealed, the worst that was ever perpetrated to help along a bad cause. It is well known that every citizen of the United States has a constitutional right to vote and can exercise it in any state in which he has resided for one year. Temporary absences do not invalidate this right, but it is necessary that he personally appear at the polling place in order to cast his vote. In times of peace this regulation was perfectly adequate, but since the outbreak of the war it has not been serviceable because no citizen on the battlefield was able to exercise his right to vote. It seemed unjust not to differentiate between those who were serving their country to the best of their abilities and were prevented by just that service from appearing at the polls and those who did not show up due to private affairs, laziness, or bad weather. Most states have therefore made arrangements for soldiers to vote where they are. State offices as well as many political organizations send out their agents to the regiments that fall under their jurisdiction and collect the soldiers' votes, which are then counted along with those of all other citizens. In order to prevent any kind of fraud, certain formalities have to be observed. A certified affidavit that has been witnessed is required and must be signed by the commanding officer.

Suddenly the almost incredible news spread that agents of the state of New York, who had been sent by Governor Horatio Seymour to collect the votes of New York citizens in the Army of the Potomac, were arrested in Baltimore and Washington. The Unionists were dismayed, and the Democrats did not want to believe it, stating that the whole affair was a trick by the administration for political advantage. But revelation followed upon revelation, and the agents were court-martialed; some of them immediately confessed, so that the most shameless fraud soon was uncovered. In most cases the affidavit was issued in the name of a soldier who had long since been killed in action or died in a hospital; signatures of officers and witnesses appeared who did not exist. In other cases, when soldiers had actually voted, ballots were removed from envelopes and substitutes placed inside. According to the agents' own testimony, these fraudulent documents had been prepared by the crateful, and of course they all benefited the Democratic party. On this occasion other edifying practices came to light: in the jargon of those who practice these things, one of them is referred to as "the marrow-fat ticket." A number of ballots are glued together with a fatty substance so that they look like a single one, but when slipped through the narrow slot of the ballot box they separate, helping the Democratic votes to multiply immeasurably.

It is perfectly clear that because the state of New York would not legally vote for McClellan, his victory was to be assured by fraud. Many former lawyers were among the agents, people who acted in full knowledge of both the crime and the consequences to which they would be exposed in case they were discovered. It is clear that they are the instruments of higher, more influential ringleaders, as it would seem unlikely that experienced, rational men would engage in such a serious crime without expectation of gain or reward and only for partisan purposes, even if the fraud had succeeded. Whatever doubt one may have had was erased when it was discovered that the criminals were carrying letters both from and to influential, high-ranking Democratic party leaders that proved their involvement. But no one honestly doubts that the key ringleader is Horatio Seymour, the governor of New York. He instigated the terrible uprising in July of last year,[2] has been an eager friend of the rebels and therefore of McClellan, and was making every effort to assure his reelection as governor. Whether his guilt can be proven will be seen in the course of the investigation. Meanwhile he sent commissioners to Washington who desperately tried to obtain the release of one of the men charged, a Colonel North. But when this effort failed, they arranged to have the investigation postponed until after the election. The two agents who had been arrested first and whose guilt is evident were sentenced by court-martial to life imprisonment, a punishment that, no matter how severe, cannot be seen as undeserved. But it is regrettable that most likely only the instruments will be punished, while the main instigators remain out of reach.

This revelation coincided with others about a conspiracy in Indiana, which I mentioned in my previous letter.[3] One of the arrested conspirators turned state's evidence and gave the most surprising testimony, revealing the extent of the whole Democratic plot for overthrowing the present government. Enough facts about the Democrats were already known to leave no doubt about their intentions, but now new fears were added about what was as yet unknown. Threats were coupled with dark rumors about an incursion of the rebels from Canada, which seemed all the more plausible because of earlier attempts of that sort.

It was no wonder, then, that besides the excitement normally associated with an election a brooding anxiety prevailed, and many people were seriously worried. Some predicted a recurrence of the bloody scenes of July a year ago, and few remained calm in anticipation of the elections in New York. It is difficult to say

Radical Passion

what might have happened had the government not put all the troops in the city under the command of General Butler.[4] He was the right man in the right place. Though formerly an energetic, died-in-the-wool Democrat, he has become one of the most active and forceful supporters of the government since the start of the war. He is now the enemies' chief dread, having become the target of their hatred when he was military governor of Louisiana, although at the same time he gained the admiration of all loyal citizens. His presence inspired even the more fearful citizens with confidence. He was like a watchful bulldog who is a friend and protector of decent people but the dreadful enemy of thieves and burglars.

On election day, New York was as calm and safe as on no other day of the year. It was a dark, rainy, and foggy day on which no one chose to be outdoors; the streets were unusually quiet and empty, and only the long lines of people in front of the polling places as well as the small shacks set up next to them for handing out ballots revealed the importance of the day. But even here everything was completely calm. The voters stood one behind the other, many with newspapers in their hands, patiently waiting their turn.[5] At night, street boys set fire to a few empty barrels as they usually do at the end of a holiday, but even here you could not hear any of the usual bursts of cheer. However, the gathering places of political clubs presented a completely different spectacle: these were places of the greatest excitement. Party leaders, club members, and crowds of supporters received reports from the various districts of the city and the state, and depending on whether these were supportive or opposed to the wishes of the crowd they were received with either much cheering or loud hissing. In the city of New York, where the worst elements of all nations are gathered, the Democrats came out on top as usual, winning by 36,000 votes. A large number of these were fraudulent because of the impossibility of strict supervision. But this majority was soon transformed into a minority as a result of the brilliant success scored by the Union party in other parts of the state. Lincoln would have been elected even without the votes of the state of New York, but the Republican victory accomplished the fall of Horatio Seymour and his henchmen, who have wrought so much disaster during the past few years.

The Democrats have become noticeably quiet now that the people, despite all the threats and attempts at intimidation, have spoken so firmly. Perhaps they are finally beginning to understand that the course of events and the spirit of the century cannot be held back by conspiracies, intrigues, and fraud. One of the most vicious Democratic journals, the *Journal of Commerce*, recently told its readers that after the outcome of this election it will no longer deal with politics but dedicate itself exclusively to commercial interests, criticism of literature and art, and other such harmless subjects. This almost looks like desperate surrender, but knowing the tenacity, stubbornness, and arrogance of the American politician from experience, one cannot be so easily convinced that this resignation is entirely honest—and that the seemingly expired copperhead will not bite and spread its poison once again.

It will be interesting to see what position McClellan will assume after his defeat. When Frémont was nominated in Cleveland he resigned from his military position because he considered it beneath his dignity to serve a government that he felt he had to criticize, a government that had carefully kept him without responsibilities. McClellan has also been inactive for two years but has drawn his full salary of 6,000 dollars annually during this entire period, even after he had become a presidential candidate. He resigned only a few days ago.

The Germans deserve the highest tribute for their behavior during the campaign. Largely thanks to them, overwhelming majorities were achieved in Ohio, Missouri, and Wisconsin. In general, the radical, educated Germans were not in favor of Lincoln, and as long as there was any hope that Frémont or some other radical and capable man would be nominated in Chicago, they did not want to participate in the campaign. But as soon as it was determined that the choice was to be between McClellan and Lincoln, they worked tirelessly and with unanimity. In many of their political clubs some of the best speakers of the campaign gave addresses. Carl Schurz was the best among many, and no one in this country, according to the Americans themselves, is equal to him in the power of oratory, in profundity of thought, and in clear, rational perception of present conditions. His speeches of the past few weeks have lasting value and open for the listener or the reader such a depth of insight into the character and activities of the so-called Peace Democrats, they explode the opposition's arguments so effectively, and are so perfect in form and expression in English and in German that they deserve to be saved with the works of the first American statesmen.

A few days before the election Schurz spoke to a large gathering of Germans. The hall of the Cooper Institute was filled to bursting (even the hallways were crowded), and the brilliantly lit room presented a truly beautiful sight. All the pillars and the platform were decorated with the red-white-and-blue national flag, and instead of a lectern they had piled up cannonballs, which were also covered with the flag. Schurz spoke beautifully and brilliantly, and the audience, consisting mostly of working-class people, listened to him with an attention and enthusiasm that proved with how much interest and commitment Germans participate in the conditions of their new home country. It cannot be denied that particularly in the larger cities there are Germans who, out of stupidity, ignorance, or innate meanness, are loyal to the Democratic party. Some of the wealthy merchants belong in this category, but I am happy to say that not a single German who has been known either here or at home for his intellect, talent, and knowledge has ever strayed into their ranks. Without exception, the truly outstanding men, the representatives of the German mind and of German education in America, are actively engaged in the struggle for freedom, humanity, civilization, and progress.

Notes

1. New York, November [1864], *Morgenblatt*, 58:52:1243–1246.

2. For Assing's account of the draft riots in New York, see Essay 66.

3. Assing is referring to her article, also dated "November [1864]," and published three weeks earlier in the *Morgenblatt,* in which she mentions a "wide-reaching, well-organized Democratic conspiracy" in "the West." It was allegedly designed to "tempt [Union] soldiers to desert, to give the enemy important information, to supply him with war materials, to assist him in recruitment efforts, and to support his incursions into the loyal states. . . ." She claims that the head of this conspiracy was "Vallandigham, the president of the [Democrats'] Chicago convention, who first proposed McClellan as the presidential nominee. . . ."

4. Benjamin Franklin Butler (1818–1893), a Democrat who became a firm Unionist, was known as "Beast Butler" for his strong rule as military governor of New Orleans. Later, as a member of Congress, he belonged to the radical Republicans.

5. In Springfield, Massachusetts, a 109-year old man, accompanied by his 80-year old son, came to the polls to vote for Lincoln. He is one of the few living people who helped elect Washington and who has voted in every election since [Assing's note].

73

Christmas and New Year's—Slavery—Everett—A New German Book[1]

The capture of Savannah was the great Christmas present that the courageous Union forces gave to the nation at the end of a year of successes and victories. Although this event had been anticipated for some time and rumors had spread the news of it more than once, it was the certainty conveyed by official announcement that released the excitement and the holiday mood all around. This achievement, which has since been followed by others, is particularly gratifying because it happened without shedding blood and because it clearly proves the rebels' complete powerlessness and hopelessness. That is all they were able to put in the way of General Sherman's three-hundred-mile march through the state of Georgia, which resulted in taking one of their few remaining ports without firing a single shot. We are starting this new year with greater hopes than any year since the outbreak of the war.

***

Unfortunately, the much-expected announcement that an act of Congress has forever banished slavery throughout the country has not been made. The Senate passed it in last year's session, but intrigues and endless counter arguments by the Democrats have temporarily defeated it in the House of Representatives. It was taken up again in the current session, but after repeated speeches for and against, the vote has been postponed for two weeks, so that it is entirely possible that the present Congress will come to the end of the session without passing the measure that will determine the future of the country. Even though the next session of Congress, beginning on March 4, will have an overwhelming majority in its favor, the postponement and the possible failure (not to mention the loss of time) are among the most troublesome and undesirable symptoms of a fundamental flaw of the American people: the lack of principles, of firm and clear concepts of right and wrong, human dignity, justice, and barbarism.

Even if the nation were to rid itself of the curse of slavery, it would be wrong—as I have mentioned before—to ascribe such an action to the people's virtue or to see it as an expression of their honest moral outrage against this crime of long standing. It would be merely the result of the pressure of circumstances and of the long overdue realization that slavery is the greatest obstacle to a lasting peace as well as the enemy of material growth and progress. Instead of having lawmakers, politicians, and members of the administration vie with each other for the glory of freeing this country from its dark stain, most of them evade that decision and retreat timidly as if sidestepping a grave responsibility. The abolition of slavery is the responsibility of the individual states, they say, and Congress has no right to intervene; and since there is no reason to doubt that the states would take care of this problem out of their own free will, it is more practical and effective to let them do it rather than to have Congress pass an act of abolition, as Congress can pass laws but cannot enforce them.

But these are only the sophistries with which the semi-loyalists try to hide their lack of conscience and honesty under the cloak of conservatism, making great efforts to quash any attempt at emancipation, any act of justice toward the Negroes. True, each state can discontinue slavery within its own boundaries, as in fact Missouri and Tennessee recently followed Maryland's example; and even Kentucky, the breeding ground of the most vicious traitors in the loyal states, promises soon to do the same. But things are different in the rebellious states, which now are being subjected one by one to Union rule. For them, of course, the decisions of those individual states that have abolished slavery are irrelevant, and if today the citizens of one or the other of them should wish to abandon the hopeless cause of the slaveholders and want to return to the Union, the conservatives would be free to admit them even with slavery if that were their request. They would be able to do so in spite of the Emancipation Proclamation, which in such a case would simply be declared a temporary war measure, so as to achieve something that might look like peace but would actually lay the foundation for a renewed rift in the future. The abolition of slavery on the part of Congress, however, would once and for all forbid any reconstruction of the Union without removing the cause of the rebellion.

Everyone knows that the president and his cabinet, all their comments and declarations to the contrary not withstanding, are prepared to accept any kind of peace, with or without slavery, as long as it means the preservation of the Union. We also know that every step they have so far taken against slavery has been forced on them by necessity. Under these circumstances, the postponement of negotiations and of the possible passage of an act of emancipation is most significant just at the moment when yet another emissary with peace proposals has left for Richmond. It is equally significant that only the papers of the most absolute opponents of slavery are courageous and honest enough to oppose absolutely any such weakness and willingness to compromise. These are neither justified nor called for at a time when Union forces are everywhere victorious, taking one essential installation after another, when discouragement, weakness, and hopelessness among our enemies are revealed in their own newspapers and in their internecine conflicts. Even the *New York Tribune*, generally regarded as the organ of the most radical emancipationism, not only fails to say a word of rebuke against the latest peace efforts but openly expresses its support for them.

As in former days, our best hopes are not founded on the virtue and firmness of our own leaders but on the suicidal blindness and rigidity of the rebel leadership. Although they have risked everything, although they are facing certain disaster, although they are violating the will of the majority of the oppressed people of the South, the rebel leaders will not entertain a peace that does not recognize their independence; for them it is "All or nothing!" Jefferson Davis has done more for the abolition of slavery than the most dedicated abolitionist of this century.

One of America's famous men, Edward Everett, recently died at an advanced age. He is one of those fortunate men who, through personal assiduousness and favorable circumstances, was able to develop his natural gifts to the fullest extent and to apply them widely. Everett was a minister, statesman, diplomat, author, and member of Congress, and his performance in all of these positions had a certain brilliance. He was a man of important and noticeable talent, but if his admirers count him among the greatest men of this country or even of this century, they reveal their own limitations or a very one-sided nativism. Although a master of form and style, Everett was no creative genius. He does not leave behind any single great and coherent work, and he spent many years giving the same speech about Washington in every town and hamlet of the Union.

His speeches were more noted for their polish than for depth and originality of thought, and it is not doing him an injustice to say that in his ideas and views he did not dare to go beyond the limits of the traditional and accepted, being careful not to offend the prejudices and errors of his contemporaries. In general, he was more a man of concession and conciliation than a fighter for any great idea. For that, he lacked passion, dedication, enthusiasm, and courage, and I do not believe that in his long career he ever dedicated his strength to a truly great purpose, to a solution of the most important problems of the age, except for defending the *status quo*. In Congress he sullied his reputation forever when he, a son of the free state of Massachusetts and the product of European civilization and learning, stood up in defense of slavery. He resigned from his professorship after only three years because he could not get the admiration of his students—but how could their hearts warm to a teacher who seemingly had no heart for them?

During the election of 1860, Everett was nominated as the vice-presidential candidate of the party that then called itself Conservative Unionists and wanted to elect Bell as president. Without having a clear goal, without believing in progress, basing their program only on the rotten foundation of existing conditions, that party had hopes not to prevent but simply to delay the imminent dissolution of the Union for a few years by making concessions of all sorts. It did not occur to them to go to the root of the problem, a process that sooner or later would have to result in bloody conflict. Valiantly ignoring it or covering it up with noble phrases and common- places, they eagerly prepared glue, plaster, and bandages in the form of settlements and compromises to cover up the incurable wound. The fact that Everett was chosen by such a party as a suitable candidate, to say nothing of the miserable demise of the party, did not raise his reputation among the better sort of people. Inane, somehow floating between Republicans and Democrats, ridiculed by both as an "old gentlemen's party," it failed gloriously in the election. Looking at Everett's long career, one cannot discover any substantial and lasting achievement or come to the conclusion that his death has left a noticeable gap, except perhaps among his personal friends.

Among the many German books that report every year about life and conditions in the United States, Adolf Douai's recently published *Land und Leute in der Union*[2] has received due attention also among the Germans over here. The author, who is at present the principal of a German school in Hoboken across the Hudson from New York, is well qualified by his many years of residence in this country and his thorough knowledge of it. Different from so many Germans writing about conditions here whose observations are limited to New York or some western state, he had the opportunity to get to know the land and the people in all sections: he knows New England, the large cities, the middle states and those of the West, and the South as far as Texas, where he once published a German newspaper and was driven out as an abolitionist by the slavery party. He is also to be credited with a clear, sharp-eyed perspective on things, an objective analysis of conditions and people, and a lively style that makes it easy for the reader to follow him.

The author does not share that disagreeable bitterness into which so many Germans fall partly out of personal disappointment and failure and partly due to seeing so many unsolved problems that they are unwilling to recognize what is undeniably good; but he is also free of any shallow, unqualified admiration and imitation of everything American, including slavery. He presents both the bright and the dark side of things with the same objectivity and is particularly clear and concise in his description of the conflict that is as old as the republic itself—the central issue of political life that has to be seen if one is to understand the United States; the struggle between the true Republicans, the party of freedom and progress, and the aristocracy of slave holders, who call themselves Democrats and thus were able to recruit the rabble and govern the country for many years; the contest that has reached its crisis in the present war. Even anyone unfamiliar with conditions here can get a good overview through this book, and that is particularly desirable now that the eyes of the world are fixed on this continent. The knowledgeable German-American, on the other hand, has the satisfaction of seeing his own perspectives and judgments confirmed and elaborated. This little volume is useful and entertaining for German readers on both sides of the Atlantic.

Notes

1. New York, January [1865], *Morgenblatt*, 59:11:262–264.

2. *Land und Leute in der Union* (The Country and the People of the Union) by Alfred Douai (misspelled "Donai" in the *Morgenblatt*) was published in Germany in 1864. Douai (1819–1888) was one of the liberal German intellectuals who emigrated to the United States after the failed revolution of 1848. He edited and published the *San Antonio Zeitung* (1853–1856) but was driven out for his strong abolitionist views. In New York, he later supported the labor movement, editing the *Arbeiter Union* (1869–1871), and was active in the Socialist Labor Party, founding the *New Yorker Volkszeitung* (1878). Since he was living in Hoboken at the time of this article, Assing knew him personally. See Peter Connolly-Smith, "The Translated Community" (Ph.D. diss., Yale 1996), 113–116.

74

The Constitutional Abolition of Slavery[1]

January 31 was the great day—the greatest in the history of the country since the Declaration of Independence—the day on which the American people rid themselves forever of the curse of slavery by the action of Congress, thereby truly joining the ranks of civilized and enlightened nations of the world. The news itself has long since crossed the ocean on the wings of steam power to be spread to all corners of the world, but the mere announcement could hardly have given a sense of the joyous excitement and enthusiasm that have seized a majority of the people. The courageous fighters for freedom and justice, who continued the struggle undeterred despite hostilities and persecutions at a time when public opinion considered the mere mention of the slavery issue a crime and any self-confessed abolitionist was virtually declared an outlaw, can be content to see the goal of their efforts realized. Anyone who has not been demoralized by the poison of slavery will feel the deepest joy at this sudden and fateful blow against the most heinous of crimes with which any nation could have besmirched itself in this century of progress and humanitarianism. Even most of those who are motivated more by circumstances than principles have by now come to understand what only two or three years ago was still a much-challenged fact: that slavery is the only cause of the rebellion and that its total annihilation is the only security against similar future insurrections.

It is well known that the Senate passed the amendment to the Constitution for the abolition of slavery last spring with a decisive majority of thirty-eight to six, but in the House of Representatives it failed with ninety-five votes in favor and sixty-four opposed, an amendment to the Constitution requiring at least a two-thirds majority. However, in the present session Representative Ashley of Ohio[2] resubmitted the issue for a vote and, after long drawn-out debates in which about thirty members spoke both for and against the measure, January 31 was set as the date for the final vote. On that day, one could feel in the halls of the House of Representatives that an important decision was about to be made.

From the very start, the visitor galleries are filled, and unusual excitement and tension are in the air. The Unionists are hopeful and confident, but the friends of the South and of slavery walk about with somber faces. The debate begins. A number of Democrats who previously voted against this measure but have since then either seen the light or come to understand the impossibility of successfully opposing the will of the people now speak in its support. The unbending admirers of slavery get up and deliver a few rambling and boring speeches but without presenting the much-repeated justifications that were formerly adduced in behalf of slavery: that it is a divine institution; that it is necessitated by the Negro's natural inability to learn; that it is to the slaves' own benefit—and whatever other arguments of this kind are commonly made. Today, no one dares to be so heavy-handed in violating the spirit of this century, and the gentlemen of the defense are trying to hide their sympathy for the rebels and their institutions behind theoretical objections. One of them avers that the abolition of slavery depends solely on the will of the individual states, and that Congress has no power to pass laws in this regard, hence that the whole proceeding is unconstitutional. Another states that passage of the amendment would hinder the restoration of the Union. And a third, attempting to make those Democrats who favor the measure look laughable, feebly tries to drive them with withering wit back into the fold of the righteous.

Meanwhile the movement is growing, and while the Republicans are pleased to watch the rift among the Democrats, the old proslavery guard increasingly reveals its annoyance. The crowds get thicker: senators, Supreme Court justices, officers, high government officials, other well-known men and even women mix with the crowds; the galleries are packed, and even the newspaper reporters are in danger of being forced to give up their seats. After more than three hours of opposing arguments the debate ends, and the crucial moment is near. But the Democrats are not yet conceding victory, as they make a last desperate effort, letting one of their own move "to table" the whole thing—the usual trick to kill an inopportune measure before it is voted on. The motion is defeated by one hundred and twelve to fifty-seven votes. However, this does not guarantee passage of the constitutional amendment because not enough members are present to make a two-thirds majority. By and by, however, the stragglers arrive. There is a vote to reconsider the motion that failed in the earlier session because of an insufficient majority. As expected, it passes, but the Democrats are making a renewed effort to turn aside a final decision, asking for a delay until tomorrow, which is, however, denied. Finally there is a vote on the constitutional amendment, which reads: "Neither slavery nor involuntary servitude, except as punishment for crime whereof the party shall have been duly convicted, shall exist within the United States, or any place subject to their jurisdiction."

The roll is called, and the Democrats who vote "Yea" are loudly applauded. Then, with breathless anticipation settling over the House, the votes are tallied. Finally, the speaker announces the result: the amendment passes one hundred and nineteen votes to fifty-six, seven more than the required two-thirds majority. A long and thunderous expression of joyful elation welcomes the announcement. Representatives, senators, judges, soldiers, and women are shouting "Hurrah," clap their hands, wave their handkerchiefs, and congratulate each other, as a hundred cannons add their thunder from the batteries.

Now that this great event has taken place, the constitutional amendment has to be submitted to the legislatures of the individual states for ratification; only after its acceptance by three-fourths of the states will it be the law of the land. The assent of the loyal states is all but assured, except for Delaware, Kentucky, and New Jersey, and many have already passed it. The recaptured states of Louisiana, Tennessee, and Arkansas can also be counted on, so that there is little doubt about the final outcome.

After this great victory over barbarism and oppression, which must be seen as the beginning of a new era, and after the brilliant successes in the South by Union forces during the past weeks and months, some of which were won without shedding blood, the breakup of peace negotiations must be seen as a stroke of good fortune. These negotiations were strange from the very start: they were not initiated by the nation's most respected men but by those ingratiating smoothies who curry favor with all parties and place success above principle. Francis Blair,[3] the first emissary of peace dispatched to Richmond, is representative of this type, and together with his sons and others of the same ilk he exercises far too much influence over the less than firmly committed president. Sending such an emissary was a mistake in itself because, even if he went without official powers, it was well known that such a step could be taken only with the president's approval. But why and for what purpose, one would ask. Why such efforts at a time when one military success is following upon another, when the fall of Charleston is just a matter of weeks or days, when the complete exhaustion and hopelessness of the rebels is so self-evident that no one with any sense can have doubts about their imminent defeat? Why the concessions, if we can soon dictate with the victor's sword?—especially since the president's proclamation of amnesty has informed the South of his conciliatory disposition, giving assurances that all who are willing to cease fighting and return to the Union will be welcomed with open arms. Blair went to Richmond twice in the span of a few days, and right away it became known that Jefferson Davis had sent three peace commissioners, and that the president and Secretary of State Seward had gone to Fort Monroe to meet with them.

The radical Unionists and opponents of slavery were deeply concerned about these events because of the president's well-known conservative and overly conciliatory attitude. They trembled in expectation of a patchwork peace and of the possibility that the president would simply readmit the rebel states with their legislatures into the Union, thereby giving them the power to block the ratification of the constitutional amendment and laying a foundation for renewed discord and armed conflict. No good was to come from that quarter, and the sudden discontinuation of the peace negotiations came as a great relief. Now that these negotiations have been made public, it is even more difficult to understand what expectations and goals had led to them in the first place, since neither party was willing to abandon any of its demands. Not considering the basic mistake of entering into these useless negotiations, one must credit the president for demonstrating more firmness than expected. He did not want to hear of any peace or armistice until the rebels had altogether laid down their arms and dissolved all their military forces, and in regard to slavery, he declared that the congressional passage of the constitutional amendment had removed the whole issue from his influence. On the other side, Jefferson Davis's commissioners made the recognition of their independence their first unnegotiable demand.

So, what in the world was there to negotiate? The most likely answer is that Blair as well as Jefferson Davis were bluffing: Blair, in his eagerness to make peace at any price, tried to convince Jefferson Davis that Lincoln would be disposed to make all sorts of concessions; Jefferson Davis, on the other hand, pretending to believe Blair, used the occasion of the inevitable failure of the peace negotiations to spur his people to a last desperate effort on the battlefield. The ridiculous temper tantrums by which his party organs vented their rage about allegedly inflicted insults seem to confirm this surmise.

At any rate, it is becoming ever more evident that the majority of the people in the South are tired of the war, the unbearable despotism, the horrors of conscription, the threats to property, the increasing costs, and the worthlessness of paper money. They would be happy to return to the security of the Union, especially since there can be no doubt about the outcome of the war and the realization that any future effort would only prolong the final agony of death and make it all the more painful. To silence this growing peace faction, Jefferson Davis is directing the papers under his control to rant about the impudence, the brutality, and tyranny of the Yankees in that characteristically southern style of crude and ridiculous bombast, claiming that the North will not consider anything but total subjection and Negro emancipation. But in their anger they actually give away what they have always stubbornly denied so as not to arouse public opinion among the civilized nations of Europe against them: that they are mostly fighting for the continuation and expansion of slavery.

The rebel leaders are fighting furiously among themselves and in their Congress about how to deal with the decimations of their regiments. Whole companies are deserting, and the ruthless enforcement of conscription has been so successful that there are no more men able to bear arms. The very people who seceded from the Union to rid themselves once and for all of the nagging Negro question, are now engaged in a bitter debate over whether or not to emancipate and arm their slaves. "We have to arm our Negroes," some of them are shouting. "General Lee says he cannot stand up against the Yankees if he does not get reinforcements, and the Negroes are our last resource." "We cannot arm our Negroes," comes the answer just as loudly. "We cannot do without them in our fields and workshops; and they would not fight for us unless we emancipate them, but emancipation would turn their masters against our cause, and the whole rebellion would come crashing down on our heads. This is a rebellion by the slaveholders, and to place its defense on the shoulders of the slaves would make it the butt of ridicule."

It cannot be denied that the reasons on both sides are equally convincing and sound. "But don't you see," says a third one, "that we are exposing ourselves to the whole world and contradicting ourselves if we were to arm the Negroes? You all know and admit that we cannot for a moment think about arming them without promising them their freedom. But how much sense would that make with all we have said so far? Doesn't the first article of our southern credo state that slavery is the most rewarding and useful condition for the Negro, that the slave loves his master beyond all else, that it is his highest pride to serve, and that he would under no circumstances accept his freedom even if it were offered? Would not the mere promise of emancipation amount to a confession that we have lied to the world and that the Negro desires his freedom like all other men?"

This argument, however, is not made consistently. To deal with the internal conflicts and the pressures from outside, some offer the most bizarre and unreasonable propositions. A member of the southern Congress suggests to emancipate all the men who are able to bear arms but to retain their wives and children in slavery. "Because," he adds with maddening insolence, "what kind of freedom would it be to burden the Negro with the support of his family! No, the Negro does not care about freedom for his wife and children as long as he is free himself! He would come soon enough asking his master to feed them for him."

Another subject that offers itself to southern journals for exercising their wit and power of invention are the reasons they offer to console their readers for all the recent defeats and losses. Instead of expressing dejection like any other mortal, they discover a silver lining around each dark cloud of loss, turning it into a source of strength and a proof of future success. One paper gives its readers the comforting news that with the fall of Fort Fisher the Confederacy's last seaport had been closed, but that this was a blessing in disguise because the South would be much stronger without the coast. Another journal tries to assuage its readers' fears by assuring them that Wilmington, which has come under the control of Union cannons due to the fall of Fort Fisher, was in no danger. Yet a third paper proves that the total loss of Wilmington would actually amount to an immeasurable gain. Withal, it is easy enough to discover behind all this bragging the hopelessness and desperation that have seized the rebel leaders. The Confederacy was founded on lies, fabrications, and treason; it is fitting that a lie be its dying breath.

Notes

1. New York, March [1865], *Morgenblatt*, 59:15:356–359.

2. James M. Ashley (1824–1896), a radical Republican from Ohio then in his third term in Congress, had effectively gotten the support of a number of border and northern Democrats for passage of the Thirteenth Amendment.

3. Francis P. Blair (1791–1876), one of the founders of the Republican party and an important political adviser to Lincoln, had engineered the Hampton Roads Peace Conference (February 3, 1865), in which President Lincoln and Secretary of State Seward tried unsuccessfully to reach a peace accord with the South. His sons were Montgomery Blair (see Essay 70, n. 2) and Francis P. Blair (1821–1875), a former congressman and Union general.

75

A Public Celebration—Corruption[1]

***

In New York, the joy over the fall of Charleston expressed itself at first by a general display of the national flag. Public buildings and private houses, the ships in the harbor, and the horses of the streetcars were decorated with the red-white-and-blue, just as they had been in those spring days of 1861 at the beginning of the war that would determine the nation's existence and unity. The official victory celebration, however, was planned for March 4, the day on which the president's inauguration for another four-year term was to take place in Washington. A public parade with much military fanfare is one of the great pleasures New York has to offer. Crowds of rich and poor, young and old are on their feet, waiting for hours with utmost patience in heat and cold and in great discomfort, just to witness such a heavenly spectacle.

As usual, soldiers and firemen were to march in the procession, but this time craftsmen, factory owners, and other representatives of industry had also been asked to join in the parade and show their products. But on the designated day it rained so relentlessly that the celebration was postponed until March 6, a cool but sunny spring day without wind, perfect for the occasion. Thousands of flags flying on roofs and balconies against a dark blue sky were a pretty sight. The grand procession, although several miles long, looked rather childish and meager; as usual on such occasions, there was a lack of good organization and tasteful arrangement to achieve an imposing impression with the available means. Horses, wagons, and people often did not keep up with each other; the horses shied at the cannons that were positioned here and there and kept banging merrily away, considerably embarrassing the riders. The spaces between the various sections were often so large that you often wondered whether more was to come.

But all these faults were nothing compared to the happy and joyous mood of the hundreds of thousands who crowded streets and windows. What inspired the masses was the consciousness that this was truly a national holiday, not just for the celebration of individual victories but for the preservation of unity, freedom, and the nation's future; it shed a glowing light like sunshine over the entire day and all its events. The wounded soldiers, whose carts made up one section of the parade, were greeted with the warmest applause. The navy was represented by a ship's model that, together with its crew, was drawn on wheels; it was followed by a rowboat seemingly propelled by rowing sailors, much to the delight of the big and small children among the spectators.

Many of the representatives of commerce, industry, and the crafts seemed to take this celebration merely as an occasion for a rather tasteless display and exhibition of their goods, although there were some attempts at jokes, puns, and allusions. One manufacturer of steel pens had written on his cart: "Any pen, but a slave pen!"—a pun that cannot be translated because in English a "pen" for writing is the same word as a "pen" for imprisoning slaves. Cannons and cannonballs were presented as "the best peace makers." An iron money box ("safe") carried the punning inscription: "The Union's safe." The manufacturer of a beauty potion used the names of cities that had been reclaimed—Wilmington, Charleston, Savannah, etc.—to advertise the "restoration of the lost bloom of youth."

One of the largest and grandest sections consisted of firemen, who—like the national militia in this country—are not a group of paid professionals but volunteers. With their brand-new, fire-red shirts and shining steam engines, ladders, and hoses, they stirred up much excitement at first; but because one company looked like another and all the engines were the same, the length and monotony of this section soon tired the spectators; only the animals that some of the companies strangely enough had tied to their engines provided a little variety. Looking down at the hubbub with more puzzlement than delight, a bear cub stood on one of the engines; three racoons had made themselves comfortable on another, and a badger on a third. Van Amburgh's menagerie provided the two elephants and camels near the end,[2] and Barnum, the great national humbug, showed his patriotism with a cart full of stuffed animals that brought up the rear. The obligatory mass rallies, speeches, and fireworks in Union Square concluded the day's festivities.

After four years of fighting, the complete victory of the national cause, the restoration of the Union, the abolition of slavery, and the subjection of the Confederacy can finally be regarded as moral certainties. Looking back over that four-year history, one can only be amazed at the incredible good luck that attended the people and its leaders along the way, especially considering all the mistakes, fraud, and bad intentions that accompanied the process leading to these great results. The long equivocations of the president and the people, their reluctance to comprehend the demands of the times, which called for arming the Negroes and abolishing slavery; the terrible defeats brought about by treasonous or incompetent generals like McClellan, Buell, or Fitz John Porter[3]—all these are shameful memories and facts known to the world and a part of history. But, in addition to these, there are almost daily revelations of the most unbelievable incidents of fraud, bribery, and all manner of vileness practiced at the country's expense by high and low government officials, speculators, merchants, and such ilk—and there seems to be no end to them.

In violation of the laws of a reasonable policy, widespread trade with the rebels is one of the worst evils. The rebel states have horded large stores of cotton and tobacco, which constitute the chief wealth and major resource of the Confederacy. Shipped to England by the "blockade-runners," these goods provide them with European money, which is the only element capable of holding together the whole rotten structure for a short while. However, since the most recent successes of the Union forces, which succeeded in cutting the rebels' access to the sea, this wealth has become a burden and an embarrassment. They cannot ship it abroad and, at the approach of the Union troops, are forced to the burn their stores to keep them from falling into enemy hands. No wonder, then, that they deem themselves fortunate when they realize that the hated Yankees are so greedy and unconscionable as to help them out of their predicament by buying their valuable treasure. Some time ago, this was done secretly and only on occasion here and there, but it has now taken on enormous dimensions under the very eyes of the government, which often conveniently winks at what it doesn't want to see. When it comes to mutual profit, not one in a thousand Americans has enough hatred or virtue to pass the trial by fire.

***

Notes

1. New York, March [1865], *Morgenblatt*, 59:18:425–428.

2. For Isaac Van Amburgh, see Essay 65, n. 4.

3. Assing frequently expressed her disdain for McClellan and Buell; Fitz-John Porter (1822–1901), another Union general, had distinguished himself in McClellan's Peninsular Campaign in 1862 but was later court-martialed for disobedience in the second battle of Bull Run.

76

Thrills of Victory and Depth of Mourning[1]

Enormous events have come and gone in such rapid succession over the past few weeks that one looks back over them with amazement at how much has been compressed into a short time: glorious victories, the destruction of slavery, the end of a four-year war, the restoration of the nation's unity, and the joy over all these accomplishments. But a pall of mourning and shock fell over them—like the red-white-and-blue flag draped with black ribbons.

When Charleston fell, when thousands of flags were unfurled, when the cities of the North resounded with the hiss of fireworks and the jubilant thunder of cannons, it seemed that we were witnessing the loudest and most enthusiastic expressions of joy of which the American people—usually so calm and often criticized for being so cold—are capable. But all of this paled compared to the boundless jubilation, the wild and passionate expressions of joy, that followed the news of the occupation of Richmond and Petersburg, signaling the complete collapse of the rebellion. Although the great event had been expected, the news came as a momentary surprise for most, raising the pitch and level of the excitement. On Wall Street, the great center of business, the telegraphic dispatch announcing the fall of Richmond and Petersburg caused a remarkable scene that will always remain with those who witnessed it. Cool and seasoned businessmen hugged each other, tossed their hats in the air, and shouted "Hurrah!" and "the Union forever!" at the top of their lungs. As if on command, all businesses closed to celebrate the great event with a general holiday, and thousands of people rushed to a mass meeting that had been organized with such fabulous speed that it seemed to occur by spontaneous inspiration. Accomplished speakers, officers, businessmen, and government officials instantly arrived, addressing the masses impromptu and with great effect. But the most moving moment came when all these thousands bared their heads to sing the national anthem—a scene I will never forget.

But even more tumultuous and ecstatic was the reception of the Union forces a few hours earlier, as they marched into Richmond and Petersburg, making more than ten thousand colored people free and independent human beings who needed to pour out their happiness in every conceivable manner. They hugged the soldiers, danced around them, sang, jumped, shouted, laughed and wept all at once; and the following day, when the president appeared and, like the true representative of a great republic, walked from the steamboat pier through the streets to the former residence of Jefferson Davis accompanied only by a few friends and soldiers, the happy shouting and clamoring seemed to have no bounds. Since the start of the war, "Lincum," as they call him, has been the messiah on whom they based their hopes for liberty and support even long before he issued the Emancipation Proclamation or gave any sign that would justify expectations of his willingness to lay a finger on slavery. At the time when abolitionists had lost almost all faith and hope, when Union generals were still returning fugitive slaves to their masters, the Negroes' faith in him remained unshaken.

Many of the white citizens of Richmond, incidentally, are also heartily tired of Davis's regime of terror and tyranny, the relentless system of conscription, the cessation of commerce and industry, and the hunger and poverty caused by the war. Hence, far from seeing the Union forces as enemies and oppressors, they greeted them as liberators. The majority of prominent traitors and rebels had joined Jefferson Davis as he left the city in which they no longer felt secure; among those who remained were many, of course, who accepted the inevitable with the clenched teeth of suppressed rage.

***

April 20 had been designated to be the day of the grand victory celebration, and New York was to shine in the glow of a general illumination, greater than anything that had ever been seen before. People were busily making preparations when the terrible news arrived: the president had been killed at the theater on April 14 and Secretary of State Seward had been shot. In an instant, all expressions of joy turned into shrieks of pain, and the whole country fell into deep mourning. Every murder evokes horror and disgust, but these feelings become a thousandfold stronger when the atrocity is aimed at the nation as a whole, when the bullet reaches the nation's heart—its first and highest representative, whom it had just reelected as its leader with greater unanimity than before. Lincoln had become a personal friend to all who had voted for him, thereby making the president the representative of their own deep convictions, wishes, and goals. Even if the stalwart and radical abolitionists—the vanguard and the guiding lights in the fight for freedom, justice, and progress—were often displeased with his temporizing and indecisiveness in moving toward these goals, their discontent contained much of the sorrow one feels for errors committed by a friend and ally. Not for a long time has a man's death caused such universal grief. This atrocity was the last deed of the rebel slaveholders, the final agony of slavery's death. Hopelessly moribund, they wanted to strike their opponents one final time, even if it meant their own destruction. There can be no doubt that the president's murder and the plot against Seward are not the work of individuals but the result of an organized conspiracy. It is now evident that Vice President Johnson, General Grant, and all the members of the cabinet were all targeted to die, so as to rid the country of its leaders in one stroke and to set it adrift in a storm like a ship without rudder or mast. Wilkes Booth, the brother of the famous actor Edwin Booth, is the murderer; a third- or fourth-class actor, he grew up in Maryland under the poisonous influence of slavery and, as was revealed in recent days, was an active participant in the arrest and execution of John Brown.

From the moment the South seceded from the Union it has been blindly and constantly moving towards its own destruction; and as secession was in reality the first act of suicide, so the South has sealed its own fate with the present atrocity. The president, as I have said, was lenient and conciliatory to a fault, and it was only a matter of days before a proclamation of general amnesty would have been issued, amnesty for all who would submit to the authority of the Union and take an oath of loyalty. The general population held similar views, which resulted from a certain lack of conscience and firm conviction as well as the inability to rise to the higher level of moral indignation. The rebels almost seemed to become popular, and Lee in particular was praised for capitulating, as if it had been an act of free will rather than an inevitable necessity. Indeed, there were people who went so far as to propose a reception for him if he were to come to New York.

It was as good as settled that the government would proceed with utmost mildness in dealing with the recaptured states and even give the rebel leaders every opportunity to escape, so long as it would be relieved of the irksome task to charge and punish them. On the other hand, there was considerable danger that this excessive and inappropriate leniency toward the enemies of the Union and its government could easily lead to injustice against its true friends, the colored people: that the latter would not be given their full and deserved civil rights—particularly the right to vote—out of undue consideration for the prejudices of the former. All that has now changed. These most recent murders have accomplished what the massacre of troops at Fort Pillow[2] and the starvation of prisoners of war in the South had failed to do. These murders have so clearly exposed the bottomless corruption and evil of the South, they show in such broad daylight what we can expect from "our misguided brethren," that voices in all quarters are calling for severity and justice.

Because of the particular circumstances in which it was carried out, the attempt on Seward's life seems to have been even more despicable and abominable than the murder of the president. Lying helplessly in bed, with severe injuries sustained in an accident in which he broke an arm and his jaw, Seward was wounded together with his two sons and his attendant, who tried to intervene. Besides being brutal and vicious, these murderous deeds reveal the vilest cowardice. All ages have seen honest, misguided fanatics who, for the sake of liberating the world from some real or imagined tyrant, will believe they must become the instrument of his destruction. But at least their courage equaled their deeds. They were willing to give their lives for the service they thought they had rendered mankind, and their followers worshiped them as heroes and martyrs. These murderers, however, seem mostly intent on escape and are no better than assassins.

These events will have consequences. Lincoln's successor, former Vice President Johnson, promises to move against open and secret traitors with the requisite determination and severity. All in all, Lincoln's death cannot diminish the country's condition and prospects. The joy of victory has of course been dampened by mourning, but the fruits of victory remain the same. The Union forces are still on the battlefield ready to overwhelm the remnants of the enemy at the first encounter. Having emerged victoriously from a rebellion and a four-year war, the country's institutions are too strong for a man's death to threaten public security and well-being, no matter how much the people depended on him. Nothing can stand in the way of a great future for the nation as long as it will use its victory in the true republican spirit to confer equal rights on *all* citizens, without regard to race or color....

As much as one mourns Abraham Lincoln's death, it is a comfort to know that he died one of the happiest of men. After four years of battle he had finally achieved the goal of his efforts: the nation was victorious, assured of its unity, on the verge of a happy new era, and he himself at the peak of success and popularity. A longer career would have brought new clouds casting shadows over the glory that had gathered around him; his death even reconciled his opponents and erased his errors; and his name will henceforth shine in the annals of history as that of a martyr to the liberty, greatness, and unity of his people.

Notes

1. New York, April [1865], *Morgenblatt*, 59:22:520–523.

2. When Confederate troops stormed Fort Pillow near Memphis on April 12, 1864, they killed a large number of black soldiers. Charged with ruthlessness, the commander claimed that the soldiers had been killed trying to escape, but the incident became known as an example of southern vindictiveness toward black Union troops.

77

The Trial—A Funeral Procession—Reconstruction[1]

The sorrow and excitement over the assassination of the president have gradually given way to a renewed interest in more recent developments and events. The arrest and execution of the murderer, the discovery and arrest of several conspirators and accessories—who are, like him, the mere instruments of the real leaders of the plot—have done much to alleviate the tension that more or less everyone has been feeling. Their trial has begun, and the public is following it with great attention and curiosity, particularly since the court proceedings have revealed that the government has got to the bottom of the conspiracy and will sooner or later reveal its entire network. In some quarters people have expressed regret that Booth was not captured alive, but these are expressions of a certain barbaric longing for vengeance rather than a desire for justice.

The murderer had no right to continue living on earth; there was no room for him after his deed; and it was a fortunate coincidence rather than a loss that fate removed him without requiring the government to take the repugnant step of executing him. Also, Booth was much too calculating and careful a criminal and he had too much presence of mind to ever confess anything; he was much too proud of his crime (which he considered a patriotic deed) to forego taking full credit for its accomplishment. He would have seen it as a diminishment of his fame to present himself as even the most willing of instruments. A true creature of slavery, he was the representative of a whole class in the South that sprang to life under that poisonous breath, a class that after a few decades will be buried with the past, now that the underlying evil has finally been plucked up by its root.

The people's affection for Abraham Lincoln and their grief over his violent end found genuine and sustained expression during his long funeral procession, which literally covered a thousand miles from Washington via Philadelphia and New York all the way to Springfield, Illinois. As is the custom here, the president's body was embalmed so that it could be transported to his home in the distant West after the funeral service in Washington. But in deference to the people's urgent demand to be part of the final procession and to see his face for the last time, the train stopped for one or two days in all larger cities—Baltimore, Philadelphia, New York, Albany, etc.—where the body was placed on a bier and taken in solemn procession to the railroad station. A large retinue of the president's family, military officers, members of Congress, and delegates from many different states served as an escort for this unparalleled cortege, which lasted for two weeks. It was a march of triumph by the deceased.

Whatever one may think of ornate funerals, this occasion was grand and inspiring because vanity, pomp, and officiousness had no place in it. It was a nation's free expression of genuine homage for its foremost citizen, who had suffered death in service to the people. All of the railroad stations had been decorated with triumphal arches, and government officials, representatives of civic groups, choral ensembles, musical bands, and vast numbers of ordinary citizens attended. The crowd in New York was larger than on any previous occasion, as the body lay publicly in state for twenty-four hours. During this entire time the streets leading to City Hall were crammed with people, each person patiently waiting for hours to take his turn. Even the dark of night brought no relief, and although nearly sixty persons were admitted every minute, many thousands were forced to leave disappointed when the time came to close the coffin. All the houses and many flags were draped with crepe. Many hours before the arrival of the procession, which moved from City Hall up Broadway and Fifth Avenue (New York's most beautiful street) and then west toward the railroad station, every front stoop and every roof were packed with spectators. Carts and carriages of all kinds stood at the corners with seats for rent; every tree carried its living load; every elevated lookout—every mailbox and lamppost—was occupied by people willing to wait for many hours in discomfort. The number of those who followed the coffin is estimated to have been at least 100,000, and as incredible as this number may seem, it is surely not an exaggeration because all government offices, corporations, Free Mason lodges, political and other clubs, universities, schools, academies, faculties, public and charitable organizations, foreign consulates, and many more were represented.

For the first time at such an occasion, delegations of colored people could be seen in the procession, showing a complete reversal in public opinion. It has to be said that in this city, where the Irish dominate the elections, color prejudice is even more pronounced and vicious than elsewhere in the North, so much so that a meanspirited and contemptible city council refused to grant the colored population's request for permission to follow the body of the deliverer of their race. It took a special order from the chief of police to make room for them in the procession. The force of events has changed people's attitudes so much that there was dissatisfaction in all quarters, and when the black delegations appeared at the end of the procession they were greeted with applause, cheers, and waving handkerchiefs. Afterwards, some members of the city council made a few hapless efforts to explain their refusal on tenuous grounds and with feeble excuses, but to no avail.

It is an old truth that war is one of the greatest evils that hinder—or even destroy—the growth and well-being of nations. But it is no less true that the satisfaction and joy permeating a people who have just gained the greatest and most deserved victory in a war over the nation's unity and future totally compensate them for all they have suffered. This is especially true when such a struggle and victory succeed in removing the cause of all evils and the single obstacle on the path to ever higher development. Hope and optimism, vitality and strength, the spirit of enterprise and the industriousness that is so typical of the American people will then flourish everywhere. The prophets of doom who predicted that the wealth of the United States would be destroyed for generations to come are now just as red-faced as those who asserted until recently that the North could never defeat the South.

Everywhere you look, railroads and bridges destroyed during the war are being rebuilt; enterprising Yankees are traveling to the South to buy up abandoned and confiscated plantations; commerce and traffic are starting up again; and thousands of busy hands are working to remove the traces of destruction. True, four years of war have placed a heavy burden of debt on the people, but it takes only a superficial knowledge of the wealth and variety of products in this country to be convinced that there are more than enough funds to pay not only the interest but, in the course of time, also the principal. Also, this debt is different from that of other nations because instead of foreign financiers and speculators exploiting the financial embarrassment of the government for their own profit, the people themselves have furnished the funds for conducting the war. Thus, the nation is in debt only to itself, and repayment is simply a process of moving money from one hand to another; the debt is therefore not a source of weakness for the government but of strength. The high degree of confidence that prevails in this matter is demonstrated by the ease and speed with which the latest bond issue was sold: on a single day, subscriptions amounted to the immense sum of thirty million dollars.

The central issue in the reconstruction of the nation, the issue that will determine a permanent peace in both the North and the South, is again—just as it was before, albeit in different form—the Negro problem. The constitutional amendment, which will certainly be ratified sooner or later, has of course put an end to slavery; the slaves had surely been legally declared free by Lincoln's earlier Emancipation Proclamation; and they in fact received their freedom when the Union forces occupied the slavery states. However, none of these measures have given the colored people the same civil rights that white people enjoy, because color prejudice—this national mark of shame—has so far withheld these rights from the Negro, not only in the slaveholding South but even in the free North. Only in New England, where education and enlightened, civilized thought are most advanced, do Negroes enjoy the right to vote; in all the other states of the North and West they are either completely disenfranchised or their right is limited through special conditions, ownership of real estate, or similar restrictions, whereas in the slavery states they were completely and forever excluded from all civil rights and subjected to a thousand limitations and injustices.

The educated European does not need to be told that humanitarianism and justice demand that the Negroes should immediately be given the same rights that the white population enjoys; anything less makes a mockery of the so-called republican idea of equality. But even without considering this general principle, the enfranchisement of the Negro is such an absolute political necessity that nothing but ill will or incurable stupidity can oppose it. The South is defeated, and the masses of people who had nothing to gain and much to lose from the rebellion, who were seduced by the fabrications of their leaders or forced by conscription, are heartily tired of the war and long to return to their former occupations. The true rebels—that is, the ambitious, the powerful, and the wealthy—on the other hand, have been defeated but not reformed; they submit to the force of circumstances only with gnashing teeth and a heart full of bitterness. Hence, there can be no doubt that, if they were permitted to reestablish their form of government even with the exclusion of slavery, they would again subject the Negroes to a condition only a step above true slavery. They would also continue to be, as they have always been, the opponents of progress and salutary innovation; they would be the enemy of the popularly elected government, resisting it with a thousand abuses and by secretly instigating and fomenting disturbances. The only counterweight against this destructive influence lies with the Negroes. Without exception, they are loyal and patriotic, the most faithful friends and most reliable supporters of the government that gave them their freedom; they always vote for the right party and thus defeat all onslaughts from former slaveholders and rebels.

At the annual meeting of the American Anti-Slavery Society in New York this issue was raised. Some, including William Lloyd Garrison, the founder of the organization, said that the abolition of slavery had fulfilled the purpose of the society, which could therefore now be dissolved. The other side, led by Wendell Phillips, the great and tireless fighter for freedom and human rights, replied that the work of abolitionists has only been half completed as long as prejudice continues to deprive Negroes of their civil rights. This point of view—the only one that is correct—prevailed, and the society will continue to function under the direction of Wendell Phillips, who was elected to replace Garrison as president. Frederick Douglass, the most gifted and prominent representative of the colored race and one of the nation's foremost orators, is now dedicating the full power of his irresistible eloquence to this task; indeed, it seems beyond comprehension that any person who is at all receptive to truth and reason should not see the justice of a demand when it is presented by a man who in his own person, talent, and conduct so brilliantly contradicts all those hateful, hackneyed sophistries and old saws about the "Negro's incompetence" and an "inferior race."

***

Notes

1. New York, May [1865], *Morgenblatt*, 59:27:645–647.

78

Lincoln's Assassins—Jefferson Davis—Emancipation[1]

The trial of the assassin Booth's accomplices is over. Four heads have fallen. A military court sentenced them to die: Payne—or, rather, Powell—who tried to assassinate Seward; Herold, who was with Booth at the time of his arrest; Atzerodt, who was to have killed the president now in office but failed to carry out his assignment; and a woman, Mrs. Surratt, whose house served as the conspirators' meeting place. They were executed together a few days after receiving their sentences. Two others were found guilty, receiving life sentences, and another two were sentenced to long years in prison. The investigation had fully established the guilt of all the accused, and most people believe that it was conducted fairly and objectively and that the sentences were just and lawful; only the friends of the rebels are clamoring about judicial murder, saying that Mrs. Surratt was innocent, Powell insane, and Herold dimwitted.

However, regardless of the repugnance anyone in this century must feel at the use of the death penalty, neither the people's sense of justice nor their longing for vengeance has been satisfied. No matter how criminal these conspirators may have been, they were—as everyone knew and the investigation eventually confirmed—merely the instruments of the rebel leadership. In Canada, Booth himself was in close contact with Sanders, Thompson, and other southern leaders.[2] Not only did they know about and participate in Lincoln's assassination, but they had a hand in the incidents of arson in New York and other big cities as well as in the despicable attempt to introduce yellow fever and smallpox "to exterminate the masses of the North," as the official documents reveal. These facts have been proven to be so incontrovertibly true that the extradition of these men could hardly be denied, if it were requested. So far, Jefferson Davis is the only instigator of these crimes who is in the custody of the government, and the investigation of his case is expected with great anticipation.

The main question is with what crime he should be charged. At first it seemed that he would be accused of high treason, and it would be easy to convict him of that. But the best lawyers and statesmen are now trying to prove that such a step would be a dangerous mistake. They are showing that a rebellion of such magnitude as that of the southern slaveholders lies far outside the limited concept of high treason and has to be regarded as a revolution, which will be judged—as to its legality or illegality—only by its outcome. They stress the importance of drawing a clear line between revolution and high treason, as otherwise some people might call high treason what others regard as a courageous and justified uprising against insufferable tyranny. Charging Jefferson Davis with high treason would be tantamount to an indirect admission that, if Washington or Thomas Jefferson had been apprehended by the British, the British government would have been justified in treating them as traitors. It would also mean that high treason, whatever one may think of it, is merely one of the many smaller offenses in Jefferson Davis's career and that he would still have to be charged with the atrocities he committed, especially since the government has documentary evidence proving his role as an accessory in the assassination plot.

One hopes that this view will prevail and become the basis for the proceedings against Jefferson Davis. Sentencing and executing him as a traitor would, at any rate, be an embarrassment abroad. The friends of the South would try to represent him as a fallen hero and martyr, eliciting sympathy from some who would otherwise repudiate the convicted criminal and instigator of so many horrors. Incidentally, Jefferson Davis is doing everything in his power to destroy the aura that his supporters have tried to give him: while in prison, he is acting with such pettiness, bitterness, and rancor that one cannot even feel the pity normally extended to the vilest of men after he has lost the power to inflict suffering. Although Davis is treated with utmost consideration and forbearance, he—the very man who condemned many thousands to suffer in his cruel prisons, whose horrors have no parallel in the civilized world of this century—vents his foul temper on his guards. He tries their patience in every possible manner, quarrels with them, and curses the food, so that many southerners are now ashamed of the once dignified head and chief representative of a confederation that was founded on slavery.

I have repeatedly expressed the opinion that the abolition of slavery was not a measure arising from the nation's sense of humanity and justice but simply an act necessitated by circumstances; one has to worry, therefore, that the task of emancipation will for the near future remain little more than a fragmentary patchwork. The lack of concern about the future of the freed slaves and the rest of the colored population in the South as well as the general refusal of the masses to grant them their civil rights are dark and ominous clouds on the horizon. The abolition of slavery is, of course, a first step, but the great work of liberation remains incomplete unless further, equally necessary steps follow. All of the southern states have barbaric laws of long standing that put a free colored person completely at the mercy of whites. He is subjected to a thousand oppressive limitations: he cannot sue a white person; he cannot bear witness against him in court unless his testimony is corroborated by a white man; and he is excluded from the right to vote that the Constitution guarantees to every American without reservation, provided he has not forfeited it by committing a crime; and thus he is forever excluded—not only in the South but in the western and middle states—from this mighty bulwark of liberty, which is the strongest warrant against tyranny and oppression of all kinds. Only New England is a noble exception.

In reorganizing the seceded states, the president had the power of the victor to remove all vestiges of barbarism; to establish freedom and equality, which had hitherto been nothing but a lie and a mockery in the slave states; and, for the sake of the nation and himself, to build a mighty party and set a counterweight against the angry slaveholders who had become doubly embittered in defeat. It is difficult to decide whether justice or public benefit demands such a measure more urgently;

and I do not know whether fear of southern hatred and clamor from the Democrats in the North, lamentable blindness, or deep-rooted, ineradicable color prejudice has caused the president to adopt the opposite policy. Instead of discarding to the ash heap of the past not only slavery itself but all institutions that have sprung from slavery, instead of placing the administration of the readmitted states in the hands of experienced, liberal, and patriotic men, he has permitted their citizens to organize themselves by the old laws that were invalidated by the rebellion. He has let them proceed with elections and arrange local conditions according to their own discretion, and he even appointed several of the most venomous and vicious rebels as governors, even though they subjected themselves to the Union only at gun point, gnashing their teeth.

The inevitable consequence of this policy is that rebels and traitors are everywhere elected to important offices and are using them to establish conditions that differ little from those of the days of slavery. Not being permitted to reestablish the actual system of slavery, they exercise revenge by oppressing and abusing the former slaves in all possible ways. Not a day passes on which the papers do not report abominations against the freed slaves throughout the South. Their former masters cheat them of their wages, organize themselves to keep wages down, and even engage in the cruel beatings of the past, so that in the end—when the Negroes abandon their work in anger and despair, and poverty and confusion reign everywhere—they can blame it on the abolition of slavery and start a general hue and cry about the failure of the experiment with free labor and proof that the Negro will work only under the lash. Meanwhile, in all areas that have troops stationed nearby, the military authorities have managed to hold the angry slaveholders in check; every day they have to intervene against excessive acts of injustice and violence or put a damper on the arrogance and presumptuousness of the southern knighthood.

A rather amusing exchange of letters between Henry A. Wise, the former governor of Virginia and executioner of John Brown, and General Turner has recently found its way into the papers.[3] A rabid secessionist from the start, who had made a name for himself among the rebels not for his deeds but for demagoguery, loud boasts, and threats, Wise had been released as a prisoner of war on the promise that he would return to his place of residence. However, he was greatly enraged to find his country home in the hands of the government, being used as a school for freed slaves. He immediately wrote Turner an arrogant, imperious letter demanding the removal of the blacks and the return of his property. General Turner replied calmly that, having freely chosen to change residence at the outbreak of the war so as to be of greater service to the rebellion, Wise could no longer consider his former property as his home and should, therefore, remove himself to his more recently chosen abode.

But the assistance of the military authorities is only temporarily effective in one case at a time. An entirely new set of laws is required that will once and forever abolish all restrictions based on race and color; only such legislation can bring about orderly conditions that will benefit all segments of society. But since no step in that direction is to be expected from the president, having declared that he will stay with his present plan of reorganization, all hopes for the future lie with the next Congress that will start its session near the end of the year. It has the power to reorganize the readmitted states and declare all previous measures null and void. Of course, the southerners, with the help of their copperhead allies in the North, will use all their wonted intrigues, lies, and flattery to regain power and influence, and it is astonishing to see with what audacity the defeated rebellion is again raising its head.

The friends of Jefferson Davis recently arranged a meeting to confer about his imminent investigation and the choice of advocates for his defense. Several southerners were in attendance speaking of rebellion and treason as freely and frankly as they had in Richmond during the days of the former Confederacy. They called Booth's execution judicial murder; they tried to justify secession with all sorts of legal sophistries; and they prophesied a future in which the South, adhering to its traditional institutions, would be more independent, respected, and powerful than ever before. This kind of talk proves that the southern knighthood and the northern copperheads have neither learned nor forgotten anything; like the Bourbons of old, they have been utterly blind to the logic of events and the spirit of progress that, in the course of a four-year war, have wrought a total social transformation.

Whatever storms and turmoil may lie ahead and harm the nation's development, there can be no doubt that we are moving towards the great goal of full emancipation, of civil equality of all blacks. Slavery has received its death blow and will never again grow into a dominating power, and civil equality is the logical and inevitable consequence of this initial great step. Despite all opposition, it will sooner or later be the law of the land, for the spirit of the century, of civilization, and of progress sternly demands it, and because it is the precondition for the republic's greatness, stability, and survival. The only question is whether a just and wise policy will guide the people to this great goal, thereby assuring the blessings of an enduring and fortunate peace, or whether such a condition can be achieved only by further battles and turmoil.

***

Notes

1. New York, August [1865], *Morgenblatt*, 59:39:929–932.

2. George N. Sanders (1812–1873) was a Confederate agent in Europe and Canada; although he was probably not connected with Lincoln's assassination, President Johnson offered $25,000 for his arrest. Jacob Thompson (1810–1885) had been a congressman from Mississippi and secretary of the interior under James Buchanan;

as a Confederate commissioner to Canada he had plans to seize Chicago and was charged with plots to burn northern cities.

3. For Assing's earlier comments on Wise, see Essays 41–43 and 55, n. 4. During the period June 1865 through April 1866, John Wesley Turner (1833–1899) was the Union commander of the district of Henrico, which included Richmond, Virginia.

Presidential Policies—Persecution of Negroes—Embittered Southerners[1]

"This land belongs to the white man, and, by God, as long as I am president its government shall be a government of white men!" With these words, President Andrew Johnson recently announced his political program to the world. Explanations are unnecessary, and his words are too much of a piece with his actions and his reorganization of the southern states as to leave any doubt that he is completely serious. He has now dropped the mask of respect for states' rights with which he had hitherto disguised his reconstruction policy by pretending that he wanted to leave the treatment of the Negroes to the laws—that is to say, to the caprice—of each state. He did so although he knew as well as anyone North or South that this would return the former slave holders to power, especially those who had rebelled against the republic because they favored the extension of slavery. It would have empowered them, not literally to reintroduce slavery itself, but to subject, exploit, and treat as social pariahs the entire colored population of the South. With this declaration, the president has voiced his hatred of the Negroes; he has clearly expressed his unwillingness to confer civil equality on the only class of people in the South who from the beginning to the end of the war were loyal to the Union and its rightful government—the colored people, who had taken up arms by the hundreds of thousands to save the unity of the republic and fought with great valor on its behalf.

Meanwhile, black soldiers are everywhere dismissed from service, but the rebellious slaveholders are given the freedom to exercise their former tyranny. The governor of the state of Arkansas, for example, has been allowed to organize the former rebel troops into a state militia, with the argument that it will be used to establish law and order and prevent illegalities and crimes, making it possible for the federal government to reduce its military and lower its expenses. But what in the world can you expect from troops that had originally been recruited for the most nefarious and illegal purpose and have a history of innumerable excesses and cruelties? It is well known that especially in Arkansas the military presence of the United States has for many months been insufficient to prevent disorder and protect the freed slaves from mistreatment by their former masters. Nevertheless, the president intends to withdraw all those forces and to have them replaced by just such troops as have a history of persecuting, torturing, mistreating, and murdering Negroes.

The old embittered spirit of rebellion, reemerging more strongly and audaciously with every day that goes by, proves how the South is in no condition to be left to its own devices. In North Carolina, Negroes are literally hunted down:

the plantation owners have made known their intention to exterminate the colored population if they cannot own them as slaves, and they take pride in shooting them with their own hands. As the Alabama state convention, which just began, refuses to declare the Confederacy's debt null and void, substantial opposition is developing in the South to recognize and pay the national war debt; and the friends of the rebels in the North have the audacity to speak out in favor of assuming the southern debt.

Our excellent fellow countryman Carl Schurz, who is now traveling in the South at the request of the government, has on many occasions experienced the hatred against the North and the new order of things; in a series of letters appearing in a Boston journal he provides most interesting descriptions of the mood and conditions there. Moderate southerners concede their defeat and know that all they can do is accept the new circumstances, but they barely conceal their displeasure and are unable to suppress the remark that they will turn things their way as soon as they are put in charge of their internal affairs. Others, especially younger men, are just as loudmouthed and boastful as in the golden days of the southern knighthood and their quondam Confederacy. They have not been defeated, only overpowered, and they prophesy that war will resume within five years. They curse what they call military dictatorship and "are simply waiting for the Yankees to withdraw" to show us what stuff southerners are made of. They promise to send people of their own kind to Congress and that they will teach us to respect their former rights. They keep a rope ready for this or that Unionist and will take care of the carpetbaggers "as soon as they are rid of the Yankees." They are determined to spare neither tar nor feathers. They take pleasure in persecuting the "nigger" and are going to teach him a lesson about freedom "as soon as they don't have to look at Yankee bayonets under their noses."

With many, this may just be southern braggadocio, but they will revenge themselves whenever they can, and black and white Unionists have good reason to be concerned. The women, however, are the most extreme. Their hatred shows itself everywhere, sometimes loud and crudely, sometimes in the most laughable way. It is quite common to witness the amusing spectacle of women from the first families in southern cities sticking out their tongues at Union officers or ostentatiously leaving the sidewalk and crossing over to the other side of the street just to avoid brushing past one of the hated uniforms. There is great excitement among the women of South Carolina in regard to the "veil question." In the good old days of slavery, black women were not allowed to wear veils, but the new order of things put an end to this silly restriction, so that colored women are now wearing veils as much as they please. In the eyes of the white ladies, however, this is an intolerable affront, and they are in an uproar about it. Some have said they would tear the veil from the face of any colored woman who dares to wear one. Others, fearing the consequences of such violence, have sworn to abjure veils as long as colored women are permitted to have them. In several towns, women who have provided lodgings for Union officers are ousted from good society and are no longer invited to balls or other social occasions.

These are rather petty matters, but every detail contributes to shine more light on the anger and unquenchable desire for revenge that fill the souls of the southern masses; it also suggests what fate awaits the hapless colored people. No doubt, the demoralized and dehumanized people of the South can be controlled only by strictness and severity; all attempts to gain their good will through leniency and concessions are as ridiculous as they are unworthy. The president, nevertheless, extends amnesty to hundreds of the most active and vicious rebels every week, if they take the required loyalty oath, which several respected southern lawyers have declared nonbinding because it is given under duress.

It goes without saying that such an alarming state of affairs causes acute and painful concern among all the right-thinking friends of liberty and justice. They see the dearly gained spoils of war in danger of being taken from them, and they see that the solution to the problem, which under a conscientious and just administration would be easily achieved, is once again removed to an uncertain distance and is likely to become the cause of future eruptions. The best patriots and most outstanding men are rising everywhere demanding in the name of justice, humanity, and the well-being of the nation that colored people should be given their civil rights, especially the right to vote. Even many of those who in their prejudice used to waver and temporize have come to the correct insight as a result of the danger. Civil equality for colored people is now the center around which all true patriots gather, and people are looking eagerly to the next Congress, in which this issue will be hotly debated and possibly resolved, if there is a majority with enough courage and honesty. Meanwhile the atmosphere is heavy and charged and filled with whispers of pain and outrage: Johnson has betrayed us to the South.

Unfortunately this is the truth, but not the whole truth. Half of the blame and half of the treason fall on the shoulders of the unscrupulous party leaders who nominated Johnson as vice president and forced his election by connecting him with Lincoln. Johnson's nomination was no mistake but a carefully conceived machination, a moral and political crime, because his entire career showed nothing deserving the confidence of the party of freedom and progress. Born in Tennessee as the son of poor parents, he was nothing but a tailor and belonged to the "poor white trash," as white working people are called by the slaveholders in the slavery states, where work is considered shameful. They are looked down upon, despised, and treated not much better than slaves by the upper class. Like the poor classes in general, he hated the rich; he hated the slaveholders but not slavery, being glad to see in the Negro an even more despised member of society, against whom he could from time to time vent his bitterness with impunity. His actions reflected his beliefs, because as soon as he had advanced himself by his labor he became a slaveholder himself, hated and persecuted the abolitionists, and regularly voted in Congress for the most vicious and unworthy measures with which the ruling party of slavery at that time tried to secure its institution for all eternity.

At the beginning of the Civil War he was sharp enough to see the foolishness and destructiveness of the secessionist lie, and he came out in support of the Union. But one cannot point to a single deed or a single word that would have given him any claim whatsoever on the heart and the confidence of the people. No political necessity could justify his nomination, as Lincoln's popularity was strong enough in and of itself to win over McClellan, who had already been stripped of all his pretenses, revealing his hollowness. Lincoln's election was assured, no matter who the candidate for vice president, even if he had been the most radical man in the country. The most powerful party really did not have to make any concessions to gain a brilliant victory. But because of this lack of principle and morality (a general characteristic of politicians and their henchmen) and this eagerness to make concessions, to stay on good terms with all parties, to talk out of both sides of the mouth—because of all this, the people may have to suffer new turmoil for years to come.

***

Notes

1. New York, September [1865], *Morgenblatt*, 59:45:1072–1075.

80

Victorious South—Half- and Whole-hearted—Black Literary Institute[1]

"The South Victorious" is the title of the great antislavery orator Wendell Phillips's latest lecture that he recently gave in New York in front of a supportive and admiring audience of several thousand persons. Such a phrase may appear strange after all the victories of the Union forces over the South and after the collapse of the rebellion, and yet it expresses a larger truth. The South is returning to the Union with all its old demands and privileges—except for slavery proper—with its old arrogance and presumptuousness, and President Johnson is opening the way for it. The South has not abandoned the destructive theory of states rights and secession, that dangerous political heresy, and they have found the president to be among its chief supporters. According to it, the individual states, having freely transferred their sovereign rights to the federal government, are just as free to take them back; the right to secede was not—as some would argue—the cause of the rebellion but the pretense with which the southerners and their friends have justified their past actions and will do so again for any future rebellion.

Because the president, given his position, cannot concede the right of secession itself, he has articulated a deplorable theory: because secession is against the law, no state *can* in fact abandon the Union; it cannot, therefore, lose its sovereign rights as a result of treason and rebellion by a majority of its citizens, so that in all internal decisions and affairs—notably the Negro question—each state remains a sovereign entity. From this point of view it is of course possible to justify every repressive measure against the colored people: forcing them to work for set, nominal wages; preventing them from suing whites; disallowing their testimony in court; not permitting them to vote; shutting them out of the schools to enforce their ignorance. In all these matters, the sovereign state is doing nothing more than exercise the right to determine its internal affairs—never mind that as a result a loyal majority, which took up arms and gave its own blood for the survival of the nation, is virtually delivered in chains to the whims of a criminal minority!

It may be an open question whether this theory is based on an erroneous but honestly held conviction, or whether it is perhaps no more than a smokescreen with which the president attempts to hide his betrayal of the Union cause and of the great Union party in the North that elevated him to his position. But one thing is clear: all his policies and actions are aimed at giving as much power as possible to the South. Meanwhile, the process of amnesty continues, not only letting thousands of the most vicious rebels go free but returning to them in many cases confiscated land on which freed slaves have settled with the permission and at the behest of the government. Those who have devoted time and energy to its cultivation are now driven off the land and are left to look out for themselves.

The government is generally treating the rebels with such tender regard and concern as contrasts sharply with the indifference and ruthlessness it displays towards the courageous, patriotic colored people. There is much twaddle about the *rights* of southerners, but it is always the *duties* of the Negroes one hears about; and governors and government officials of all kinds take every opportunity to lecture the Negroes on morality and all the virtues of which their former masters were day in and day out the living opposite examples. Some time ago, the president addressed one of the colored regiments returning from the war. In the course of a long speech he congratulated them on their newly won freedom, but the only reward, the only fruit of it that he was able to mention was "the right to work"! Yet he had a thousand uplifting lessons to teach them, particularly on the importance of morality and the sanctity of marriage.

If it were not for the occasion itself or for the president's general position on the Negro question, one would like to think that his speech about the sanctity of marriage was ironic, because—as the whole world knows—it was not the Negroes but the slaveholders who cruelly violated all family bonds to slake their greed and lust, forcefully separating children and parents, tearing a woman from her husband's arms if she aroused their passion, and even breeding and selling hundreds of thousands of light-skinned girls, mulattoes, and quadroons for vile purposes. In the end, the president left it to time to determine whether the two races could live peacefully together in the same country, or whether it would be necessary for the colored people to find a new homeland—that is to say, whether slaveholders, rebels, and traitors would some day choose to drive the industrious and patriotic Negroes from their own country.

As great as the pain, the disappointment, and the outrage may be among true patriots and all friends of liberty, who see that the precious rewards for victory over the South are snatched from them and deliberately squandered, dissatisfaction and indignation are rarely voiced in public. Anyone who does not have the opportunity to make his own observations and has no other way to gauge the public mood than by reading newspapers and listening to speeches at political gatherings and conventions would get the very erroneous idea that the better part of the nation sees eye to eye with the president. No one in the press exposes his reconstruction policy, and even the *New York Tribune*, the most powerful and influential organ of the Unionist and antislavery party, while continuing to call for civil equality for Negroes and to uncover the injustices and cruelties occurring in the South in the name of the law, does not face up to the fact that the president's policy is the true cause. On the contrary, they heap praise on him, twist his most unambiguous statements, and present him as favoring equality for the Negroes just to spare themselves the unpleasantness of generating opposition against him.

It was just the same at the recent Republican convention in New York that chose the candidates for the upcoming state elections. The delegates—state and national party leaders—mouthed some well-worn cliches against slavery, oppression, and southern arrogance but never said a word in favor of Negro equality. Yet they could not speak loudly enough about their full satisfaction with the government and their unlimited confidence in the president. Even Senator Wilson of Massachusetts, one of the most outstanding leaders of the Republican Unionist party, tries to accommodate himself with the remark that equality for Negroes is not really the central issue at present. And Henry Ward Beecher, brother of the author of *Uncle Tom's Cabin* and generally considered to be the most decided abolitionist and friend of the Negro among this country's ministers, believes that we should try to woo the people of the South with conciliatory steps and do nothing that might upset them, since they have the power to oppress the Negroes completely and to "grind them into the dust," as he says.

Everything is being done to distort the perspective, to confuse the issues, and to conceal the present danger. Only the most resolute and independent of men, the most determined abolitionists, take every opportunity to open the public's eyes to the true condition of things and to point out the abyss to which current policies are leading. Men like Charles Sumner, Wendell Phillips, Frederick Douglass, Gerrit Smith, and Parker Pillsbury[2] have become strong by a life of fighting the prejudices of the masses and therefore have no need to curry favor with either the people or the government. The attention and applause they receive prove that the better part of the nation stands behind them. When Wendell Phillips used the occasion of his lecture, "The South Victorious," to express his opinion that the next Congress should impeach the president, the audience erupted in enthusiastic applause—an important signal in a city like New York that is known for its general moral apathy.

Why, then, this silence from a mighty press that is fully capable of naming presidents and destroying them? Why the silence from men who have worked most of their lives for the abolition of slavery and the rights of the Negro? Cowardly and selfish considerations, the fear of losing power, influence, and lucrative offices, are stronger than all basic principles and stronger than the obligations of gratefulness and justice that these men recognize. The great Republican Unionist party has been in office for five years, and with the sweet habit of governing it has learned the fear of ownership that sees the hobgoblins of riot and ruin in every great change, in every revolution. The leaders fear that, if Negro equality becomes the central issue, color prejudice will cause the broad mass of the people to jump ship and go over to the Democrats, whose hatred of the Negro can always be counted on. They have been particularly afraid of this development since Connecticut followed this plan and it was rejected by a large majority. They also fear that the president might turn away from them and throw himself completely into the arms of the Democrats and the southerners if his own party firmly denounced his reconstruction policy.

So it is better to remain silent, to blame others for injustices, and—as usual—to sacrifice the Negroes. Concessions made in the name of what is known as practical politics but at the expense of principled conscience have already unleashed one civil war; they are the curse that lies on American statesmen and politicians. Lacking clear vision and worthy goals, they try to cobble together irreconcilable differences, and only because there is no immediate clash they persuade themselves and others that the experiment has succeeded—until, to the detriment of the country, a new catastrophe sooner or later proves the hollowness and wretchedness of this theory of pragmatic politics.

***

The colored people of Baltimore have provided their own funds to start a literary institute, which they have named for their most gifted representative, Frederick Douglass. "The Douglass Institute" contains a library, journals, a reading room, and a meeting hall for literary and political lectures. It is the first enterprise of this kind that has been launched *only* by colored people. At its opening ceremony this fall, Frederick Douglass gave the keynote speech. Considering that Maryland has been a free state for only three years and that many obstacles are put in the path of Negroes who aspire to improve their training and education, one must greet such an institution as a most welcome sign of their sense of progress and their commitment to the life of the mind.

Notes

1. New York, November [1865], *Morgenblatt*, 59:50:1200 and 59:51:1220–1222.

2. Parker Pillsbury (1809–1898), an active antislavery advocate from Massachusetts, was known for his fervent and effective oratory, a man "who tears up words like trees by the roots" (J. R. Lowell).

Appendix

Letters to Frederick Douglass, 1870–1879

Of the many hundreds of letters that were exchanged between Frederick Douglass and Ottilie Assing over twenty-eight years (Assing speaks at one point of her "weekly allowance") only those printed in this Appendix have survived. The fire that destroyed Douglass's Rochester house in 1872 burned many of Assing's letters accidentally, but both correspondents later saw to it that their letters would not be left to posterity. All of the letters printed below are in the Frederick Douglass Papers, Library of Congress. They are transcribed here with a minimum of editorial intrusion: Assing's often erratic punctuation has not been corrected, and occasional misspellings that the reader might mistakenly take for typographic errors have been identified by the addition of "[sic]" within the text. Although Assing's command of English was excellent, there are some instances of unidiomatic usage that the reader should not attribute to errors in setting the present text, even though they are not identified by editorial insertions. A very small number of editorial emendations have been added in brackets to make some words and sentences comprehensible. The information provided in the annotations is largely based on Maria Diedrich's biography, *Love Across Color Lines: Ottilie Assing & Frederick Douglass.*

Hoboken April 14. 1870

My dear Friend:

To be sure, one'[s] room does not look as cheerful when entered after a dear guest has left it as it looked when he was in it, and yet there seemed to be left something in it as if it were in the very atmosphere—a little seasoned perhaps with the fragrance of cigars—that made it a better place than it would have been if that guest had not been in it. I feel rather inclined to enter on some details about that matter, but as I know that you would call them incendiary, I shall not say anything more except that I think it was a delightful time, admirably spent, though it ought to have been at least one day longer in order to allow us to see Macbeth together. There being however no prospect of enjoying that pleasure in this season, I went on Tuesday with Mr. Lange and Mrs. Werpup.[1] Booth was splendid in it, equal to any of his other parts. One feature that I appreciate particularly in his performance is the tact and skill with which he knows to bring out all that is yet good and human in Macbeth, so that notwithstanding all his bloody deeds one cannot help feeling interested in him, even attracted, nor is it possible to deny him pity with his sufferings. The effect would have been much greater yet if he had been more ably supported, but the others being altogether quite inferior actors, there was quite a painful contrast and Lady Macbeth was such an abomination that she kept me in constant indignation. Such ugliness, such grimacing and raging, such utter lack of gracefulness can hardly be outdone by any other bad actress, while the only redeeming feature, the real deep love and affection she has for Macbeth, so that indeed the desire to see him great is the chief cause of her fall, this affection did not come to the light at all, or rather was utterly and entirely wanting, so that the whole character became merely a horrible and repulsive caricature. Does not that tragedy show more than any other the terrible power of women? A power that the right of suffrage can neither increase nor diminish. With a good wife by his side—though possibly warranted to kill at forty paces—Macbeth would very soon have overcome the temptation thrown out by those bad women, the witches, and would have lived as a famous and happy man—might even live now-a-days if he had not died, to use the style of the fairy tales, and that is the "moralité" which I attach to it.—To me it appeared very objectionable too to see the witches performed by men. The witch—such has [sic] popular superstition and tradition have handed her down to us, is the very personification of all that can be bad, mean and repulsive in *woman*, not in human nature generally, and therefore cannot be acted by men without damage being done to the conception. Other things that I utterly dislike are first the English custom of turning one's back to the spectators—a real outrage according to German and French stage rules, and the coarse tastelessness of displaying wounds by smearing one's face all over with red paint. It looks bad, but not natural. This is an article which—with some slight alterations might fill its place in a paper, but you know, I am almost an actor myself and imagine besides that the matter interests you somewhat and that you have time for reading. Of course, we should have talked it all over together, if we had seen it in common.

Another matter which certainly will interest you and give you pleasure is: that coming home on Monday I found a letter from Lewis with a money order of 25 dollars and the promise to pay the rest in a month or so. He shows his good intentions anyhow, and does the best he can. I should like to know what figure a Border State will play.[2] A pity that you won't get any direct information about it and that we shall have to go merely by induction, to use a philosophical expression in a very unphilosophical affair.

Good night my Friend and everything good to you! I am now looking forward to Anniversary week[3]; you know I must have something to look forward too [sic].

Yours ever
Ottilia[4]

New York, June 18 1870

My dear Friend:

I find that by taking the train that leaves here at half past ten in the morning I can save several hours of railroad travel, besides having the pleasure of riding in a drawing room car and enjoying the scenery.[5] I shall therefore start as early as *Tuesday* morning and reach Rochester between nine and ten in the evening. I don't wish however to keep anybody in the house awake beyond his usual time, and shall only expect to find the door of the back dining room unlocked, a lamp burning and a piece of bread and a glass of milk below in the dining room, and everything else the following morning. Good bye meanwhile!

Yours ever
Ottilia

Hoboken May 1. 1874.

My dear Friend:

You will believe me when I tell you that all these days I have been reading all the news about the bank with the greatest anxiety.[6] Certainly, there are many reasons for wishing that the institution would stand the shock and prove able to brave the storm, yet I acknowledge that above all others I am influenced by personal motives. I thought it such a pleasant and easy occupation for you, and the difference between the income derived from it and that earned by lecturing, more than balanced by the gain in comfort and health. Your name may yet achieve great things however.

I have come to the conclusion that my new quarters are utterly unfit for me. The close proximity with the inevitable piano is becoming more and more odious, but there is another real evil just as great if not greater. Those good people keep the most miserable table without exception that it ever was my bad luck to share. Not only that the food is of the plainest kind, but everything is utterly spoiled by rascally bad cooking and made more unpalatable by the slovenly manner in which it is served up. Dirty tableclothes [sic], broken dishes, German silver spoons the plating of which has come off, are the ornaments of the table, and it has come so far that instead of looking at meals as a pleasant part of the day, I dread going down and consider it an inevitable evil. Of course, if I have to stay in Hoboken next winter, I shall go back to Mrs. Werpup, who was quite happy when I made the announcement to her last night, and told me that she felt quite lonely without me. So far all will be right, but I am so disgusted with this slovenly concern that I would rather go today than tomorrow and Mrs. Werpup would also like me to come the sooner the better, but the difficulty is to get away without giving offense, and there does not seem to be the slightest idea that I should not be perfectly satisfied. Today I made an attempt and expressed the fear that my close proximity might be rather troublesome to them, but was assured by Mrs. Fehr that such was not the case at all, and I saw but too distinctly that she wants to keep me by all means.[7] Of course, I could not mention the bad food, since this is always the most sensitive point of a housekeeper's heart, and thus see no escape before the end of the month, when I shall escape to Boston and stay there untill [sic] you call me, never to go back save to the fleshpots of Egypt at Mrs. Werpup's. The best part in this starvation comedy however is that the people in Mrs. Fehr's employ, the clerk and porter bless me as if it were, and heartily wish that I should stay, since, as they say, they now get better and more food than ever before! How then must it have been? As after all, these inconveniences are but of secondary importance and the end is certain to come, I can well afford to take a humorous view of the situation, yet I am so impatient that for a moment I formed the adventurous idea of giving out that I was going to Boston in a week and to hide away meanwhile at Mrs. Werpup's. The evident desire to make me comfortable is the great difficulty, otherwise I should be off by next Monday. A kingdom for a good, plausible pretext!

In fact, I ought not to have entertained you so long with these little miseries, but you know, we share great and small things, and besides I think you want to know how I am off.

Snow and cold one day and wind and cold the next, such is the bill of fare in the weather department. When shall we have spring? All good things to you!

Yours ever
Ottilia

Boston July 3. 1876.

My dear Friend:

Thanks for your dear letter! Indeed, it is a sacrifice to write letters when the thermometer is in the nineties, and I can well imagine how oppressive it must be in Washington, since even here, in cool New-England we had yesterday ninety-one degrees, accompanied by intolerable sultriness and swarms of most malignant muskitoes [sic]. Yet I am going to tax you once more just with one line. Please to drop me a note directed [to] 29 10th St. Hoboken, informing me whether and when I may expect you on a visit, in order to enable me to devote those days which you will appoint entirely to you and to fix some other day for the numerous other friends who will doubtless call to bid me farewell.[8] You see, it is in your own interest that I am asking for that little exertion, for I know how you dislike a rush of visitors as is likely to take place.—People here declare my plan for traveling in Europe excellent, almost envy me and predict great enjoyment to me. I think I should look forward to the trip with some expectation if I only could rely that my large-bird would follow me in due time.[9] Without this confidence it is just one degree above going into exile.

You will have noticed that Schurz is attempting to regain favor with the Republicans and has already declared fealty to Gov. Hayes.[10] Well if he can whip in those weakminded Germans who still believe in him, he is welcome to do so, since their votes count just as much as those of the most intelligent, but no impartial person can fail to perceive that he only comes back because he found apostasy not a paying business. He has kept long enough on the fence to find out in which direction the wind blows, and that the Democrats—even if successful, would have no reward for him.

This time I don't wish you as much sunshine as usually, but rather a fine cooling breeze.

Yours ever
Ottilia

Steamship Frisia, Ocean July 25. 1876.

My dear Friend:

Tomorrow morning early we shall reach Plymouth and therefore I send you hearty greeting over the waters. Our journey has been most lucky in every respect.

The 25. we hope to land in Hamburg from where I shall write you at length. I am awkward writing on a rocking table.

Yours ever on land or water
Ottilia

Rome January 5. 1877.

My dear Friend:

Wherever in the world I may be, how many marvels of art or nature I may have all around me, a letter from you is always the most welcome guest that can come to me either from far of [sic] or from the neighborhood, even though the news should not be all of a cheering nature. I can't indeed think it but a real calamity that Nathan[11]—disgraced villain that he is—should again be near you and even be admitted as a member of your family. He will never be anything but a scamp, for he is by no means a man who once yielded to passion or strong temptation, but one absolutely destitute of moral feelings and perceptions, who will not shrink from any crime if he expected to derive any advantage from it. A thousand times rather would I undertake the task to teach a cat or even Border States grammar than to impress him with a sense of truthfulness and honesty. Before long he will get into a new scrape and matters will be worse than before, the family possibly even somewhat larger than now!—Rose too unfortunately shows traces of the long demoralizing contact with him; otherwise she could not have consented to live with him again, for even if she could have forgiven his rascality, his treachery towards her must have opened her eyes. I am much afraid you committed a grave mistake in selling the house to him and thus planting him as if it were, right on your nose. To be sure, I don't know how much either the one or the other property is worth, but you know that notwithstanding his mental inferiority he has always had low cunning enough to cheat you in every money transaction, just because you are of a high, noble disposition, above all littleness and trickery. I beseech you therefore to practice the greatest caution and prudence you are capable of, and thus let this disagreeable topic be dismissed for the present, especially as that which has been done, can not be undone.

As you see, I am in the "eternal city" feasting and revelling in its marvels. It is indeed the most wonderful thing to see the monuments of so many different civilisations side by side, nay in many instances piled on each other—a church built on the foundations of an antique temple, for instance. There are first the glorious remnants of antiquity, then those of the early times of Christianity, of the Middle Age [sic], of the Renaissance, of the decline, and finally we have our own whole variegated modern civilisation with all its bustle, its joys and heart burnings. None of the works of later times—great as they may be—however equal the remnants of antiquity. By the side of those gigantic, collossal [sic] structures, the Coliseum, the palaces of the Emperors and their temples, all the palaces and churches of Papal Rome appear small and almost brittle, and as for the beauty of the ancient statues, it is truly overwhelming. We have seen several beautiful casts together, but excellent as they may be in their way, they convey but a very imperfect idea of the immortal splendor of the originals. Today I was almost overcome with delight when all at once I found myself face to face with the Olympian Jupiter. Of all things those ruins and statues attract me most irresistibly again and again and over them I almost forget the rest of the world, save a few good friends whom to have here and enjoy this magnificent world with me, I should give more than a little. Another inexhaustible source of delight is this beautiful climate and the luxuriant, tropical vegetation. In the gardens and on the promenades you would think yourself in midsummer among all those southern evergreen trees.

As I intend to stay yet a good while here and intended so from the first, I have taken chambers—two pleasant rooms—for the small sum of fourteen dollars a month at the house of a very kind and good woman, the widow of a Colonel, with whom I am on pleasant social terms. I make myself agreeable by teaching one of her daughters German and they all seem to like me, and consequently don't think me the monster as that my sister would have me appear.[12] They even offered to get me an introduction to the Pope, the great object of so many American ladies. Yet, curious as I should have been to see the old gentleman and the whole ceremonial of the Papal court, I declined with many thanks for her good intentions, since with my convictions it would be a piece of untruthfulness towards myself as well as hypocrisy towards him if I should seek him and kneel down to receive his blessing. The more however I have seen of Churches and Catholic worship in all its features. The Italians are very liberal and don't object at all to visitors moving about in their churches and looking at the paintings and monuments even during service. How tired however one grows of all that empty ceremonial, the hypocrisy that is displayed and how one learns to abhor this whole church fabric after looking at the state of ignorance, poverty and general backwardness to which it has reduced the people.

I am rather a little isolated here and of course should like to have some good friend with whom to enjoy in common and exchange thoughts about the impressions received,[13] yet I don't complain and feel comparatively happy since I can again move about freely without having constantly to endure those outbreaks of temper, of great rudeness and all the petty malices, of the kind that only a woman is capable of. Sometimes I think myself that there must be some motive behind that I don't know, but whatever it may be, it doesn't change the matter. I don't deny that this experience has left a shadow and that I can't help thinking it over again and again, but fortunately I have friends enough to compensate me and have besides the satisfaction to know not to have slighted any affection, any heart beating warmly for me and shall as I hope, manage to get away in peace.

Mrs. Werpup had already informed me of your visit and of the great pleasure it has been to her. She writes to me faithfully and tells me of all that is going on in the Hoboken circle among men and animals. I am glad you showed her so much attention as to go over to see her in my absence. She is really so kindhearted as to consider my friends hers also.

I had just moved in my present quarters when I was much surprised by the unexpected visit of a lady whom I had very well known in old times, and who had found my name in the list of arrivals at the hotels. From her I learned one of those stories which seem more novels than reality. I shall tell it to you when we meet again—wherever that may be—and it will interest you, since it has a sweet bearing on the whole shape my life has assumed, and shows on what slight chances our fate may frequently depend.

Now good night and a thousand good wishes for the new year! May it be kind to both of us! Write me soon and don't forget to send me your autograph and if possible those of some other interesting public men.

Hayes' election seems certain, according to the Times, but I doubt that the Democrats will quietly abide by the result.

Yours ever
Ottilia

Rome Feb. 11. 1877.

My dear Friend:

If I could have followed my feelings I should have answered directly your letter of the 3d of January, but since you wrote me that you did not expect to be at home before the 4th of March, I thought you would be more pleased on your return to find a fresh letter rather than a stale one. You can easily imagine the solicitude and apprehension with which I accompany you in mind on your trying and fatiguing winter trip. The extraordinary severity of the season in our always rigorous climate and first and above all the state of your health and the terrible strain on your constitution by constant work and railroad traveling are so many causes of anxiety to me that I shall be happy to learn that the principal work is over and that you are none the worse for it. The improvement of your eyes is certainly a matter of great gratification to me, and the more so as it is something rather unexpected and out of the common way, for it is generally assumed that the inability to read and write without glasses to which most far-seeing people are more or less subject after they are over forty, after it has once made its appearance is something permanent, to be neutralized only by good spectacles well adapted to the eyes. If yours nevertheless show such uncommon elasticity and recuperative power it is I think, proof of an excellent constitution and makes me hope that other troubles will also gradually disappear in the course of time.

As you see, I am still in this wonderful city, enjoying its marvels and its glorious climate. I am now rather familiar with the chief points of interest, for in my first delight I set out with such an indefatigable intensity that I "did" Rome in comparatively a very short time and now have the pleasure to revisit at leisure the main attractions, to impress them on my memory and conclude firm and lasting friendship with them. This whole day again I spent among the ruins of the palaces of the emperors on Mount Palatinus, under evergreen trees. I did not know myself formerly that I should be so enthusiastic about antiquity, but for an old mosaic, a fresk [sic] or a ruin I run frequently many miles, and—you will be glad to learn it, am as indefatigable as ever. Up and down mountains, to the spires and domes of the highest churches, nothing seems too much to me and frequently I find in the evening that I was five or six hours or even more in constant motion. Lately, on an excursion I saw for the first time this season any snow close by. Of course it was on a mountain, and as it was under the warm sun of noon and everywhere surrounded by evergreen trees it did not produce the saddening impression which it always has made on me in our less favored climate.

I have also made some very pleasant acquaintances. Lately I met quite refined Germans on a cemetary [sic] and as we happened to be the only visitors at the time and were looking for the same graves, we naturally got in conversation and finally I discovered that they are intimate old friends of the Koehlers.[14] Thus the living meet among the dead!—It is quite gratifying to me to notice that wherever I go I make friends, and whom I once have won I hold. From all my American friends I receive frequent and hearty letters. Kind Mrs. Werpup and Mrs. Nickert even have visited my green child and Mr. Fehr has had the nice idea of sending me some of his feathers.[15] Recently I had a very fine and interesting letter from Dr. Loewenthal, and inclosed one from Maja and one from my good comrade Willy. Even good little Albert Heyne has written me a letter, probably the first he ever has accomplished in his life.[16] Ludmilla is the only exception. Even her letters are disagreeable and always contain some hit intended to produce an unpleasant feeling. I have pretty strong circumstantial evidence that she is actually hostile to me and is doing her best to poison other people against me. But enough for the present of this unwholesome matter!

We are just now on the height of the carneval [sic]. I was very anxious to see it, but find it simply childish and trifling and it is a riddle to me how steady and sensible people can spend days and nights looking on a spectacle which to them has not even the charm of novelty. There is however one thing which really is a pleasure to contemplate; this is the uniform good behavior of the people, the contentment they evince, the gift to derive great enjoyment from very small sources. All are peaceable, goodnatured and cheerful and on this account it is that I like to mix with the crowd. I shall probably stay here about a fortnight longer and then start for Naples. Now my Friend, how about your own schemes? May I hope yet to see you in spring? If you only let me know exactly the time when you expect to touch this continent, I shall be ready to start and receive you at the landing. Otherwise my traveling schemes for this spring and the first part of summer are almost completed, but I shall reshape them with the greatest pleasure in order to adopt [sic] and accomodate [sic] them to your own. You can form no adequate idea of the enjoyment in store for you if you can once determine to undertake the trip. Impressions so grandiose, truly tending to enlargen [sic] one's mental horizon that they may properly be called experiences of life. I should be delighted of course to have you here. At all events however you can rely that in the latter part of August my name will be in the passenger list of the Hamburg Steamer touching at Havre and bound for New-York.

When you write me, please don't forget to send me your autograph for the young gentleman I mentioned to you. The difficulty is that I can't stand behind you, put it in the envelop [sic] and direct it as I do when near you in order to satisfy other collectors. If also you would send one of Sumner and one of Grant, you would really bestow a great favor and much oblige a young man whom I think to be friendly to me.

Through a new blunder of the bookseller in Hamburg I have not received the Times for the last four weeks and have to rely only on the telegrams. Today I read that the vote of Florida has been awarded to Hayes. I need not tell you that I am looking forward for the decision with the greatest anxiety.

Now my dear Friend fill up the space with all that genuine and warm friendship can think of. Good night to you and pleasant dreams! Half past one o'clock here will make about half past seven in Washington.

Yours ever
Ottilia

It just occurs to me: did you receive my hasty note written on the Ocean and mailed at Plymouth?

Munich July 12. 1877

My dear Friend:

I have your dear and interesting letter of the 25 of June, and after getting it at the Post Office swallowed it in an omnibus. The meeting with your old master naturally was one of the chief points of interest and under the circumstances you met him in, loaded with honor, one of the most prominent men in the country, it must have been quite gratifying to you and rather an act of condescention [sic] on your part than otherwise.[17] If I only for once could see the Eastern shore in your company! Now as we see that you can venture to go there, I dare to hope that I may yet have that pleasure. Your encounter with Schurz too is rather a pleasant affair, if—as I think it quite natural, you like each other's society, why not do so! I do not object either to associate superficially once in a while with people of whose character and fidelity to principle I have not exactly the highest estimate, provided they are interesting company.—As a matter of course I am delighted that the malignant pro-slavery element of Washington has failed in the attempt to oust you from your position,[18] once for the sake of principle and the precedent established for the first time, and further because I want you to keep the office as long as possible on account of its pecuniary advantages, and just as much because I cannot bear the idea of your going on lecturing trips any more to the far West in midwinter. There is nothing surprising in the fact of my being so soon informed of your troubles, since I have had all the time the "Times," our good and faithful ally to keep me posted about affairs at home. Today however I received the last number of the semester and do not want to renew my subscription for the few weeks which

I have yet to stay on this continent. I shall not fail to read Grace Greenwood's letter which doubtless is to be found in this number though I have not yet found time to look for it. It is great comfort to me that you take a hopeful view of the situation. At a distance matters look terrible and I should give up Republicanism not exactly for dead but for paralyzed at least for many years, thanks to Hayes, Schurz and others of the same tendency if it were not for your hopefulness. Every number of the paper records new deeds of crime and violence—Judge Hilton's dastardly attempt against the equal rights of the Jews reveals prejudice of race in a quarter from which I expected it least and I wonder what will be the result. It is an ugly feature in human nature that the lower the stage of development which either a race or an individual has reached, the more it is oppressed, the more it will yearn to oppress some one more humble in its turn. The Jews and the Irish, so long downtrodden in their own country are foremost among the negro haters and the slaves used to vent their superiority on poor defenseless animals.

This has been a very rich day for me, quite aside from the daily revelling in works of art, in which this city is overrich. First I received your letter and all the afternoon I had a call from the wife and the daughter of Feuerbach,[19] who are spending some months of the summer in a country place in the neighborhood and had come to the city for the sake of making my acquaintance. It was a great treat to me, and I also felt quite gratified to think that it is largely owing to our exertions when they now can afford the luxury of going in the country at all. They are two very good, warmhearted and genuine women, intelligent and receptive though a little depressed and kept down by years of care and privation. I made them feel directly quite at home with me and we talked about everything. It is surprising how entirely aside from opinions and principles we agree in taste and sympathies; they are about as great lovers of animals as I am and so too was Feuerbach. Particularly he had a great liking for cats, large and little ones, and they all like myself too, liked to raise and fondle mice, frogs, lizards and all such little usually despised people. They send you a hearty greeting and would be delighted to make your acquaintance. In Nürnberg they are quite isolated and suffer from the lack of friends whose society would give them any gratification.

Did I or not tell you in my last letter that I had seen my old friend who had promised me disclosures about Ludmilla's behavior towards me? I think I have, and won't risk to tell you the same thing over again. If I am mistaken, let me know and I shall tell you.

I regret that I told you to direct next to Paris, because not expecting to be there before the first week of August, it will last a good while before I shall get it and now it is too late to mend or alter the matter. Safe it is at any rate, only that for a while it will lie at anchor. My stay in Hamburg ended as pleasantly as it began and it required a greater resolution to tear me away from new and old friends. Everywhere kindness and attentions too from beginning to end. Mr. Susmann too, who first had been absent and whom I saw only one day before leaving, wants to be kindly remembered to you.

Good night this time! It is long after midnight, about five in the afternoon with you, and your nightowl has yet much to do in order to be ready in time for tomorrow.

Yours ever
Ottilia

Boston Aug. 21. 1878.

My dear Friend:

Your letter, which came this morning, produced a very keen feeling of disappointment and regret among all of us, for your telegram *not* having reached us, I imagined that you had been detained and would yet arrive some day this week. That hope has now vanished to be superseded by unmitigated sorrow, especially since your determination to go home in such hot haste was prompted by the bad condition of your health. So many excursions had been planned and your presence was looked forward to as the great event, the culminating point of the season. I think you hardly realize how devoted the Koehlers are to you, among the hundreds and thousands who profess friendship for you, none are more genuine more free from any selfish motives though they are less noisy in their demonstrations than many others who will occasionally have an axe of their own to grind.— Unfortunately nothing has yet turned up for Mr. Koehler, although he has written to all publishers and other people through whom he could possibly hope to get an opening. The plan of which I wanted to tell you when you were here, without finding a chance however to do so, consisted in the establishment of an Art Journal, of which Mr. Koehler would have become the chief editor. There could not have been an activity more congenial to his tastes and inclinations, but it has come to nought, the publisher whom he addressed on the subject, being afraid of taking the risk in the present unsettled state of business. Today he has made the same proposition to the Harpers, in order not to omit anything, without however expecting a favorable result. His great mistake was not so much his leaving Mr. Prang's business, who really seems to be a thoroughly whimsical and unreliable man, but his running away from New-York, where he had quite a secure and well paying position. It would be but little short of a misfortune if they had to go away from Boston and start life again in another place now, after they have taken root here and the children found their associations.

Mrs. Werpup staid here two days on her way back from Plymouth and greatly enjoyed her visit. She staid in the room at the neighbors' which indeed is as comfortable as any in this house besides being larger and higher. When she left we all felt confident that you would come to occupy it the same evening or the next day at the latest. I regret the more your staying away because I had hoped to persuade you to consult for once Dr. Martin, who has done such excellent service to Mr. Koehler, who is suffering from the same complaint.

I shall start whenever it will be convenient for you. I don't fully understand your apprehensions, if they refer to me I have only to remind you of all which I wrote you months ago and which then you thought quite satisfactory. My *feelings* for you can never change, but if all this, after all, is nothing to *you*, or if *you* anticipate for yourself more pain than pleasure, you know that you may shake me off whenever you please. Border State is my smallest trouble. I think I have shown my diplomatic tact by getting along with her nearly twenty years without any serious trouble. She is amiable compared to Ludmilla.

One thing I yet wanted to remind you of since I know how easy-going you are in such matters: *Are you sufficiently insured?* Love from us all! Write soon again.

Yours ever
Ottilia

Boston Sept. 6. 1878.
My dear Friend:

You know by this time that I was here early enough to receive your last good note directly out of the letter carrier's hands. I have no fear of the "experiment" as far as I am concerned, and the question is only whether and how *you* will stand it?[20] I know exactly my own feelings, but from all which you have told me about yourself and others I have come to the conclusion that in some respects I am so entirely unlike the majority of men that I cannot well consider myself at all a standard by which to measure the feelings and sensations of others. A queer and unfortunate mixture of earthly and unearthly matter!

Last night I made my annual pilgrimage to Mr. Garrison. He seemed quite pleased to see me, had thought that it was about time for me to come and the evening was spent in very interesting and animated conversation. He is strong and fresh and looks nearly as he did twenty-four years ago when I saw him the first time.[21] He seems to like wonderfully to be—as if it were interviewed about the political situation and I was delighted to find that we agreed about every question. He too is of opinion [sic] that Grant is the only man who can save us from a crushing defeat in 1880 unless something quite unexpected should turn up. About Butler whom he too defended yet a year ago, he thinks now as we do and I think, almost all decent Republicans. I feel satisfied now that he never left the Democratic party for the sake of conviction and principle, but simply because as a shrewd trickster that he is, he judged it played out and foresaw that further adherence to it would have been a barrier to his further success in Massachusetts in those days.[22] Strange that Wendell Phillips—honest and truthful as he is, yet indorses the demagogue and his inflation humbug with which he caters to the illusions and vagaries of the ignorant masses.

I was allowed to take possession of the house without any formality because Mr. Fehr himself wished me to do so. He is none the worse for it and I am spared a great deal of delay, vexation and expense, since the sale could not take place but six months after the foreclosure and meanwhile the house would stand half empty in its present neglected and unsightly condition without yielding any interest. Even as it is, matters look ugly enough and I don't expect anything like comfort and quiet until I shall succeed to get rid of this ponderous millstone.[23]

Have you noticed what a cruel monster the orthodox are again making of their god on the occasion of the yellow fever calamity? A wise and kind father who just for his own private pleasure and amusement inflicts such horrible suffering on his children, and yet notwithstanding all his wisdom and justice is so whimsical and open to outside influences that they hope to coax him by prayer! And yet this is evidently what the Episcopal bishops recently assembled in New-York are trying in ordering a prayer for the occasion. Such notions are natural enough for peoples in the infancy of civilization, but in the present state of science and enlightenment! The old prostitute dies hard but doomed she is none the less.

Mary Ann must indeed be capable of a degree of devotion for which I should hardly have given her credit. Her assistance will certainly be of great value, for there is not a speck of hope for poor Libbie, as Frauenstein tells me, and consequently more and more nursing will be needed.[24]

The Koehlers have now all their children at home. The house is crowded but all are cozy and merry. They all send love to you. A rivederci amico mio!

Yours ever
Ottilia

Boston Sept. 14. 1878.

My dear Friend:

I can't help feeling uneasy for not receiving my weekly allowance, since I have no doubt that my last letter which I mailed a week ago, has duly reached you. My apprehensions are chiefly aroused on account of your health, because I know that even under the pressure of business you always find leisure to send me a longer or shorter message. Meanwhile the time for my departure has come near; on Tuesday the 17th. I shall start for a visit of about a week to my old friend in Stamford, so that your next letter will have to be directed: *Care Mrs. Huntingdon. Box 105. Stamford Conn.*[25] After that I shall fly southward with the same feelings of longing as twenty years ago, intense as ever, the old pigtail that hangs behind him,[26] but perfectly reliable as to self-control.—I feel thoroughly sad to leave the Koehlers just as I found them, that is: in the same precarious condition, without any better prospects for something to turn up. I really think that Mr. Koehler in view of his responsibilities and duties toward his family had no moral right to give up an honorable position which yielded him over 4000 dollars a year, because it did not suit his taste, and because Mr. Prang, though thoroughly honorable and respectable is rather a whimsical and selfish man, and consequently at times disagreeable to deal with. The higher a man stands in knowledge and intellect, the harder it is to find proper and congenial occupation for him, while the laborer who can only do the coarsest work, will almost always find it. I am much concerned about it and don't know what is to come of it.

For the last two days I have been deeply engaged in Frothingham's life of Gerrit Smith, a copy of which has been fortunately preserved in the Boston library. I think it gives a very faithful and vivid picture of the man which cannot fail to interest and attract those who did not know him and rejoice those who knew him and will recognize all his characteristic features in it. For those who have taken a more or less active part in the events and movements of those times, known some of the prominent men who appear in it, of course it is the more interesting and thus naturally all the reminiscences of the antislavery movement are particularly attractive to me. Mrs. Miller and Col. Cochrane have acted very unwisely in making so much noise about the book and displaying such a degree of indignation at the mere *supposition* expressed by Frothingham, that Mr. Smith had known more of John Brown's schemes than he thought fit to acknowledge afterwards. That is very different from the Chicago Tribune's assertion that he had feigned insanity. I should think that Mrs. Miller herself must have known a good deal of those schemes.

Kind Providence seems particularly bent just now to convince poor humanity of its benevolence. Yellow fever in its most terrible form, hurricanes, tornadoes, floods, explosions, accidents, devastations everywhere! One actually must dread to take up the paper, lest there may be new calamities recorded.

This afternoon an excursion—the first and last since the one we made together—is to be undertaken and as I am a little in a hurry, I send you my best wishes, hoping that these lines may meet you well and in good spirits.

Yours ever
Ottilia

Hoboken Sept. 26. 1878

My dear Friend:

I just receive your telegram but don't know myself whether I "see fit" or not. You certainly judged my feelings correctly in writing me not to come at once, and first I forgot to thank you for it. I do it now, only that you sent your telegram to the place where it could not but place me in a very uncomfortable position. To have that person opposite me at the table is just as if every mouthful of food were over salted, when she is on the left side it seems peppered, when on the right burned or cooked with bad butter, without mentioning the flavor. Now, since I don't know when she will leave, in order to allow a fair time, unless I receive orders to the contrary from you, I shall start on *Monday* morning, as I hope that at any rate I shall have to be together with her only one day or two at the worst. I shall *probably* take the Limited Express Train, possibly the earlier Train if I can be early enough, but since both arrive within a few minutes [sic] difference, you will not have to wait long at any rate. Many thanks to you for kindly rescuing my trunk. It is real relief. I am invited to spend the afternoon and am in great haste, and a thundershower is coming up too.

Everything good to you and at length au revoir I hope.
Yours ever
Ottilia

Stamford Nov. 18. 1878

My dear Friend:

It is with the old feeling of something like homesickness which I always experienced when leaving you after spending a considerable time with you, that I am thinking of you now. Whatever there may be distressing in the conditions under which we only can meet, yet your company for me has such a charm and afford me a gratification the like of which I never feel elsewhere. Aside from other attractions it is such comfort to be allowed to communicate anything and everything to each other, to confide unconditionally without the least reserve or distrust. I might continue yet much longer in variations on this subject, were it not for the fear that you could accuse [me] of using incendiary language in spite of honest intentions and promises to the contrary.

The difference of climate is quite conspicuous at this stage of the season, not so much perhaps in temperature as in appearance. The trees are entirely stripped of their foliage and the cold wind and rain of the last two days contribute to give a bleak and winterlike appearance to the landscape. In Hoboken everything is about the same as usual. My Maca flew down from his stand the moment I entered my room, rushed at me and could find no end of caresses and demonstrations of delight. Though excellently cared for and caressed by the children, he had been perfectly silent all the time, yet almost from the moment he saw me again as his audience he began to talk as finely and distinctly as ever. I really feel almost like doing wrong in leaving him again after so short a stay. All my other friends too are cordial and hearty as always. I saw the Loewenthals, Kudlichs[27] and Mrs. Werpup, yet the whole place has become disagreeable to me on account of that "varmint" of a house. Miss Fehr's failure to take a house in New-York is owing to the disappointment caused her by a young couple who after having engaged themselves to board with her through the winter, deserted her almost at the last moment. To be sure, she can't risk the experiment without having at least her rent and expenses secured and thus some weeks or months may yet elapse before we shall move over. Dr. Frauenstein however is safe for the first of May, and by that time if not before, the way will be clear. Mr. Fehr is getting deeper and deeper entangled and behaves like a madman. His foolish anger against his successor seems to have completely blinded him and may yet lead to some catastrophe.

As I shall stay at least a week here I shall as a matter of course expect a letter from you, directed here, care Mrs. Huntingdon, Box 105. As the two ladies go to bed with the chickens I hope to do a good deal of letterwriting in my long evenings and to manufacture also an article about the Corcoran Gallery.—I should much rejoice if you would employ your leisure hours in writing the sequel of your autobiography. I have no doubt you could make it a highly attractive book. John Brown, political and abolitionist reminiscences, intercourse with prominent men, such as Lincoln, Sumner, Grant, etc. deliverance from religious bondage and so many other interesting topics you might treat. The long winter evenings are just favorable for such work and I think that writing would strain your eyes much less than reading.

My love to your glorious place and all who walk on it either on two or four legs, to its trees, hills and valleys.[28] I don't dare to inquire after the poor unfortunate piece of humanity since I expect none but sad news. All good things to you!

Yours as much as ever
Ottilia

Hoboken Nov. 28. 1878.

My dear Friend:

You would have received the answer to your dear letter several days earlier if you had not written me that you intended to go to the Eastern shore and to stay away probably most of the week, so I thought better to retain it in my mind than to have it lie in wait for you in the office. I reached here yesterday after a pleasant visit in Stamford. Everything was as comfortable as possible, warm rooms, abundance of books and paper and above all as warmhearted, cordial and amiable hostesses as one can meet anywhere, yet in the long it would be rather too quiet and uniform for my taste. They live entirely isolated without any but the most superficial intercourse with the people in the place and refined, intelligent and excellent as the ladies are, there is but one animal in the world with whom I could live even on a desert island without ever missing other company. Besides I thought with a feeling like homesickness of your place with its glorious view and of the splendid southern sky and vegetation and also of my charming, devoted, affectionate Maca. My old friend too feels the seclusion, the more so as myself excepted she has no friend in this country with whom she can talk of the past and of her relatives and friends in Europe, the living and the dead and just on that account is the more affectionate and rejoices in being together with me. Before leaving I had the gratification to see my detective's work crowned with success, in spite of wrong directions and all the difficulties that one will encounter in dealing with people who can neither read nor write. A letter from the lady with whom the woman in question was staying two years ago, has informed us that she is well and contented and going to remain there for life. I am really proud of my achievements.

I am staying for the present with Miss Fehr and her married sister, comfortable enough although the house is of the narrow wardrobelike kind and seems the more compressed to me after staying so long in your palace and that in Stamford which is built in the same style. I need not tell you that whenever you come you will be welcome and in one respect you will even feel more at home, for Mr. and Mrs. Cronemeyer although not blessed with abundance of intellect, are a great deal more pleasant than Mr. and Mrs. Heyne. If later the arrangement with Miss Fehr and Dr. Frauenstein should not turn out quite satisfactory the least hint on my part would suffice for Mrs. Werpup to urge me to come back to her. She is as cordial as ever and complains of being lonely.

Just after reaching home I received a letter from Mrs. Koehler. Nothing has turned up thus far for Mr. Koehler. He hopes however that Mr. Prang will give him another year such literary work as he has done of late, which—though not sufficient in the long run, keeps them at least above water for the moment. I cannot cease wondering at the utter recklessness with which he gave up an honorable and lucrative position without anything like certainty for the future. It has been a most unlucky step and I doubt whether he will ever again find such lucrative employment.

The most painful excitement prevails here on account of the loss of the Pommeranian. Hardly anything else is spoken of and just here people are particularly excited and distressed because a many year's [sic] resident of Hoboken, a very popular man, Mr. Lücke with his wife and three children are among the missing. It seems they were in the first boat that left the ship and which was lost. He was an intimate friend of Mr. Heyne and the Captain and officers too have many friends here and have always been uncommonly popular among the travelers. This is the second time that acquaintances of mine have thus been lost. The greatest anxiety however I experienced in those days when rumors were afloat about the Tennessee. Dark days they were, yet I can afford now to recall them.

I should think that a book from your pen would always be a success and find readers. We shall yet discuss this matter face to face; for the present I bid you good night.

          Yours ever
          Ottilia
          302. Garden Street.

          Hoboken Dec. 2. 1878
My dear Friend:

With intense interest I followed you on your wanderings to all those places which are so familiar to me through your descriptions that I am under the impression as if I myself had once seen them in childhood. Your feelings I can perfectly interpret; I know what it is to visit such old haunts from my own experience and should have given a great deal to be the pigtail that hangs behind him during this trip as elsewhere. That you should pick up Perry is just like you and natural enough under the circumstances.[29] Among all the leeches that feed on you he is one of the most harmless and least expensive, and since you are wisely going to put him in the little house you will not be greatly troubled by his presence. But how then about the gardener? Shall I answer advertisements and see applicants while the house is occupied at least for the present or do you intend to build another if a suitable man should present himself?

Saturday I received a letter from Ludmilla[30] in which she mentions the suicide of her former husband and also the rumor about her stopping a small annuity. This she declares to be untrue and says that it has been contradicted. So much the better for her, yet there remains the disagreeable fact that he would be living today if he had not resigned his position in the army in order to marry her. To be sure, the world does not lose anything in him, but nevertheless I would not be in her shoes.

Queer people the Osbornes! When they lived in our neighborhood they did not return my call and now, when I ignored them they went such a distance to see me. This shows at least that there is no prejudice of color behind, but some people act most strangely when natural, inborn tact clearly points the way. Mr. Lange recently furnished a striking illustration in this line. When Dr. Kudlich's daughter died he merely sent a card, the coolest manner in which the most distant acquaintances can manifest their sympathy, although the summer before last, when he was engaged to his wife, the two came almost every fortnight to spend Sunday afternoon with the Kudlichs. I have not seen him since the evening when you were here, but yesterday had a very pleasant call from Frauenstein. I told him of your glorious place and he said that he would much like to see you there some time in a favorable season.

No better prospects yet concerning the disagreeable house,[31] and matters are even so far worse that the druggist who occupies just half of it, has not yet paid his rent for November, and if then he could not pay fifty dollars, I don't see how he will raise a hundred now. I don't anticipate to get anything from him and don't judge him a conscientious man, or else he would not have taken the large and elegant upper story, furnished it in fine style and even bought a piano that his wife might thump it and jingle for the edification of mankind. This is too much in the style of Charles and of Mr. Beneck to expect much good. We both acted differently in former days. A most painful disappointment it is to me that under the circumstances I have yet to postpone buying cigars for you. It has always been endless gratification to me to see you smoke and enjoy them and I feel the deprivation most keenly.

On Saturday I called on Mrs. Nickert. The old lady bears the weight of her ninety-four years remarkably well. If only she could have a little more company and be free from care, but Mrs. Nickert's earnings fall shorter every year, and all which I can do for the present is to give them a few articles of clothing. Need everywhere!

Everything good to you!

Yours ever
Ottilia

Hoboken Dec. 10. 1878.

My dear Friend:

Anything in the line of success or praise and acknowledgment you win, very naturally gives me pleasure and consequently I felt gratified in reading the article of the Easton Gazette, although I think that aside from that part which treats exclusively of you the author takes a view by far too sanguine and rosy of the condition of the South and the prospects for the future. True, we are rid of slavery, but that is about all and no likelyhood [sic] of any progress for many years to come. A solid South, the Republican party there virtually dead, the Blacks virtually disfranchised even where they form the majority, ku-kluxed, defrauded, really, without any rights which white men are bound to respect, there is indeed no cause to boast and crow over. Your own position is entirely an exceptional one, owing to your exceptional gifts, to your being a unique specimen of mankind, a y. m. in short, yet we know very well that just on that account you are the more a thorn in the flesh of every good Democrat Yet the article is well intended, friendly to you and that is always to be appreciated.[32]

I anticipated nothing better on the part of the Pitts set and those connected with them. Mrs. Pitts is a crafty plotting woman, not at all better or less unscrupulous than any of the Colman family. I only wish you will not hesitate to take possession of the land which they have bought with your money. Lending is a bad business anyhow and far from making friends and earning thanks those whom you have obliged are but too ready to turn against you the moment they find that you don't mean to make them a present of the amount. The falling off in Mrs. Pitts' visits I should however consider a gain at any rate. There is a distressing lack of genuineness about her, which I imagine even to notice in her face. I should rejoice anyhow to see you keep aloof from anybody and anything at all connected with that infamous Alpha. If you had read it as I have, notwithstanding my disgust, just for the sake of having a right to denounce it, you would agree with me that no good and pure-minded woman can advocate those monstrous doctrines, allow her imagination to run always in that same channel, read all that obscene stuff hidden under religious cant without being shocked unless she is so incurably and irredeemably stupid as to be considered altogether irresponsible.[33]

If it were not for the proximity of the fatal house,[34] I should be quite satisfied with my interim state. To be sure, the house and the street are far inferior to 300 Washington Street, but what a contrast between warm-hearted, kind and cordial Mrs. Cronemeyer and empty, shallow, indolent and selfish Mrs. Heyne. Indeed, I almost wonder how patiently I stood company so entirely uncongenial to me for so many years merely out of friendship for Mrs. Werpup. The children too are quite amiable and never disturb by their presence like young Heynedom. Mr. Fehr is running into debt in New-York and seems doomed to ruin. It is a pity; there are so many truly good and noble qualities in him but so much mixed up with folly, confusion in his ideas and the like that he makes either enemies or is laughed at. I keep yet on good terms with him, although he has ruined me.—Mr. Lange has forfeited his claim to atheistic saintship by consenting to be married by a clergyman. Queer that a sensible man should allow himself to be thus henpecked by such an inferior woman!

I rejoice that your menagery [sic] is so well provided and I thank you in their name. For any kindness done to animals I feel personally thankful. My Maca is the favorite of the children and allows them to play with him. If the poor little piece of humanity should live, it will be chiefly owing to Madame's and Louisa's care.[35]—It is a great thing that you can yet write without spectacles, though I don't know whether you would not benefit your eyes by using them.

Yours ever
Ottilia.

Hoboken Dec. 18. 1878

My dear Friend:

I am glad to learn that notwithstanding the election frauds and outrages in the South, notwithstanding the virtual disfranchisement of the Blacks you are yet capable of taking a hopeful view of the political situation, since thus far I have always found you a trustworthy barometer, quite as reliable—to say the least, as the men in the houses "where the weather is made" which we can see from your hill. Although I cannot entirely share it I find it a comfort that you don't despair of the future. The other day I had a talk with Mr. Wehle, whom—though he is by no means a man of deep intellect, I have thus far found correct in his political anticipations, and consequently felt alarmed to learn that he is by no means confident about our power to carry the next Presidential election, and what outrages and abominations will be perpetrated before that time by a Congress with a Democratic majority in both houses!—Did I tell you that I am again a regular reader of the Tribune and that we are on the very best terms? Is Whitelaw Reed [sic] still the chief editor?[36]

I never thought Charlotte Forten more than one of the half and half ones who may always be made to crawl back to the old sheep pen if brought under retrograde influences.[37] It is on this account that I never can assent to anything short of unconditional, radical unbelief. If you leave the smallest backdoor, nay, a mere rathole open for the old faith you always risk that the whole devil with horns and hoofs, Trinity, hell, salvation and all the other articles of the old gospel shop will again force his way in.

I wish you will remain faithful to your good resolution not to lend money again. When I saw all those little scraps of promissory notes I knew that they were no more than so many pieces of waste paper, Mr. Osgood's of all others since he knew very well that you would not strip him of the old rag carpets, boot jacks and cloth horses which he has pledged as security. As for feeding the other hangers[-]on who claim relationship, I should not object if only I felt certain that you were laying by enough to dispense entirely with lecturing even if your term of officeholding should come to an end with that of the present Administration. Provided you have enough through life, I shall neither worry about the rest since I too feel convinced that all that you have acquired by your labor will be squandered without benefit to anybody.—No improvement concerning the fatal house. The store still vacant and the druggist does not pay his rent. The other day I have had to pay hundred dollars taxes out of my pocket, making an irretrievable loss of 550 dollars since the first of

May. Miss Fehr can have a convenient house in New-York whenever she chooses, and is determined to take it by the first of May at the latest, and even earlier if she finds some other boarders before that time. You are mistaken in supposing that Dr. Frauenstein had any plans about going to Washington this winter. He told me and I wrote you that he might possibly think of such a trip by next spring.

The inclosed pictures are for the two little girls in the place of the pictures that I used to cut for them or to draw on the slate. They are not too much spoiled yet to be amused by such trifles. My Maca sends his best thanks to Mrs. Douglass for the walnuts and is passionately fond of them. He was silent all the time I was absent and has been talking charmingly from the moment I came back. He is convinced that I belong to him exclusively; what do you think of it? My love to my fourlegged good daughter, Rock and Nellie Grant!

Yours ever
Ottilia

Hoboken Dec. 26. 1878

My dear Friend:

Christmas work, fabricating presents that I had to make as well as assisting others in the manufacture of it, have for once delayed my weekly chat with you and I don't feel sorry that there is quiet again, leisure for reading and writing, though everything passed off pleasantly enough. Christmas eve I spent at the Loewenthals, where we had lively and interesting conversation about politics and the world in general and in particular. The Doctor is quite as confident as you are about our ability to carry the next election and has hardly any doubt that Grant will be nominated, for whom he is just as enthusiastic now as he was opposed to him some years ago.—Yesterday I was invited to dine with the Kudlichs and was much reminded of the pleasant day which we spent there together over a year ago and that you enjoyed so much. The young Doctor, of whom you saw but little, is the very type of a handsome and attractive young Teuton and the young girls are crazy after him, while he consequently remains only the cooler and the more unimpressed.

Two days before Bayard Taylor there died in Germany and old friend of mine, Karl Gutzkow,[38] whose acquaintance and intellectual influence on me I shall always count among the most precious treasures which life has vouchsafed me. His life was one of disappointment bitterness and struggle, for although perfectly happy in his marriage and family relations he never found the appreciation, never obtained the success to which he was entitled. As a dramatic poet and novel writer he had no equal among living authors, but since his turn of mind was too profound and ideal for the multitude he never achieved popularity and some of his best productions were but little appreciated while much inferior, superficial stuff was highly praised by the shallow millions. In consequence he became embittered and misanthropical and when I visited him two years ago he was not much more than a ruin—though an imposing one—of his former self. He was the one who asked me about the story of my affections as I then duly related to you and how I circumvented answering by telling him that it was no subject to be treated in presence of the young generation, well knowing that he would not have a chance to repeat his question.

It is terribly cold here, as everywhere, but my room is as sunny and warm as I can wish and my Maca is sitting on my shoulder, caressing me, playing, cleaning his plumage and manifesting in his own demonstrative way that he is one of the happiest birds living. I feel truly thankful to you for your kindness to the cow child. The more you humanize her the more you will be rewarded by her affection and the more attractive qualities you will develop in her. The warm stable is a great benefit for the whole four-legged and two-legged menagery [sic] and Mrs. Cow will manifest her gratitude by a larger supply of milk than she would yield otherwise.

Notwithstanding the cold I travelled uptown the other day to see Mr. Fehr and carry some cake and sweetmeat for his boy, as I correctly thought that he was sitting there like a poor, put-away cat, with nobody to look after him save his creditors with whose attentions he would rather dispense. He took it very kindly and I am glad that I went and still think him an honest, generous though very foolish fellow.

May the stars grant us a tolerable year, since anything better is denied to us. If you think fit, you may present the inclosed card to Madame.

Yours ever
Ottilia

Hoboken Jan. 6. 1879.

My dear Friend:

All these cold days I had been thinking of you and of the inconveniences which the arctic enemy would cause you in your exposed place and even anticipated the accident to the water pipes. We too had them frozen, yet [sic] were thawed before any misfortune had occurred. As a preventive it is recommended to set the water feebly running in the kitchen during the night and to turn it off altogether in the upper story. As there may be yet other polar waves in store within the next two months, you will perhaps have to try the experiment. You need not give yourself any uneasiness about me, for my room is as warm and comfortable as I can ever wish, so warm indeed, that only by looking at the thermometer outside the window and by hearing the wind blow through the stovepipe I am informed of the state of affairs. To be sure, I don't venture much out of the house, only twice since the beginning of the year and then only a few blocks but with abundance of work, reading matter and pleasant company I can patiently wait for a change of temperature.

I think I have told you that Miss Fehr has gone to stay some weeks in New-York with friends, a renowned physician and his wife. A while ago she borrowed my translation of your book of me, in order to read it to those people, and the other day when she came over again she told me that they had been quite fascinated with it, were enthusiastic and had asked anxiously for the sequel and expressed the opinion that you ought to write it by all means.³⁹ So you see that I don't stand alone with my desire about this matter. The John Brown affair in all its details and particulars as you only can write it, your relations with Lincoln, Grant, Sumner and other prominent men, your visits to Baltimore, the Eastern shore and the meeting with your old master and your trip to Dominica would furnish an abundance of of [sic] highly interesting material, and of all things your conversion to free thinking, how through your own courage and strength, with Feuerbach tendering a helping hand to you as if it were, you broke the chains of a second bondage. I think that after once having found an opening everything would come quite easy, superabundance rather than lack of material.

How unlucky you are with your houses on Capitol Hill! How I sympathize with you I need not tell and I worry over it almost as much as over that fatal house of mine, which poisons every moment and is dragging me into irretrievable ruin. Any kind of real estate above the house in which a man may decide to live is an absolute, unmitigated curse. Just today I received a very hearty and amiable letter from Mrs. Kapp,—she and her husband [were] my traveling companions in the South of Italy and old friends of the Koehlers—and she too tells me that the entire crop of a farm which they own in Southern Germany has been destroyed by inundation, so that they too have lost the income of a whole year. It is highly gratifying however how all my traveling acquaintances thus far have remained faithful to me, short and hasty as my whole trip was. The letter is so long, gives such full particulars about all their circumstances and experiences as if written to an old friend of many years standing.

Have I told you that Mr. Koehler is expected any day and is coming for the purpose of looking for "something to turn up"? I much fear that he will meet with no better success than in Boston, since there is still general stagnation and prostration in business and in a subordinate position he will always feel unhappy.

Warmer weather for both of us! The most appropriate wish for this season!

Yours ever
Ottilia

Hoboken Jan. 15. 1879

My dear Friend:

Winter seems to have treated you this year even more roughly in that usually gentle latitude than it has behaved toward us, some degrees higher north. I was quite prepared too to learn some bleak and chilly morning that the water pipes in that fatal house had been burst by the frost but until now I have been spared this mishap at least. Everything else is just as it has been all the time, that is, the druggist is in arrears for two months, without the smallest particle of prospect of any improvement. Thus we are about equally unfortunate in this respect as in others, with the only difference that I don't entertain any sanguine hopes of this worthless pile of wood and stone being ever anything to me but the cause of endless vexation, anxiety and absolute ruin. If I had been foolish enough to buy it out of my own free will, I should really hate myself for my stupidity and give myself a whipping every night as a monk will castigate himself for his sins.

I should have liked very much to see and hear the two Mormon women. I can't help taking them for great frauds, for I don't believe that they possibly can be sincere in their glorification of Mormonism. Whatever may be a man's views and inclinations on the subject—and I readily believe that one does not need to go round with a lantern to find many who would prefer a score of wives to monogamy—the institution goes too diametrically against woman's feelings and instincts as to make it at all credible that any should advocate it in good faith. On this point, the stupid and the intelligent, the refined and the ignorant women are all alike and even where their own judgment has been perverted by Mormon teaching and education, inborn inclination and instinct will supply the place of sound reasoning. Anything may be shared and enjoyed in common save a man's affection! I have frequently been told how visitors to Salt Lake City are struck with the woebegone subdued expression of most of the women.

I am glad of your determination to abstain from any attempt in Nathan's favor, and only wish you may carry it through. You have done ten times your full share to help him along with no result at all. He never will be anything but a lazy scoundrel, bound for the workhouse at best and very likely for a worse place. The sooner he goes out of your way, the better for you and the better too for his children, since the stain on their name is kept the more fresh by his presence. How I wish that Charles' prospects may become realities! How many starts and chances he has had and how differently he might be situated if he had only improved them!

Mr. Koehler has been in New-York for the last week and on Sunday we spent at the Kudlichs another day of the kind you have had a sample of. He looks very well and is seemingly in good spirits but care and anxiety must necessarily lurk behind. I should think it indeed a rare piece of luck if in the present depressed state of business he should find remunerative employment which at the same time would suit his taste. It is really most fortunate that notwithstanding all your losses through bad tenants, vacant houses and reckless children you are kept afloat by your salary. Your appointment has been about the best thing which Hayes has done,[40] yet it [is] not the only good one.

It now turns out that Karl Gutzkow did not die a natural death, but was suffocated by smoke. As he suffered terribly from sleeplessness he used to take large doses of Chloral, and in order not to be interfered with by his family who did not approve of this habit, he had banished his wife from his bedroom and always firmly locked and bolted the door. In that fatal night it seems that he rose too and lighted his lamp to take his usual narcotic, and probably threw the burning match on a sofa which set it to burn, not at a blaze, but slowly, causing a terrible smoke. Several pieces of furniture were thus consumed and early in the morning when the smoke and smell spread alarm he was found dead on the floor, where he probably had fallen on his way to the door. Rather a sad death, yet considering the unfortunate disposition of the man, his feelings of unhappiness and dissatisfaction and his undermined constitution it seems almost a mercy to me that he was spared the sufferings and infirmities which must infallibly have increased with age.

I rejoice to see you as well as most of my friends take a hopeful view as to the result of the election in 1880, though even in that case the "solid South" cannot be prevented from managing their affairs precisely as they have done, by murder and fraud. The State Rights' heresy is the very carricature [sic] of republicanism, but the reverse of its essence. If there were only the right under the Constitution for the Government to send a few regiments south, declare a state of siege and martial law in the most unruly states and have every one convicted of political murder shot within twenty-four hours! A few weeks would be amply sufficient to restore peace and security. How finely Grant would accomplish such a task!

My love to your whole live stock [sic]! Is there no prospect of your coming here in the course of the winter? You will feel more comfortable in this house, as far as the people are concerned, than at the Heynes.

Yours ever
Ottilia

Hoboken Jan. 29, 1879.

My dear Friend:

So you have now a larger number of mouths to feed than ever in your younger days! This is decidedly too much of family bliss and it is indeed a piece of luck that you should be able at all to be equal to the demand. I think however that with so large a family claiming your charity, there ought to be the absolute end of extending it also to neighbors who have no title to show but that of being Republicans, and yet are rewarded with lucrative situations by a republican Administration. Such republicanism is no martyrdom and there is no excuse for using it as if it were as a pump handle to draw on your kindness.—I am truly happy to know Hattie under your protecting wing.[41] Until I learned it from you I always imagined to see her on the farm neglected, neither understood nor appreciated and made to serve as a drudge to the smaller children. She needs the tenderness and affection which within your circle are bestowed on her only by yourself.

I am confident that the conversation with Hamilton Fish, filling several columns of the Tribune has received due attention from you. It is a significant document and unmistakably shows the direction of the wind. The reminiscences of Henry Clay, Marcy etc. are evidently but the pretext for such a eulogy on Grant as is very natural coming from a friend like Mr. Fish, but quite a surprise to meet in the columns of the Tribune, heretofore as bitter and inveterate an enemy as any democratic paper. Conklin [sic] too has been treated respectfully since his triumphant reelection and since he now controls the vote of New-York the Tribune is evidently ready to throw it for Grant if he chooses to carry the state for him.[42] These are encouraging signs indeed!—How will the probable rejection of Mr. Merrit affect Charles' chances for employment?[43] It is time he should find means of support dependent or independent of political patronage.

Yesterday I have made the acquaintance of a highly attractive woman, well known in literary and artistic circles, who once was the cause of a duel in which a former lover of hers was killed, is now at her third husband, and although no longer young still turns the heads of old and young men. She is a German, as much of an atheist and lover of animals as myself and you can imagine that we made friends at once.[44] Mrs. Kudlich too patronizes her although her reputation is a little bit tainted. You know however that such people are frequently the most amiable companions.

No news yet from Mr. Koehler although he has been seen on Broadway by an acquaintance a few days ago. Thus he is yet in search of employment. You are right, there must be some constitutional infirmity, that of taking too seriously the inevitable evils of daily life and rather than putting up with them flying to more serious ones. My affairs are yet in the same cheerless state. The druggist does not pay his rent, is a cheat and liar from head to foot who speculates on the credulity of other people and will be ejected some fine day in the first half of February, but that does not bring me another tenant. I wonder indeed how it is possible that people should buy any real estate except the homestead in which they expect to live and die.

You had only written me that you were laying up ice without mentioning how. I don't understand enough of the matter to have an opinion whether the experiment may turn out well. If so it would be an invaluable convenience.

I am reading a novel the scene of which is laid in ancient Egypt, som [sic] 3000 years before the Christian Era. It is wonderfully attractive. A pity that it is not translated into English; you would enjoy it.

Yours ever
Ottilia

Hoboken Feb. 12. 1879.

My dear Friend:

Who would think that independant [sic] as I am, with nearly eighteen hours out of the twenty-four at my disposal, I should have to wait anxiously for and eagerly to seize the first moment to write a letter, and yet such is the fact. Social life, a few lessons to give, some literary work, reading of books and papers, the making and mending of clothes and my duties to my dear green fowl, who even now is sitting on my shoulder, caressingly pinching my hand and seizing even my pen, that I have to be truly miserly with my time in order to keep up with all demands without getting too much behind with my correspondence, which is more extensive than ever before. I like however to be thus kept busy, especially since I find that the more work I have, the more I can accomplish and the less time there is left for meditating and reflecting about our tragic fate, our hopes and disappointments and the exceptional, unparalleled injustice and cruelty practiced on us by nature itself, the better it is.—I need not tell you that during the last few days I devoted to the reading of the testimony before the Investigating Committee. It is truly refreshing and exhilarating to a sound republican heart and the deepest disgrace to the democratic party that ever has fallen on any party in the persons of its standard bearers. And this exposure at the very moment when they were fishing for Republican frauds! If Tilden had any sense of honor—only as much as a dog usually has in his tail—he would have blown out his brains rather than go on the witness stand and perjure himself without convincing a single cat in the country of his innocence. If only the Party would proclaim its utter indifference to honesty, truth and decency by renominating him in 1880!—Windom's resolution is utterly unsound,[45] as all legislation which discriminates between races and classes, since it is incompatible with republican principles and institutions. Unless Blacks, Chinese and Indians are allowed all the rights and privileges of all other races there will be antagonisms to liberty and equality which sooner or later must result in fatal conflict.

You can hardly wish more heartily that Charles may at length become selfsupporting than I wish it for your sake. To be sure, it will only be for a while since such appointments are not given for life and depend largely on politics as well as on personal favor, but at least there will be some temporary relief. You know that frequently, when speaking of the demands and exactions of your children I reminded you of King Lear and told you how the story never would become antiquated and alway[s] be revived by similar cases. Only a few days ago I heard of a very striking instance of the kind. There is an old, estimable lady living in this place, nearly stone deaf, who has three daughters, two of them married, comfortably situated and living in fine houses, the third a widow, whose husband has lost the mother's little fortune in business, and none of them is willing to give her shelter and provide for her! Does this not even outdo King Lear, since there are three Gonerils and Regans without one redeeming Cordelia. "Put money in your purse" Iago says to Rodrigo; "Hold your own purse strings firmly" I say to you.

Much as I like the prospect of moving to New-York, there is one thing which I shall greatly miss: I mean the frequent company of my good comrades, the Loewenthal boys, for although they will come to see me there, it makes a great difference whether there is a distance of four blocks or a river to be crossed and at least half an hours [sic] walk. They usually come one evening in the week to improve their German and English a little, in which they are rather deficient. After correcting their exercises I let them read together and it is a real treat to see them enjoy it, tease each other in a goodnatured way, and laugh and roar about nothing that I first wonder at their hilarity and then catch the contagion myself. Besides this Willy usually spends nearly the whole of Sunday afternoon with me, to the great amusement of his family and of my good landlady and her husband, who delight in seeing his fresh, beaming face at the coffee table. Is it not rather gratifying that those young fellows, with plenty of friends of their own age should resort to me as a companion? As long as we are sought by young people, we may be sure not to have survived to our freshness of mind and feeling[.]

Some terrible stories are told of the "Red Countess" not "Red Lady" as you make it. I shall try to find out whether they are true or not and should be very sorry for it, because in that case one would have to set her down not merely as passionate, emotional and eccentric, but as mean and shameless. Her love story as related by herself is truly thrilling.

All good stars with you!

Yours ever
Ottilia

Hoboken Feb. 17. 1879.

My dear Friend:

This time I answer your rich letter directly, partly because it always gives me pleasure and partly because I want you to help me carry the load of care that is just now troubling me on account of our good friends the Koehlers, although I don't entertain any sanguine hopes that you may be able to accomplish something for them through your influence. The other day I received a letter from Mr. Koehler which made my heart ache. In [a]ll his expectations he has met with disappointment and seems as despondent and low-spirited as he was sanguine and confident when he left Mr. Prang's business. He says that he has altogether given up the hope of finding a position suited to his abilities, but would accept *anything* to keep the wolf from his door. They are living now on money kindly lent by Mr. Lange, so that indeed matters look about as bad as can be. In receiving the letter I went directly to see Dr. Loewenthal in order to hold counsel with him, but all that either of us could advise was to go and speak to Mr. Hallgarten, since he is the only business man among those who count their money by the hundred thousands, with whom we are on familiar terms.[46] Consequently I went, received promises which I have no doubt are sincere, in case "something should turn up" but was told the familiar story that it would be very difficult to find an opening. In his own office it is already overcrowded, two clerks who are superfluous since there is an end to gold speculations, whom he retains only out of kindness and who would do him a favor if they would leave out of their own impulse.—Now, do you think that it would be possible for Mr. Koehler to find employment in some one of the departments? You know, he is more than up to anything that might be required and as it is I think he would jump at anything of the kind at a salary of 1000 or 1500 Dollars. To be sure, all those positions are precarious and there is never any security for the next month, but they are good places for watching until there is an opening for something better, the islands, provided with water and bananas where the wrecked mariner can wait for the passing ship to take him ultimately into port. Since Mr. Koehler himself wants me to ask you to think of him, I have felt bound to lay the case before you at full length. If only a favorable result could be hoped!

You had written me your opinion about the Windom resolution and I only stated my perfect assent. I shall certainly look for the interview in the Tribune. Much worse than that resolution and an unmitigated disgrace to the Republican party is the fact that Republicans are taking an anti-Chinese position and that the infamous bill prohibiting Chinese immigration has been passed through Republican votes and that as prominent a man as Blaine should soil his record by advocating it. It is the very antagonism of republican principles, slapping right in the face the past of the nation, ignoring on purpose the causes that contributed to its greatness and displaying an absence of consistency which in his case—since it is not the consequence of prejudice and narrow notions—can be owing only to lack of principle and honesty. He fully deserved the rebuke administered to him by the Southerner.

Hoping [sic] cough is a horrible guest, and if the genuine article, certain to make a very long stay, I pity those afflicted with it and those who have to take care of them nearly as much.—How dreadful that plague in Russia and at the same time how significant! Nothing good has ever come to Europe from Russia, and now it is even the very worst of all diseases, one which was thought to be almost extinguished with which thanks to Russia! the civilized world is threatened once more.—Mrs. Werpup shall learn that you kindly remember her.

Yours ever
Ottilia

Hoboken Feb. 24. 1879.

My dear Friend:

Thanks for your prompt answer! It is exactly what I expected, from the outset I had no hope and wrote you only in order not to leave undone anything that might possibly lead to a favorable result. I hardly think that under the circumstances Mr. Koehler will make an application—a very disagreeable step at the best—and I would hardly advise him to do so with so slight a chance of success. Since I wrote you on his behalf, I got another letter from him, informing me that he would be in New-York again one of these days, probably for the object of making another attempt to obtain employment. He says that his prospects are getting every day "beautifully less." It is most distressing and none of his numerous friends—notwithstanding the best intentions is able of doing anything more than sympathize heartily, do some fruitless steps and wish for a piece of good luck.

Miss Fehr has at length taken the house in fifteenth Street. It is situated nearly opposite Dr. Frauenstein's present residence, right between the eig[h]th and ninth Avenues horse car line, the West side elevated Railroad and a Cross Town horse car which passes from Union Square to Christopher Street Ferry. Frauenstein is ready to move in about the middle of April and I shall therefore leave Hoboken at the same time. Everything thus far looks as pleasant and convenient as possible and my only fear is that Miss Fehr may be too sanguine in her expectations and entertain illusions which must result in disappointment in regard to financial success. I have not yet seen great results from such enterprises but wish for her sake as well as my own that things may go smoothly.

This seems to be an endless winter. Snow, cold and piercing winds day after day and if it is so cheerless, chilly and bleak in the city, how much more so it must be on your hill! The true "Bleakhouse." Today I ventured out the first time for more than a week to have a good chat with Mrs. Kudlich. It amuses me greatly to hear her pass Hoboken society in review; a little bit of gossip and malice is a good seasoning of conversation. During the very cold days I staid indoors very busy alternating between literary work and dressmaking as nearly all of this winter. When I have just dispatched a long article for the Art Journal, there will always be some article of clothing that needs rejuvenating and by the time that is accomplished, the material for another article has accumulated and the same round is gone through again. I propose to write a little biography of our gifted and humorous ally Th. Nast for the Art Journal. As a matter of course I shall duly describe and explain all those incomparable carricatures [sic] of Andrew Johnson swinging round the circle and of Greeley while a candidate. It is a subject into which I shall go with a true vim.

The attempt of the Democrats to repeal the Election Laws is one of the outrages most characteristic of the party. We all know and indeed the whole nation must know by this time that the Democracy won't stop at any outrage, be it murder, fraud or bribery, provided it leads to success, yet that public men in open Congress should as much as openly admit that they don't want any honest election, reveals a degree of impudence and shamelessness never equalled by any other party or individual. They are evidently growing desperate, particularly since the exposure of Tilden and the coparceners.

How about Charles' prospects? Love to all our fourlegged friends!
                Yours ever
                Ottilia

                Hoboken March 19. 1879.
My dear Friend:

As a matter of course your description of the sensible funeral which you gave to the poor little piece of humanity has been highly gratifying to me,[47] although in fact I did not expect anything less of my dear, enlightened boy. It never occurred to me that you might feel tempted to make humiliating concessions to superstition and prejudice; I felt perfectly sure of you and have been right in my anticipations as almost always. You will remember how frequently I told you in former years that even in respect to worldly success—entirely aside from the gratifying consciousness of intellectual and moral independence—you would make your career just as well outside as inside of the Church, no matter whether denounced or blessed by the pious and now you are the "bloated officeholder" appointed even by a praying President and the more honored for your moral courage by all sensible, enlightened people.

It is a great grief and serious source of care to me that your financial affairs should nevertheless be in so unsatisfactory and precarious a condition. I had hoped that these four years in office would be amply sufficient to secure to you a modest independence and freedom from financial cares for the remainder of your life and I still think that you might have accomplished it if it were not for all the hangers-on and parasites who abuse [you] of your kindness either on the plea of relationship or on that of being allies in opinions. No opening yet for Charles I suppose? How much longer does he expect to be supported in idleness?

No, you really wrong me in supposing that I underestimate the ailments of others and yours in particular. It is just the reverse, for since I consider physical suffering the greatest, most absolute and unconditional evil for which there is no compensation whatsoever, I feel deeper pity with those afflicted in that line than with any others. When after waiting most anxiously I received your note in which you informed me that though yet suffering from a cold, you expected to be all right again within a few days I rejoiced of course to learn that it was nothing worse. If then you yourself underestimated your ailment, I am heartily sorry for it, yet could not anticipate it.

You give expression to a thought which I have entertained for some time without uttering it thus far: yes, war would be the best thing to save us from another edition of the bad old times! In my opinion it would also be the only means for preventing the final dissolution of the Union, since I don't see any possibility of a solid North and solid South of living together peaceably in the long-run under the conditions now existing for which redress can only be had through another war. I am truly delighted to see you take such a hopeful view of the political outlook, for I trust your judgment and need it to brace me up, since I feel almost despondent in view of a Congress Democratic in both branches with vast powers for mischief.

A note from Mr. Koehler to Dr. Kudlich announces his arrival toward the end of the week. He adds that there is now a prospect for the realization of his favorite plans. That would be a great thing, too good indeed to conceive great hopes, since in the case of failure the disappointment too would be the more bitter.

I shall have a severe strain on my time. The other day Willy Loewenthal came to me and told me that he was going to leave the public school, that there was no discipline, that he had no respect for his teachers and consequently wasted his time without learning anything. He therefore asked me to teach him the languages for a while previous to and in preparation for his entering some kind of business. All this winter I have devoted a whole evening of the week to him, but in the future I shall have to give him another, for I cannot well refuse under the circumstances, especially since the dear fellow has an unbounded confidence in my ability as well as in my friendship for him and in that confidence he must not be disappointed. He is indeed like a faithful comrade to me.

Good health and all other good things to you!

Yours ever
Ottilia

Hoboken April 1. 1879.

My dear Friend:

I am now standing as if it were with one foot in New-York and with the other in Hoboken. Miss Fehr has gone, as she intended and carried my baggage over with her and most of the furniture of my room, so that I am now quartered in three nearly empty rooms, with my mammoth trunk which you know, my sewing machine and the bird's stand, yet perfectly comfortable, for besides the most perfect stove which keeps me in summer temperature I have yet a bed, two tables and chairs, a washstand and a little looking glass at my disposal, and that is about all that is truly needed for physical comfort. Most of our costly pieces of furniture after all, are mere objects of luxury, very pleasant to be surrounded by and serving an excellent purpose in promoting taste and sense for fine forms and colors, even assisting in developing artistic dispositions but quite easily to be dispensed with if necessary. I intended to move over the day after tomorrow but on account of the disorder and cheerlessness which prevail yet in the new house and even more of the terrific wind and bitter cold of the last two days I have postponed the final move and enjoy some days longer the company of my excellent iron friend. You may consequently direct me another letter to this place.

I fully share your apprehensions concerning Mr. Koehler's success and I find the same feeling among his other friends too. It is a risky affair since in the case of failure he will have sacrificed time as well as money. He has now gone to Philadelphia and I have mailed him a card yesterday, in which I have informed him that he will be welcome to you and directed him to go to City Hall on his arrival, and in case that he should not find you at the office, to inquire for Lewis or Fred in order to be forwarded to your house.

There is never an end to cares and trouble. The latest in that line is the dangerous illness of poor Mrs. Nickert. Over three weeks she has been sick with what seems to be nervous fever and only a few days ago the disease has taken a favorable turn. I anticipate great misery, since the small income which she derived from the few lessons which she has had to give, is barely sufficient to provide for the absolutely necessary and there is no prospect that she will be able to resume them before the summer vacations. The poor old mother is almost despondent, herself helpless with old age and entirely dependant [sic] on her daughter! All the burden falls on Mary who behaves admirably and notwithstanding her own household and her four little children yet finds time to nurse her mother and grandmother. In such an emergency I feel the strait doubly painfully in which I am placed through Mr. Fehr's unequalled stupidity. Of course, I have given the little that I could afford and hope to be able to give even a little more in a while, yet all that I can do will never amount to more than a slender palliative.

I always rejoice when I know you are planting and setting out fruit trees. It shows that you are making the best of existing circumstances. I hope however that not only posterity but yourself will yet enjoy rich crops of pears and peaches from those striplings. Oh, what a home yours would be if only all the surroundings and conditions could be set right which actually are all wrong and out of joint.

I should certainly not miss a single day in the Oliver trial if I could reach the Court House by passing over the bridge. It must be a treat to see Butler thus in his own element. Of course, that monster of a woman will lose her suit, but will the matter stop there? I think the Grand Jury ought to indict her as a forger and blackmailer. Indeed, the State Prison would be almost too respectable a place for her.[48]

Love to the whole animal company!

Yours ever
Ottilia

Hoboken April 22. 1879.

My dear Friend:

At length warmer weather seems to set in and I think consequently that I may venture to draw my other foot over the large ditch called the North River. Dr. Frauenstein is installed at 359 West 15th Street since last Saturday, and although he and Miss Fehr get along together perfectly well I notice that both—not being much acquainted—think it rather a little dull and are quite anxious that I should join them. If there is no change in the weather to cold I shall therefore move next Saturday and you may accordingly direct your next letter there, as a good inauguration, in place of the bread and salt which superstitious people in the old country use to carry first of all things to a new residence.—You need not trouble yourself about *sending* the seeds. If you only are so kind to *order* them, the Department will send them to us post free.

I am very sorry about your difficulties with Nellie Grant,[49] as much on your account as on her own, since she will hardly be treated as tenderly by any other owner as she has been treated by you. I apprehended some mischief from the first, although I could not tell which, since you got her through Nathan, who will always take even greater advantage of you than of anybody else, because he knows that he can do so with impunity.

The day before yesterday I went to look after the old lady, Mrs. Nickert's mother and found her surprisingly well and cheerful. Mary and her husband have given up their bedroom, the back parlor to her and do all they can to make her comfortable. In fact, she complains but of one thing and that is something for which there is no help in narrow quarters, namely: the noise made by the children.—When I entered I found her holding the four months old baby on her lap; indeed a rare and interesting sight, the extremes of old age and early youth thus together, with nearly a century between them. I really begin to think now—and Mary confirms my opinion—that much of Mrs. Nickert's ill feeling against her son-in-law arose from the religious difference, although she was cunning enough not to tell me so, since she doubtless apprehended that it would prepossess me in his favor. To her it was of course a terrible thing to see her only daughter, the daughter of an orthodox clergyman fall from grace and become an infidel, converted through the influence of a lover, who was frank enough to tell her from the outset that even for love's sake he would never make any religious concessions and consent to go to church. With Mary's permission I searched her mother's writing table and picked out a whole badge [sic] of letters from Ludmilla. They are a real curiosity, overflowing with empty, sentimental gush, yet bristling with malignant hits and falsehoods about me, although none of them equals the one you know, in perfidy and audacity in lying. It is truly disgusting reading, a mixture of molasses for Mrs. Nickert and rat's poison for me. From these letters it is quite evident that during the first years of her and my stay in this country before I knew you Mrs. Nickert, who was not remarkable for perspicacity and acuteness, not only believed all that stuff but really played a little of the informer's part, until adversity befell her and I stretched out a helping hand to her and gave her more assistance than any one else ever has given her, while Ludmilla kept on dealing out molasses.

I think that in principle you are perfectly right in opposing the stampede of the negros [sic],[50] but what shall men do when their lives are in jeopardy? It is one thing to recommend and advise a measure on general grounds and quite another to resort to it as the only means of escape from a violent death. Formerly it was a question of liberty and slavery, now it is one of life and death, and besides, what do those poor, ignorant men know of the political situation, whether it is only temporary or permanent? A man will jump right in the sea to escape from a burning steamer. It is a terrible state of things to which we have come and I yet can look in the future only with feelings far from confident.

Mr. Koehler was more than moderately pleased with his visit at your house. What I said about his criticisms of Washington only refers to the style of architecture of the city, the public buildings and the like, while he knows to enjoy the beauty of your place, notwithstanding the drawbacks of cold weather and a grey sky.

There is no end yet to the loss and vexations on account of that fatal house. The occupant of the third story had to be ejected for non-payment of his rent from the middle of January, and has made such a pig-sty of the dwelling that it will take about seventy dollars to set it in order for the new tenant. I shall never forgive myself for the blunder which I committed in allowing myself to be persuaded to take the house instead of disposing of it directly by auction and investing the little it would have brought in safe bonds instead of feeding it out of my pocket and suffering from want myself. You have not told me whether your houses are rented for the first of May? I fear you will feel them to be a terrible incumbrance. I don't know anybody owning real estate, who after enjoying the curse for a while—although he may have brought [it] on himself voluntarily, would not be glad to part with it if it could be done without loss. Dr. Kudlich, Dr. Loewenthal, Mr. Koehler, Mr. Fehr's brothers-in-law, they all would rejoice if they could get back the money that they invested in that manner. Any number of houses and stores here are yet to let for the first of May, with nearly the certainty of remaining vacant through the year.

All good things to you! So I shall look for a letter on Monday or Tuesday in 359 W. 15th St. New-York.

Yours ever
Ottilia

Notes

1. Mrs. Werpup was Assing's landlady in Hoboken at this time and Johannes D. Lange one of Assing's Hoboken friends.

2. Lewis Henry, the Douglasses' second child, was born in 1840; "Border State" was Assing's term for Anna Murray Douglass.

3. Assing always looked forward to "anniversary week," in May, when various reform organizations, including the American Anti-Slavery Society, would conduct their annual meetings in New York, with Douglass attending.

4. Ottilie Assing signed herself "Ottilia" in letters she wrote in English; in her German correspondence she kept to her given name, "Ottilie."

5. Starting in 1858, when Assing was working with Douglass on her translation of *My Bondage and My Freedom*, she spent three or four months every summer with the Douglasses in Rochester and later in Washington.

6. Early in 1874, Douglass had been chosen to serve as the president of the newly chartered Freedman's Savings and Trust Company; it failed only a few months later.

7. Mrs. Werpup, Assing's former landlady, had retired, and Assing took rooms with Mrs. Linn Fehr, who seems to have been Mrs. Werpup's daughter and the wife of Julius Fehr.

8. Ten days later Assing departed to go on an extended European tour that she had planned for some years.

9. The "large-bird" is, of course, Douglass; Assing had long delayed her European trip in the hope Douglass would accompany her.

10. Carl Schurz, having broken with the radical Republicans and with President Grant, formed the Liberal Republican party, but in 1876 became a supporter of Rutherford B. Hayes.

11. Nathan Sprague was Rosetta Douglass's husband, hence Frederick Douglass's son-in-law.

12. The severe tension and animosity between Ottilie and her sister Ludmilla, dating back to their childhood, marked their encounters during this European trip. Ludmilla had established her residence in Florence some years earlier.

13. Before Assing's departure from the United States, Douglass had suggested that he would join her early in 1877.

14. Sylvester Rosa Koehler and his wife, Amalie, were particularly close friends of Assing in Hoboken; after they moved to Boston, she spent a week or more every summer with them.

15. Emilie Nickert, Assing's cousin, had also emigrated to America in the 1850s; later references indicate that she lived with her daughter (Mary) and mother (Mrs. Reihl). The "green child" was Assing's macaw.

16. Dr. Loewenthal was part of the German-American community in Hoboken; Maja, Willy, and Albert Heyne appear to be children of friends and acquaintances in Hoboken.

17. For the first time since his escape in 1838, Douglass had a meeting with his former master, Thomas Auld, at St. Michaels, in Talbot County, Maryland.

18. Douglass had been appointed Marshal of the District of Columbia in March 1877.

19. Ludwig Feuerbach was the author of *Essence of Christianity*, which Douglass and Assing had read together; Assing claimed that her introducing Douglass to Feuerbach's ideas made him a freethinker and atheist like herself.

20. Maria Diedrich, Assing's biographer, comments that the nature of the "'experiment' . . . is impossible to decipher; it is clear, however, that central to it was the role Assing would play in the new Douglass home [Cedar Hill] during her next visit to Washington."

21. Assing's first meeting with William Lloyd Garrison had been at the American Anti-Slavery Society anniversary meeting in May, 1854.

22. Benjamin Franklin Butler, a former Union general, was then an independent Greenbacker in Congress (1877–1879) and was elected governor of Massachusetts in 1882.

23. Assing had come into possession of a house in Hoboken because Julius Fehr had defaulted on a loan she had given him.

24. Libbie (Mary Elizabeth) was Charles Douglass's wife, hence Frederick Douglass's daughter-in-law; Dr. Gustav Frauenstein was a Hoboken physician.

25. Assing had met Mrs. Huntingdon on her travels in Italy.

26. "Pigtail" is Assing's reference to herself, Douglass's appendage, so to speak.

27. Hermann C. Kudlich had been Assing's pupil; he and his wife, Luise, were among her closest friends in Hoboken.

28. Assing had just returned from a visit to the new Douglass home, Cedar Hill, in the Anacostia hills on the outskirts of Washington.

29. Apparently Douglass had gone to pick up his half-brother, Perry Downs, who came to live in a small house on Douglass's property.

30. Assing's sister, who lived in Italy.

31. See note 23, above. Assing apparently wanted to sell the house but could not find a buyer.

32. On his recent trip to Easton, Maryland, Douglass had given a speech ("The Self-Made Man") in which he advocated a bootstrap approach to dealing with the problems of the freedmen. Assing's reference to "y. m." remains unclear.

33. According to Maria Diedrich's biography of Assing, Hiram Pitts had recently become a neighbor of the Douglasses at Cedar Hill; Pitts's niece, Helen Pitts, was in Washington (where she was involved with the feminist journal *Alpha*), visited her uncle, and met Frederick Douglass in the summer of 1878. Assing refers to her in this letter as "Mrs. Pitts."

34. See notes 23 and 31, above.

35. Anna Douglass and Louisa Sprague were at this time caring for Libbie, Charles Douglass's wife, who died a few months later.

36. Whitelaw Reid became editor and publisher of the *New York Tribune* in 1872 and remained in control of the paper until his son succeeded him in 1905.

37. Charlotte Forten was a black teacher and abolitionist, who wrote about her experiences working with freed slaves in "Life on the Sea Islands," *Atlantic Monthly*, 1864; she married Francis J. Grimké, the pastor of the Fifteenth Street Presbyterian Church in Washington, in December 1878.

38. The radical German writer Karl Gutzkow had been Assing's close friend since her days in Hamburg; she read his novel *Die Ritter vom Geist* on her first transatlantic voyage in 1852.

39. Assing had translated Douglass's second autobiography, *My Bondage and My Freedom*, which appeared in Germany as *Sclaverei und Freiheit* (1860); Douglass was soon to begin writing his third autobiography, *Life and Times of Frederick Douglass (1881)*.

40. See note 18, above.

41. Possibly a reference to Douglass's sister, Harriet Bailey, who had come to live at Cedar Hill.

42. Having served as secretary of state during both Grant administrations, Fish was among the most prominent men pursuing a third term for Grant in 1880. Henry Clay and William L. Marcy had been secretaries of state in previous decades. Roscoe Conkling, a U.S. senator from New York, was also active in the third-term movement for Grant.

43. Possibly a prospective appointee to a position in the Treasury Department, where Charles Douglass occupied a clerkship.

44. The "Red Countess," Helene von Racowitza, had caused a scandal in 1864 when her lover, the German Socialist Ferdinand Lasalle, was killed in a duel with her fiancé.

45. Senator William Windom's resolution of January 16, 1879, was designed to establish a committee to inquire "as to the expediency and practicality of encouraging and promoting . . . the partial migration of colored persons" from states "where they are not allowed to freely and peacefully exercise and enjoy their Constitutional rights as American citizens, into such States as may desire to receive them, and will protect them in said rights, or into such Territory or Territories of the United States as may be provided for their use and occupation. . . ."

46. Assing sometimes wrote her letters on stationery of Hallgarten & Co., Bankers and Brokers, 28 Broad Street, New York, and may have from time to time worked for that company.

47. Libbie, Douglass's daughter-in-law, had recently died.

48. The Oliver trial, in which Mary S. Oliver unsuccessfully sued the prominent politician Simon Cameron for breach of promise of marriage, took place in Washington, March 17–April 1, 1879. Benjamin Franklin Butler was one of the attorneys representing Cameron.

49. Douglass had taken into his already crowded household a needy young woman.

50. Because of the terrible living conditions to which the freed slaves of the South were exposed at this time, a mass exodus of African Americans to the North and the West was underway, a development that Douglass opposed.

Index

Abolitionism (see also American Anti-Slavery Society, Brown, Douglass, Garrison, Phillips, Slavery), 56, 94-95, 97-98, 274-275, 277
   increasing popularity of, 225, 236, 288
   southern fear of, 171
   unionists and disunionists, 158
Academy of Music (NYC), 119
Academy of the Sacred Heart (NYC), 52-53
African Americans
   Assing meets, 8, 15, 19, 41-44, 57, 62
   benefits of freedom, 217-218, 224-225, 237, 262-263
   camp meeting, 41-44
   capture in Wisconsin, 33-34
   characteristics, 58, 61-62
   and citizenship, 125-126
   colonization, 141-142, 237-238, 244-245, 280
   colony in Canada, 99-102
   equal rights, 308, 312-313, 315-317, 319-322, 355
   expectations of development, 59
   free in Maryland, 139
   heroism, 217-218, 241, 269
   lack of education, 57-58
   at Lincoln's funeral procession, 311
   menial employment, 58
   migration to West, 362
   mistreatment in Maryland, 347
   prejudice against, 54-55, 73, 237-238, 245, 263, 269, 277-278, 325
   protest NYC streetcars, 124-125
   as soldiers, 240-241, 269-270, 280-281
   speaking Pennsylvania Dutch, 62
   unequal army pay, 269-270
   violence against, 49, 126
African Colonization Society, 141-142
Alboni, Marietta, 6, 7 n. 2
Albrecht Brethren, 31
Albrecht, Jacob, 32 n. 2
Alpha, 347, 365 n. 33

American Anti-Slavery Society, 35-38, 94-95, 95 n. 3, 123-124, 274-275, 313, 363 n. 3, 364 n. 21
American Medical College (Philadelphia), 126 n. 6
American national characteristics, 60-61, 79, 108
American Tract Society, 123, 152-153
Anderson, Major, 207, 221
Andrews, John, 240
Antioch College, 81
Anti-Semitism, 338
Anzeiger des Westens, 219 n. 3
Arbeiter Union, 297 n. 2
Arcole (Italy), 250, 251 n. 4
Art Journal, 358
Ashley, James M., 298, 302 n. 2
Assing, Ludmilla, 193 n. 3, 334, 336, 338, 340, 346, 362, 364 n. 12
Assing, Rosa Maria, 24 n. 2
Atchison, David Rice, 86-87, 87 n. 5
Atlantis (Effelen's journal), 33
Auld, Thomas, 337, 364 n. 17
Austerlitz (see Slavkov)

Bailey, Harriet, 353, 366 n. 41
Banks, Nathaniel P., 72, 76 n. 2
Barnum, P.T. (see also Barnum's American Museum), 11 n. 4
Barnum's American Museum, 9, 17, 31, 120-122, 218, 262, 304
Beecher, Henry Ward, 150-151, 184, 274, 325
Beethoven, Ludwig van, 120
Bell, John, 190, 198, 201 n. 2
Bennett, James Gordon, 208
Blackwell, Lucy (see Stone, Lucy)
Blackwell, Samuel C., 115 n. 3
Blaine, James G., 357
Blair, Francis P., 300-301, 302 n. 3
Blair, Francis P. (Jr.), 302 n. 3
Blair, Montgomery, 280, 282 n. 2, 302 n. 3
Bloomerism (see women's dress reform)
Booth, Edwin, 307, 329

Booth, John Wilkes, 307-309, 310
   and conspirators (Atzerodt, Herold, Powell, Mrs. Surratt), 314
Börnstein, Heinrich, 217, 219 n. 3
Boston-Journal, 79
Boucicault, Dion
   The Octoroon, 183
Bowers, Mr., 133, 139
Breckenridge, John C., 198, 201 n. 2, 234
Bremer, Fredrika
   Homes of the World, 160, 162 n. 2
Brittan, Professor, 260-261, 264 n. 3
Britten, Emma Hardinge, 264 n. 3
Brooks, James, 267, 268 n. 2
Brooks, Preston S., 79, 83 n. 2, 86, 87 n. 3, 97
Brown, Ann Leah, 264 n. 2
Brown, Antoinette (Rev.), 113-114, 115 n. 3
Brown, John , 163, 170-173, 215, 223 n. 3, 235, 307, 316, 342, 351
   execution and martyrdom, 175-179
   hero in the North, 171
   northern reaction to execution, 177
   raid on Harpers Ferry, 165-169
   trial, 170-171
Brown, John, Jr., 214
Brown, Mary, 176-177
Brownlow, William Gannaway, 130-131, 131 n. 3, 135-136
Buchanan, James, 71, 78, 84, 139, 166, 202 n. 2, 221, 223 n. 3, 234, 317 n. 2
Buell, Don Carlos, 244, 249, 257, 304, 305 n. 3
Burnside, Ambrose E., 253
Butler, Benjamin Franklin, 214, 291, 293 n. 3, 340, 361, 364 n. 22, 367 n. 48
Butt, Bob, 148

Cameron, Simon, 221, 223 n. 3, 367 n. 48
Cass, Lewis, 125
Charleston (S.C.)
   destruction by fire, 225-226
Charlestown (Va.), 165-178
Chase, Salmon P., 72, 221, 223 n. 3
Chapin, Edwin H., 184, 186 n. 2

Chapin's Church (Broadway), 35-36
Cheever, George Barrell, 229, 231 n. 2
ChicagoTribune, 342
Child, Lydia Maria, 171, 173 n. 3
Children's upbringing, 48
Chinese-Americans, 62-63
Chinese immigration, 356-357
Christy, Edwin P., 18 n. 5
Christy's Minstrels (see Minstrelsy)
Church, Frederick Edwin, 185, 186 n. 4
Citizen, 39 n. 2
Civil War
   administration's mismanagement, 253, 304
   arming the slaves, 301-302
   Antietam, 244
   Beaufort Islands, 224-225
   benefits of, 311-312
   blockade runners, 304-305
   Bull Run, 220-221
   Charleston taken, 303
   draft, 248
   draft riots (NYC), 265-268
   early skirmishes, 208, 211
   and England, 224
   Fort Pillow (Tenn.), 308, 309 n. 2
   Fort Sumter, 207, 221, 226, 233
   and German-Americans, 217, 220-221, 230, 232-233
   Gettysburg, 266
   impact on North, 248-249, 257-258, 271
   impact on South, 249, 257-259, 301
   incompetent generals, 252
   northern defeats, 220, 252
   northern indecisiveness, 215-216, 220
   northern superiority, 212-213
   northern victories, 232, 302
   officers' intrigues, 230, 252-253
   peace negotiations, 300-301
   political intrigues, 221
   popular support, 207-209, 210, 211, 220
   preservation of the Union, 277
   profiteering, 231, 276-277
   Richmond occupied, 306
   Savannah captured, 294
   slavery the true issue, 210-214, 215, 234, 236

South's brutality, 216-217, 234-235, 270-271
South's corrupt motives, 212-213, 308
South's lack of heroism, 235
victory celebration (NYC), 303-304, 306-307
Clay, Cassius, 86
Clay, Henry, 353, 366 n. 42
Cochrane, John, 286, 287 n. 2
Colleges and universities, 50-51
Conkling, Roscoe, 353, 366 n. 42
Cook, Bill, 168
Cook, John E., 169 n. 3, 178, 180 n. 2
Cooper, Falathea, 65
Cooper Institute (NYC), 185-186, 292
Cooper, James Fenimore
  The Last of the Mohicans, 9, 21
Cooper, Mr. and Mrs., 64-65
Cooper, Ociola, 65
Cooper, Peter, 185, 186 n. 5
Cooper Union (NYC), 186 n. 5
Coppoc, Barclay, 180 n. 2
Coppoc, Edwin, 178, 180 n. 2
Copeland, John Anthony, 177, 180 n. 2
Corrie, Captain, 155
Cotta, Johann Friedrich, 102 n. 1
Crime (NYC), 97, 117, 223
Croly, David Goodman, 278 n. 2
Cronemeyer, Mr. and Mrs., 344, 347
Crystal Palace (NYC), 79, 89
Cuba, 146
Culver, Erastus Dean, 105, 127, 131 n. 2
Curtis, George
  The Potiphar Papers, 124

Daguerrotype (see photography)
Davis, Jefferson, 209, 212, 217, 223, 223 n. 3, 233-234, 265, 284, 295, 300-301, 306-307, 314-317
Declaration of Independence, 71, 88, 121, 148, 298
Defoe, Daniel
  Robinson Crusoe, 52
Democracy
  distinct from Democratic party, 144
  enjoyment of liberty in, 10
Democrat and Observer (Rochester), 174 n. 8

Democratic party, 71, 103, 105, 106
  attacks on blacks, 125, 265-268
  and Civil War, 207-209, 233
  conspiracy in West, 290, 293 n. 3
  corruption of, 139, 289-290, 354-355, 358
  defeat in 1860, 198-201
  gains in state elections, 249-250
  and John Brown, 168, 172, 177-178
  not democratic, 144
  origin and decline of, 84
  platform of 1864, 283-284
  presidential nomination, 188
  routed in elections, 139, 194, 266
  rowdyism, 195, 200-201
  and slavery, 84, 190, 266, 283-284, 298-299
  and the Union, 204, 284
  victory celebration (NYC), 143
Dimmick, Colonel, 214
Dix, John Adams, 257, 259 n. 2
Doane, George Washington, 247 n. 5
Doane, William Croswell, 246, 247 n. 5
Douai, Alfred
  Land und Leute in der Union, 296-297, 297 n. 2
Douglas, Stephen A., 35, 85, 87, 143-144, 145 n. 2, 188, 190, 191, 198, 201 n. 2, 217
Douglass, Anna Murray, 69, 329, 333, 340, 347, 349, 350, 363 n. 2, 365 n. 35
Douglass, Charles, 352, 353, 355, 358, 359, 365 n. 24, 365 n. 35, 366 n. 43
Douglass, Frederick, 58, 95 n. 2, 102 n. 1, 143, 159, 163-64, 174 n. 7, 174 n. 8, 180 n. 2, 184, 204, 274, 278 n. 2, 325, 326
  appointment as Marshal of D.C., 337, 352
  Assing's first meeting with, 69
  Assing's letters to, 329-363
  and black civil rights, 313
  Cedar Hill home, 364 n. 20, 365 n. 28, 365 n. 33, 366 n. 41
  and "exodusters," 362, 367 n. 50
  failed military appointment, 270
  financial situation, 358-359

Freedman's Savings and Trust Co.,
  331, 363 n. 6
home in Rochester, 163
influence of Ludwig Feuerbach, 351
irreligious views, 344, 351, 358
Letters from Assing, 329-263
*Life and Times of Frederick
  Douglass*, 343-344, 350-351, 366
  n. 39
meets Carl Schurz, 337
My Bondage and My Freedom, 68-70,
  70 n. 1, 130, 350-351, 363 n. 5,
  366 n. 39
opposed to colonization, 142, 244-
  245
opposed to compensation, 98
optimistic views, 348, 359
participation in John Brown
  conspiracy, 173
possible visit to Canada, 102
possible visit to Europe, 336-337
possible visit to Haiti, 210 n. 2
physical appearance, 69
"The President and His Speeches,"
  247 n. 2
pro-Constitution, 95
provides home for Nellie Grant, 361
quality of oratory, 68-69, 94-95, 125
Sclaverei und Freiheit (see *My
  Bondage and My Freedom*)
"The Self-Made Man," 365 n. 32
vision problems, 335
visits Thomas Auld, 337, 351
Douglass, Frederick, Jr., 360
Douglass Institute (Baltimore), 326
Douglass, Lewis H., 330, 360, 363 n. 2
Douglass, Libbie (Mary Elizabeth), 341,
  358, 365 n. 24, 365 n. 33, 367 n. 47
Douglass, Rosetta (Sprague), 333, 364 n.
  11
Downs, Perry, 345, 365 n. 29
Draft riots (NYC), 265-268
Dred Scott decision, 125, 126 n. 5, 154,
  157 n. 2, 282 n. 2
Dr. Robin (play), 92
Drummond, Captain, 3, 6
Dumas, Alexandre (*père*), 109 n. 2

Edmonds, Laura, 263-264 n. 2

Education (American), 47-53
  Catholic, 53
  for freed slaves, 100
Elgin Association, 99-102, 102 n. 1
Emerson, Ralph Waldo, 111
Emigration ships, 117-118
"Erie" (slave ship), 235
Erie, Lake, 34, 99
Erie Railroad, 96
Ethiopian Opera Co. (see Minstrelsy)
Everett, Edward, 108, 109 n. 3, 184, 296

Fehr, Linn, 331, 363 n. 7
Fehr, Julius, 336, 340, 343, 347, 350,
  360, 362, 363 n. 7, 365 n. 23
Fehr, Miss, 344-345, 349, 350-351, 357,
  360, 361
Feuerbach, Ludwig, 338, 351
  Essence of Christianity, 364 n. 19
Fifty-fourth Massachusetts Regiment,
  126 n. 6, 269, 273 n. 2
Fig, (?), *Leonora*, 119
Fillmore, Millard, 87 n. 2, 227
Financial crisis (1857), 96-97, 104, 106,
  116
Fish, Bowman, 263 n. 2
Fish, Hamilton, 353, 366 n. 42
Fish, Leah (Fox), 263 n. 2
Fish Sisters (see Fox Sisters)
Fiske, Professor, 260-261, 264 n. 3
Floyd, John B., 223, 223 n. 3, 234
Forbes, Hugh, 172, 173 n. 4
Formes, Karl Johann, 104, 105 n. 3, 119,
  122 n. 2
Foster, Abby Kelley, 37-38
Foster, Stephen, 18 n. 5
Fox, Margaret, 263 n. 2
Fox Sisters, 260, 263 n. 2
Frauenstein, Dr. Gustav, 341, 343, 345,
  346, 349, 357, 365 n. 24
Free-love advocates, 132
Frémont, John C., 77 n. 6, 169, 194,
  232-233, 239, 240, 244, 251 n. 3,
  281, 287 n. 2
  actions in Missouri, 221-222
  candidate for presidency, 71-76, 78,
    86, 286-287, 291-292
French-Americans, 91, 92
Fugitive Slave Act, 55, 104, 134

Gaeta (Italy), 207, 210 n. 3
Garrick (David?), 92,
Garrick, David, 93 n. 2
Garrison, William Lloyd, 36, 56, 95 n. 4, 123, 204, 274, 340, 364 n. 21
   dissolution of Anti-Slavery Society, 313
   opposed to Constitution, 94
   opposed to Union, 98
   and women's rights, 124
Gartenlaube, Die, 102 n. 1
Gazette (Easton, Md.), 346-347
German American, 281
German-Americans, 5, 26-28, 29-31, 33, 34
   and assimilation, 38-39
   and Civil War, 217, 232-233, 268
   and Democratic party, 73, 84, 145, 197, 292
   denial of ethnic identity, 38
   disparagement of America, 38, 47, 74, 156-157
   and franchise, 112
   in Hoboken, 91-92
   in Missouri, 129-130, 217, 259
   and nativism, 84
   and Republican party, 73, 128, 197, 292, 332
   and slavery, 38, 73, 84, 128-129, 145, 259, 268, 281
   in Texas, 128
   in Wisconsin, 33
Giddings, Joshua R., 173, 174 n. 6
Gignoux, Régis-François, 185, 186 n. 4
Gilbert, Marie (see Montez, Lola)
Goethe, Johann Wolfgang von, 83
Goodwin, Daniel Raynes, 246-247, 247 n. 7
Gordon, Nathaniel, 235
Grant, Ulysses S., 76 n. 2, 251 n. 2, 268 n. 3, 307, 337, 340, 344, 349, 351, 353, 363 n. 10, 366 n. 42
Greeley, Horace, 80, 81, 111, 172-173, 174 n. 5, 229, 277, 358
Green, Shields, 178, 180 n. 2
Greenwood, Grace, 338
Grimké, Charlotte Forten, 348, 366 n. 37
Grimké, Francis J., 366 n. 37
Grimké, Sarah, 160

Grow, Galusha W., 76, 77 n. 7, 106-107
Guide des voyageurs, 121
Gutzkow, Karl, 349-350, 352-353
   Blasedow und seine Söhne, 21-22, 24 n. 4
   Die Ritter vom Geist, 3, 6 n. 2, 8, 11 n. 3, 366 n. 38
Gypsies, 66-67

Haiti, 207, 210 n. 2, 238
Hale, John Parker, 73, 76 n. 4, 172, 174 n. 5
Halleck, Henry W., 250, 251 n. 3, 252, 257, 259 n. 2
Hallgarten & Co., 366 n. 46
Hamburg (fire of 1842), 227 n. 3
Hamilton, Alexander, 133
Hamlin, Hannibal, 205
Harper and Brothers, 339
Harpers Ferry (Va.), 165-179
Harvard College, 50
Harvard School of Medicine, 114 n. 2
Hatch, Cora, 264 n. 2
Hawks, Francis Lister, 246, 247 n. 3
Hayes, Rutherford B., 332, 335, 337-338, 352, 363 n. 10
Hecker, Friedrich, 76 n. 3
Helper, Rowan Hinton
   Impending Crisis of the South, 181
Heyne family, 336, 345, 347, 353, 364 n. 16
Higginson, Thomas W., 82-83, 111, 124
Hilton, Judge, 338
Hoboken (N.J.), 90-93
Homestead Bill, 241-242
"Howard" (steamer), 118
Hudson River, 8, 19, 40-41, 44-45, 90-91, 160
Humboldt, Alexander von, 192, 192 n. 3
Humbugs and scams, 89
Hunt, Harriot, 112-113, 114 n. 2, 162 n. 2
   Glances and Glimpses, 115 n. 2, 160-161
Hunter, David, 239-240, 244
Huntingdon, Mrs., 341, 365 n. 25
Hutchinson family (musicians), 120, 228-229

"Indian Queen" (steamer), 3-6
Indians (see Native Americans)
Irish-Americans, 10-11, 40, 45, 92, 96, 116
   characteristics of, 61
   and crime, 267
   and draft riots, 265-268
   and franchise, 112
   politics in NYC, 104

Jackson, Andrew, 226
Jahreszeiten, 102 n. 1
Jefferson, Thomas, 51, 84, 314
Jencken, Kate (Fox), 263 n. 2
Jenckes, Thomas Allen, 74, 77 n. 5
Jenkins, Jane Lydia, 124, 126 n. 4
Johnson, Andrew, 231 n. 4, 307-308, 317 n. 2, 321-322, 358
   abandons black Americans, 319, 324
   impeachment, 325
   on state sovereignty, 323-324
   Reconstruction policies, 315-317, 319-322, 323
Journal of Commerce, 291
Julius, Nicolaus Heinrich
   Die amerikanischen Besserungssysteme, 14, 17 n. 2
Justice system (American), 13-15, 97

Kamehameha, King, 238
Kansas
   Lecompton Constitution, 123, 126 n. 2
   slavery in, 78, 84-85, 106-107, 123, 154, 163, 166-168
Kansas-Nebraska Bill, 35-37, 55, 84-85, 143, 145 n. 2
Kapp, Friedrich, 192, 192 n. 3
Keitt, Lawrence M., 86, 87, 87 n. 3, 106-107
Kemble, Charles, 147
Kemble, Fanny (Butler), 147-148
King, William (Rev.), 99-102
Kinkel, Gottfried, 6, 6-7 n. 2
Know-Nothing party, 71, 73, 103, 128
   in Boston election (1856), 78-79
   and rowdyism, 128
   and the Union, 207
Koehler, Sylvester Rosa, 336, 339, 341, 345, 351, 352, 354, 356, 357, 359, 360, 362, 364 n. 14
Kossuth, Louis, 6, 7 n. 2
Kudlich, Hermann C., 343, 346, 349, 359, 362, 365 n. 27

Labor unrest (NYC), 271-272
Ladies Physiological Society, 114 n. 2
LaGrange, Anna De, 119, 122 n. 2
Lamar, Charles, 155
Lane, Joseph, 199, 201 n. 3
Lange, Johannes, D., 329, 346, 347, 356, 357 n. 1
Lasalle, Ferdinand, 366 n. 44
Law, George, 74-75, 77 n. 6
Lee, Ann, 22, 24 n. 5
Lee, Robert E., 301, 308
Leo X, Pope, 121
Leutze, Emmanuel Gottlieb
   "Washington Crossing the Delaware," 15-16, 18 n. 3, 186 n. 3
   "Battle of Princeton," 185
Liberia, 141-142, 238
Lincoln, Abraham, 131 n. 3, 202-204, 205, 215, 223 n. 3, 251 n. 2, 258, 282 n. 2, 287 n. 2, 293 n. 5, 302 n. 2, 317 n. 2, 321-322, 231 n. 4, 344, 351
   assassinated, 307-309
   and black soldiers, 240
   candidate for president, 190-191, 283-287
   compromise with South, 295, 300-301, 307-308
   conspiracy to assassinate, 307, 310, 314
   election, 198-201, 288-292
   and emancipation, 239-240, 243-245, 256-257, 295, 306-307, 312
   funeral procession, 310-311
   indecisiveness, 209-210, 215-216, 220, 229, 240, 250, 285-286
   as martyr, 309
   treatment of Frémont, 222, 239
Lind, Jenny, 11 n. 4, 121
Liszt, Franz, 109 n. 2
Lodging houses (see poverty)
Lodi (Italy), 250, 251 n. 4
Loewenthal, Dr. E.J., 336, 343, 349, 356, 362, 364 n.16

Loewenthal, Willy, 355, 359
Lowell, James Russell, 326 n. 2
Ludwig I (of Bavaria), 109 n. 2
Luze, Anna (see Ann Lee)
Lyon, Nathaniel, 220-221, 223 n. 2

Mann, Horace, 81, 111
Marcy, William L., 353, 366 n. 42
Marie Antoinette, 121
Marvin, Judge, 155
Mason, Murray, 224, 227 n. 2, 234
Massachusetts Anti-Slavery Society, 95 n. 3
McClellan, George, 229, 232, 257, 304, 305 n. 3, 322
    defeat in election, 288-292
    presidential candidate, 283-287
    removal from command, 250, 252-253
    sympathies for South, 244-245, 249
Meyerbeer, Giacomo, 122 n. 3
    Les Huguenots, 119, 122 n. 3
Middle Ages, 127, 128
Miller, Mr. and Mrs., 159-160, 161, 342
Millerites, 10
Minstrelsy, 16-17, 18 n. 5, 120
Miscegenation, 277-278
"Miscegenation . . .," 279 n. 2
Missouri, 101
    raids on Kansas, 78, 85-86, 106, 166-167
Missouri Compromise, 84-85
Mitchel, John, 35, 37, 38, 39 n. 2
Mitchel, Ormsby M., 257, 259 n. 3
Monroe, James, 133, 288
Montez, Lola, 107-108, 109 n. 2
Morgan, John Pierpont, 231 n. 4
Morgan, Junius Spencer, 231, 231 n. 4
Mott, Lucretia, 81, 83 n. 3, 114, 274
Mount Vernon Association, 148
Musard's Orchestra, 119
Music and Opera, 119-120
Mutt, Commodore, 262

Nast, Thomas, 358
National Abolitionists, 95
National American Woman's Suffrage Association, 83 n. 4
National Anti-Slavery Standard, 173 n. 3

National Compensation Convention, 97
Native Americans, 64, 71, 91
    assimilation to white culture, 65
    in Chapequaw (N.Y.), 64-65
    in New York City, 64, 132
    in Wisconsin, 33
    medical practices, 65
    oral narratives, 66
    resistance to assimilation, 66
Nativists, 71
Negroes (see African Americans)
New York Daily News, 268 n. 2
New Yorker Vokszeitung, 297 n. 2
New York Express, 268 n. 2
New York Herald, 9, 172, 208, 233
New York Times, 267
New York Tribune, 80, 174 n. 5, 223, 229, 270, 277, 295, 324, 348, 353, 365 n. 36
New York World, 278 n. 2
Niagara Falls, 160
Nickert, Emilie, 336, 346, 360, 361-362, 364 n. 15
Nicolai, Gustav,
    Italien wie es wirklich ist, 11, 12 n. 6
Non-Resistance, 95 n. 4
Nott, Eliphalet, 11 n. 2
Nott, Urania Sheldon, 11 n. 3

Oberlin College, 115 n. 3, 180 n. 2
Oliver, Mary S., 361, 367, n. 48
Oliver trial (see Mary S. Oliver)
Orr, James L., 143, 145 n. 2
Owen, Robert Dale, 83 n. 5

Painting
    Corcoran Gallery, 343
    Hudson River School, 186 n. 4
    Washington Exhibition, 15
    Leutze's "Washington," 15-16, 18 n. 3, 186 n. 3
    Leutze's "Battle of Princeton," 185
    and sculpture exhibit, 185
Parker, Theodore, 36, 56, 98, 114, 124, 151
Pate, Henry Clay, 166, 169 n. 2
Patterson, Robert, 216, 219 n. 2
Pearce, James Alfred, 134, 134 n. 2
Pennington, Almira, 59 n. 2

Pennington, James W.C., 59 n. 2, 62
   The Fugitive Blacksmith, 58, 59 n. 2, 59 n. 3
   meeting with, 59
Peyne, Abraham, 136
Phelps, John Smith, 244
Phillips, Wendell, 36-37, 38, 56, 8, 83, 124, 177, 184, 191, 204, 229, 278, 286, 325, 340
   and black civil rights, 313
   greatness of oratory, 88, 147
   lecture on Toussaint l'Ouverture, 147
   "On the Philosophy of Reform," 88
   opposed to Constitution, 94
   opposed to Union, 98
   "The South Victorious," 323
   and women's franchise, 111, 124
Photography, 80, 120, 223
Pierce, Franklin, 85
Pierpont, John, 137, 138 n. 2
   Airs of Palestine . . ., 138 n. 2
   Anti-Slavery Poems . . ., 138 n. 2
Pillsbury, Parker, 325, 326 n. 2
Pitts, Helen, 347, 365 n. 33
Pitts, Hiram, 365 n. 33
Pius XII, Pope, 53
"Planter" (steamer), 241
Pomare, Queen, 238
Poore, Perley, 78-79
Porter, Fitz-John, 304, 305 n. 3
Poverty (in NYC), 116-117
Powell (Chippewa chief), 65, 66
Prang, Mr., 339, 341, 345, 356
Presidential election (1856), 71-76, 78-79
Psychology (see Spiritualism)
Public lectures, 146-147, 184-185
Public schools, 49
Purvis, Robert, 36, 39 n. 3

Quincy, Edmund, 94, 95 n. 4

Racowitza, Helene von, 354, 355-356, 366 n. 44
Reconstruction policies (see Andrew Johnson)
Reform societies, 191-192
Reid, Whitelaw, 348, 365 n. 36

Religion
   and American society, 109, 253-254
   Baptists, 100, 110, 127, 254
   H.W. Beecher's popularity, 150-151
   camp meeting, 41-44
   Congregationalists, 110
   diversion from cares, 44
   Episcopalians, 246-247, 254, 341
   freethinkers, 196-197
   importance of atheism, 348
   Methodists, 40, 81, 99, 100, 110, 254
   Mohammedanism, 188
   Mormons, 187-188, 352
   Presbyterians, 99
   Quakers, 81, 99, 112, 114, 139, 160, 274
   revivals, 110, 137, 151
   sectarian proliferation, 31
   Shakers, 21-24, 24 n. 5, 132
   and slavery, 56, 123-124, 127-128, 152, 171-172, 246-247
   superstitious humbug, 341
   Unitarians, 109, 110, 137, 254
   Universalitsts, 110, 254
Remond, Charles Lenox, 94, 95 n. 3
Republican party, 71, 87, 104, 106
   campaign rallies, 194-195
   and Chinese immigration, 356-357
   conciliation of South, 325
   party convention, 190
   and the Union, 204, 207, 285-286
   victory in 1860, 198-201
Rock, Dr. John Sweat, 125-126, 126 n. 6
Rocky Mountain Club, 74
Roman art and culture, 333-334, 335-336
Rose, Ernestine Potowski, 82, 83 n. 5, 114, 124, 126 n. 3, 197
Rose, William E., 83 n. 5
Rosecrans, William Starke, 268, 268 n. 3
Rosencrans (see Rosecrans, W.S.)
Rosenthal, Adolph, 28 n. 2
Rossini, Gioacchino, 122 n. 4
Rowdyism (political), 128, 195-196, 204, 205-206, 212, 265-268
Royal Italian Opera (London), 105 n. 3
Ruggles, Samuel Bulkley, 246, 247 n. 6
Ryan, Dick, 196
Rynders, Isaac, 201

San Antonio Zeitung, 297 n. 2
Sanders, George N., 314, 317 n. 2
Schonau, Adalbert von (see Amalie Schoppe)
Schoppe, Amalie, 11 n. 2, 11 n. 3, 20-21, 24 n. 2,
Schurz, Carl, 6 n.2, 197, 232-233, 292, 320, 332, 337-338, 363 n. 10
Secession of South (see also Civil War)
  beginnings of, 205-206
  criminality of, 234
  origins of, 226-227
  supported by women, 230
  threatened, 86, 106, 143, 179, 202-204
Seward, William Henry, 85, 190, 221, 223 n. 3, 300, 302 n. 3, 307-308, 314
Seymour, Horatio, 249, 251 n. 2, 265-267, 289-290
Shaffer, Chauncey, 74
Shakespeare, William, 4, 147
  King Lear, 355
  Macbeth, 329-330
  Othello, 355
Shaw, Robert Gould, 269, 273 n. 2
Sheboygan (Wis.), 25-28, 29-32, 33, 64
Sherman, William Tecumseh, 294
Shilo Presbyterian Church (NYC), 59
Siegel, Franz (see Sigel, Franz)
Sigel, Franz, 217, 219 n. 3, 230, 233, 259, 268, 268 n. 3
Sing Sing (N.Y.), 40-41, 44
Sing Sing prison, 44-45
Slavery
  abolished in District of Columbia, 237
  abolition by Congress, 294-295
  abolition only a first step, 315
  African slave trade, 135, 142, 148, 152-153, 154-156, 179, 202, 235
  black hatred of, 224-225
  certain end of, 228, 275, 276
  and Cuba, 146
  effects on country, 228, 253
  effects on South, 181-182, 211-213
  emancipation, 239-240, 243-245, 256-257
  extension of, 72-73, 78, 84-87
  fear of slave insurrection, 195-196,
  203, 205-206, 214, 226
  and federal government, 228-230, 257, 263
  hatred between North and South, 179
  in Kansas (see Kansas)
  and labor, 139
  legality of, 179
  in Missouri, 129, 259
  mistreatment of opponents, 133
  North's complicity in, 55
  and presidential election (1856), 71
  proslavery propaganda, 86, 130-131, 224
  public debate over, 135-136
  reenslavement in South, 316, 319
  rising prices for slaves, 154
  suppression of antislavery literature, 182
  Thirteenth Amendment, 298-299, 312
  and viticulture, 129
Slavkov (Czech Rep.), 250, 251 n. 4
Slidell, John, 224, 227 n. 2, 234
Smith, Gerrit, 56, 97, 98 n. 3, 325, 342
  meeting at F. Douglass's, 159
  and philanthropy, 158-161
  politics and characteristics, 158-160
  supports women's rights, 111
Smith, Joseph, 187
South Carolina, 87, 225-227
Southern Rights Association, 227
Spandau (prison), 25, 28 n. 3
Spiritualism, 132, 137, 260-262, 263-264 n. 2
Sprague, Louisa, 348, 365 n. 35
Sprague, Nathan, 333, 352, 364 n. 11
Staatszeitung (New York), 73, 145, 157
Stanton, Edwin M., 232
Stanton, Elizabeth Cady, 83 n. 3
Stephens, Alexander, 234
Stevens, Aaron D., 168, 169 n. 4, 170
Stone, Lucy, 38, 81-82, 83 n. 4, 112-114
Stowe, Harriet Beecher, 150, 278
  Uncle Tom's Cabin, 68, 325
Stratton, Charles (see Tom Thumb)
Sue, Eugène, 67 n. 2
  Martin, l'enfant trouvé, 67
Sumner, Charles, 56, 79, 83 n. 2, 85, 86, 87, 87 n. 3, 97, 106, 238, 325, 337, 344, 351

Tammany Hall, 105 n. 2
Taylor, Bayard, 349
Technology, 80
Temperance laws, 31-32, 34
Thalberg, Sigismond, 119, 122 n. 4
Thompson, Jacob, 314, 317 n. 2
Thorwaldsen, Albert
    "Christ and the Apostles," 80
Tilden, Samuel J., 355, 358
Tillman, William, 218
Tom Thumb, 11 n. 4, 92, 121, 262
Tombs, The (NYC prison), 13-15, 120
Toombs, Robert A., 87, 87 n. 6
Townsend, Captain, 135, 155
"Trent Affair," 224, 227 n. 2
Trollope, Frances,
    Domestic Manners of Americans, 11 n. 5
Turner, John Wesley, 316, 318 n. 3

Underground railroad, 105, 139, 163, 224
Union College, 11 n. 2, 20-21, 24 n. 3, 50, 53 n. 2
University of Virginia, 51

Van Amburgh, Isaac, 261, 264 n. 4, 304, 305 n. 2
Varnhagen von Ense, Karl August, 192, 192 -193 n. 3
Victor Emmanuel II, 210 n. 3
Vieuxtemps, Henri, 119, 122 n. 4
Violence, 48-49, 128, 133

Wakeman, George, 278 n. 2
Wall Street (stock exchange), 96, 306
"Waring" (schooner), 218
Warren, Lavinia, 262
Washington, George, 15-16, 18 n. 3, 108, 148, 185, 233, 293 n. 5, 314
Washington, John, 148
Watts, Thomas, 205
Welles, Gideon, 231, 231 n. 4
Wellington Regiment, 4

Werpup, Mrs., 329, 331, 334, 336, 339, 343, 345, 347, 357, 363 n. 1, 363 n. 7
West (American), 33
Westermanns Monatshefte, 95 n. 1
Williamson, Passmore, 56
Wilson, Henry, 72, 76 n. 2, 85, 125, 274, 325
Windom, William, 366 n. 45
Windom resolution, 355, 356-357, 366 n. 45
Wise, Henry A., 86, 165, 169, 171, 175-176, 223, 223 n. 3, 316, 318 n. 3
Woman's Journal, 83 n. 4
Women
    American characteristics, 60-61
    and black orphanage, 57
    convention on women's rights, 81-83, 83 n. 3, 111-113, 124
    and dress reform, 112-113, 272-273
    education, 51-52, 113, 185-186
    emancipation, 81, 111
    franchise, 111-112
    harmful excesses, 112
    male opposition, 112
    in Massachusetts, 82, 111
    and Methodists, 81
    prisoners, 14-15, 46
    and Quakers, 81
    support secession, 230
    and taxes, 112
Wood, Benjamin, 268 n. 2
Wood, Fernando, 105 n. 2, 128, 267
    elected to Congress, 249-250
    supports Civil War, 208-209
    wins NYC mayoral election, 103-104
World's Anti-Slavery Congress (1840), 95 n. 3
World's Temperance Convention, 115 n. 3

Yochplefileila, 65
Young, Brigham, 188
"Young Germany," 6 n. 2

Zecher, Wilhelm, 161

www.ingramcontent.com/pod-product-compliance
Ingram Content Group UK Ltd.
Pitfield, Milton Keynes, MK11 3LW, UK
UKHW022229230426
12048UKWH00016BA/1146